SMITHSONIAN

ATLAS OF SPACE EXPLORATION

ROGER D. LAUNIUS & ANDREW K. JOHNSTON

BUNKER HILL PUBLISHING

www.bunkerhillpublishing.com
This book has been designed and produced by
Bunker Hill Publishing,Inc.
285 River Road
Piermont, New Hampshire 03779
FIRST EDITION

The name of the "Smithsonian," "Smithsonian Institution," and the sunburst logo are registered trademarks of the Smithsonian Institution.

Designed by Sterling Hill Productions

Library of Congress Cataloging-in-Publication Data
Launius, Roger D.
  Smithsonian atlas of space exploration / Roger D. Launius and Andrew K. Johnston. -- 1st ed.
      p. cm.
  Includes index.
  ISBN 978-0-06-156526-7
  1. Outer space--Exploration--History--Pictorial works. I. Johnston, Andrew K. (Andrew Kenneth), 1969- II. Smithsonian Institution. III. Title.

  QB500.262.L384 2009
  500.5--dc22

2009000649

13   12   11   10   09   10 9 8 7 6 5 4 3 2 1

JACKET ILLUSTRATION CREDITS:

Front, Top Row(Left to Right):
Hevelius looking through telescope, Image courtesy History of Science Collections,
    University of Oklahoma Libraries.
Star, ©Tim Brown/Getty Images
Salyut 7, NASA

Front, Bottom Row (Left to Right):
Mercury 7 Astronauts, NASA
Lunar Image by Galileo Spacecraft, NASA
STS-1 on Pad, NASA

Back, Top Row (Left to Right):
Gemini EVA, NASA
Ptolemaic system, NASM
Nebula from Hubble Space Telescope, NASA

Back, Bottom Row (Left to Right):
Copernicus portrait, NASM
Soyuz, NASA
Copernican system, NASM

DEDICATION

For Monique Laney and Erin McKeen

Contents

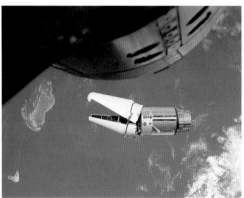

PART SIX
OTHER TERRESTRIAL WORLDS • 131

PART SEVEN
ACROSS THE SOLAR SYSTEM • 169

PREFACE

To some, the various space efforts of the world have represented both prestige and a positive image for the nations involved on the world stage. To others it has signified the quest for national security. Some others view it solely as the realm of telecommunications and other applications satellites and little else. To still others space is, or should be, about gaining greater knowledge of the universe. It represents, for them, pure science and the exploration of the unknown. In reality, it is all of these things and more.

There is no doubt that the last 50 years have witnessed numerous accomplishments in what President John F. Kennedy termed "this new sea" of space. At present Earth is encircled by hundreds of operational satellites performing a wide range of functions. Some look outward toward distant galaxies; space telescopes have continually probed the depths of the universe using all parts of the electromagnetic spectrum and brought new knowledge and new questions to the fore. Other satellites peer downward toward Earth performing duties for Earth-based observers such as reconnaissance, weather, communications, navigation, and other forms of remote sensing.

Robotic space probes have returned astonishing images of alien worlds and taught us that the universe is both more complex and more interesting than ever envisioned. Since 1957, when the space age began, every planet of the Solar System has been explored in some way at least once, and several of the moons of planetary bodies (including our own) and some comets and asteroids have been visited. We have placed spacecraft in orbit around our Moon, and the planets Venus, Mars, Jupiter, and Saturn, and landed on our Moon, Venus, Mars, Saturn's moon Titan, and an asteroid. Missions to explore the outer Solar System have yielded a treasure of knowledge about our universe, how it originated, and how it works. Such were the dazzling products of the first fifty years of the space program. Exploration of Mars has shown powerfully the prospect of past life on the red planet. Missions to Venus and Mercury have harvested knowledge about the origins and evolution of the inner Solar System. The stunningly successful Hubble Space Telescope has transformed our understanding of the cosmos. Most important, we have learned that as far as we know, Earth is the only place where everything necessary to sustain our life is, as Goldilocks found in the fairy tale, "just right."

The first years of the space age proved some of the most exciting of any lifetime. From the tentative first steps into space with astronaut flights through the breathtaking orbital missions of Mercury, Gemini, Apollo, Vostok, Voskhod, and Soyuz, the decade of the 1960s offered a vicarious thrill ride igniting the imagination of millions. But it never proved easy; perhaps that is why the term "rocket science" entered our lexicon to measure difficulty. Early on the rockets failed repeatedly; as a child at the time, one of us was about four or five years old before realizing that rockets were not supposed to explode during launch and provide really fine fireworks displays. Other problems and disasters demonstrated the extreme adventure that spaceflight offered, as the crew of Apollo 1 perished in a flash fire during ground tests in 1967 and only heroic efforts by all involved saved the crew of Apollo 13 en route to the Moon in 1970.

We have sent humans to the Moon, and are intent on doing so again. Twelve astronauts walked on the surface of the Moon between 1969 and 1972. In the more recent past the Space Shuttle has flown more than 120 missions, and the International Space Station, a cooperative effort of 16 nations, is nearing completion. In addition to Russia, which put the first human into space on April 12, 1961, China in 2003 entered the realm of human spaceflight with its first Shenzhou flight. Other nations may well develop their own human launch capability in the next quarter century, and we may see in the twenty-first century the first outposts on the Moon and perhaps Mars.

At the same time the delight of this exploration of space enlivened the imagination. Novelist Ray Bradbury captured the thrill best when he commented: "Too many of us have lost the passion and emotion of remarkable things. . . . Let us not tear up the future, but rather again heed the creative metaphors that render space travel a religious experience. When the blast of a rocket launch slams you against the wall and all the rust is shaken off your body, you will hear the great shout of the universe and the joyful crying of people who have been changed by what they've seen."

We have changed the world in which we all live through our capacity to fly in space. Who can imagine a world without global, instantaneous telecommunications, giving as it does instant information from anywhere in the world? The ability to monitor military actions from space, to warn of missile launches, and to ensure better command and control of national security assets have been a stabilizing influence on the nations of the world.

The space age was made possible by brilliant, innovative, and dedicated people who conceived, built, and operated the exquisite machines that turned our visions into reality. Some of these machines were called spacecraft. Boosted by powerful rockets into orbits beyond the influence of Earth's gravity, they could and did carry their payloads of scientific instruments to the farthest reaches of the Solar System. Other exploring machines remained on Earth to maintain a deep space connection to observe and listen to the universe beyond Earth.

And what of the thousands of scientists and engineers who made space exploration possible? Raised on an insatiable desire for knowledge and visions of the human colonization of the Moon and Mars they have pursued the dream of spaceflight for all of humanity. Thousands of them heeded the siren call of space, and they became in the poetry of Mary Jean Holmes the "everyman" who enabled humanity to explore the Moon:

> For I'm the man who took up tools and laid out the designs.
> Of starships, I'm the one who built their sleek and burnished lines.

I'm everyman who ever fashioned cold refined steel.
Into the dreams of spaceflight, I'm the one who made them real.

Humanity's venture into space has changed us. It brought us knowledge and understanding to be sure, but it also stretched our imaginations and made us believe that anything we set our minds to we could accomplish. "Yes, indeed, we are the lucky generation," commented Walter Cronkite, for we "first broke our earthly bonds and ventured into space. From our descendants' perches on other planets or distant space cities, they will look back at our achievement with wonder at our courage and audacity and with appreciation at our accomplishments, which assured the future in which they live."

The historical atlas that follows is an attempt to relate in words and photographs, illustrations and maps, the story of space exploration from earliest times to the present. It relates the quest for knowledge of the universe from the first observations from the ground to the most recent missions to other planets. It depicts the reliance of humans on spacecraft for many aspects of our daily lives. And it seeks to show the human element of exploration of the Moon and elsewhere beyond Earth.

The first fifty years of space exploration were marked by fantastic dreams and a compelling sense of destiny in space, and this thrill of exploration continues into the next half century. Who knows what transforming discoveries will be made during the second fifty years of the space age that will alter the course of the future? A limitless future for humanity in space remains the critical but elusive goal of the space age. Russian spaceflight pioneer Konstantin Tsiolkovsky said it best: "The Earth is the cradle of the mind, but we cannot remain forever in the cradle." Space exploration has taught us that this cradle is not a cage and that we can leave it.

Roger D. Launius
Andrew K. Johnston
Washington, D.C.

Space artist Chesley Bonestell painted this large three-part mural, *Lunar Landscape,* in 1956 for the Boston Museum of Science. As was the case of all of Bonestell's work, he planned the mural in meticulous detail. He positioned the viewer on a spot 1,300 feet up the south wall of an imaginary lunar crater ("similar to Albategnius, but smaller"), located seven degrees from the Moon's North Pole and five degrees to the left of the center of the lunar disc. He went so far as to specify that it was 3 o'clock, Boston time, on a late June afternoon, and calculated the position of the planets and stars accordingly (Jupiter over the central peaks, Antares below and to the right of the Earth). The painting hung in the Boston Museum of Science until 1970 when Apollo landings there demonstrated that the lunar surface looked nothing like what was depicted. The Boston Museum of Science removed it and presented it to the National Air and Space Museum in 1976.

part one
ENVISIONING SPACE

Curiosity about the universe and other worlds has been one of the few constants in the history of humankind. Prior to the twentieth century, however, there was little opportunity to explore the universe except through astronomical observations. Ancient societies watched the heavens, erecting great observatories to chart the paths of the Sun, Moon, planets, and stars. It became wrapped up in their religions, science, and philosophy.

The prehistoric people who built Stonehenge in England apparently used their observations of celestial bodies to chart planting seasons and measure other events, assigning this study a religious significance as well. To the ancient Egyptians, the Milky Way was a "heavenly Nile" that helped explain for them some of the seemingly mysterious forces of nature and build a cosmology of the immortality of the human soul. Astronomers in Babylon about 700 B.C.E. charted the paths of several planets and compiled observations of fixed stars. Later, around 400 B.C.E., the Babylonians devised the zodiac, the first mechanism to divide the year into lunar periods and to assign significance to a person's date of birth in foretelling the future. In what became the Americas the ancient Incan and Aztec cultures also built astronomical observatories. North American Indians observed the supernova of 1054, which created the Crab Nebula—not seen in Europe.

While the astronomy of the ancients may reflect mythology and religion as much as understanding of the natural universe, using by our standards crude instruments, they were successful in measuring with some precision the size of the Earth, the rising and setting of constellations, planetary motions, and distances around the globe. Artifacts of such ancient instruments as the Mayan calendar demonstrate a level of astronomical sophistication as impressive as it was prescient.

Ancient Observatories

Humans have always looked up at the sky to understand their place in the universe. Some of the earliest astronomical observatories were constructed centuries ago in Baghdad, Iraq, Jaiput, India, and Beijing, China. For thousands of years, even before structures were built explicitly as observatories, people constructed buildings that reflected their understanding of the Sun, Moon, and stars. These structures, built mostly for religious and ceremonial purposes, often measured movements of celestial objects or included walls and other structures aligned with the Earth's orbital movement.

Exact celestial alignments of prehistoric sites are usually not recorded, so the purported astronomical significance of many older sites remains controversial. However, many sites around the world demonstrate that diverse groups of ancient people developed extensive celestial knowledge. The map to the right shows sites where celestial alignments have been theorized for ancient structures.

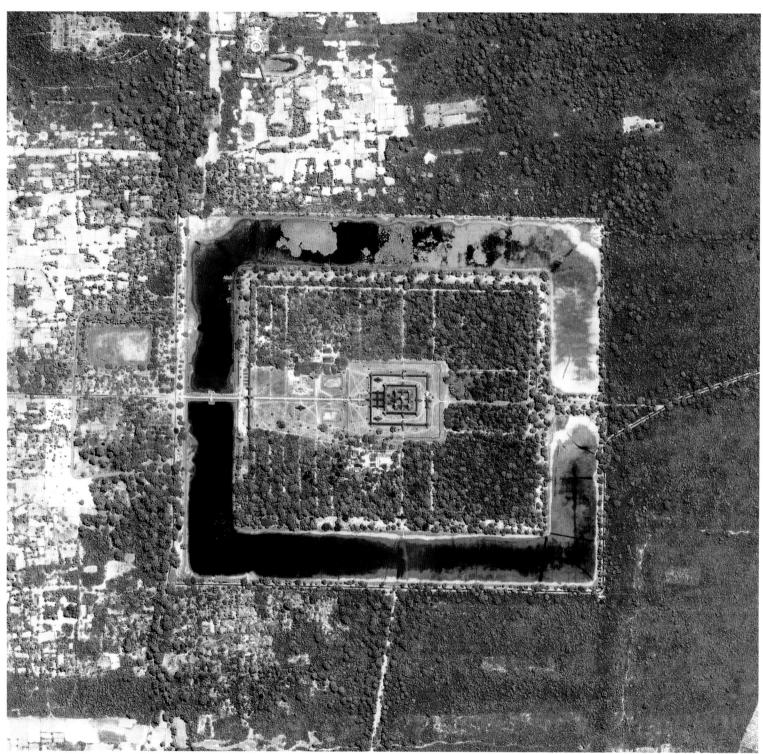

This image from the Earth-orbiting IKONOS satellite shows Angkor Wat in northwestern Cambodia. Angkor Wat was built by the Khmer Empire in the early 1100s. At first used as a Hindu temple, it was later converted for use as a Buddhist temple. Although they do not mark specific celestial movements, the temple buildings visible at the center were clearly constructed with knowledge of the Earth's orbital motion. The sides of the 630-foot-wide moat and central complex were laid out exactly along north-south and east-west directions.

Ancient Observatories

Big Horn Medicine Wheel
Big Horn, Wyoming

Chaco Canyon
NW New Mexico

Woodhenge
Cahokia, Illinois

Newgrange
Drogheda, Ireland

Brodgar
Orkney Islands, Scotland

Stonehenge
Salisbury, England

Gotland Grooves
Gotland, Sweden

Nebra Sky Disk
Goseck, Germany

The Temple of the Seven Dolls
Dzibilchaltun, Yucatan Peninsula, Mexico

Kokino Observatory
Near Kumanovo, Macedonia

Chumsungdae Astronomical Observatory
South Korea

Chichen Itza
Yucatan Peninsula, Mexico

Beijing Ancient Observatory
Beijing, China

Pyramid of the Sun
Teotihuacan, Yucatan Peninsula, Mexico

Pyramid of the Magician
Uxmal, Yucatan Peninsula, Mexico

Gaocheng
Near Dengfend, China

Chankillo
Near Lima, Peru

Tiwanaku
Bolivia

El Karnak
NE area of Luxor, Egypt

Abu Simbel
Near Aswan, Egypt

Angkor Wat
Cambodia

Easter Island
Chile

Machu Picchu
NE of Cusco, Peru

Egyptian Stonghenge
Nabta Playa, near Abu Simbel, Egypt

Jantar Mantar
New Delhi, India

Around 1000 years ago the Anasazi people, ancestors of modern Pueblo Indians, built several groups of structures in what is now northwestern New Mexico. Chaco Canyon contains a high density of these structures. Most of these buildings reflect directions on the ground or in the sky. A small structure known as the "Sun Dagger" was built to mark the passage of the Sun and Moon. Hundreds of miles of roads were constructed, sometimes running directly over topographic barriers.

This image from the IKONOS satellite (left) shows Pueblo Bonito and Casa Rinconada, two of the most significant features in Chaco Canyon.

The Beijing Ancient Observatory was constructed beginning in the 1440s to map positions and movement of stellar objects. The rooftop observatory was upgraded with more sophisticated instruments through the centuries. This hand-tinted photograph, taken in 1895, shows an armillary sphere and other instruments used to measure locations in the sky.

Pueblo Bonito is the largest group of structures in Chaco Canyon. The southern margin of the complex lies on an east-west line and the entire complex is bisected by a north-south line. It had hundreds of rooms, including several kivas, sunken circular rooms used for ceremonial purposes.

Casa Rinconada is the largest kiva in Chaco Canyon. Unlike other kivas, it stands alone just across the canyon from Pueblo Bonito. The kiva is bisected by a north-south line.

The Ptolemaic and Copernican Models of the Universe

The universe as conceived in Europe from the ancient through the mediaeval era and into the early Renaissance was predicated on the worldview of Ptolemy, a second-century astronomer and theorist. It was a geocentric model, positing the Earth as the center of the universe. In this conception, the Earth was surrounded by nine crystalline spheres, each representing the Sun and planets. From innermost to outermost, the spheres followed this order:

1. Earth (central and unmoving)
2. Mercury
3. Venus
4. The Moon
5. The Sun
6. Mars
7. Jupiter
8. Saturn
9. The Fixed Stars
10. The Primum Mobile

This explanation of the workings of the universe proved progressively more difficult to square with the observations of astronomers and over time increasingly more complex explanations cobbled together the theory and the observations. The most important of these theories was for epicycles within the spheres. Circles attached to the concentric spheres executed uniform circular motion as they went around the sphere at uniform angular velocity; at the same time the epicycles (which contained the planets) carried out their own uniform circular motion. This model allowed for observable retrograde motion and varying brightness, and satisfied the Ptolemaic universe model until the advent of the tele-

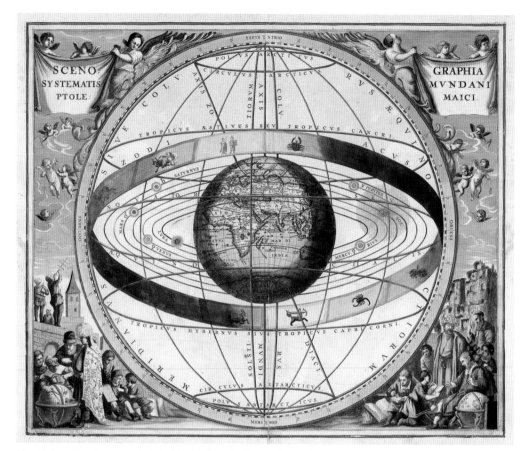

The Ptolemaic universe as depicted by Andreas Cellarius, *Harmonia Macrocosmica*, 1660/61. The chart shows signs of the zodiac and the Solar System with the world at the center.

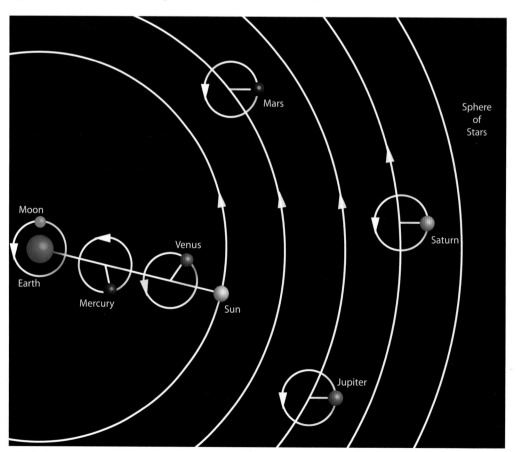

This depiction of the Ptolemaic universe shows the epicycles added to the system to explain irregularities in observations.

Claudius Ptolemy (87–150 C.E.), ancient Greek philosopher and scientist, and follower of Aristotelian ideas.

scope and the much greater clarity with which astronomers could make out what was taking place in the heavens.

It took more than 1,500 years for serious questioning of the Ptolemaic universe to take hold. Three major assumptions about this model proved incorrect: (1) that Earth was at the universe's center, (2) that uniform circular motion took place in the universe, and (3) that objects beyond Earth were perfect and unchanging. Copernicus challenged each of these.

In the book Copernicus published as he was about to die, *On the Revolutions of the Heavenly Bodies,* the great Polish astronomer proposed that the Sun, rather than Earth, rested at the center of the Solar System. This "heliocentric" model of the universe found adherents all over Europe by 1650. He ordered the planets in this new system as are now accepted. From innermost to outermost, the bodies (minus the crystalline spheres) followed this order:

1. Sun
2. Mercury
3. Venus
4. Earth (with Moon orbiting)
5. Mars
6. Jupiter
7. Saturn
8. Stars beyond

Copernicus did not view himself as a revolutionary and he was cautious in the expression of his ideas, correct though they turned out to be. Christian dogma recognized the Earth as the center of the universe and his ideas remained obscure until after his death in 1573. In the seventeenth century, however, Kepler, Galileo, and Newton built on the Copernican model of the universe and replaced the older Ptolemaic system. Commonly called the Copernican Revolution, this transformation of ideas about the universe represented some of the most fundamental shifts in cosmology until Albert Einstein in the twentieth century.

This depiction of the Copernican universe is from Thomas Digges, *A Perfit Description of the Coelestiall Orbes* (1576).

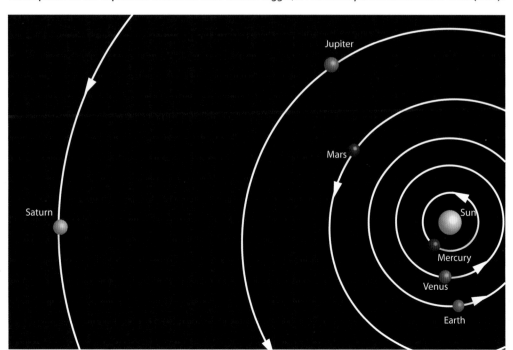

The Solar System as envisioned by Copernicus contained the Sun at the center, with planets in surrounding orbits.

Nicolaus Copernicus was a Polish astrologer, astronomer, mathematician, and economist who revolutionized human understanding of the Solar System with his heliocentric, or Sun-centered, studies.

Kepler-Newton: Something New Under the Sun

Understanding how planets move became the focus of work after Copernicus had altered conceptions of the Solar System. Johannes Kepler and Isaac Newton led the way by writing rules that govern planetary movement. Today these principles are still used in every mission into space.

Johannes Kepler worked near the time of Galileo in Germany, and developed theories to understand the movements of the planets. Kepler produced three principles that explain the orbits of the planets. Kepler himself did not use the term "law," but today these items are often referred to this way. According to Copernicus, all planets traveled in circular orbits around the Sun. Kepler and others noted that observations of the planets disagreed slightly from this prediction. In fact, planetary orbits are slightly elliptical. This observation led to Kepler's first "law" of planetary motion:

The orbital paths of the planets are elliptical with the Sun at one focus.

Today we still measure the elliptical shape of each planet's orbit. A planet's "perihelion" is its closest point to the Sun, while the "aphelion" is the most distant point. The speed with which a planet moves along its elliptical path can be explained with the second of Kepler's "laws":

A line joining a planet to the Sun sweeps out equal areas in equal intervals of time.

This describes how planets move at a higher speed when they are closer to perihelion. The total amount of time required for a planet to move in its path around the Sun is defined with Kepler's third "law":

The square of a planet's orbital period is proportional to the cube of its semi-major axis.

This describes how outer planets move at a slower rate than inner planets. Mercury requires only 88 "Earth days" to revolve around the Sun, while Saturn requires the equivalent of more than 29 "Earth years."

Johannes Kepler (1571–1630).

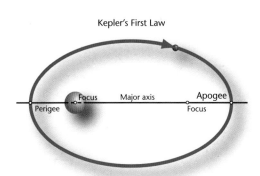

Kepler's First Law

The orbital paths of the planets are elliptical with the Sun at one focus.

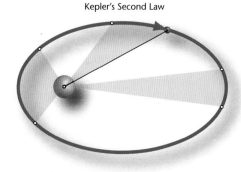

Kepler's Second Law

A line joining a planet to the Sun sweeps out equal areas in equal intervals of time.

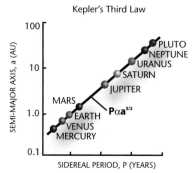

Kepler's Third Law

The square of a planet's orbital period is proportional to the cube of its semi-major axis

Isaac Newton (1642–1727).

Working in England Isaac Newton also developed three laws of motion in addition to fundamental advances in mathematical theory. His academic training began with classical knowledge inherited from ancient Greeks, but he soon moved beyond that understanding. Instead of simply describing planetary movement as Kepler had done, Newton addressed the movement of all objects in the universe. His theories updated those of Kepler, who had assumed that only the Sun had the attractive force to maintain orbits. Newton realized that all bodies in the universe containing mass, including small objects, caused gravitational attraction. The Earth's gravity holds objects to its surface, but gravity also pulls the planet upward toward those objects. Newton's first law of motion:

An object at rest will remain at rest until some force acts on it. When a force does act, the object will remain in that state of uniform motion until another force acts on it.

This describes *inertia*, the property of objects to "want" to remain still or maintain their movement. Understanding inertia is essential for spaceflight. Even in the absence of gravity, rocket propulsion must overcome a spacecraft's inertia to cause it to move. Newton's second law describes the amount of force required to overcome an object's inertia:

The acceleration of an object is directly proportional to the net applied force and inversely proportional to the object's mass.

In modern terms, a force of 1 Newton is required to move a mass of 1 kilogram with an acceleration of 1 meter/second. These units are used to calculate the firing of thrusters to navigate spacecraft into orbit and across the solar system. Newton's third law explains the interaction between two objects:

For every force there is an equal and opposing force.

This explains how rockets move spacecraft around empty space. By applying a force with rockets, spacecraft always move in the opposite direction.

Newton's First Law

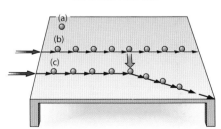

An object at rest will remain at rest until some force acts upon it. When a force does act, the object will remain in that state of uniform motion until another force acts on it.

Newton's Second Law

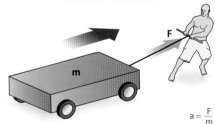

$$a = \frac{F}{m}$$

The acceleration of an object is directly proportional to the net applied force and inversely proportional to the object's mass.

Newton's Third Law

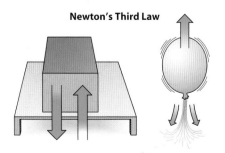

For every force, there is an equal and opposite force

Wernher von Braun, an advocate of spaceflight (right), and Walt Disney (left), 1954. They met on the set of a Walt Disney television program that helped to build public support for an ambitious space program.

part two
BEGINNING THE SPACE AGE

Until the twentieth century, study about the universe and speculation about the nature of spaceflight were not closely related to the technical developments that led to rocket propulsion. But a merging of these ideas had to take place before the space age could truly begin. The rocket represented the fundamental convergence of these ideas and the technology necessary to make spaceflight a reality. A reaction device, based on Newton's Third Law of Motion, the rocket served to enable explora-

tion beyond Earth. Without explicitly understanding this law, humanity has recognized the rocket's practicality for centuries.

While the technology of rocketry was moving forward on other fronts, some individuals began to advocate their use for space exploration. Throughout the first half of the twentieth century such advocates as Robert Goddard, Hermann Oberth, Hermann Noordung, Max Valier, Konstantin Tsiolkovsky, Luigi Gussali, Wernher von Braun, and Robert

Esnault-Pelterie worked to develop more effective rockets and to sell the idea of spaceflight to the various publics in which they lived.

A mock-up of the Sputnik 1 (PS-1) satellite is shown here on display. When the development of the first advanced scientific satellite, Object D, proved to be more difficult than expected, the Soviets decided to launch a simpler, smaller satellite, PS-1 or Sputnik 1, which began development in November 1956. The satellite's launch on October 4, 1957, signaled the beginning of the space age.

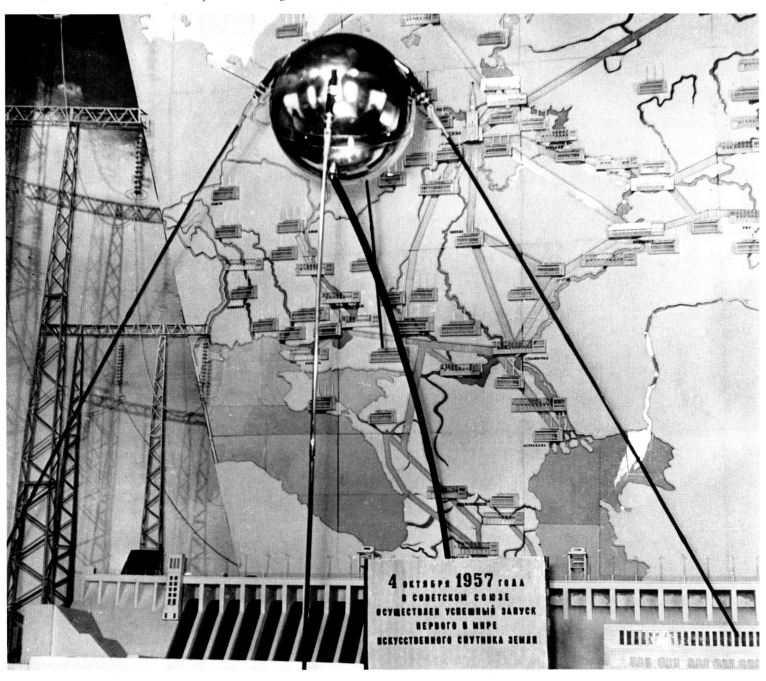

The Origins of Rocketry

Although it is unclear who first invented rockets, many investigators link the first crude rockets with the discovery of gunpowder. The Chinese, moreover, had been using gunpowder for some 1,800 years. The first firecrackers seem to have appeared in the first two centuries after the beginning of the Common Era, and the Chinese were using rockets in warfare at least by the time of Genghis Khan (ca. 1155–1227). Not long thereafter the use of rockets in warfare began to spread to the West and was in use by at least the time of Konrad Kyser von Eichstadt, who wrote *Bellifortis* in 1405, which described the use of war rockets in his day. By this time the use of rockets in military operations was reasonably well known in Europe.

The use of gunpowder rockets was refined through the first part of the nineteenth century. Essentially, the military application for rocketry—and there was little other at the time—was as a type of artillery. Sir William Congreve (1772–1828) carried rocket technology as far as it was to go for another century, developing incendiary barrage missiles for the British military that could be fired from either land or sea. They were used with effect against the United States in the War of 1812; it was probably Congreve's weapons that Francis Scott Key wrote about in the "Star Spangled Banner" while imprisoned on a British warship during the bombardment of Fort McHenry at Baltimore. The military use of the rocket was soon outmoded in the nineteenth century by developments making artillery both more accurate and more destructive, but new uses

for rockets were found in other industries such as whaling and for seagoing shipping where rocket-powered harpoons and rescue lines began to be employed.

While the technology of rocketry was moving forward on other fronts, some individuals began to advocate their use for space travel. One of the earliest pioneering figures was the Russian theoretician Konstantin Eduardovich Tsiolkovsky (1857–1935), who had been inspired by the science fiction of Jules Verne and H. G. Wells. An obscure schoolteacher in a remote part of Russia, he submitted a piece for publication in 1898 to the Russian journal *Nauchnoye Obozreniye* (*Science Review*), one that was based upon years of calculations and that laid out many of the principles of modern spaceflight. His article was not published until 1903, but it opened the door to future writings on the subject.

A second rocket pioneer was Hermann

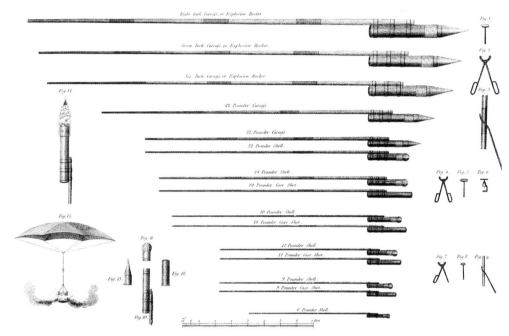

William Congreve had served in the Royal Artillery briefly in 1791 but worked as a technician at the Royal Arsenal at Woolwich, England, when he began experimenting with rockets. By 1806 he was producing 32-pound rockets with a range of more than 3,000 yards. Congreve's invention enabled artillery without the movement of heavy guns; wherever a packhorse or an infantryman could go, the rocket could provide support.

Konstantin Eduardovich Tsiolkovsky (1857–1935).

German rocketeer Rudolf Nebel built a subscale prototype for a human-carrying rocket in the early 1930s and it was flown eight times in 1933. This was the largest German rocket launched until the latter 1930s.

Oberth (1894–1989), a German who published the classic study *Die Rakete zu den Planetenraumen* (*Rockets in Planetary Space*) in 1923. It represented a thorough discussion of almost every phase of rocket spaceflight and inspired many to follow his lead. Among his proteges was Wernher von Braun (1912–1977), the senior member of the rocket team that built NASA's Saturn launch vehicle for the actual trip to the Moon in the 1960s.

Although the work of rocketeers was path-breaking, only World War II truly altered the course of rocket development. Many combatants were involved in developing some type of rocket technology. As an example, the Soviet Union fielded the "Katusha," a solid-fueled rocket six feet in length and carrying almost fifty pounds of explosives that could be fired from either a ground- or truck-mounted launcher. The United States began in earnest in 1943 to develop a rocket capability, and several efforts were focused in that direction. One of the most significant was at the Jet Propulsion Laboratory (JPL) in Pasadena, California, where a team under the brilliant Hungarian scientist Dr. Theodore von Kármán (1881–1963) began developing a rocket for use in launching aircraft on short runways and then graduated to the development of the WAC Corporal, which became a significant launch vehicle in postwar rocket research. Others built various types of handheld antitank and anti-aircraft rockets.

Hermann Oberth, along with rocketeers Ernst Stuhlinger (left) and Wernher von Braun (right), at the time of the first Apollo Moon landing in 1969.

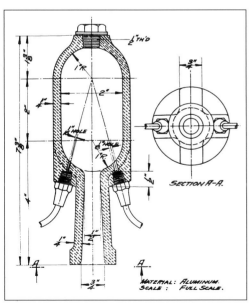

The American Rocket Society (ARS) began life on April 4, 1930, under the name American Interplanetary Society, but it soon began rocket experiments and changed its name to more effectively reflect its experimental work. Here is a plan for the ARS-2, an improvement on a German rocket design. It used liquid oxygen and gasoline propellants, and was successfully launched on May 14, 1933, although the rocket veered after takeoff and only reached an altitude of 75 miles. Successive rockets refined the design.

This image from 1941 shows a "rocket-assisted" airplane, taking off using a shorter runway than the plane still on the ground. Both planes started at the same position and time.

Robert H. Goddard and the Development of American Rocketry

The son of a machine shop owner, Robert Hutchings Goddard pioneered modern rocketry in the United States and founded an entire field of science and engineering. Goddard graduated from Worcester Polytechnic Institute in 1908 and then became a physics instructor at Worcester Technical University, where he received an M.A. in 1910 and a Ph.D. in 1911, before joining the faculty of Clark University.

Motivated by reading science fiction as a boy, Goddard became excited by the possibility of exploring space. As a youth in 1901 he wrote a short paper, "The Navigation of Space," that argued that movement could take place by firing several cannons "arranged like a 'nest' of beakers." At his high school oration in 1904 he summarized his life's perspective: "It is difficult to say what is impossible, for the dream of yesterday is the hope of today and the reality of tomorrow."

As a young physics graduate student he conducted static tests with small solid-fuel rockets at Worcester Tech, and in 1912 he developed a detailed mathematical theory of rocket propulsion. He continued these efforts and actually received two patents in 1914. One was the first for a rocket using solid and liquid fuel, and the other for a multistage rocket. In 1915 he proved that rocket engines could produce thrust in a vacuum and therefore make spaceflight possible.

By focusing his attention on liquid rocket propulsion, theorizing that liquid oxygen and liquid hydrogen were the best fuels, he asked the Smithsonian Institution for assistance in 1916 and received a $5,000 grant from its Hodgkins Fund. His research was ultimately published by the Smithsonian as the classic study *A Method of Reaching Extreme Altitudes* in 1919. Here Goddard argued from a firm theoretical base that rockets could be used to explore the upper atmosphere. Moreover, he suggested that with a velocity of 6.95 miles per second, without air resistance, an object could escape Earth's gravity and head into infinity, or toward other celestial bodies. This became known as Earth's "escape velocity." He also argued that humans could reach the Moon using these techniques.

These ideas became a great joke for those who believed spaceflight was either impossible or impractical. Some ridiculed Goddard's ideas in the popular press. The *New York Times* was especially harsh in its criticisms, referring to him as a dreamer whose ideas had no scientific validity. It also compared his theories to those advanced by novelist Jules Verne, indicating that such musing is "pardonable enough in him [Verne] as a romancer, but its like is not so easily explained when made by a savant who isn't writing a novel of adventure." The *New York Times* questioned Goddard's credentials as a scientist and the Smithsonian's rationale for funding his research and publishing his results in an editorial on January 18, 1920.

Such negative publicity prompted Goddard to become secretive and reclusive. However, it did not stop his work, and he eventually registered 214 patents on various components of rockets. He concentrated on the design of a liquid-fueled rocket (the first such design) and the related fuel pumps, motors, and control components. On March 16, 1926, near Auburn, Massachusetts, Goddard launched his first rocket, a liquid oxygen and gasoline vehicle that rose 42 feet in 2.5 seconds. This event heralded the modern age of rocketry.

Goddard continued to experiment with rockets and fuels for the next several years. A spectacular launch took place on July 17, 1929, when he flew the first instrumented payload—an aneroid barometer, a thermometer, and a camera (to record the readings). It was the first instrument-carrying rocket. The launch failed; after rising about 90 feet the rocket turned and struck the ground 171 feet away. It caused such a fire that neighbors complained to the local fire marshal and Goddard was prohibited from making further tests in the area.

Fortunately for Goddard, Charles A.

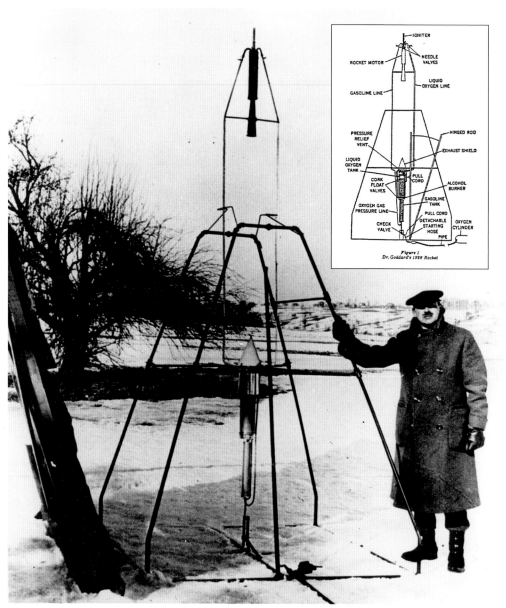

One of the most famous photographs of the twentieth century, this image shows Robert Goddard with his first liquid-fueled rocket just before its successful launch on March 16, 1926. A schematic of the design is shown inset.

Lindbergh, fresh from his 1927 transatlantic solo flight, became interested in Goddard's work. He persuaded Daniel Guggenheim, a philanthropist, to award Goddard a grant of $50,000. With this, Goddard set up an experiment station in a lonely spot near Roswell, New Mexico. There he built larger rockets and developed many theories that are now standard in rocketry. He designed combustion chambers of the appropriate shape, and he burned gasoline with oxygen in such a way that the rapid combustion could be used to cool the chamber walls.

From 1930 to 1941 he launched rockets of increasing complexity and capability. He developed systems for steering a rocket in flight by using a rudderlike device to deflect the gaseous exhaust, with gyroscopes to keep the rocket headed in the proper direction. Goddard described many of his results in 1936 in a classic study, *Liquid-Propellant Rocket Development*. The culmination of this effort was the successful launch of a rocket to an altitude of 9,000 feet in 1941. In late 1941 Goddard entered naval service and spent the duration of World War II developing jet-assisted takeoff (JATO) rockets to shorten the distance required for heavy aircraft launches. Some of this work led to the development of the "throttlable" Curtiss-Wright XLR25-CW-1 rocket engine in 1947, which later powered the Bell X-1 and helped overcome the transonic barrier, a range of speed between about .9 and 1.1 mach. Goddard did not live to see this; he died of cancer in Baltimore, Maryland, on August 10, 1945.

Robert H. Goddard at a blackboard at Clark University in Worcester, Massachusetts, in 1924.

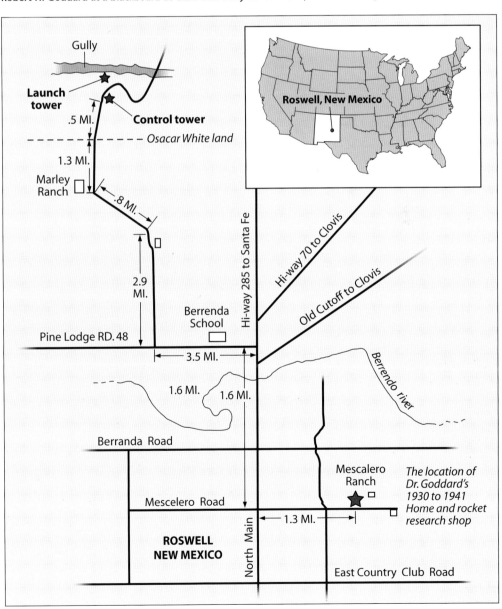

A map of Roswell and environs that shows Robert Goddard's ranch, shops, and test facilities.

This four-chamber rocket is being prepared for test launch at Goddard's Roswell launch site in 1940.

Wernher von Braun and the V-2

Germany had great success during World War II in developing a ballistic missile capability. The brainchild of Wernher von Braun's rocket team operating at a secret laboratory at Peenemunde on the Baltic coast, the V-2 rocket (the A4 in German designation) was a liquid-propellant missile extending some 46 feet in length and weighing 27,000 pounds. Throughout the 1930s von Braun worked to develop rockets for the German army, and by 1941 designs had been developed for the ballistic missile that eventually became the V-2. At its height, the Peenemunde research and development facility where von Braun was technical director for the missile program had more than 5,000 engineers and technicians working there on the V-2 and other advanced weapons programs. The V-2 flew at speeds in excess of 3,500 miles per hour and delivered a 2,200-pound warhead. First flown in October 1942, it was used against targets in Europe beginning in September 1944. On September 6, 1944, for instance, more than 6,000 German troops were deployed to Holland and northern Germany to bomb Belgium, France, and London with the newly developed V-2s.

Beginning on September 8, 1944, these forces began launching V-2s against Allied cities, especially Antwerp, Belgium, and London. By the end of the war 1,155 had been fired against England and another 1,675 had been launched against Antwerp and other continental targets.

V-2 GENERAL CHARACTERISTICS

Engine 8,380 lb (3,810 kg) of 75% ethanol and 25% water + 10,800 lb (4,910 kg) liquid oxygen

Launch mass 27,576 lb (12,535 kg)

Length 46 ft (14 m)

Diameter 5 ft 5 in (1.65 m)

Wingspan 11 ft 8 in (3.56 m)

Speed maximum: 1.6 km/s (about 3,580 mph); at impact 800 km/s (about 1,780 mph)

Range 200 miles (322 km)

Flying altitude 55 miles (88.5 km) maximum

Warhead 2,150 lb (977 kg) Amatol

Guidance Gyroscopes for attitude control; Müller-type pendulous gyroscopic accelerometer for engine cutoff on most production rockets (10% of the Mettelwerk rockets used a guide beam for cutoff)

Launch platform Mobile

At the time of launch the fuel (alcohol) and oxidizer (liquid oxygen) mixed in the rocket motor and ignited to a temperature of 4532°F–4892°F (2500°C–2700°C). Cooled by a coating of non-ignited fuel pumped along a double wall outside the main combustion burner, this was the first regeneratively cooled rocket engine. This fuel was then pumped into the main chamber through 1,224 tiny pinholes. The V-2 used four external tail fins with rudders and four graphite vanes at the exit of the rocket nozzle for control. These aided in guidance from two gyroscopes providing stabilization. The first models used an analog computer to adjust the rocket's azimuth, and range depended on engine cutoff controlled either by Doppler radar or by an on-board accelerometer. At that point the rocket reached the top of a parabolic flight and accelerated toward the ground target. The guidance system for these missiles was imperfect to say the least and many did not reach their targets, but they struck without warning and there was no defense against them. As a result the V-2s had a terror factor far beyond their capabilities.

Initially production for the V-2s took place at the research and development site at Peenemunde, but following an air raid targeting the research and development facility German officials moved it underground

The German Army prepares a V-2 for a test launch.

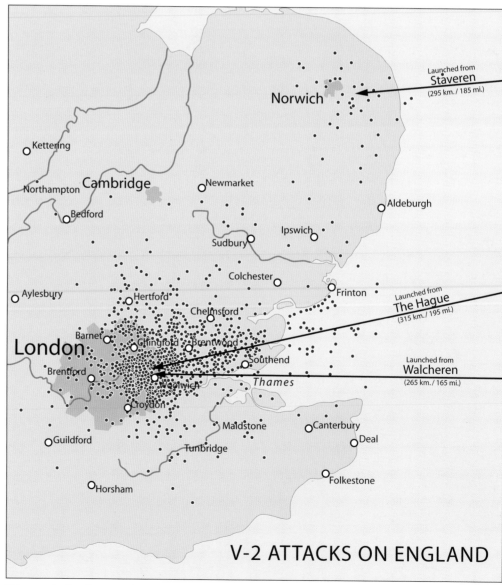

Launched from **Staveren** (295 km. / 185 mi.)

Launched from **The Hague** (315 km. / 195 mi.)

Launched from **Walcheren** (265 km. / 165 mi.)

Norwich

Kettering

Northampton Cambridge Newmarket

Bedford Aldeburgh

Ipswich

Sudbury

Colchester

Aylesbury Hertford Frinton

Chelmsford

Barnet Brentwood

London Chingford Southend

Brentford Thames

Woolwich

Croydon

Guildford Maidstone Canterbury

Tunbridge Deal

Horsham Folkestone

V-2 ATTACKS ON ENGLAND

This map depicts the more than 2,000 impact sites in England of the V-2 during its wartime use.

to production facilities at Mittelwerk, and assigned production to the SS. In 1944 and 1945 this facility built about 6,000 V-2 rockets using concentration camp labor. Some 20,000 forced labor workers died there, nearly three times the 7,000 killed by the missiles themselves.

Clearly the technology employed in this weapon was worthy of American study and as the war was winding down, U.S. forces brought captured V-2s back for study. Along with them—as part of a secret military operation called Project Paperclip—came many of the scientists and engineers who had developed these weapons, most notably Wernher von Braun, who made a point of surrendering to the Americans so he and more than 100 colleagues might continue their work after the war. They were installed at Fort Bliss in El Paso, Texas, and launch facilities for the V-2 test program were set up at the nearby White Sands Proving Ground in New Mexico. The first successful American test firing of the captured V-2s took place at White Sands on April 16, 1946, and between then and 1951, 67 captured V-2s were test launched.

WAC CORPORAL GENERAL CHARACTERISTICS

Overall dimensions
Diameter: 1 ft (0.30 m)
Total length: 24 ft (7.34 m)

Tiny Tim booster
Loaded weight: 759.2 lb (344.3 kg)
Propellant weight: 148.7 lb (67.4 kg)
Thrust: 50,000 lbf (220,000 N])
Duration: 0.6 s
Impulse: 30,000 lbf·s (130,000 N·s)

WAC Corporal sustainer
Empty weight: 296.7 lb (134.6 kg)
Loaded weight: 690.7 lb (313.3 kg)
Thrust: 1,500 lbf (6,700 N)
Duration: 47 s
Impulse: 67,000 lbf·s (300,000 N·s)

Propulsion
Sustainer: Aerojet liquid-fueled rocket, 1,500 pounds for 47 seconds; booster: Tiny Tim solid-fueled rocket, 50,000 pounds for 0.6 seconds

Speed 3,000 feet per second

Range 50 miles

One of the most important and innovative efforts of post–World War II rocketry was Project Bumper, which mated a smaller WAC Corporal missile as a second stage on a V-2 to obtain data on both high altitudes and the principles of two-stage rockets. An important successful launch took place on February 24, 1949, when the V-2/WAC Corporal reached an altitude of 244 miles and a velocity of 5,150 miles per hour. A final launch of the combination on July 24, 1950, Bumper 8, was the first successful flight to take off from Cape Canaveral, Florida.

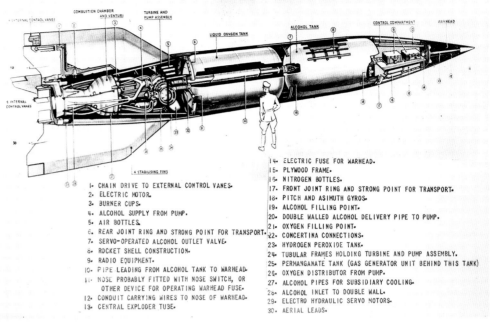

1. CHAIN DRIVE TO EXTERNAL CONTROL VANES.
2. ELECTRIC MOTOR.
3. BURNER CUPS.
4. ALCOHOL SUPPLY FROM PUMP.
5. AIR BOTTLES.
6. REAR JOINT RING AND STRONG POINT FOR TRANSPORT.
7. SERVO-OPERATED ALCOHOL OUTLET VALVE.
8. ROCKET SHELL CONSTRUCTION.
9. RADIO EQUIPMENT.
10. PIPE LEADING FROM ALCOHOL TANK TO WARHEAD.
11. NOSE PROBABLY FITTED WITH NOSE SWITCH, OR OTHER DEVICE FOR OPERATING WARHEAD FUSE.
12. CONDUIT CARRYING WIRES TO NOSE OF WARHEAD.
13. CENTRAL EXPLODER TUBE.
14. ELECTRIC FUSE FOR WARHEAD.
15. PLYWOOD FRAME.
16. NITROGEN BOTTLES.
17. FRONT JOINT RING AND STRONG POINT FOR TRANSPORT.
18. PITCH AND ASIMUTH GYROS.
19. ALCOHOL FILLING POINT.
20. DOUBLE WALLED ALCOHOL DELIVERY PIPE TO PUMP.
21. OXYGEN FILLING POINT.
22. CONCERTINA CONNECTIONS.
23. HYDROGEN PEROXIDE TANK.
24. TUBULAR FRAMES HOLDING TURBINE AND PUMP ASSEMBLY.
25. PERMANGANATE TANK (GAS GENERATOR UNIT BEHIND THIS TANK)
26. OXYGEN DISTRIBUTOR FROM PUMP.
27. ALCOHOL PIPES FOR SUBSIDIARY COOLING.
28. ALCOHOL INLET TO DOUBLE WALL.
29. ELECTRO HYDRAULIC SERVO MOTORS.
30. AERIAL LEADS.

This German illustration showing a cutaway of the V-2 was modified after the war, with an English legend for the use of American engineers.

The Popularization of Space

Beginning in the 1920s a space craze gained popularity worldwide as science fiction and science fact reinforced each other to make the dreams of spaceflight seem more real than ever before. While meanings shifted significantly over time—in ways that reflected similar shifts in politics, culture, and society—the level of interest and excitement for the possibilities of spaceflight remained constant through the World War II era. In Germany Hermann Oberth published in 1923 his classic book, *Die Rakete zu den Planetenräumen (The Rocket into Interplanetary Space)*. The book explained the mathematical theory of rocketry, applied it to possible designs for practical rockets, and considered the potential of space stations and human travel to other planets.

The success of the 1923 book prompted Oberth to consider writing a more popular, and less technical, treatise on the possibilities of spaceflight, but because of his teaching load in a secondary school, German spaceflight enthusiast Max Valier condensed and published one for him. This book inspired a number of new rocket clubs to spring up all over Germany, as hardcore rocket enthusiasts tried to translate Oberth's theories into practical space vehicles. The most important was the Verein für Raumschiffahrt (Society for Spaceship Travel), or VfR. Oberth became a sort of mentor for the VfR during the 1920s, encouraging the efforts of Valier, Willy Ley, and the young Wernher von Braun.

One man who foresaw the possible outcomes of the space craze was the silent movie maker Fritz Lang. After reading Oberth's book, he decided to film an adventure story about space travel. The result was the 1929 feature *Die Frau Im Mond (The Woman in the Moon)*. Lang wanted his movie set to be technically correct, so he asked Hermann Oberth to be his main technical advisor. Oberth and Willy Ley helped Lang with his sets and built a spacecraft that looked very realistic. Ever the dramatist, Lang even invented the countdown to increase tension for the audience and to add drama to the rocket flight.

As a publicity stunt for Lang's film, Oberth also agreed to build an actual rocket that would be launched at the premier of *Die Frau Im Mond*. Two days before the premier, however, Oberth discovered that the rocket would not be completed in time. At that point he went to Romania to soothe his nerves. Regardless, the movie and Oberth's role in it served as a powerful merging of space technology with imagination.

Also in 1929 Austrian engineer Hermann Noordung (a pseudonym for Slovenian-born Hermann Potôcnik) elaborated on the concept of an orbital space station as a base for voyages into space. In Noordung's case, the technical attributes of a space station to support planetary exploration took up the bulk of his 1929 book, *Das Problem der Befahrung des Weltraums (The Problem of Space Travel)*. An obscure engineer in the Austrian Army who was inspired by the work of Robert Goddard and Hermann Oberth, he prepared the first detailed technical designs of a space station. He described the use of orbiting spacecraft for detailed observation of the ground for peaceful and military purposes, and described how the special conditions of space could be useful for scientific experiments. Unfortunately, Noordung died of tuberculosis in 1929 not long after the book's publication and failed to follow up on his early conceptions.

Other aspects of spaceflight captured the imagination of many people in this same era. Capitalizing on the success of Buck Rogers, in 1934 Alex Raymond created the *Flash Gordon* comic strip, and a host of toys, games, movies, and other items appeared thereafter.

What may be concluded from this mixing of science fiction with science fact is how closely the dominant trends in science fiction literature and film, as well as public perceptions, reinforce actual events in spaceflight and therefore fundamentally affect public support for the activity. As the relationship between reality and perceptions drew tightly together they created an expectation that allowed the accomplishment of an aggressive space agenda.

Flash Gordon pursued adventures on land and sea as well as in space. This record from 1948 played a story titled, "City of Sea Caves."

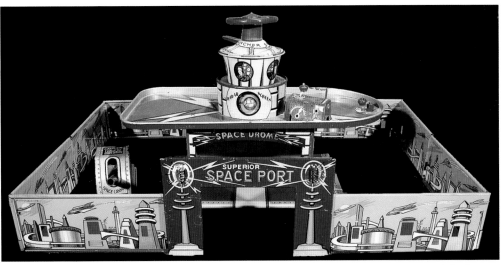

This metal toy set dating from the 1950s consisting of nine separate pieces depicts a spaceport of the future.

These Flash Gordon and other ray gun toys date initially from the 1930s but were also produced by such companies as American toymaker Louis Marx & Co. into the 1950s.

This Buck Rogers Solar Scouts Badge was a popular children's item produced in the 1930s.

This Buck Rogers pin from 1934 was given to attendees to the Buck Rogers show at the Chicago's World's Fair, known as "A Century of Progress."

This Buck Rogers comic book popularized the adventure of space travel for children throughout the United States.

Considering the Moon

What is it about the Moon that captures the fancy of humankind? A silvery disk hanging in the night sky, it conjures up images of romance and magic. It has been counted upon to foreshadow important events, both of good and ill, and its phases for eons served humanity as its most accurate measure of time. Since ancient times, people have watched the Moon wax (appear to grow larger) and wane (appear to shrink) and wondered at its beauty and mystery. The Moon holds an important place in many of the world's religions, and once had a part in other religions—such as Christianity—that no longer assign it special significance. Many of those religions see the Moon as a deity, with many names and many incarnations.

The Moon is by far the most dominant and changeable element in the night sky. It has kindled enthusiasm, joy, lust, fear, and horror upon generations of peoples of all races and cultures who have lived out their lives under its silvery reflected light. Defined differently from culture to culture and age to age, humankind remains captivated by its power. We have characterized it by its features, by its phases, and by its influence over Earthly entities whether they are animate or not. Moongazing is one of the oldest pastimes in the human experience.

Ancient civilizations assigned the Moon dominion over their lives through supernatural intervention; others have envisioned it as a home for extraterrestrial life. It inspires poets and artists, scientists and engineers, creators and destroyers. With the invention of the telescope at the turn of the seventeenth century—coinciding with the rise of the Scientific Revolution—the Moon took on new meaning as a tangible place with mountains and valleys and craters that could be named and geological features and events that could be studied.

The first truly modern science fiction writer, Jules Verne, specifically focused on the Moon in his novels. For example, in 1865 Verne published *De la Terre a la Lune* (*From the Earth to the Moon*). The scientific principles informing this book were very accurate for the period. It described the problems of building a vehicle and launch mechanism to visit the Moon. At the end of the book, Verne's characters were shot into space by a 900-foot-long cannon. Verne picked up the story in a second novel, *Autour de la Lune* (*Around the Moon*),

describing a lunar orbital flight, but he did not allow his characters actually to land.

The Moon is often seen as a gift of intense romance from one lover to another. This is a part of our cultural heritage and accepted as an expression of intense affection. For instance, in the classic Frank Capra motion picture, *It's a Wonderful Life* (1946), the leading character George Bailey, played by Jimmy Stewart, tells his future wife, played by Donna Reed:

George: What do you want, Mary? Do you want the moon? If you want it, I'll throw a lasso around it and pull it down for you. Hey! That's a pretty good idea! I'll give you the moon, Mary.

Mary: I'll take it! Then what?

George: Well, then you can swallow it, and it'll all dissolve see, and the moonbeams would shoot out of your fingers and your toes and the ends of your hair . . . am I talking too much?

As spaceflight became a possibility in the twentieth century the Moon took on added meaning as Earth's nearest astronomical neighbor and a relatively easy place for humankind to visit and explore. The Moon was early on an

Lukian of Samosata wrote "A True History," or "Vera Historia," about 165 C.E., telling the story of a vessel sailing with 50 Greek soldiers to the Moon. It is widely viewed as the first work of science fiction. Here one of the scenes from the book is depicted as the people living on the Moon are surprised by "Cloud Centaurs." This illustration was first published in the 1880 edition of the work translated by Alfred J. Church.

This map of the Moon was made by Hevelius, one of the most famous astronomers of his time. Hevelius built an observatory in 1641 and spent the rest of his life observing the Moon and other celestial objects. While Galileo had been the first to observe lunar mountains, Hevelius made the first detailed drawings and published the first selenographical atlas. This is one map from his larger atlas, the most accurate possible at that time. Hevelius's atlas remained a standard work until the nineteenth century.

attractive target for both the United States and the Soviet Union in their rocket-propelled space programs during the latter 1950s and 1960s because it was so comparatively close. There were also numerous opportunities every month for a launch from the Earth to the Moon.

In the desperate rivalry between the United States and the Soviet Union during the Cold War it held enormous potential as a public relations coup for the nation reaching it first. The number of spaceflight "firsts" associated with the Moon in the 1950s and 1960s clearly demonstrates the significance assigned to various lunar exploration efforts during this first heroic era of the space age. From the first clear images of the Moon to the last landings in the 1970s and to the present, this celestial body has held a fascination that propels the space program.

In 1887 Andre Laurie (a pseudonym for Paschal Groussey) published *Les exiles de la terre (Exiles from the Earth)*, a strange plot in which Earthlings use an electromagnet in the Sahara to pull the Moon toward Earth, give it an Earth-like atmosphere, and make it more accessible for exploration. This illustration depicts an artist's conception of the lunar surface from that work.

Artist Pierre Mion's 1979 painting entitled *Astronauts Explore the Moon* dramatizes the immense size of the lunar craters and mountains on the lunar surface, with astronauts at the bottom dwarfed by the landscape.

This mosaic picture of the Moon was compiled from 18 images taken with a green filter by the Galileo spacecraft's imaging system during its flyby on December 7, 1992. The north polar region is near the top part of the mosaic, which also shows Mare Imbrium, the dark area on the left; Mare Serenitatis at center; and Mare Crisium, the circular dark area to the right. Bright crater rim and ray deposits are from Copernicus, an impact crater 96 kilometers (60 miles) in diameter.

The Lure of the Red Planet

Like the Moon, Mars has long held a special fascination for humans who pondered the planets of the solar system—partly because of the possibility that life might either presently exist or at some time in the past have existed there. Italian astronomer Giovanni Schiaparelli published a work in 1877 that laid the foundation for the belief in canals on Mars. His map of Mars showed a system of what he called canali; in Italian this meant "channel" and carried no connotation of being an artificial feature. Even so, the word was commonly translated into English as "canal" and began the speculation that Mars held beings that were changing the planet's features for their own purposes.

American astronomer Percival Lowell became interested in Mars during the latter part of the nineteenth century, and built what became the Lowell Observatory near Flagstaff, Arizona, to study the red planet. His research advanced the argument that Mars had once been a watery planet and that the topographical features known as canals had been built by intelligent beings. Over the course of the first forty years of the twentieth century others used Lowell's observations of Mars as a foundation for their arguments. The idea of intelligent life on Mars stayed in the popular imagination for a long time, and it was only with the scientific data returned from probes to the planet since the beginning of the space age that this began to change.

Lowell published in 1908 *Mars as an Abode of Life* based on his extensive visual observations and what has proven to be an exceptionally active imagination. He offered a compelling portrait of a dying planet, whose inhabitants had constructed the vast irrigation system of canals to distribute water from the polar regions to the population centers nearer the equator. Despite its popular appeal, many astronomers refused to accept Lowell's theory. They could not confirm his observations and many soon concluded that he had been fooled into seeing the canals.

Lowell's observations gave rise to the Martian myth, one of the most powerful ideas motivating human curiosity about the solar system during the twentieth century. People

Following the 1898 publication of *War of the Worlds,* by H. G. Wells, an artist envisioned how intelligent creatures on this low-gravity world might appear for a 1908 serialization of the novel in *Cosmopolitan.*

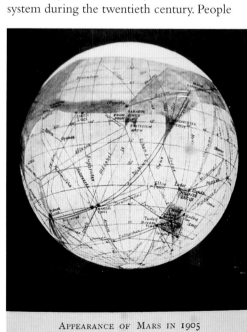

APPEARANCE OF MARS IN 1905

This map from Lowell's *Mars as an Abode of Life* shows the canals that he thought existed on the Martian surface.

genuinely expected explorers to find life on Mars. Magazine illustrations commonly portrayed the planet as a network of canals. Editors at *Life* magazine informed readers of a 1944 issue that the canals served to irrigate patches of vegetation "that change from green to brown in seasonal cycles." Willy Ley, one of the most popular science writers of that time, assured readers of a 1952 issue of *Collier's* magazine that primitive plant life "like lichens and algae" surely existed on Mars. Where plants exist, Ley added, animals must have followed. Walt Disney, in a widely viewed 1957 television broadcast, showed animated drawings of flying saucers skimming over fields of Martian plants and animal life.

Such speculations fueled a powerful conception in the first half of the twentieth century that theorized that the Sun had gradually been cooling for millennia and that as it did so each planet in the Solar System had a turn as a haven for life of various types. While it was now Earth's turn for life to exist, the theory suggested that Mars had once been habitable and that life on Venus was now just beginning to evolve. Beneath the clouds of Venus, this theory offered, was a warm, watery world and the possibility of aquatic and amphibious life. "It was reasoned that if the oceans of Venus still exist, then the Venusian clouds may be composed of water droplets," remarked JPL researchers as late as 1963; "if Venus were covered by water, it was suggested that it might be inhabited by Venusian equivalents of Earth's Cambrian period of 500 million years ago, and the same steamy atmosphere could be a possibility."

Near the same time, British science fiction writer H. G. Wells's novel, *The War of the Worlds* (1898), describes an invasion of England by Martians. It is one of the earliest, best-known, and most influential stories of alien invasion ever written, and it has influenced many other works of film, radio, television, and fiction since that time. One 1938 radio broadcast by Orson Welles caused public outcry, as many listeners believed that an actual Martian invasion was in progress. That hysteria said more about the American public in the years just before World War II and the general belief in life on Mars than perhaps any other piece of evidence.

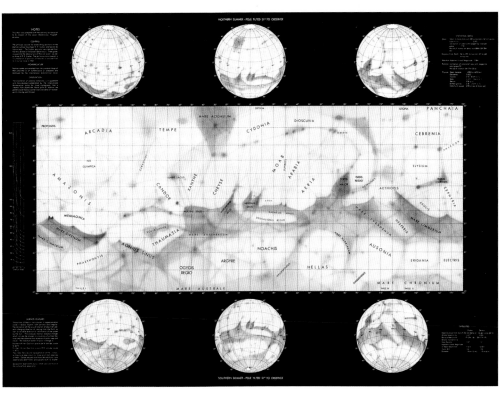

This Mars map from 1967 shows the most detailed information about the surface of the planet available at the time. A 1:35M scale at the equator, this global, color map has six orthographic projections of Mars. Even at this time, the features could still be interpreted as canals.

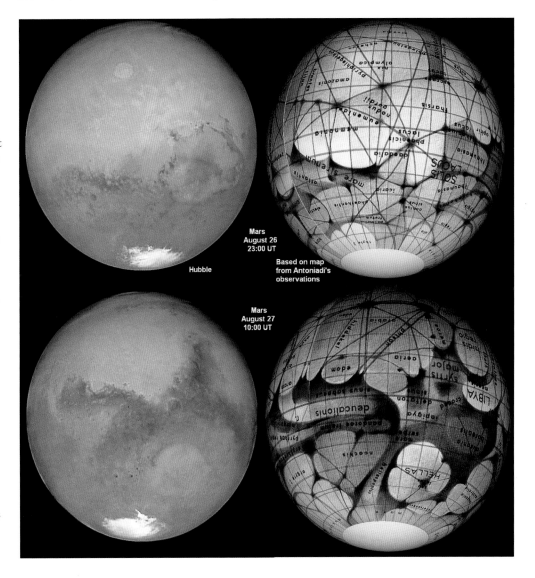

These maps, constructed from Viking orbiter images in the 1970s in the same format as Schiaparelli's—south is up—shows no sign of the canals, though a few features may have been interpreted as such.

Concepts for Missions to the Moon and Mars

In the middle part of the twentieth century, as spaceflight appeared on the verge of reality, several individuals began speculating on how to fly to the Moon and Mars. No one was more eloquent in this effort than German engineer Wernher von Braun, the godfather of the V-2 rocket and a postwar immigrant to the United States with a contingent of associates who had built this first ballistic missile in human history.

In essence, von Braun envisioned an expedition much like that conducted by Lewis and Clarke on the American frontier. In a 1952 plan, outlined in *Collier's* magazine, von Braun described a fifty-person expedition on a six-week reconnaissance of the Moon. Technicians in space suits, von Braun proposed, would assemble three very large spaceships in the vicinity of an orbiting space station. Each spaceship would measure 160 feet in length and, fully fueled, weigh more than 4,000 tons. Two of the ships would carry sufficient fuel to land on the Moon and return to the Earth orbiting station. The third would carry a 75-foot-long cargo container to the lunar landing zone. Once on the lunar surface, astronauts would unload supplies from the cargo container using large construction cranes. The empty cargo container would be removed from the landing craft and split in half to create two ready-to-use Quonset huts for the expedition's base camp.

Von Braun proposed that astronauts set up their base camp in a crevice beneath a towering mountain range, so as to protect the expedition from cosmic radiation. To do this, astronauts would need to tow their equipment from the landing site to the base camp using three pressurized tractors. "The principal aim of our expedition during this first lunar exploration will be strictly scientific," von Braun and astronomer Fred Whipple promised, by which they meant that military objectives would not dominate the mission. (At the time he outlined his proposal, von Braun designed missiles for the U.S. Army.)

Expedition leaders would probe the origins of the Moon, conduct experiments, and search for raw materials. They would dispatch ten persons on a ten-day round trip excursion to Crater Harpalus, 250 miles away, proceeding in a convoy of tractors and trailers. Plans called for the expeditionary corps to remain on the Moon for forty-two days.

Eventually, most thinkers on spaceflight believe that the effort must be self-sustaining and mining Helium-3 (He-3) on the Moon has been advanced by many, especially Apollo 17 astronaut Harrison Schmidt, as a commodity that could pay for itself many times over. It is a light, nonradioactive isotope of helium with two protons and one neutron sought after for use in nuclear fusion research. Virtually unknown on Earth, it is thought to be embedded in the upper layer of the lunar regolith by solar wind bombardment over billions of years. Many conceptions of lunar exploitation involve mining this or other rare materials.

In 1948, Wernher von Braun developed specifications for a Mars expedition which he hoped to present in a science fiction novel. The novel was never published in his lifetime, but the technical plans were.

In von Braun's view, the first expedition

Cover of *Collier's* magazine, April 30, 1954. The ultimate objective for the first set of pioneers was a human expedition to Mars, the arrival of which is depicted in this painting by Chesley Bonestell. It helped to energize public excitement for the possibility of a wondrous future in space.

Artist's depiction of humans exploring the Martian system, after 2020, by Ren Wicks. Mars advocates would like to dispatch the first expedition before 2030, but the cost and technical complexity of the mission will likely delay it.

This illustration by Chesley Bonestell from 1949 depicts astronauts disembarking from a modified V-2 rocket during the first expedition to the Moon. The painting appeared on the dust jacket of a 1949 book by Bonestell and Willy Ley, *The Conquest of Space,* which laid out a realistic program of space exploration for the following fifty years.

would travel to Mars in a flotilla consisting of ten spaceships. Once in orbit around Mars, von Braun recommended that the expedition team fly to the surface in three airplanelike spacecraft. The first of the three landing craft would descend to the polar ice cap. Its crew would use skids instead of wheels to stop on the ice, the only surface thought sufficiently smooth for a safe landing. Unloading tractors and supplies, the crew would drive 4,000 miles to the Martian equator, where they would prepare a landing strip for the other two planes. For one of von Braun's books on the exploration of Mars, Chesley Bonestell painted a famous landscape incorporating the winged space planes and the expeditionary corps surveying a desertlike terrain.

According to von Braun's plan, the expedition would remain on Mars for 15 months, waiting for the two planets to realign themselves for a return voyage. Removing the wings from their landing craft, ground crews would set the space planes on their tails. The expedition team would gather on board, blast off, rendezvous with the spacecraft in which they had come, and head home.

These initial scenarios for missions to the Moon and Mars have evolved over time, but the desire to undertake them has not abated.

Artist's conception of lunar mining, after 2020. Artwork by Pat Rawlings. Many believe that the resource-rich Moon may one day sustain human efforts to remain in space indefinitely.

The Space Age Begins: Sputnik and Explorer

Although space science went back to the early twentieth century and advanced significantly during and after World War II (with the development of the German V-2 rocketry, for example), the history of U.S. space exploration really began in 1957 when the first artificial satellites were launched as part of the International Geophysical Year (IGY). This space age originated after the decision in 1955 by the U.S. National Security Council to approve development of a small scientific satellite "under international auspices, such as the International Geophysical Year, in order to emphasize its peaceful purposes; . . . considerable prestige and psychological benefits will accrue to the nation which first is successful in launching a satellite . . . especially if the USSR were to be the first to establish a satellite."

This commitment was followed by competition between the Naval Research Laboratory and the Army's Redstone Arsenal for government support to develop an IGY satellite. Project Vanguard, proposed by the Navy, was chosen on September 9, 1955, to carry the standard in launching a nonmilitary satellite for the IGY effort; the Navy's project was chosen over the Army's "Orbiter" proposal. The decision was made largely because the Naval Research Laboratory's candidate would not interfere with high-priority ballistic missile programs (it had the nonmilitary Viking rocket as its basis), whereas the Army's bid was heavily involved in those activities and proposed adapting a ballistic missile launch vehicle. In addition, the Navy project seemed to have greater promise for scientific research because of a potentially larger payload capacity.

Sputnik 1, launched on October 4, 1957, from the Soviet Union's rocket testing facility in the desert near Tyuratam in the Kazakh Republic, proved a decidedly unspectacular satellite that probably should not have elicited the horrific reaction it wrought. An aluminum 22-inch sphere with four spring-loaded whip antennae trailing, it weighed only 183 pounds and traveled an elliptical orbit that took it around the Earth every 96 minutes. It carried a small radio beacon that beeped at regular intervals and could by means of telemetry verify exact locations on the Earth's surface. Some U.S. cold warriors suggested that this was a way for the Soviets to obtain targeting information for their ballistic missiles, but that does not seem to have actually been the case. The satellite itself fell from orbit three months after launch on January 4, 1958.

With the launch of Sputnik 1, however, the space age was born and the world would be different ever after. This satellite was the Soviet entry into the IGY program, and its success spelled crisis in the United States.

This combination of technological and scientific advance, political competition with the Soviet Union, and changes in popular opinion about spaceflight came together in a very specific way in the 1950s to affect public policy in favor of an aggressive space program.

During the furor that followed in the Sputnik crisis many people accused the Eisenhower administration of letting the Soviet Union best the United States. The Sputnik crisis reinforced for many people the popular conception that Eisenhower was a smiling incompetent; it was another instance of a "do-nothing," golf-playing president mismanaging events. G. Mennen Williams, the Democratic governor of Michigan, even wrote a poem about it:

Oh little Sputnik, flying high
With made-in-Moscow beep,
You tell the world it's a Commie sky
and Uncle Sam's asleep.

You say on fairway and on rough
The Kremlin knows it all,
We hope our golfer knows enough
To get us on the ball.

On that same evening of October 4, Senate Majority Leader Lyndon B. Johnson, Democrat-Texas, presided over one of his patented barbecues at the LBJ Ranch in Texas.

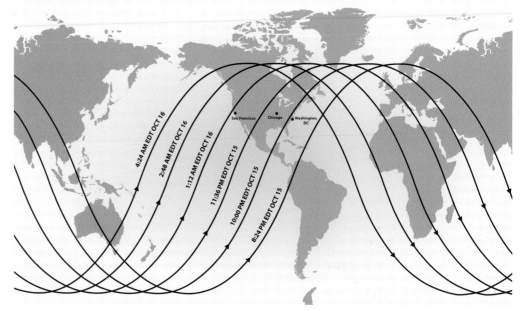

This exploded view of Sputnik 1 shows the inner parts of the Sputnik spacecraft.

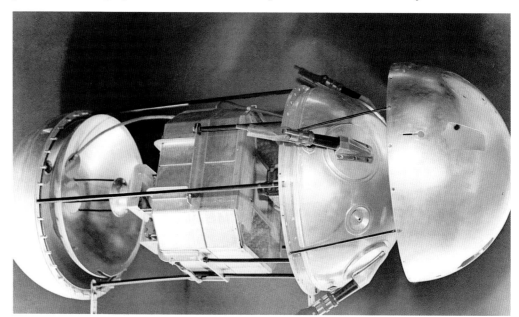

This plot showing the orbital track of the Sputnik 1 satellite was computed by scientists at Washington's Naval Research Laboratory and released on October 15, 1957.

While at the gathering he heard the announcement of Sputnik 1's launch on the radio. He led his guests on a nighttime ramble about the ranch to the nearby Pedernales River, as he commonly did at such affairs, but Johnson's mind kept returning to the heavens as he pondered the Soviet triumph. Johnson realized something had to be done about this problem.

As a result he opened hearings by a subcommittee of the Senate Armed Services Committee on November 25, 1957, to review the whole spectrum of American defense and space programs in the wake of the Sputnik crisis. This group found serious underfunding and incomprehensible organization for the conduct of space activities. It blamed the president and the Republican Party. One of Johnson's aides, George E. Reedy, summarized the feelings of many Americans: "the simple fact is that we can no longer consider the Russians to be behind us in technology. It took them four years to catch up to our atomic bomb; it took the Russians one year to catch our hydrogen bomb; now we do not even have a timetable for catching up to their satellite. We started out the race four laps ahead; we fell back to less than a lap; now all we can see is the dust."

Seeing this, the Eisenhower administration had to move quickly to restore confidence at home and prestige abroad. As the first tangible effort to counter the apparent Soviet leadership in space technology, the White House announced that the United States would test launch a Project Vanguard booster on December 6, 1957. The media was invited to witness the launch in the hope that it could help restore public confidence, but it was a disaster of the first order. During the ignition sequence, the rocket rose about three feet above the platform, shook briefly, and disintegrated in flames. Project manager John Hagen, who had been working feverishly to ready the rocket for flight, was demoralized. He felt even worse after the next test. On February 5, 1958, the Vanguard launch vehicle reached an altitude of four miles and then exploded. Hagen was tearful at the very public failures and some of his associates thought his career ended then and there, for he never again held an important post.

In this crisis the Army, featuring the handsome and charismatic Wernher von Braun and his rocket team of German immigrants to the United States after World War II, dusted off an unapproved plan for the IGY satellite effort, Project Orbiter, and flew it within a 90-day period of time. After two launch aborts that made observers nervous that the United States might never duplicate the Soviet successes in spaceflight, the Juno 1 booster carrying Explorer 1 lifted off from the Cape Canaveral, Florida, launch site at 10:55 p.m. on January 31, 1958. The tracking sites marked the course of the rocket to the upper reaches of the atmosphere, but they had to wait to learn if orbit had been achieved. It was, and Americans celebrated this success as the U.S. entered the space age.

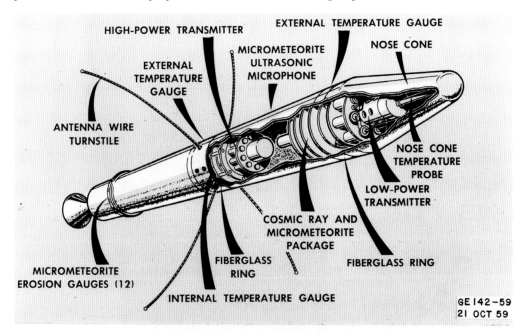

EXPLORER I

This 1959 drawing of the Explorer 1 spacecraft shows the internal components of the orbital vehicle.

The spectacular nighttime launch of Explorer 1 on January 31, 1958, the first U.S. Earth orbital satellite.

The Discovery of the Van Allen Radiation Belts

James A. Van Allen was a pathbreaking astrophysicist best known for his work in magnetospheric physics, and was the lead on the scientific instrument package on the Explorer 1 spacecraft that discovered the belts of radiation that now bear his name. In school Van Allen loved everything relating to science and mathematics, and he excelled in those areas as well as in wood shop and other classes where his mechanical skills were used. He enrolled at the California Institute of Technology in the fall of 1935 and completed an M.S. the next year. From there he proceeded to the Ph.D., defending his dissertation in June 1939.

After World War II, Van Allen began working in high-altitude research, first for the Applied Physics Laboratory and then, after 1950, at the University of Iowa. Using captured V-2s and other rockets developed in the postwar era, Van Allen continued studying the magnetosphere of Earth in a series of increasingly complex upper-atmosphere experiments. These investigated the properties of cosmic rays, solar ultraviolet, high-altitude photography, atmospheric ozone, and ionosphere current systems. By the mid-1950s, Van Allen had developed a reputation as a pathbreaking scientist in these increasingly important areas of research.

Van Allen's career took an important turn in 1955 when he and several other American scientists developed proposals for the launch of a scientific satellite as part of the research program conducted during the International Geophysical Year (IGY) of 1957–1958. Van Allen supported the proposal of both the Army's Redstone Arsenal and the Naval Research Lab, offering a satellite to study terrestrial magnetism. But Project Vanguard, proposed by the Navy, was chosen over the Army's Explorer satellite on September 9, 1955.

After the success of the Soviet Union with Sputnik 1, the Explorer spacecraft was approved for launch on a Redstone rocket. It flew with Van Allen's experiments on January 31, 1958, and returned critical data about the radiation belts encircling Earth. Van Allen became a celebrity because of the success of this mission, and he pursued other important scientific projects in space thereafter. The radiation belts he discovered now bear his name, and the discipline of magnetospherics became important in part because of his initial work. In one way or another Van Allen was involved in the first four Explorer probes, the first Pioneers, several Mariner efforts, and the orbiting geophysical observatory.

Project Vanguard also received additional funding to accelerate its activity, and Vanguard

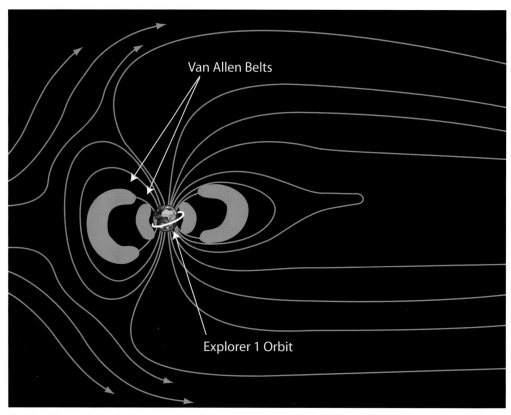

The Van Allen radiation belts are a series of concentric arcs that ring the Earth, trapped by the planet's magnetic field. The magnetic field serves as a shield for the surface of the Earth from deadly cosmic rays and radiation from the Sun. It is one of the major reasons why life as it exists here is able to survive.

1 was finally orbited on March 17, 1958. Vanguard 1 and its successor satellites in 1959 conducted geodetic studies of the Earth, explored further the Van Allen radiation belts, and discovered the Earth's slightly "pear" shape. Both the Vanguard and the Explorer series of satellites were enormously important in collecting scientific information about the universe. They were also partially successful in salving the nation's wounds at not being first in orbiting a satellite.

Since Explorer 1, measurements by numerous spacecraft have calculated the size and intensity of this field, showing that it contains two belts of very energetic, charged particles. At its upper limits the magnetosphere encounters charged plasma particles thrown off by the Sun, known collectively as the solar wind, which create a boundary where the two come into contact. These electromagnetic fields interact and create shock waves, some of which are responsible for auroral phenomena such as the aurora borealis, or northern lights. Perhaps as important as the discovery of the radiation belts and the rise of magnetospheric physics, Explorer 1 demonstrated that a team of academic scientists could design and build instruments that worked well in space.

This front page of the *Hunstville Times*, from Huntsville, Alabama, where the builders of the Redstone rocket that launched Explorer 1 into orbit lived, ballyhoos the accomplishment for the local audience.

This iconic image from the launch of Explorer 1 on January 31, 1958, was taken at a press conference at the National Academy of Sciences building in Washington, D.C., in the dead of night after the launch. The next day, this image appeared in newspapers around the world. Pictured (L-R) are William Pickering, director of the Jet Propulsion Laboratory and lead on the science effort for Explorer 1; James Van Allen, scientific principal investigator for the mission; and Wernher von Braun, technical director of the Army Ballistic Missile Agency that built and launched the Juno 1 rocket that placed Explorer 1 into orbit. Two points about this image are important. First, the inclusion of the U.S. flag on the left is no accident; it demonstrates that this was a national effort. Second, military officers such as Army General John B. Medaris deserves to be in this photo but his uniform would signal the military nature of the launch.

This image shows the nighttime launch of the Cassini spacecraft to Saturn in 1997 aboard a Titan IV launch vehicle from Cape Canaveral, Florida.

part three
GATEWAYS TO SPACE

In 2008 there were more than 60 space-faring nations on Earth. Each engaged in space activities in several realms ranging from human spaceflight to Earth applications technologies to scientific missions beyond Earth. Several of these nations have their own launch complexes and engage in space-access activities. Worldwide as of 2008 24 specific spaceports were in operation and another 8 were in development. The largest of these, at Cape Canaveral, Florida, and Baikonur, in the former Soviet Union, undertake many orbital launches per year, some of which are human missions. The European Space Agency's massive launch complex at Kourou, French Guiana, confines itself to the launch of commercial and scientific missions. Israel's launch complex on the eastern shore of the Mediterranean Sea is the only site where space launches are sent east to west. Other launch complexes are intermittently used at best. On the pages that follow are images and maps, along with descriptions, of many of these spaceports.

Equally important, the rockets launched from these sites have provided space access for the nations of the world for a host of activities in Earth orbit and beyond. The rockets used for these flights are also discussed below.

This overview from the rear of the Russian Mission Control Center shows flight controllers of the International Space Station in 2007.

Antecedents of Space Launch: The X-15 and Dyna-Soar Programs

One of the dreams of space access came with the lessons learned from the X-15 program, operated between 1959 and 1968. It has been lauded loud and long for two specific reasons: its outstanding technology and its exceptionally brave and proficient pilots. The program began in earnest in 1954 with the issuance of preliminary specifications for this vehicle. The National Advisory Committee for Aeronautics (NACA) made these unusually concise, only four pages in length, with six additional pages of supporting data.

The X-15 that emerged from this effort had a long fuselage built by North American Aviation, Inc., with short stubby wings and an unusual tail configuration. A Reaction Motors, Inc., XLR99 rocket engine generating 57,000 pounds (253,549 newtons) of thrust powered the aircraft. This engine used ammonia and liquid oxygen for propellant and hydrogen peroxide to drive the high-speed turbopump that forced fuel into the engine. This rocket could be throttled like an airplane engine, and was one of the first such throttleable engines that was "human-rated" or declared safe to operate with a pilot aboard.

The X-15 first flew on June 8, 1959, on a glide flight. It was dropped from under the wing of a specially modified B-52 "mothership." The first powered flight took place on September 17. Once the X-15 fell clear of the B-52, pilot Scott Crossfield ignited the rocket engine and flew to a relatively pokey Mach .79. But the X-15 was soon traveling many times the speed of sound. The X-15 continued flying until October 24, 1968. In all it made 199 flights divided among three aircraft and established many records.

During its early years of flight, the X-15 confirmed hypersonic models developed by U.S. aerodynamicists. These models of flight were later used to design other missiles and spacecraft, such as the Space Shuttle. This program proved enormously productive in that capacity. In October 1968 NASA engineer John V. Becker summarized 22 accomplishments from the research and development work that produced the X-15, 28 accomplishments from its actual flight research, and 16 from experiments carried by the vehicle. The X-15 actually achieved Mach 6.7, and an altitude of 354,200 feet, a skin temperature of 1,350 degrees Fahrenheit, and dynamic pressures over 2,200 pounds per square foot.

Once the NACA achieved the original research goals, moreover, because of its abil-ity to reach such high speeds and altitudes the X-15 proved useful as a high-altitude hypersonic test bed for 46 follow-up experiments. For approximately the last six years of the program, the X-15 supported various types of technology development programs that required high-speed flight. Among other things, it carried micrometeorite collection pods and ablative heat shield samples for Project Apollo and various other experiments.

Much more important, however, the joint Air Force-Navy-NASA-North American program investigated all aspects of piloted hypersonic flight. Yielding over 765 research reports, the program "returned benchmark hypersonic data for aircraft performance, stability and control, materials, shock interaction, hypersonic turbulent boundary layer, skin friction, reaction control jets, aerodynamic heating, and heat transfer," as well as energy management.

The X-15 program pioneered materials, aerodynamics, guidance and control, propulsion, and avionics associated with high-speed aircraft and spacecraft, as well as the techniques to construct them. Lessons learned with its rocket engine proved critical to the development of later rocket engines, such as the Space Shuttle Main Engine. As one other example, Inconel X, developed as a heat-resistant skin for the X-15, was used for some critical parts of the Space Shuttle structure.

Also during the 1960s, the U.S. Air Force pursued the X-20 Dyna-Soar, a military space-plane that would provide long-range bombardment and reconnaissance capability by flying at the edge of space and skipping off the Earth's atmosphere to reach targets anywhere in the world. Begun on December 11, 1961, the Air Force intended to use the Titan IIIC to launch its military orbital spaceplane. This winged, recoverable spacecraft did not possess as large a payload as NASA's capsule-type spacecraft and was always troubled by the absence of a clearly defined military mission. Accordingly, in September 1961 Defense Secretary Robert S. McNamara questioned whether Dyna-Soar represented the best expenditure of funds. This resulted in numerous studies of the program, but in 1963 McNamara canceled the Dyna-Soar program without it ever reaching the prototype stage.

Neil Armstrong, the first person to set foot on the Moon in Apollo 11 in 1969, was a civilian NASA research pilot for the X-15. Here he is standing with his vehicle in 1960.

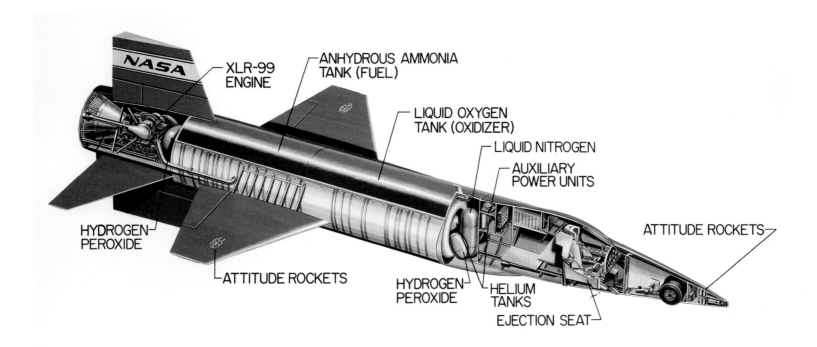

XLR-99
ENGINE

ANHYDROUS AMMONIA
TANK (FUEL)

LIQUID OXYGEN
TANK (OXIDIZER)

LIQUID NITROGEN

AUXILIARY
POWER UNITS

ATTITUDE ROCKETS

HYDROGEN
PEROXIDE

ATTITUDE ROCKETS

HYDROGEN
PEROXIDE

HELIUM
TANKS

EJECTION SEAT

This cutaway drawing of the X-15 was created by North American Aviation in 1962 to show the basic features of this exceptionally important hypersonic research vehicle.

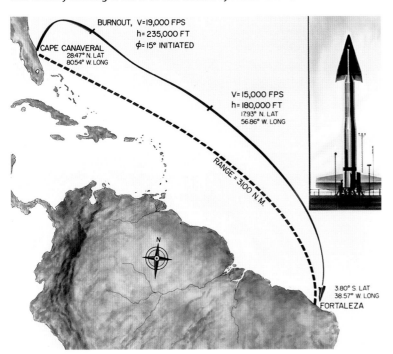

BURNOUT, V=19,000 FPS
h= 235,000 FT
φ= 15° INITIATED

CAPE CANAVERAL
28.47° N. LAT
80.54° W. LONG

V= 15,000 FPS
h= 180,000 FT
17.93° N. LAT
56.86° W. LONG

RANGE = 3100 N.M.

3.80° S. LAT
38.57° W. LONG
FORTALEZA

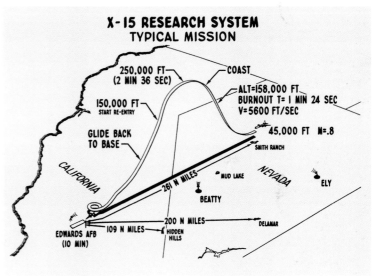

X-15 RESEARCH SYSTEM
TYPICAL MISSION

250,000 FT
(2 MIN 36 SEC)

COAST

150,000 FT
START RE-ENTRY

ALT=158,000 FT
BURNOUT T= 1 MIN 24 SEC
V= 5600 FT/SEC

GLIDE BACK
TO BASE

45,000 FT M=.8

SMITH RANCH

CALIFORNIA

261 N MILES

MUD LAKE

NEVADA

ELY

BEATTY

200 N MILES

DELAMAR

EDWARDS AFB
(10 MIN)

109 N MILES

HIDDEN
HILLS

Left: A projected mission profile for the first phase of suborbital tests for the Dyna-Soar. Above: This flight shows a typical mission of the X-15 superimposed over a map of southern California and the NASA flight research center.

This X-15 in flight in the early 1960s shows the vehicle passing the speed of sound as the air shock wave forms around the vehicle.

How Do We Reach into Space? Launch Means and Methods

Throughout the late 1940s and early 1950s scientists and engineers worked to learn more about accessing space. They conducted ever more demanding test flights and explored the idea of orbiting spacecraft. One of the most important efforts they undertook was Project Bumper, which mated a smaller Army WAC Corporal missile, produced at JPL, as a second stage on a V-2 to obtain data on both high altitudes and the principles of two-stage rockets.

Additionally, the Naval Research Laboratory was involved in sounding rocket research—nonorbital instrument launches using a Viking launch vehicle built by the Glenn L. Martin Co. Viking 1 launched from White Sands on May 3, 1949, while the twelfth and last Viking took off on February 4, 1955. The program uncovered significant scientific information about the upper atmosphere and took impressive high-altitude photographs of Earth.

The Army also developed the Redstone rocket during this same period, a missile

capable of sending a small warhead a maximum of 500 miles. Built under the direction of Wernher von Braun and his German rocket team in the early 1950s, the Redstone took many features from the V-2, added an engine from a Navaho test missile, and incorporated some of the components from other rocket test programs in its electronic components.

The first Redstone was launched from Cape Canaveral on August 20, 1953. An additional 36 Redstone launches took place through 1958, notably one on August 8, 1957, testing blunt-body shapes and ablative materials used to combat the rigors of superheating during reentry. This rocket led to the development of the Jupiter C, an intermediate-range ballistic missile that could deliver a nuclear warhead to a site after a nonorbital flight into space. Its capability for this mission was tested on May 16, 1958, when combat-ready troops first fired the rocket. The missile was placed on active service with American

The crawler-transporter approach as used for the Saturn V launch process has been followed by the Space Shuttle program. Here the Space Shuttle rides on the crawler transporter en route to LC-39. Note the vehicles shown for the scale of this transporter.

From the earliest times of the Soviet Union's space program it decided to move launchers horizontally by rail from the assembly building to the launch complex. Presently at Baikonur Cosmodrome, the principal Russian spaceport, payloads to be fired into orbit are prepared for launch in a processing center a few miles from the launch site. The overall testing as well as fueling and pneumatic pressurization of the spacecraft takes place there, and then the payloads are integrated with the rocket's upper stage. All of the rocket stages are sent by rail from the production plant, and mated for launch at this assembly point, before being loaded by cranes on a flat railroad transporter that takes it to the launch site, raises it vertically, and fires it into space. Here the Russian TM-31 Soyuz spacecraft approaches the launch complex on the horizontal rail car in preparation for its launch with a crew of three on October 31, 2000.

The Pegasus, the U.S.'s first air-launched orbital launch vehicle, is carried by a modified B-52 to its launch altitude of 12,000 m (39,000 ft.). The three-stage, solid-fuel Pegasus is then released and free-falls for five seconds in a horizontal position until it reaches a safe distance from the aircraft before its rocket engine ignites and accelerates it to orbital velocity. The vehicle's delta wing fins give additional lift as it travels through the upper atmosphere. It can place a small 450 kg (1,000 lb) satellite into Earth orbit. Developed by Orbital Sciences Corp., Pegasus was first launched on April 5, 1990. Since that first flight, it has orbited 70 satellites in more than 30 missions. Designed as a low-cost vehicle for launching lightweight satellites, it is often launched over the ocean, away from population centers, with spent stages falling safely into the sea. Of course, the idea of an air-launched space vehicle was not new—in 1956 the Italian Aurelio Robotti proposed one and in the 1980s both the Soviet and U.S. Air Force developed anti-satellite missiles that were air launched from high-speed aircraft.

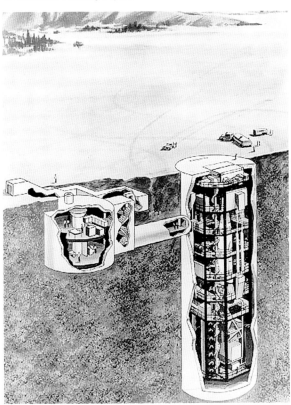

One of the truly significant advances in ballistic missile basing was its placement in nuclear-attack hardened silos to protect them from a Soviet first strike. This image shows the configuration of the silo as it was constructed. The missile would be stored and prepared for launch underground, but then elevated above the silo for launch. First deployed in the early 1960s, there were three types of operational Atlas missiles, each reflecting upgrades in technology. At the height of their deployment there were 8 Atlas D, 27 Atlas E, and 72 Atlas F operational missile complexes. They were controlled by ten different Air Force bases located throughout the United States. Each base had a Strategic Missile Squadron, reporting to the Strategic Air Command at Offutt Air Force Base near Omaha, Nebraska, which operated the silos. Missile crews rotated on alert assignments underground continuously throughout the Cold War era, but advancements in solid fuel rocket technology made the Atlas liquid-fueled missile obsolete by the mid-1960s and all of the Atlas missile sites were decommissioned. They were replaced by another liquid-fueled ICBM, the Titan II, and especially by the Minuteman solid-fueled ballistic missile that did not require as much care for its operations as the liquid-fueled launchers.

units in Germany the next month, and served until 1963.

During this same era all the U.S. armed services worked toward the fielding of intercontinental ballistic missiles (ICBM) that could deliver warheads to targets half a world away. Competition was keen for the development of an intercontinental ballistic missile. The first-generation ICBM was the underground-siloed Atlas, followed quickly by the Titan missile in the early 1960s. To consolidate military efforts, Secretary of Defense Charles E. Wilson issued a decision on November 26, 1956, that assigned responsibility for land-based ICBM systems to the Air Force and sea-launched missiles to the Navy. The Navy immediately stepped up the development of the submarine-launched Polaris ICBM, which first successfully fired in January 1960.

The U.S. Air Force did the same with land-based ICBMs. The Atlas received high priority from the White House and hard-driving management from Brigadier General Bernard A. Schriever, a flamboyant and intense Air Force leader. The first Atlas rocket test fired on June 11, 1955, and a later version became operational in 1959. These systems were followed in quick succession by the Titan ICBM and the Thor intermediate-range ballistic missile. By the latter 1950s, therefore, rocket technology had developed sufficiently for the creation of a viable ballistic missile capability. It effectively shrank the size of the globe, and the United States—which had always before been protected from outside attack by two massive oceans—could no longer rely on natural defensive boundaries.

With the development of ICBMs, some launched from underground silos and submarines, a range of launch methods emerged thereafter. These involved transport from an assembly facility to a launch complex on either a crawler as was done for the Saturn V Moon rocket or on a rail system as used by the Soviet Union. There were also a range of options for an air-launched rocket, first seen with the test missions of the X-1 and the X-15 research aircraft, and later manifested with such modern rockets as the Pegasus.

Mission Control Centers

From the dawn of the space age, operators had to develop a means for ensuring the success of their launch and orbital missions. The Mission Control Center (MCC) was the result and over time it has emerged as the central unit that manages spaceflights. These are often part of a governmental agency. There are several such agencies in the world and many locations from which control might take place. The main task of any MCC is to handle all aspects of the space mission from the point of liftoff until landing or end of the operation. The MCC is staffed by a set of flight controllers, as well as supporting technicians in other locations, and the entire effort is overseen by a flight director who has overall responsibility for the success of the mission.

Depending on the complexity of the mission the MCC might range from a series of computer interfaces with a small number of controllers to a carefully defined set of procedures and processes choreographed in considerable detail and with large numbers of participants. The most well known of all MCCs was established for NASA's human spaceflight activities. It operated from Cape Canaveral for Project Mercury, but in 1965 moved to the Manned Spacecraft Center (renamed the Johnson Space Center in 1973) in Houston, Texas.

The look of MCC has changed over the years, but has consisted of a standard approach since the beginning. One wall has maps and large display screens depicting basic information about the flight. Rows of flight controllers sit facing those screens with the flight director occupying a central desk in an upper tier. Behind these controllers is a viewing area for observers who have no role in the operations taking place. Most of the time the MCC had about 20 or so controllers normally working there during a flight. Even so, there are usually about 50 people on a team, with three teams working nine-hour shifts each. Each team has a flight director responsible for all activities in the MCC.

NASA's historic MCC consisted of two identical rooms with a unique pattern and arrangement that bespoke the structure of NASA's approach to human spaceflight. Each console in the MCC is the base of operations for a flight control team and there are side rooms with staff dedicated to supporting the individual controllers working in the MCC. Early on a tradition emerged at NASA to affix to specific consoles the initials or abbreviated names for the functions carried out there. The MCC leadership called on people not by name but by their abbreviations—done initially because of the shift changes and the need to

keep straight who was doing what function at all times—and these call signs now signify all aspects of every spaceflight. Controllers referred to themselves and others by their call signs during all communication.

"The Trench" is the popular name for the first row of consoles, with four controlling stations present. These are for the propulsion systems engineer (BOOSTER), the retrofire officer (RETRO), the flight dynamics officer (FIDO), and the guidance officer (GUIDO). The BOOSTER monitors the propulsion system, while the RETRO, FIDO, and GUIDO handle spacecraft trajectory, course changes, and control.

The left side of the second row had the flight surgeon monitoring the health of the

This overall view of the NASA Mission Control Center (MCC), Houston, Texas, was taken during the Gemini V flight of August 21–29, 1965. Note the screen at the front of the MCC which is used to track the progress of the Gemini spacecraft.

The Mission Control Center at NASA's Johnson Space Center during the flight of STS-99, February 11–22, 2000. The recently built facility features a workstation-based operating system and considerable flexibility in flight control operations. This workstation-based system replaced a much older mainframe system, reducing maintenance costs and increasing capability.

astronauts and the capsule communicator (CAPCOM), which has always been responsible for voice transmissions between the ground and the spacecraft. CAPCOM is virtually always an astronaut, and except in emergencies no one else in MCC can speak directly to the astronauts. On the right side of an aisle are monitors for specific systems, including the EECOM, the electrical, environmental,

and consumables manager; the guidance and navigation engineer; the propulsion controller; the EVA staff; the payload and experiments controllers; and the INCO, the monitor for the spacecraft's communications and instrumentation.

On the third row are the communication officer, the operations and procedures engineer charged with coordinating with other teams

and assuring continual "go" conditions, an assistant flight director, and the flight director in a center console, with controllers assigned to flight operations and network issues on the right side of the row.

The final row includes representatives of public affairs charged with communicating to the media, flight operations management, liaison with other organizations, and the overall mission director. Often during human spaceflight missions this row included desks for the Johnson Space Center director, the Director of the Astronaut Office, and NASA headquarters officials.

Over time the specific seats and their placement in this mission control center has changed in response to new conditions and capabilities. For example, when the Space Shuttle began flying in 1981, increased emphasis on payload deployments and associated issues required that more emphasis in the MCC be placed on those responsibilities. When the international cooperation that led to the International Space Station emerged in the 1990s the MCC changed to reflect and incorporate into it representatives of other nations with their specific contributions to each mission.

The Historic Mission Control Center at the Johnson Space Center that had served so well during the Gemini, Apollo, and early Space Shuttle era was replaced in 1998 by a new MCC nearby while the old facility was frozen in time and made available for public tours through the Johnson Space Center Visitor's Center. Once opened, the new MCC had two rooms. The first was known as the "White" flight control room (FCR) and focused on Space Shuttle flights. A "Blue" FCR, somewhat smaller, handled International Space Station operations until moved to another facility in 2006. The ISS facility had a smaller crew of about twelve controllers and was set up for continuous operations since the space station had a rotating crew in permanent Earth orbit. A counterpart to the ISS MCC is also located in Korolyov, Russia, near the RKK Energia plant that built much of the Russian contribution to the station.

For scientific, national security, and commercial space missions, MCCs are usually located at the organization managing the effort. For NASA's robotic space explorers this is often at the Jet Propulsion Laboratory in Pasadena, California, although control may be distributed to other sites as necessary. Generally these are less elaborate operations with only a few controllers and places for the science team to participate in the activities of the mission controllers.

1 Booster	9 LM/EVA	14 Flight Director	16 Network Controller	18 Flight Operations Manager
2 Retrofire	10 LM G&N/Prop	15 Flight Activities	17 Public Affairs	19 Mission Director
3 Flight Dynamics	11 Comm Systems			20 Department of Defense
4 Guidance	12 Operations & Procedures			
5 Life Systems	13 Assistant Flight Dir			
6 CAPCOM				
7 CSM EPS/ECS				
8 CSM G&N/Prop				

This illustration shows the general configuration of the Mission Control Center at the Manned Spacecraft Center, Houston, Texas, during the Apollo era of the latter 1960s. Over time the positions have shifted but every aspect of the mission was represented by a controller in the MCC.

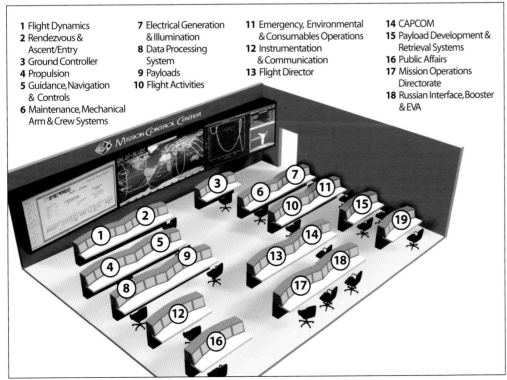

1 Flight Dynamics	7 Electrical Generation & Illumination	11 Emergency, Environmental & Consumables Operations	14 CAPCOM
2 Rendezvous & Ascent/Entry	8 Data Processing System	12 Instrumentation & Communication	15 Payload Development & Retrieval Systems
3 Ground Controller	9 Payloads	13 Flight Director	16 Public Affairs
4 Propulsion	10 Flight Activities		17 Mission Operations Directorate
5 Guidance, Navigation & Controls			18 Russian Interface, Booster & EVA
6 Maintenance, Mechanical Arm & Crew Systems			

This conception of mission control shows a configuration of the new facility since 1998. It features a workstation-based operating system allowing greater flexibility in flight control operations.

A Suite of Major Nonpiloted Launchers

After five decades of effort, access to space remains one of the most difficult issues space-faring nations face. The technical challenge of reaching space with chemical rockets—particularly the high costs associated with space launch, the long lead times necessary for scheduling flights, and the less than spectacular reliability of rockets—has demonstrated the slowest rate of improvement of all space technologies.

Of course, a key element in the space-faring vision long held is that inexpensive, reliable, safe, and easy spaceflight is attainable. Indeed, from virtually the beginning of the twentieth century, those interested in the human exploration of space have viewed as central to that endeavor the development of vehicles for flight that travel easily to and from Earth orbit. The more technically minded recognized that once humans had achieved Earth orbit about 200

miles up, the vast majority of the atmosphere and the gravity well had been conquered and that humanity was then about halfway to anywhere else they might want to go.

These pages offer a suite of major launchers used for robotic space missions over the history of spaceflight.

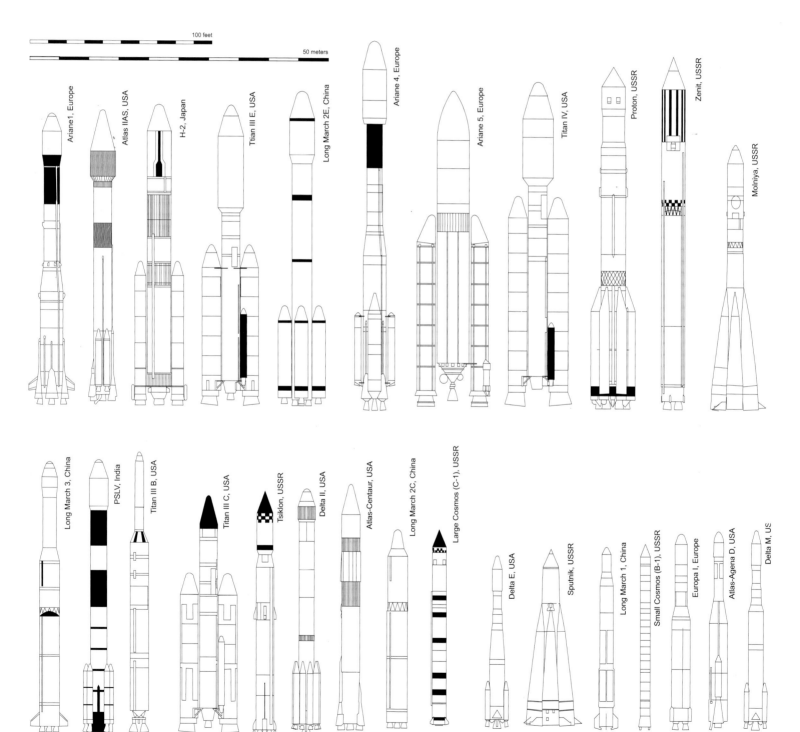

This Atlas/Centaur rocket ascends to orbit during a launch from Cape Canaveral on May 4, 1979, carrying the Fltsatcom 2 satellite into orbit.

This Titan IV is being prepared for its October 15, 1997, launch, when it carried into orbit the Cassini spacecraft bound for Saturn, lifting off from Launch Complex 40 at Cape Canaveral.

On November 20, 1998, this Proton launch from the Russian complex at Baikonur lifted into orbit the Zarya module of the International Space Station, the first component to be placed in orbit. The Zarya module was funded by NASA and built by Khrunichev in Moscow under subcontract from Boeing for NASA.

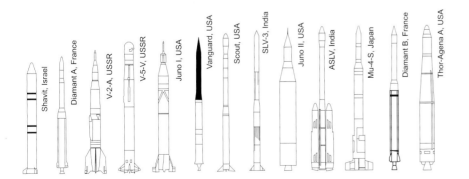

A Suite of Major Human Spaceflight Launch Vehicles

The human spaceflight endeavor has sparked considerable effort in both the United States and the Soviet Union/Russia in the period since the first launch of Sputnik 1 in 1957. The first human, Yuri Gagarin, flew a one-orbit mission on April 12, 1961, and the U.S. followed with its first human spaceflight, a suborbital ride by Alan Shepard, on May 5, 1961. A rivalry between these two superpowers in space followed throughout the 1960s as each sought to best the other with space spectaculars. The United States eventually achieved recognition for winning this contest with its stunning Apollo program, landing Americans on the Moon six times between 1969 and 1972.

All of these efforts required the development and operation of space launch vehicles capable of carrying human spacecraft. Although based largely on technology developed for the military intercontinental ballistic missile (ICBM) programs of these nations, launchers for human spaceflight required greater reliability and capability. In the United States the Redstone, Atlas, and Titan, which had begun development as ICBMs in the 1950s, provided the muscle that made possible the Mercury and Gemini astronaut programs of the 1960s. In 2008, the United States still relies on the descendants of these missiles for much of its space-access requirements. Even though the families of space boosters—each with numerous variants—have enjoyed incremental improvement since first flight, there seems no way to escape their beginnings in technology (dating back to the 1950s) and their primary task of launching nuclear warheads.

As a measure of governmental investment in that first generation of launchers, the Eisenhower administration undertook a study in the summer of 1957 and learned that through fiscal year 1957 the nation had spent $11.8 billion on military space activities in then-year dollars. "The cost of continuing these programs from FY 1957 through FY 1963," Eisenhower was told, "would amount to approximately $36.1 billion, for a grand total of $47 billion." In 2008 dollars, for comparison, this would have represented an investment of more than $235 billion.

Likewise, the Soviet Union's human space launchers were based on ICBM technology, and its current Soyuz launch vehicle is closely related to its ICBM antecedents. The U.S. and the Soviet Union did develop some rockets absent any military requirements, especially the two nation's Moon launchers, the Saturn family of vehicles for the U.S. (Saturn IB and V) and the N-1 for the Soviets, as well as a space shuttle. The U.S.'s Space Shuttle program served as the workhorse of its human spaceflight program between 1981 and the present—with a projected retirement in 2010—as did the Soviet Buran for the Soviet Union, which flew only one test mission before retirement in 1989.

Finally, the People's Republic of China (PRC) has developed its own human spaceflight capability and thus far has flown three missions—in 2003 with a single pilot, a two-person flight in 2005, and a 2008 mission—with launch vehicle technology also coming out of its ballistic missile effort. Other nations may join the human spaceflight community in future years, but thus far none has announced hardware development programs to make this possible.

These pages offer a suite of major launchers used for human space missions over the history of spaceflight.

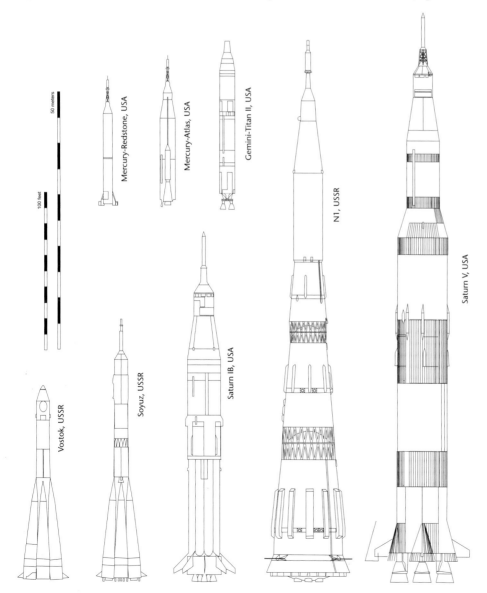

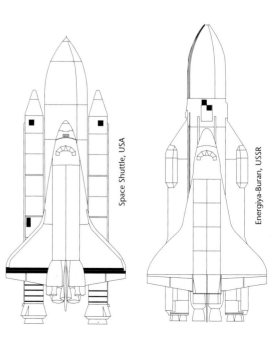

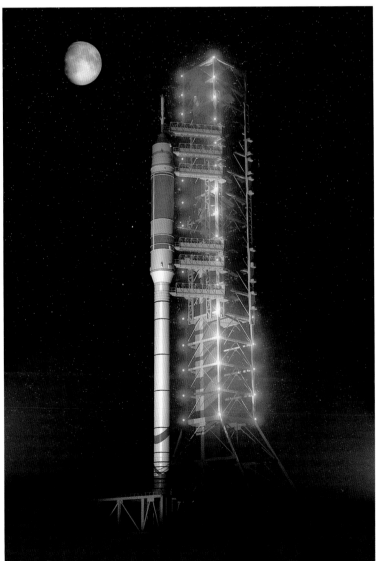

TOP LEFT: The R7 was a ballistic missile used for the launch of several space vehicles, both human and robotic, into Earth orbit. A vehicle similar to this was used to launch Yuri Gagarin on April 12, 1961. TOP RIGHT: The Soyuz TM-31 launch vehicle is shown in the vertical position for its launch from Baikonur, carrying the first resident crew to the International Space Station in 2000. The Russian Soyuz launch vehicle is an expendable spacecraft that evolved out of the original Class A (Sputnik). From the early 1960s until today, the Soyuz launch vehicle has been the backbone of Russia's space launch fleet. BOTTOM LEFT: This artist's conception of the Ares I launch vehicle is the vehicle under development in the first decade of the twenty-first century to replace the Space Shuttle. BOTTOM RIGHT: The launch of Apollo 11 on July 16, 1969, the first human-landing mission on the Moon.

The World's Spaceports

In the more than fifty years since the beginning of the space age, the most remarkable and visible installations created have been the launch facilities. These spaceports are not numerous, numbering only 24 active sites worldwide, but they have been active. Many of them are the sites where history was made. There are the well-known launch sites, such as those at the Kennedy Space Center and Cape Canaveral Air Force Base on the east coast of Florida. Some are popular places open to the public, while others are top secret closed sites shrouded in mystery, such as the Palmachim launch site in Israel. These various spaceports are national facilities, located at various places around the globe in response to political realities and geographical considerations.

Each of these sites offers the capability to launch satellites into various orbits around the Earth, most often in a west to east equatorial orbit, but for national security satellites usually in a polar orbit. Some launch sites also have concentrated on nonorbital flights, engaging in sounding rocket research in the upper atmosphere, such as that conducted at NASA's Wallops Flight Facility on the coast of Virginia. Since 1957, more than 5,000 satellites have successfully launched into orbit from these various sites.

The busiest spaceports are operated, as should be obvious, by the most aggressive nations involved in spaceflight. The space programs of the United States and Russia have long been comparable in size and operation and their spaceports account for the lion's share of the global launch activity. Among these Cape Canaveral, Vandenberg, Baikonur, and Plesetsk are the world's busiest spaceports. Close behind are the launch sites of the European Space Agency at Kourou, French Guiana; Tanegashima and Kagoshima, Japan; and Sriharikota, India.

As the twenty-first century progresses, the activity of these current spaceports will probably increase, and new sites will be added to fulfill future requirements for space access.

Worldwide Launch Sites

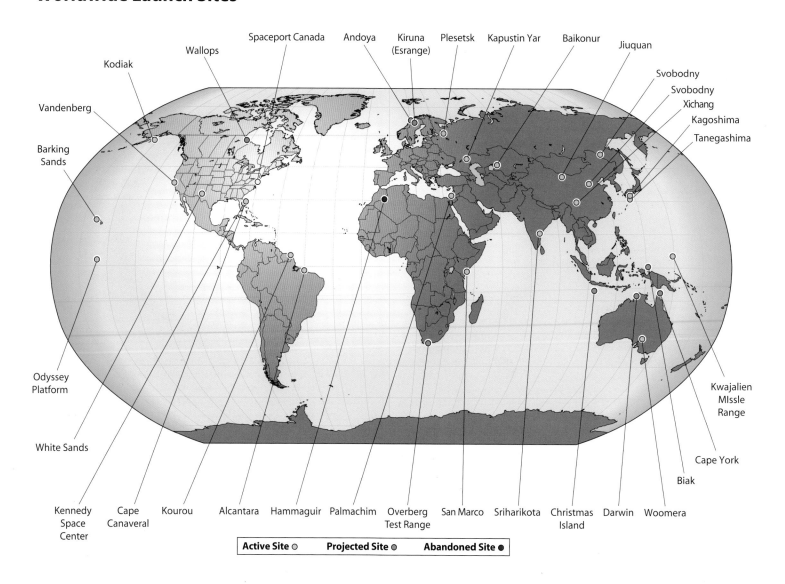

This test of the Titan II ICBM took place on September 12, 1962, at Launch Complex 15, Cape Canaveral, Florida.

This launch of the Titan IVB/Centaur launch vehicle from the Cape Canaveral Air Station, Florida, started the Cassini orbiter and its attached Huygens probe to Saturn. Launched on October 15, 1997, from Launch Complex 40 it would undertake a 2.2-billion mile journey that included two swingbys of Venus and one of Earth to gain additional velocity, arriving at Saturn in July 2004 where it entered orbit and soft-landed Huygens on Titan, one of Saturn's moons.

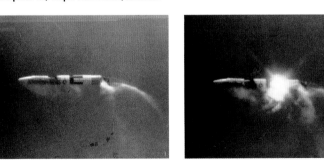
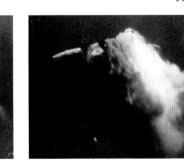

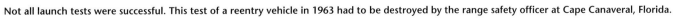

Not all launch tests were successful. This test of a reentry vehicle in 1963 had to be destroyed by the range safety officer at Cape Canaveral, Florida.

The Cape Canaveral Launch Complexes

On July 24, 1950, the first rocket lit up the sky above Cape Canaveral, Forida, a region on the east coast of the state known for its picturesque beaches, incessant mosquitoes and alligators, and ubiquitous orange groves. It was the launch of Bumper 8, a modified German V-2 with a WAC Corporal second stage—the first instance of an event that would become common in future years. At a fundamental level the "Cape," as it would universally come to be called by those in the space community, is as much a state of mind as it is a physical place. With high-technology enterprises resting side by side with a wetlands refuge it is an eerie place, what Ann Morrow Lindbergh referred to as the abode of both the "heron and the astronaut."

There are three central components to the Cape's space-access efforts. The one that is best known is the Kennedy Space Center, the NASA installation that serves as the site for the preparation and launch of the nation's human spaceflight effort. The Apollo and Space Shuttle launches have both taken place from there. In the future the Constellation program's space launches will take off from there as well. The military also has a huge presence at Cape Canaveral, with Air Force and Navy facilities engaging in all manner of test and evaluation in the Eastern Test Range into the Atlantic Ocean as well as firing NASA's Mercury and Gemini launcher. In recent years, finally, there has been a major effort to establish commercial space operations in the area and a growing number of nongovernmental launches have been flown from the Cape.

Throughout its history, the launch facilities on the Florida coast have been used for research and development with launches into the Atlantic Ocean missile range. Those flights included the ballistic missiles so well known in history—the Atlas, Titan, Minuteman, Polaris, Trident, and Poseidon—as well as cruise missiles such as the Matador, Snark, Bomarc, and Navaho. They also included scientific rocket launches, as well as the human space-flight missions, and the construction and operation of the facilities that supported them.

The Army missile development program housed in Huntsville, Alabama, established a formal presence at Cape Canaveral in 1951 by designating the spit of land east of mainland central Florida the Experimental Missiles Firing Branch, a subordinate unit of the Army Ordnance Guided Missile Center. Following the earlier launch of Bumper 8, it supervised test flights of the U.S. Army's Redstone intermediate-range ballistic missile (IRBM). In January 1953, upon expanding its responsibilities, the Army renamed this Cape Canaveral

This overall aerial view taken in the 1960s of Missile Row at Cape Canaveral Air Force Station is looking north. The Vertical Assembly Building (VAB) may be seen under construction in the upper-left-hand corner.

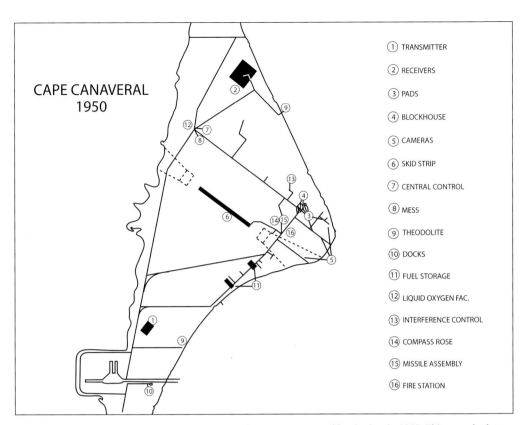

The first space launch capabilities were constructed at Cape Canaveral beginning in 1950. This map depicts the spaceport as it existed early in the space age.

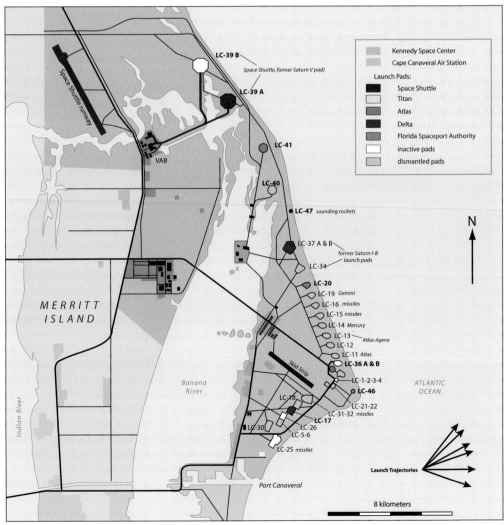

The modern Kennedy Space Center in its current configuration.

facility the "Missile Firing Laboratory." It went through a series of redesignations, expansions, and facilities until it achieved status on July 1, 1962, as the Launch Operations Center, a part of the National Aeronautics and Space Administration (NASA). After the assassination of President John F. Kennedy on November 22, 1963, his successor, Lyndon B. Johnson, renamed the Launch Operations Center the "John F. Kennedy Space Center," declaring that this was an especially fitting tribute since President Kennedy had "lighted the imagination of our people when he set the Moon as our target and man as the means to reach it." The spaceport, he added, would be a "symbol of our country's peaceful assault on space." Near the same time, the U.S. renamed Cape Canaveral Cape Kennedy, a designation that remained until 1973.

As NASA pursued its lunar landing program in the 1960s it acquired a 324-sq.-km tract of land on adjacent Merritt Island for assembling and launching its mighty Saturn V Moon rockets. Between 1962 and 1968 NASA built the Vertical Assembly Building (VAB) and Launch Complexes 39A and B for this purpose. After the last Apollo flights, launch complexes 39A and B were refurbished for Space Shuttle operations, and the VAB, renamed the Vehicle Assembly Building, was modified for the shuttle. Over time, this was expanded with additional Space Shuttle support facilities and other components for a one-stop spaceport for NASA and other entities. It now houses NASA's processing, launching, and landing facilities for the Space Shuttles and their payloads, as well as processing for the components of the International Space Station.

Meantime, the nearby Cape Canaveral Air Force Station and Patrick Air Force Base also played key roles in the development of the U.S. space launch infrastructure. Under the control of the U.S. Space Command's 45th Space Wing, these military installations have active Atlas and Delta launch complexes, as well as previous launch complexes used by earlier expendable launch vehicles and ICBMs. It also oversees the Eastern Test Range and provides support for military, NASA, and commercial launch operations. Throughout its history more than 400 space launches have been made from these installations. Currently, between 10 and 20 launches take place from this site on the east coast of Florida each year. The Spaceport Florida commercial launch site is also located at Cape Canaveral Air Station, operated by the Spaceport Florida Authority (SFA), and it has converted the Navy's Launch Complex 46 for firing medium commercial launchers. That Navy site was originally used for testing the Trident II submarine-launched ballistic missile (SLBM).

Not all events connected to Cape Canaveral have been positive. Three accidents—the Apollo 1 fire on January 27, 1967; the Challenger explosion on launch on January 28, 1986; and the Columbia breakup on reentry on February 1, 2003—have cost the lives of 17 astronauts. This image shows the grid on the floor of the RLV Hangar at KSC as workers in the field bring in pieces of Columbia's debris. The Columbia Reconstruction Project Team attempted to reconstruct the bottom of the orbiter as part of the investigation into the accident that caused the destruction of Columbia and the loss of its crew as it returned to Earth on mission STS-107.

This launch of Atlas-Centaur 10, carrying the Surveyor 1 spacecraft, lifted off from Pad 36A at Cape Canaveral on May 30, 1966. The Surveyor 1 mission scouted the lunar surface for future Apollo human lunar landing sites.

Looking up at the massive 363-foot-high Saturn V rocket, the launch vehicle is emerging from the VAB's High Bay 3 at the start of the 3.5-mile rollout to Launch Complex 39A on September 8, 1969. The transporter carried the 12.8-million-pound load along the crawlerway at speeds under one mile per hour.

This Delta II on the launch pad at Cape Canaveral is being prepared to launch NASA FUSE satellite on June 24, 1999.

The timed exposure of the Space Shuttle, STS-1, at Launch Complex 39A, depicted the space vehicle and support facilities in a unique way on April 12, 1981.

The Baikonur Soviet/Russian Launch Facility

At the height of the Cold War, on October 4, 1957, the Soviet Union made history by launching the first artificial satellite into orbit above Earth. That satellite, Sputnik 1, rode into orbit atop a modified R7 ballistic missile, known to its builders as "Old Number Seven," from the Baikonur Cosmodrome. Located on the steppes of Kazakhstan in central Asia,

near the Baikonur/Tyuratam area, this facility became the premier spaceport of the Soviet Union throughout the Cold War, and of Russia thereafter. The Soviets constructed the launch pad where Sputnik 1 and the flight of Yuri Gagarin originated in 1955. Sergei Korolev, Chief Designer of the Soviet R-7 ICBM, selected the site because of its remoteness,

accessibility within a few hundred miles by rail, and generally clear weather. The Soviet Union invested heavily to build assembly, checkout, and launch facilities; housing and offices; and a transportation and utilities infrastructure to support its operations.

In the closed society of the Soviet Union nothing was said about the remote site where

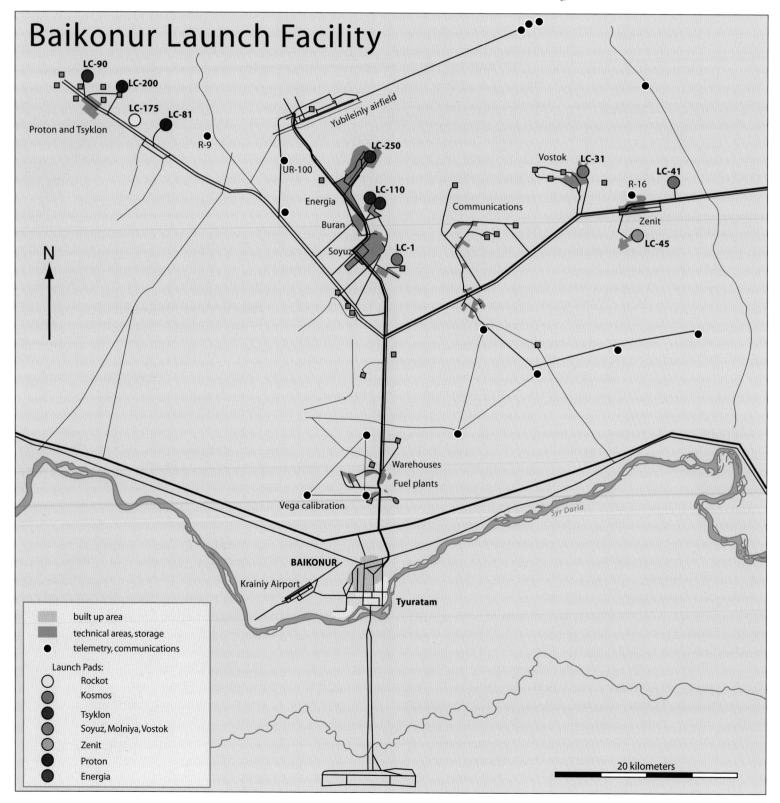

Soviet rocketeers tested their vehicles until the Sputnik 1 launch, which was so public that the world demanded details about this base. The Baikonur Cosmodrome is the oldest and largest operational space launch facility in the world. About 200 km (124 miles) east of the Aral Sea, secrecy drove Soviet officials to declare that the launch site was near Tyuratam, in reality more than 300 km (230 miles) southeast of the actual spaceport. With the breakup of the Soviet Union and the establishment of the state of Kazakhstan, in 1992 that government officially renamed the facility Tyuratam. Old names die hard, however, and the space community still refers to it as Baikonur Cosmodrome.

Over time the spaceport has grown in sophistication. It has nine expansive launch complexes encompassing fifteen launch pads and the support structures necessary to their operation. All of Russia's human spaceflights have been launched from the site, as has its interplanetary space probes. It remains important as the launch site for the Proton, Zenit, Energia, and Tsyklon SL-11 rockets. Baikonur Cosmodrome is, in essence, the Soviet/Russian equivalent of the American Cape Canaveral launch facilities. Even so, because Baikonur is not on a coast its rockets have to launch at a high inclination to avoid Chinese territory since a due east launch would mean that lower

rocket stages would fall there. By the end of the Cold War in 1990 the steppes to the northeast of Baikonur had many toxic spent booster stages littering it. Since that time efforts have been underway to mitigate this environmental hazard but the problem persists to some degree.

Two N1 Moon rockets appear on the pads at Baikonur in early July 1969. The N1 was designed for the Soviet space program's human lunar missions. In the foreground is booster number 5L with a functional payload for a lunar-orbiting mission. In the background is the 1M1 ground test mock-up of the N1 for rehearsing parallel launch operations. Attempting take-off the rocket collapsed back onto the pad, destroying the entire pad area in a massive explosion.

This image from the U.S. Corona reconnaissance spacecraft shows an N1-L3 (1M1) Moon rocket, on the launch pad at Baikonur. This picture was taken on September 24, 1968.

The Soyuz TMA-9 spacecraft launches from the Baikonur on September 18, 2006, carrying a new crew to the International Space Station. Among those aboard was spaceflight participant Anousheh Ansari, who spent nine days on the station as an adventure tourist.

Three Major Launch Sites: Kourou, Vandenberg, and Wallops

The Centre Spatial Guyanais (CSG) has existed as a French spaceport near Kourou, French Guiana, since 1968. It presents an ideal launch site because of its closeness to the equator and its location on the eastern coast of South America, thereby maximizing the launch capability of the rockets involved. The European Space Agency, the French space agency CNES, and the commercial Arianespace company conduct launches from this spaceport. Originally surveyed in 1964, CSC presently consists of a total of 850 square kilometers (330 sq mi). France used it for all manner of launch operations through the later 1960s and into the 1970s, as well as thereafter. With the creation of the European Space Agency (ESA) in 1975, ESA negotiated an arrangement to use Kourou for its space launches. The Ariane rocket, a commercial and scientific launcher, operates from this site, and the managing authority also leases commercial launches to non-European companies. The current arrangement has ESA paying two-thirds of the spaceport's annual budget while France has responsibility for the remainder.

While several rockets have launched from Kourou, the centerpiece of operations there are the flights of the Ariane family of space vehicles. The first of these took off from the spaceport on December 24, 1979, when ESA launched a scientific satellite into orbit. Supporting the more than 250 launches of the various rockets of the Ariane family, the largest and most recent of these, the Ariane V, has thus far been flown 38 times from the spaceport. Ground facilities supporting these flights include rocket (*l'Ensemble de Lancement*) and satellite processing buildings, launch control centers and support equipment, and a propellant installation. A major upgrade effort in the first decade of the twenty-first century involved the building of an l'Ensemble de Lancement Soyouz (ELS) to prepare and launch Russian-built Soyuz rockets from this spaceport about 10 km (6.2 mi) north of the launch complex used for the Ariane V.

Vandenberg Air Force Base (VAFB), on the Pacific Ocean 19 km (12 mi) north of Lompoc, California, and 241 km (150 mi) northwest of Los Angeles has long been the principal military launch complex of the U.S. Department of Defense. Operated by the U.S. Space Command 30th Space Wing, Vandenberg is the only military installation in the United States from which satellites may be launched into a polar orbit. Launching due south, recon-naissance and other polar-orbiting satellites

have embarked on their various missions since the first successful launch in 1960. Vandenburg has also served as the home of a variety of intercontinental ballistic missile test launches, firing them westward toward the Kwajalein Atoll in the Marshall Islands. It also manages the Western Range tracking network, extending into the Indian Ocean to meet an Eastern Range tracking network operated by Patrick Air Force Base in Florida.

Although it was never used for that purpose, in the early 1980s the Air Force intended to launch a military Space Shuttle similar to that operated by NASA on high-inclination orbital missions, mostly for satellite recon-naissance deployment operations, but after the Challenger accident of 1986 that program was scrapped. Space launch complex 6 (SLC, pronounced "slick") was under construction at that time and it sat vacant and unfinished for several years until refurbished for Delta IV launches beginning there on June 27, 2006. Other Delta rockets are flown from SLC-2W, Titans from SLC-4, and Atlas from SLC-3.

Control room personnel during the launch of ESA's ECS-1 and AMSAT's P3B from Europe's spaceport in Kourou, French Guiana, on June 16, 1983, aboard an Ariane 1. The ECS telecommunications satellites each operated up to nine Ku-band transponders working simultaneously through five beams across Europe, with a capacity equivalent to 12,000 telephone circuits or 10 TV channels. Five ECS satellites were built; ECS-3 was lost due to a launcher failure. After in-orbit testing, ECS-1 was handed over to Eutelsat by ESA on October 12, 1983. It was retired from service in December 1996, having been in service for almost twice its design lifetime of seven years.

An Ariane V ECA launcher lifted off from Europe's spaceport near Kourou, French Guiana, on its mission to place two telecommunications satellites, Skynet 5A and INSAT 4B, into geostationary transfer orbits, on March 11, 2007.

Other entities have used Vandenberg over the years for sounding rocket and commercial orbital launches. Without question, one of the most important of the launch operations of Vandenberg has been the reconnaissance satellites that observed the Soviet Union, China, and other nations on behalf of U.S. security efforts. The Corona program provided the first space-based overhead imagery. While the first 12 launches failed, on the launch from Vandenberg on August 18, 1960, the rocket and satellite performed as intended and two days later returned the first film canisters to Earth for development and analysis. With a variety of code names—(Keyhole) KH-1, KH-2, KH-3, KH-4, KH-4A, and KH-4B—there were a total of 144 Corona satellites launched, of

which 102 returned usable imagery. Corona as a program ended in 1972 but the reconnaissance satellite mission, performed with successor systems, has been continued from Vandenberg to the present.

The Wallops Flight Facility, located on the eastern shore of Virginia, is a NASA site inherited from the agency's successor, the National Advisory Committee for Aeronautics (NACA), upon the space agency's creation in 1958. Originally called the Pilotless Aircraft Research Station, it is one of the oldest launch sites in the world. It has been used by NACA and NASA continuously from the time of its first rocket launch on July 4, 1945, to the present.

Following Cape Canaveral and Vandenberg Air Force Base, Wallops became the U.S.'s

third space launch site in 1961 when NASA shot into orbit the Explorer 9 balloon aboard a solid-fueled Scout rocket. Over the course of its operations, NASA and other organizations have flown more than 14,000 rockets from Wallops. The principal rocket flown from Wallops was the Scout, its many variations being fired 118 times with an overall 96% success rate. Until retired in 1994, the Scout accomplished 94 orbital missions (27 Navy navigational and 67 scientific satellites), 7 probe missions, and 12 reentry missions. In addition to the Scout program, NASA has used Wallops for the launch of many other sounding rockets and other commercial and experimental launchers.

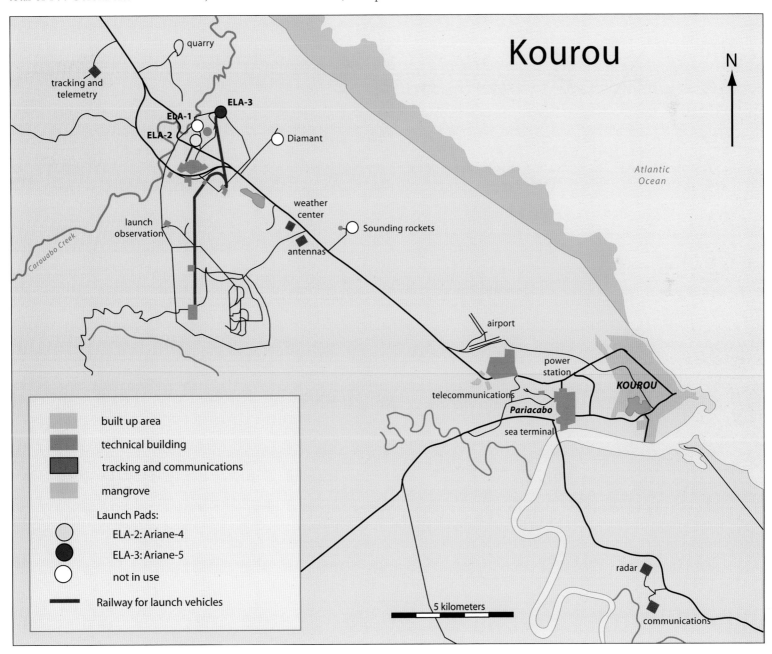

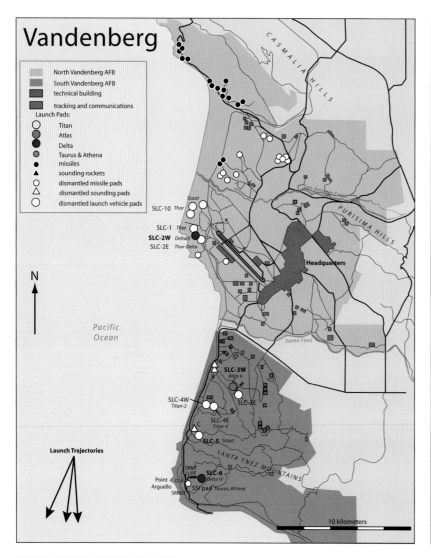

Vandenberg

Legend:
- North Vandenberg AFB
- South Vandenberg AFB
- technical building
- tracking and communications

Launch Pads:
- ○ Titan
- ◐ Atlas
- ● Delta
- ● Taurus & Athena
- • missiles
- ▲ sounding rockets
- ○ dismantled missile pads
- △ dismantled sounding pads
- ○ dismantled launch vehicle pads

CASMALIA HILLS

PURISIMA HILLS

San Antonio Creek

Headquarters

N

Pacific Ocean

Santa Ynez

SLC-10 Thor
SLC-1 Thor
SLC-2W Delta II
SLC-2E Thor-Delta

SLC-3W Atlas V
SLC-4W Titan-2
SLC-3E
SLC-4E Titan-4
SLC-5 Scout

SRMF
IPF
Point Arguello
OSB
SRMSF

SLC-6 Delta IV
SSI pad Taurus, Athena

SANTA YNEZ MOUNTAINS

Launch Trajectories

10 kilometers

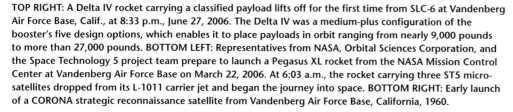

TOP RIGHT: A Delta IV rocket carrying a classified payload lifts off for the first time from SLC-6 at Vandenberg Air Force Base, Calif., at 8:33 p.m., June 27, 2006. The Delta IV was a medium-plus configuration of the booster's five design options, which enables it to place payloads in orbit ranging from nearly 9,000 pounds to more than 27,000 pounds. BOTTOM LEFT: Representatives from NASA, Orbital Sciences Corporation, and the Space Technology 5 project team prepare to launch a Pegasus XL rocket from the NASA Mission Control Center at Vandenberg Air Force Base on March 22, 2006. At 6:03 a.m., the rocket carrying three ST5 microsatellites dropped from its L-1011 carrier jet and began the journey into space. BOTTOM RIGHT: Early launch of a CORONA strategic reconnaissance satellite from Vandenberg Air Force Base, California, 1960.

Wallops Island

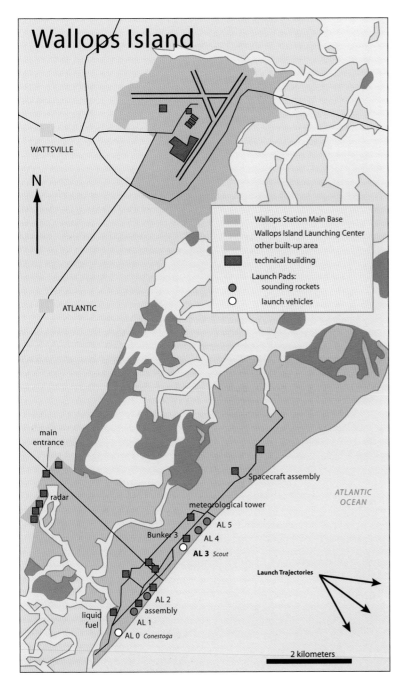

Wallops Station Main Base

Wallops Island Launching Center

other built-up area

technical building

Launch Pads:
sounding rockets
launch vehicles

WATTSVILLE

N

ATLANTIC

main
entrance

radar

liquid
fuel

Bunker 3

meteorological tower

Spacecraft assembly

AL 5

AL 4

AL 3 Scout

AL 2
assembly

AL 1

AL 0 Conestoga

ATLANTIC
OCEAN

Launch Trajectories

2 kilometers

The launching of the first rocket at the NACA's Wallop's Island Facility on June 27, 1945. Joseph Shortal described this launch as follows: "The initial operations on June 27, 1945, on Wallops were to check the tracking station location and operation, check the use of CW (Doppler radar for measuring velocities of missiles and to gain experience with actual rocket). Five 3.25 inch rockets were fired at 39.4 elevation angle, and one each at 33.7, 29.3, and 21.5. All were fired in a direction parallel to the beach to simulate the first Tiamat missile launching. Four of the eight rockets were tracked satisfactorily by the SCR-584 radar located at the mainland tracking station 2 and a strong signal was obtained on the CW radar."

Launching of the Little Joe launch vehicle on October 4, 1959, took place at Wallops Island, Va. This was the first attempt to launch an instrumented capsule with a Little Joe booster. Only the LJ1A and the LJ6 used the space metal/chevron plates as heat reflector shields, as they kept shattering. Little Joe was used to test various components of the Mercury spacecraft, such as the emergency escape rockets.

This B4-988/S-138R sounding rocket is shown on its launcher in a horizontal position at Wallops Island in 1965.

Other Worldwide Launch Sites

Like Vandenberg Air Force Base in the United States, the Soviet Union established a launch site specifically for military space missions at Plesetsk, in the Archangel Region approximately 500 mi (800 km) north of Moscow and east of St. Petersburg (formerly Leningrad). The 1,094-square-mile (1,762 km) site of the Plesetsk Cosmodrome was built from virtually nothing, and all logistics had to be created from scratch. It was the location of the first operational base for the R-7 intercontinental ballistic missile (ICBM) first deployed in 1960, and the intended launch point for over-the-pole ICBM strikes against the U.S. Named the Plesetsk Cosmodrome, it began operations in 1957 when the first launch pads were constructed and it soon became one of the busiest spaceports in the world. Between 1966 (when its first launch occurred) and 1993 (when it found its workload shifting to newer launchers operated from Baikonur), the Plesetsk Cosmodrome supported more than 1,300 launches, or more than a third of all orbital or planetary mission launches from all the other sites in the world. It remains an important military launch facility—an ideal

launch site for polar flights and many other high-inclination orbits (63 to 83 degrees). Critical to its operations during the Cold War, launches from Plesetsk did not pass over any other countries during the boost phase so other nations had no reason to protest Soviet operations or make claims against the Soviet state should an accident take place. Increasingly important in the aftermath of the Cold War, in contrast to Baikonur this launch site is on inherently Russian soil and therefore secure from any diplomatic machinations of the now independent Kazakhstan.

For many years the Plesetsk Cosmodrome was a state secret. That changed when the first launches took place from there. On March 17, 1966, the Soviet Union launched Cosmos-112 from Plesetsk atop a Vostok-2 booster. Carrying a Zenit reconnaissance satellite, it was essentially the counterpart of the American Corona spacecraft already flying. Less than a month later, on April 6, the Soviets launched a more advanced Zenit (Cosmos-114) from Plesetsk onboard a larger Voskhod rocket. These launches excited Soviet spaceflight observers in the West. A team of British students under Geoffery Perry at the Kettering School saw that these two spacecraft were in a very

high-inclination orbit, 73 degrees, that had not been seen previously in Soviet operations. They monitored the spacecrafts' trajectories and analyzed radio signals to deduce that they had been launched from a site north of Moscow and east of Leningrad. A third launch (Cosmos-129) on October 14, 1966, allowed the Kettering team to determine definitively that a new launch site existed in the far north of the Soviet Union and to come close to pinpointing its location. On November 3, 1966, Perry and his team officially announced the existence of the Plesetsk launch complex. It became a location much watched thereafter. Even so, the Soviet Union refused to acknowledge Plesetsk's existence until 1983 while wits in the West referred to it as the worst kept secret ever attempted by the Soviet Union since launches from their were so readily tracked.

A total of four launch pads were built for R-7 missiles during the 1960s along the Yemtsa River; the steep cliffs above the river served as natural flame ducts. The first military unit to serve operational ICBMs R-7A was officially formed on May 19, 1958. The unit would be housed in barracks of Site 41, near the yet-to-be-built launch complex at Site 1. The checkout and assembly of R-7 missiles for the pad #1 were conducted at Site 142. After the R-7s, for many years the Plesetsk Cosmodrome

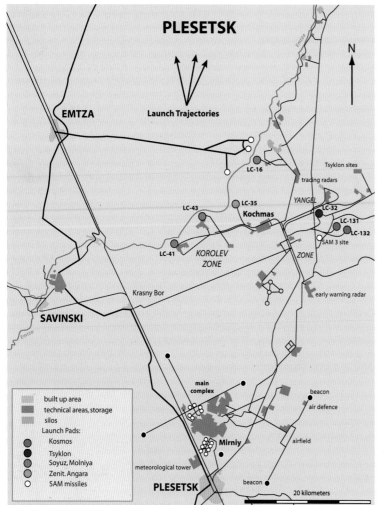

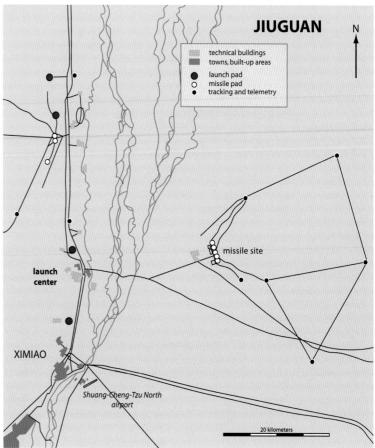

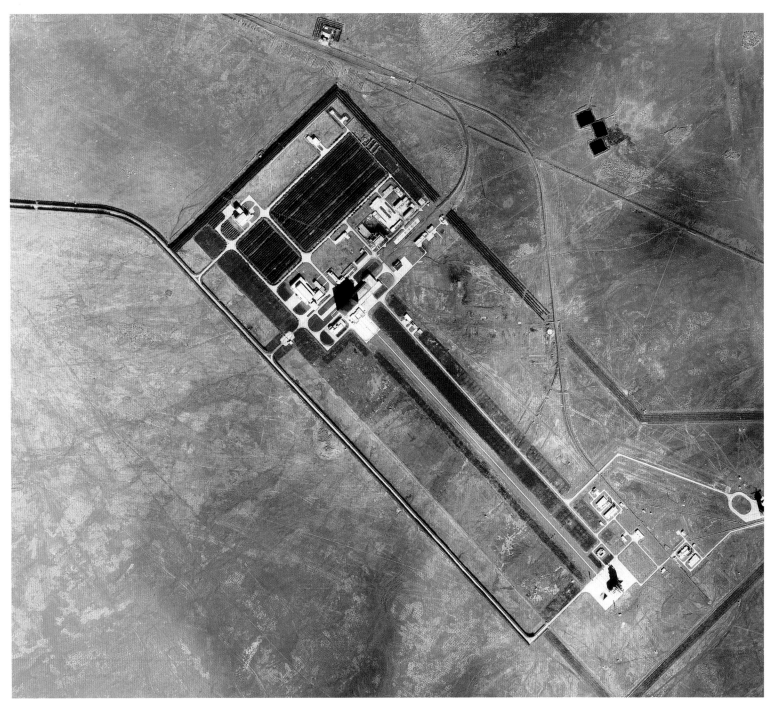

The IKONOS satellite operated by GeoEye, Inc., captured in one-meter resolution this image of China's expansive Jiuquan Space Launch Center in northwestern China on October 4, 2003. It shows the vehicle assembly area and launch pad.

The range control room of the Takesaki Range Control Center in 2001.

This launch of the H-II took place in 2003.

H. S. Tsien, far right, stands with Hugh L. Dryden, Ludwig Prandtl, and Theodor von Kármán on the steps of the Kaiser Wilhelm Institute in Göettington, in occupied Germany at the end of World War II. Tsien, a Chinese national, had come to the United States in the 1930s to study engineering under von Kármán. He became interested in rocketry, and soon became one of the leaders in the field in the U.S. during World War II. He was implicated in the "Red Scare" of the 1950s, deported to the People's Republic of China in 1954, and eventually became the godfather of the Chinese space program.

This launch of the Chinese LM-2C launch vehicle in the 1990s is a publicity photo advertising the commercial launch services of the Great Wall Industry Corp. The LM-2C is a direct descendant of the Long March ICBM. The development of this launch vehicle was started in 1970 and its first successful test flight in 1975 allowed it to emerge as the main vehicle launching China's satellites.

concentrated on launching four basic vehicles: Kosmos-3M, Soyuz/Molniya, Tskylon-3, and Start. Kosmos-3M can be launched from any of three launch pads (Complexes 132 left and right and 133). Soyuz/Molniya has three active pads (Complexes 16 and 43 left and right). There is a fourth pad (Complex 41) that is presently not in use. Complexes 32 left and right support Tsyklon launches, while Start, a program that began launching in 1993, flies from Complex 158.

Not long after the United States reached the Moon, on April 24, 1970, the People's Republic of China (PRC) launched its first satellite into orbit, becoming only the fifth nation after the Soviet Union, the United States, France, and Japan to do so. The satellite, Mao-1, flew atop a Long March-1-modified ICBM from the Jiuquan Space Launch Center in Inner Mongolia. The Jiuquan Space Launch Center was built beginning in 1958 north of Jiuquan City in the Gobi desert 1,000 miles (1,600 km) west of Beijing. Limited to southeastern launches on a 57–70-degree inclination orbit

to avoid overflying Russia and Mongolia, it has concentrated on operations for the Long March family of rockets and for smaller sounding rockets. Sometimes Westerners refer to this launch site as Shuang Cheng Tzu, named for the region in which it is situated. Because of its orbital inclination limitations Jiuquan is used largely for recoverable Earth observation and microgravity missions. To solve that problem the PRC built two additional spaceports, Xichang for geostationary orbit launches and Taiyuan for Long March 4 rocket launches.

Remote and generally closed to anyone not associated with the Chinese space program, the 1,740-square-mile (2,800 km) Jiuquan Space Launch Center includes a technical center, launch complexes, a launch control center, mission command and control centers, and various other logistical support systems. This launch site has been used for lower and medium orbits with high orbital inclination angles, and for testing ballistic missiles. It also serves as the launch site of the Chinese human spaceflight program. On October 15, 2003,

the piloted spacecraft Shenzhou 5 flew atop a Long March 2F rocket from Jiuquan. It carried China's first taikonaut, Yang Liwei, and made China only the third nation after the USSR and the U.S. to send a human into space. In 2005 and again in 2008 it launched the second and third human spaceflight missions of the PRC.

Japan's principal launch site, the Tanegashima Space Center (TNSC), was established in 1966 as an experimental facility for launching small rockets. In 1969 Japan's recently formed National Space Development Agency (NASDA) made it its largest and most complex space facility, the counterpart to Cape Canaveral in the United States. Beginning in 1975 it launched orbital missions, starting with the first Japanese engineering test satellite "Kiku," and since then many meteorological and communications satellites have been sent into space from TNSC. TNSC is now operated by the Japanese Space Exploration Agency (JAXA). Located on the southeast coast of Tanegashima Island 650 miles (1,046

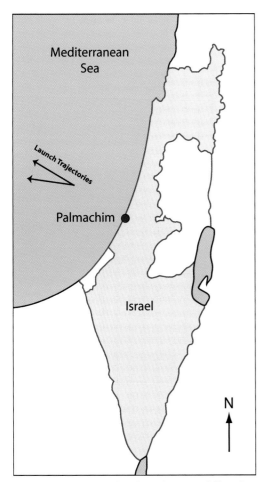

This Israeli launch site has the unique capability of launching to the west.

km) southwest of Tokyo, it has facilities for sounding rocket launches at the Takesaki Range, J-I and H-IIA heavy launchers at the Osaki Range, the Masuda Tracking and Communication Station, the Nogi Radar Station, the Uchugaoka Radar Station, and a range of support structures. There are also related developmental facilities for test firings of liquid- and solid-fuel rocket engines.

At the Palmachim Air Base near the city of Yavne in central Isreal, the Israelis have built a launch complex for its national space efforts. From this base, on September 19, 1988, Israel became the ninth nation to launch a satellite into orbit. Named Horizon 1 (Ofeq 1), it flew aboard a Shavit launch vehicle. This site is closed to all but a select few, but located on the eastern end of the Mediterranean Sea it is visible from the coast highway. It is also the only site in the world where launches toward the west take place. All other complexes launch to the east or toward the poles to take advantage of the Earth's rotation.

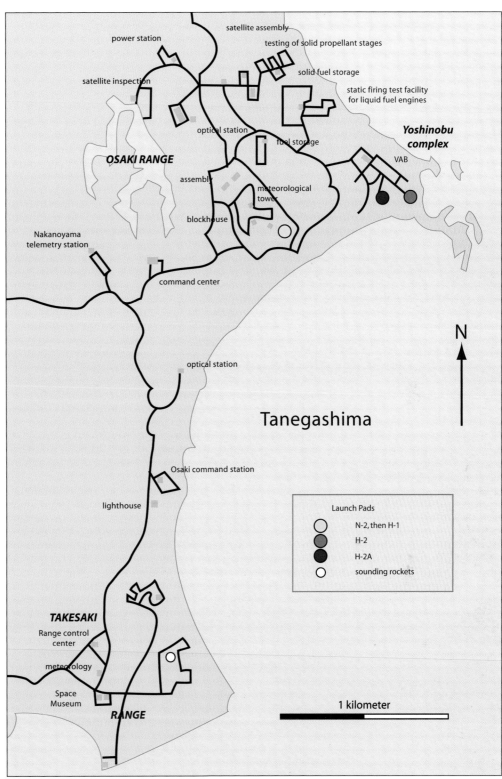

The principal Japanese launch site is located on Tanegashima Island, southwest of Tokyo.

The H-II, Japan's heavy lift launcher, on the launch pad at the Tanegashima Space Center.

This aerial photograph of Japan's Osaki J1 Launch Complex was taken in 2000.

Air- and Sea-Launch Methods

In addition to launch complexes located around the world there are two means of launching space vehicles that have been developed over the years. The first of these is an air-launched method requiring a "mothership" to take a vehicle, sometimes called a parasite vehicle often tucked under its wing, to a speed and altitude usually over 40,000 ft (1,290 m) where it is "dropped" while in flight. After clearing the mothership, the rocket will then fire its own engines and propel upward. While only a few smaller launch vehicles are possibilities for air launching, the method provides several advantages over ground-based launch facilities. First, instead of taking off from a dead stop at sea level, it offers a higher speed and altitude at the beginning of the mission. Second, this saves weight and equipment. The downside is that air launching is limited to smaller spacecraft and rockets since aircraft capabilities for such operations are weight limited.

Air launching dates back to the World War I era when some airships were equipped with parasite biplanes that could be launched for defense or escape in the event of a problem with the larger vehicle. As aircraft became more complex and heavier this system proved less useful and eventually was abandoned by World War II. The use of parasite fighters on large bombers such as the Convair B-36 was attempted in the United States but it proved virtually useless. In postwar rocket research, however, the B-29 Superfortress and the B-52 Stratofortress found use by the National Advisory Committee for Aeronautics and its successor, NASA, in ferrying vehicles to high altitude for launch. The Bell X-1 rocketplane, the first to fly faster than the speed of sound, in October 1947, employed this method of launch. So too did the X-15 research rocketplane, flown 199 times between 1958 and 1969. This vehicle also reached suborbital space flight on two occasions. First, on July 19, 1963, Air Force research pilot Joe Walker flew the X-15 to an altitude of 65.9 miles (106 km) to qualify for the international Fédération Aéronautique Internationale (FAI) definition of a spaceflight by passing the 62.1-mile (100 km., 328,084 ft.) mark. On August 22, 1963, Walker claimed an unofficial world altitude record in the X-15 with his flight to 354,200 feet (107,960 m), or 67.08 miles (107.9 km), after launch from NASA's B-52. Following in the tradition of using NASA's B-52, on November 16, 2004, researchers launched the X-43A on a Mach 9.6 record-setting flight.

Even more important, in June 1982 the United States announced the development of an Air-Launched Miniature Vehicle (ALMV) consisting of a two-stage missile deployed from a high-altitude F-15 aircraft that could reach into low Earth orbit, target a satellite, and destroy it with kinetic force. The first and only test of the ALVM against a satellite took place on October 13, 1985, when it destroyed an obsolete Solwind satellite in a 344-mile (555 km) orbit.

Similarly, in 2004 SpaceShipOne used a mothership, "White Knight," to carry it aloft for deployment on three suborbital flights. In the process it claimed the coveted Ansari

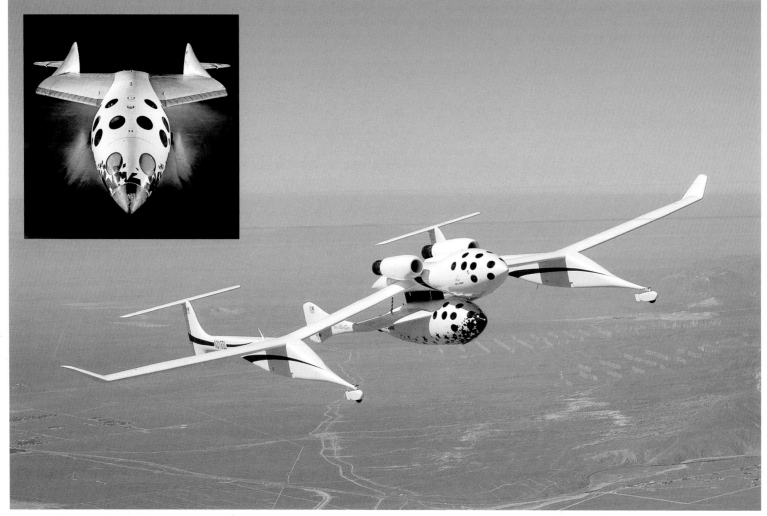

SpaceShipOne made history in 2004 by flying into space twice within a week to claim the $10 million Ansari X-Prize. Hung beneath its White Knight mothership, SpaceShipOne undergoes a flight test in June 2003.

X-Prize as the first privately developed and operated piloted craft to reach space twice within a one-week period. SpaceShipOne was a joint venture by legendary aircraft designer Burt Rutan and investor-philanthropist Paul G. Allen, cofounder of Microsoft. Rutan had for years been viewed as an innovative, and perhaps a little mad, designer of winged vehicles. He intended with SpaceShipOne to prove the concept of safe space tourism. The craft had distinctive swept wings with tail fins to accomplish a three-part flight profile. First, "White Knight" would carry the vehicle to 50,000 feet (15,240 m) for launch. Second, a hybrid rocket motor—burning solid rubber with liquid nitrous oxide—would power SpaceShipOne to Mach 3 with an altitude of 180,000 feet (54,864 m). The vehicle then coasted to an altitude of more than 62.12 miles (100 km) for a suborbital arc through space. As the craft returned to Earth the pilot

reconfigured the wing for reentry, and landed like an aircraft on a runway. Pilot Mike Melvill took SpaceShipOne to 62 miles (100 km) on June 21, 2004, and to 64 miles (102.9 km) on September 29. Brian Binnie flew it to 70 miles (112.7 km) on October 4, 2004.

For orbital space flight, the only vehicle currently being air launched is the Pegasus, flown from a Lockheed L-1011. Carrying the three-stage solid-fuel rocket to its launch altitude of 39,000 feet, the L-1011 then releases Pegasus until the first-stage rocket motor ignites, followed by the other stages. Pegasus was designed as a low-cost vehicle for launching lightweight satellites—1,000 pounds or less. Air launching the vehicle means that the operator may dispense with expensive ground facilities, elaborate launch preparations, and numerous personnel. It is also typically launched over the ocean, away from population centers.

Pegasus was the brainchild of Antonio L. Elias, who in 1987 while doodling in a "boring meeting" sketched a picture of "a little F-15 aircraft with a rocket and satellite on the rocket." The next year he patented the idea and began working on an air launch concept. On April 5, 1990, at NASA's Dryden Research Center in California, the Orbital Sciences Corp. launched the first Pegasus, carried aloft beneath NASA's B-52 aircraft. Since that first flight, Pegasus has orbited 70 satellites in more than 30 missions.

A second unique method of space launch is from a floating platform. Known as "sea launch," this method has been developed by the Sea Launch Company L.L.C. since the 1990s to enable heavy spacelift—8,818.5 lb (4,000 kg) to 13,448 lb (6,100 kg)—to low Earth orbit. Using a floating platform that operates out of Long Beach, California, this launch method reduces legal, operational, and infrastructure challenges. It also offers equatorial launches in any inclination from a single launch pad, providing maximum efficiency from the launcher. It is, therefore, often viewed as a cost-effective alternative to conventional launch operations. Established as a partnership between Boeing (USA), Aker ASA (Norway), RSC-Energia (Russia), and SDO Yuzhnoye/ PO Yuzhmash (Ukraine), the Sea Launch Company was organized on April 3, 1995. It then constructed its platform and launched its first test payload into orbit on March 27, 1999. Using a jointly produced Zenit-3SL launcher built in the Ukraine, Russia, and the U.S., it flew its first commercial payload on October 9, 1999, a DIRECTV 1-R communications satellite. Since that time Sea Launch has lifted an additional 23 satellites into orbit. Its two failures, in 2000 and early 2007, are on a par with other types of launches for a 92.6% success rate.

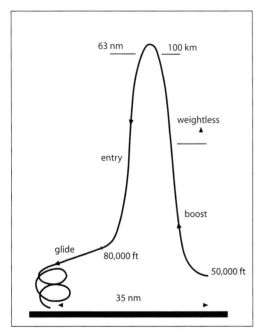

SpaceShipOne was boosted vertically to 100 kilometers, then fell back into the atmosphere with folded wings before gliding to a final landing.

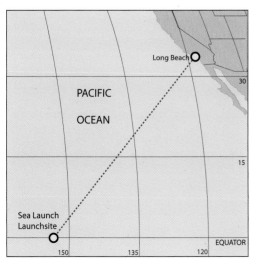

Map of launch site for Sea Launch.

The launch of Koreasat 5 on August 21, 2006, from the Sea Launch platform.

Human Space Launch Emergency Procedures

All organizations that fly humans into space are consumed with developing foolproof methods of abort and emergency escape should something go wrong with the launch. Essentially three methods have been used since the beginning of the space age for abort and crew escape. Each of these methods has been tested and determined satisfactory for surviving launch malfunctions.

First, most human spacecraft have employed launch escape systems (LES) that allowed astronauts or cosmonauts to escape danger by propelling the capsule carrying them away from a malfunctioning rocket. It was essentially an approach that allowed a flight crew to cut loose from a failing booster during any phase of the launch, or at least until the spacecraft was able to survive on its own. The Soviet Union/Russia and the People's

Republic of China used this method for their Voshkod, Soyuz, and Shenzou capsules. The U.S. employed that approach on the Mercury and Apollo spacecraft, and will do so again once the planned Orion capsule comes online sometime before 2020. This approach involves attaching a rocket tower to the capsule that may be fired either automatically or manually to separate the crew module from the rest of the rocket stack quickly in the event of emergency. This system has angled solid-rockets that exhaust away from the capsule and is only used in instances where there is an imminent threat to the crew. It may be used either on the launch pad or during ascent to orbit.

There have only been two instances of operational use of a launch escape system, both by the Soviet Union. The first came on April 5, 1975, when Soyuz 18A aborted after the

third stage's engine ignited while the second stage was still attached. This triggered a mission abort sequence and the launch escape system automatically separated the Soyuz spacecraft from the third-stage booster. The second abort occurred on September 26, 1983, during the attempted launch of Soyuz T-10-1 when the launch vehicle was engulfed by fire while still on the launch pad. Two seconds before the rocket exploded the launch escape system lifted the Soyuz spacecraft and crew away from the pad. These systems have thus proven their worth, both in tests and during actual emergencies.

A second method of space launch abort and escape is the use of ejection seats in the spacecraft. There have been several programs that used this approach to crew escape. The Soviet Union employed them in the Vostok

Return To Launch Site (RTLS) Abort Profile

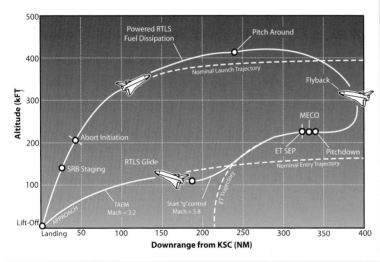

Transatlantic Landing (TAL) Abort Profile

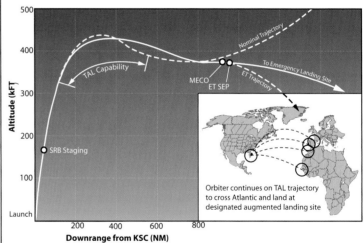

Orbiter continues on TAL trajectory to cross Atlantic and land at designated augmented landing site

Abort Once Around (AOA) Profile

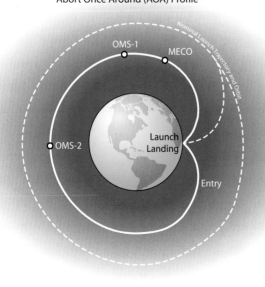

Abort To Orbit (ATO) Profile

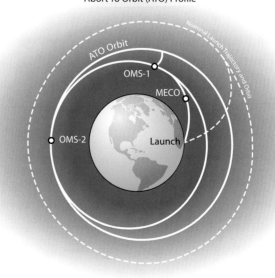

These images illustrate the abort methods of the Space Shuttle.

Space Shuttle Emergency Landing Sites

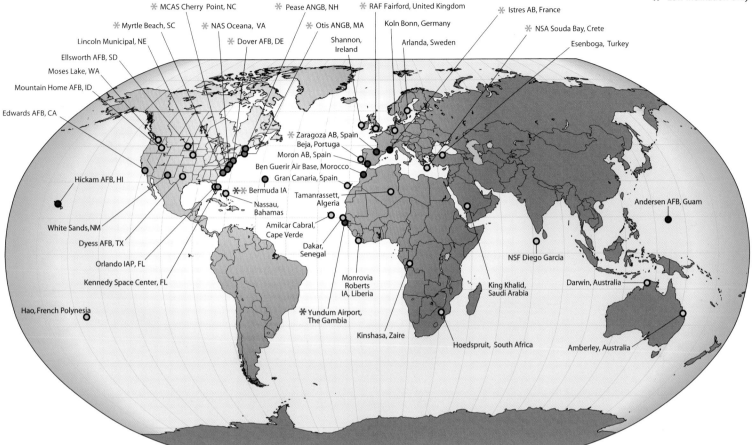

✳ High Inclination Only
✳ Mid Inclination Only
✳ Low Inclination Only

MCAS Cherry Point, NC
Pease ANGB, NH
RAF Fairford, United Kingdom
Istres AB, France
Myrtle Beach, SC
NAS Oceana, VA
Otis ANGB, MA
Koln Bonn, Germany
NSA Souda Bay, Crete
Lincoln Municipal, NE
Dover AFB, DE
Shannon, Ireland
Arlanda, Sweden
Esenboga, Turkey
Ellsworth AFB, SD
Moses Lake, WA
Mountain Home AFB, ID
Edwards AFB, CA
Zaragoza AB, Spain
Beja, Portuga
Moron AB, Spain
Ben Guerir Air Base, Morocco
Gran Canaria, Spain
Hickam AFB, HI
Andersen AFB, Guam
White Sands, NM
Bermuda IA
Tamanrasset, Algeria
Nassau, Bahamas
Dyess AFB, TX
Amilcar Cabral, Cape Verde
NSF Diego Garcia
Orlando IAP, FL
Dakar, Senegal
Darwin, Australia
Kennedy Space Center, FL
Monrovia Roberts IA, Liberia
King Khalid, Saudi Arabia
Hao, French Polynesia
Yundum Airport, The Gambia
Kinshasa, Zaire
Hoedspruit, South Africa
Amberley, Australia

⊙ End of Mission Sites
Locations with all of the necessary equipment to handle a normal landing at the conclusion of a mission. These sites could also be used for an AOA or ATO abort as well as a RTLS abort in the case of Kennedy Space Center. These are the only landing sites that have been used to date.

◉ Launch Abort Sites
Locations equipped with landing aids unique to the Orbiter and temporarily staffed with the personnel required to support a Shuttle landing during every launch. Augmented sites include those used for a TAL abort.

◉ Augmented Landing Sites
Locations along the eastern seaboard of North America that can safely support a Shuttle landing during a launch abort. These sites are used for ECAL aborts when the Orbiter is unable to return to Kennedy Space Center as in the RTLS abort. These landing sites do not contain any equipment or aids unique to supporting an Orbiter landing and are not staffed by NASA personnel. They are typically military bases or commercial airports.

● Augmented Emergency Landing Sites
Emergency sites equipped with Orbiter landing aids and staffed with the proper NASA personnel to support the Shuttle. These and the end of mission sites are preferred in the event of an AOA or ATO abort.

○ Emergency Landing Sites
Several sites around the world, including military bases & commercial airports, with runways long enough to handle an Orbiter emergency landing, if required. These landing sites are generally considered the least desirable since they are typically outside the US, not staffed by NASA, and lack the aids ideally used during a Shuttle landing. These locations could support an AOA or ATO abort if the situation were critical enough.

program of the early 1960s. The single Vostok crew member could fire the ejection seat if a launch abort was necessary, and the cosmonaut could eject after reentry and descend under an individual parachute. Yuri Gagarin did this on the first mission on April 12, 1961, although the Soviets for many years denied this because the flight may not have been recognized for a record by the Fédération Aéronautique Internationale (FAI) since the cosmonaut did not accompany the craft to a landing. As it was planned, the Vostok spacecraft would reenter the atmosphere in the capsule and descend under parachutes to an altitude of about 3,000 ft. (6,000 m) before the astronaut ejected from the capsule and descended under a personal parachute pack.

The American Gemini capsule, for two astronauts, also used ejection seats for emergency escape while it flew in 1965 and 1966. It could be fired by pulling a handle located between the astronaut's legs where it was

stowed so that it would not be inadvertently tripped. The seat had to outrun a potential fireball if a rocket was exploding for more than 800 ft (290 m). Of course, NASA recognized that ejection seats would work only up to about 3,400 mph (2,692 knots) and 130,000 feet (39,624 m). That represented a very limited portion of the vehicle's operating envelope. Tested extensively with manikins from capsule boilerplates accelerated on rocket sleds, these were never used by the astronauts. Astronauts were skeptical of this system, and Tom Stafford specifically commented on his reluctance to find out what might happen when triggering an ejection seat rocket in a cabin pressurized with oxygen. Recognizing this, for Apollo NASA returned to the Launch Escape System that had been effectively used in the Mercury program.

The Space Shuttle Columbia, when flown on its first four orbital missions in 1981 and 1982, also used ejection seats for the mission

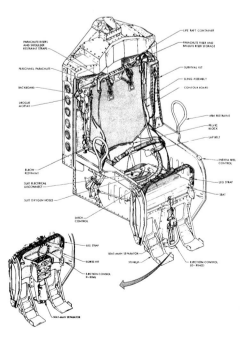

A diagram of the Gemini program's ejection seat from the Gemini Familiarization Manual of 1965.

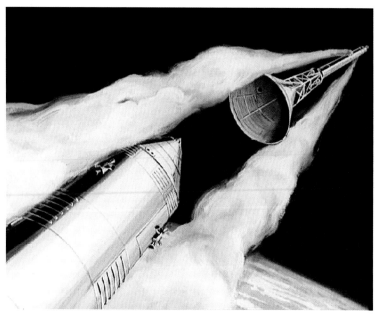

Top: A technician mounts a model of the Apollo Launch Escape System (LES) in the Unitary Wind Tunnel at the NASA Ames Research Center, Moffett Field, California, in 1963. The LES was a towerlike structure consisting of four solid-propellant motors mounted atop the Apollo command module. In the event of a contingency (booster failure or some other imminent failure), the LES would be commanded to ignite, subsequently removing the command module from the Saturn launch vehicle.

Above: This illustration shows the jettisoning of the Apollo Launch Escape System upon reaching orbital velocity.

Right: On April 29, 1961, technicians serviced the Mercury-Redstone 3 (MR-3) rocket using a cherry picker, one of many tests conducted to evaluate astronaut escape feasibility.

Launch of the Space Shuttle Atlantis on September 25, 1997.

commander and pilot. These seats, based on those included in SR-71 reconnaissance aircraft, were part of Columbia's original design, giving the crew some chance to survive a catastrophic breakup as fast as Mach 3. These same ejection seats could be used if the orbiter was declining to subsonic speeds on reentry but could not reach the runway. The system, however, was removed when NASA began flying larger crews since the remainder of the team would not be in a compartment that would allow ejection. In addition, ejection seats were heavy and would limit the payload of the shuttle. At the same time, few believed that the ejection of the crew would be survivable. Indeed, the shuttle was viewed as so safe that it did not require a crew escape capability. This proved a faulty perception when the first shuttle accident took place in 1986. After the Challenger accident, should bailout be possible, all astronauts have worn pressure suits

and parachutes during launch and reentry. Known as the Inflight Crew Escape System, this is also believed to be insufficient in the event of a true launch emergency. Because of cost and weight considerations, other crew escape systems were rejected. These ranged from a formal escape "capsule" built into the crew cabin, ejection seats for the entire crew, and even an escape system modeled after the Apollo LES. Instead, redundancy of systems, risk analysis, and firm procedures were viewed as the best defenses against having to abandon the spacecraft. Of course, in both shuttle accidents, Challenger in 1986 and Columbia in 2003, the orbiters disintegrated so quickly that virtually nothing could have been done to save the crews.

Should the Space Shuttle be required to abort the launch, but the vehicle itself not be destroyed, NASA developed several scenarios for recovery. The first of these was a return to

launch site (RTLS), wherein the solid rocket boosters are jettisoned, the orbiter pitches around, and the Space Shuttle main engines (SSME) fire to return the orbiter to the Kennedy Space Center in Florida. When the SSMEs shut down, the external tank would be jettisoned and the orbiter would make a normal gliding landing on the runway. If the vehicle is higher and nearing orbital velocity, the orbiter may undertake a transoceanic abort landing (TAL) in either Africa or Western Europe, some 45 minutes after liftoff. There is also an abort once around (AOA), allowing a suborbital flight of the shuttle around the Earth before returning for a landing at the Kennedy Space Center. Abort to orbit (ATO) allows a very low orbit and then a return to Earth. This was done in two shuttle missions, STS-51-F in 1985 and STS-93 1999. Of these options, by far the ATO is the preferred abort option.

Returning from Space

One of the most difficult tasks with which any space-faring organization has had to contend is how its space systems operate while transiting the atmosphere as they return to Earth. Coming home after a flight into space is fundamentally a challenge that has involved over the years critical contributions from engineers working in aerodynamics, thermal protection, guidance and control, stability, propulsion, and landing systems. Without this base of fundamental and applied research the capability to fly into space would not exist.

While most proposals for satellites between 1946 and 1957 avoided the difficult problem of reentry, it became obvious soon after World War II that returning to Earth represented a major step in flight. Beginning with the theoretical work of Germans Walter Hohmann and Eugen Sänger, as well as Americans such as Theodore Theodorsen and Robert Gilruth at the Langley Memorial Aeronautical Laboratory, it also included efforts to understand the heating of reentry during ballistic missile development in the 1950s. Three approaches dominated thinking at the time. The first was a heat sink concept that sought to move quickly from space through the upper atmosphere. Superheating proved a serious

problem, however, and materials to protect the spacecraft a major concern. It was initially the preferred thermal protection choice for ballistic missiles, but as range and speed grew, engineers realized that heat sink was unacceptable for orbital reentry. The second approach, championed by Wernher von Braun and his rocket team in Huntsville, Alabama, called for circulating a fluid through the spacecraft's skin to soak up the heat of reentry. Von Braun's grandiose vision foresaw astronauts returning from wheeled space stations aboard huge spaceplanes, but when challenged to develop actual hardware he realized that there was no way for the heat to be absorbed without killing the occupants. For orbital flight, both of these concepts gave way to Julian Allen's and Alfred Eggers's blunt-body concept, which fundamentally shaped the course of spaceflight research and provided the basis for all successful orbital reentry vehicles. At the same time, John V. Becker and others at the Langley Laboratory were championing the X-15, a winged research airplane intended to demonstrate the ability to fly back from near-space to normal runway landings.

All human spaceflight projects actually flown by the United States prior to the Space Shuttle

employed a blunt-body reentry design with an ablative shield to deal with the heat generated by atmospheric friction. This approach has also been used in reconnaissance, warhead, and scientific reentry successfully from the 1950s to the present. Additionally, the question of what materials to use to protect the spacecraft during blunt-body reentry emerged, and research on metallic, ceramic, and ablative heat shields prompted the decision to employ ablative technology. All of these decisions required trade-offs, and the process whereby these decisions were made and implemented offer an object lesson for current engineers involved in making difficult technical choices.

Once the orbital energy is converted and the heat of reentry dissipated, there is still the requirement to gently land the spacecraft in the ocean or on land. Virtually all of the early concepts for human spaceflight involved spaceplanes that flew on wings to a runway landing. Sänger's antipodal bomber of the 1920s did so, and Wernher von Braun's popular concepts did the same. These proved impractical for launch vehicles available during the 1950s, however, and capsule concepts that returned to Earth via parachute proliferated, largely because they represented the "art of the possible" at the time.

Human Spaceflight Landing Sites

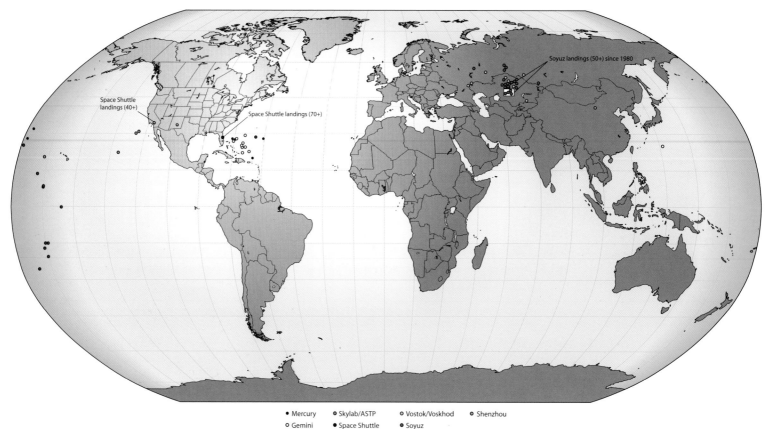

- ● Mercury
- ○ Gemini
- ● Apollo
- ● Skylab/ASTP
- ● Space Shuttle
- ○ Vostok/Voskhod
- ● Soyuz
- ● Shenzhou

This artist's rendering of the Stardust capsule returning to Earth shows it coming home with samples of interstellar dust, including recently discovered dust streaming into our Solar System from the direction of Sagittarius, under a parachute.

All of the American efforts until the Space Shuttle, and the Soviet and Chinese human capsules, all used from one to three parachutes for return to Earth. For the Americans, the capsules landed in the ocean and were recovered by ship. This exposed them to corrosive saltwater while waiting for expensive recovery efforts. Both the Soviet/Russian and Chinese spacecraft have always been recovered on land, which presented the crew with a harder landing than would be the case in the sea. For Project Gemini NASA toyed with the possibility of using a paraglider being developed at Langley Research Center for "dry" landings instead of a "splashdown" in water and recovery by the Navy. The engineers never did get the paraglider to work properly and eventually dropped it from the program in favor of a parachute system like the one used for Mercury.

The U.S. also used parachutes to return film canisters from the nation's first reconnaissance satellite, Corona, flown between 1960 and 1972. This program employed satellites with cameras and film launched into near-polar orbits to provide frequent coverage of the USSR. After the film was exposed, it was wound onto reels in a special reentry capsule that separated from the spacecraft at about 100 miles (160 km) in altitude and then at 60,000 feet (20,000 m) jettisoned its heat shield and deployed a parachute. Air Force planes flying over the Pacific then snagged the parachute and capsule, returning the film for processing and analysis.

In 2006 the first capsule, Stardust, successfully returned from deep space with samples of interstellar dust. On a previous mission Genesis had crashed when its parachute failed to deploy. The Stardust spacecraft was launched on February 7, 1999, with a primary goal to collect carbon-based samples during its encounter with Comet Wild 2. This was the first U.S. space mission dedicated solely to the exploration of a comet and delivering extraterrestrial material from outside the Earth-Moon orbit. The capsule was returned to Earth in mid-January 2006 with its precious cargo—cometary particles collected in aerogel—landing by parachute on the Utah Test and Training Range.

The Genesis and Stardust capsules were targeted for landing in an area near the Utah/Nevada border. In 2004 the Genesis parachute failed to open and the capsule crashed into the desert. However, the majority of the science goals were eventually reached, providing important insight into the nature of the Sun and early Solar System. Stardust successfully returned comet material in 2006.

Above: Soyuz landing sites in Kazakhstan used since the 1980s.

Right: During the early years of satellite reconnaissance, spacecraft ejected film canisters that reentered the atmosphere and were retrieved by aircraft such as this Corona recovery as a C-119 snatches its parachute during descent in 1962.

Below Right: In the early 1960s the Gemini program tried to develop parasails for soft, controlled landings. The program did not prove successful but is being considered again for the Orion capsule currently under construction by the United States.

Below: The Apollo program used parachutes to bring the capsules to the surface of the Pacific Ocean for a soft landing as depicted in the Apollo 15 return to Earth in 1971.

Both the American Space Shuttle and the Soviet Buran pioneered reentry and landing using wings.

Even as Apollo was reaching fruition in the latter 1960s, NASA officials made the decision to abandon capsules with blunt-body ablative heat shields and recovery systems that relied on parachutes for its human spaceflight program. Instead, it chose to build the Space Shuttle, a winged reusable vehicle that still had a blunt-body configuration but used a new ceramic tile and reinforced carbon-carbon for its thermal protection system. Parachutes were also jettisoned in favor of a delta-wing aerodynamic

concept that allowed runway landings. Despite many challenges, and the loss of one vehicle and crew due to a failure with the thermal protection system, this approach has worked since first flown in 1981. Although NASA engineers debated the necessity of including jet engines on the shuttle, it employed the unpowered landing concept demonstrated by the X-15 and lifting body programs at the Flight Research Center during the 1960s. Flying more than 125 missions since the first orbital

flight, the shuttle has been scheduled for retirement in 2010, to be replaced by the Orion space capsule, which will return to Earth using either parachutes or a paraglider.

The Soviet Union also built a space shuttle, the Buran, which flew only one mission without a crew aboard in 1988 before its retirement. Like its American counterpart, Buran landed on delta wings like an aircraft. With the demise of the Soviet Union in the latter 1980s, the Soviet Ministry of Defense realized that this system was expensive, and without a firm rationale, it was canceled. Not until 1993 did NPO Energia head, Yuri Semenov, publicly announce the end of the project. As the twenty-first century progresses, the preferred method for returning to Earth remains using an ablative heat shield for the dissipation of excess heat and speed and parachutes for soft landings.

Space Shuttle Orbits

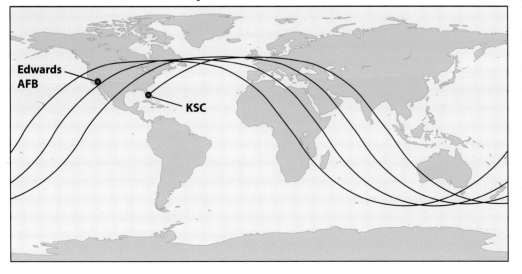

Edwards AFB

KSC

This chart shows the typical ground track of the first few Space Shuttle orbits after launch from Kennedy Space Center (KSC). The Space Shuttle can return to either KSC or Edwards Air Force Base in California only when its orbit provides the correct alignment. In the event of an emergency other sites must be used.

part four
ORBITING THE EARTH

A satellite orbiting above the atmosphere of the Earth influenced your life at some time today. Whether you checked for storms or other weather patterns, watched television, or used a credit card or wrote a check, or any of hundreds of other simple, daily acts, you did something that has been aided by a spacecraft orbiting hundreds of miles above our heads. These orbiting spacecraft travel in three general patterns. The first is a geostationary orbit that circles the planet once every 24 hours, and since the orbital time matches the rotation of the Earth, it continually views the same part of the planet. This stationary position is located 22,300 miles (35,900 km) above the equator of the Earth. At this altitude, the Earth's gravity is canceled by the centrifugal force of the rotating objects beyond. This is the ideal location to park many satellites, and geostationary satellite orbits are highly prized because they work so well for applications spacecraft used for weather forecasting, satellite television, satellite radio, and several other types of global telecommunications.

A second type of orbit is also equatorial but at a lower altitude than the geostationary satellites. One of the most popular, and the one used by all of the human spaceflight programs, is low Earth orbit (LEO) from the edge of the atmosphere about 100 miles (160 km) to an altitude of approximately 1,240 miles (2,000 km). Spacecraft in that orbit travel about 17,025 mph (27,400 km/h) (5 mi/s or 8 km/s). These usually make one complete orbit around the Earth in about 90 minutes. Medium Earth orbit (MEO) is the region between LEO and geostationary, ranging from 1,243 miles (2,000 km) to 22,236 miles

(35,786 km). One orbit by a satellite in MEO requires between 2 and 12 hours. These orbits are especially useful for navigation satellites and the constellation of satellites making up the Global Positioning System (GPS) are located in this region. So, too, was one of the most famous of the early satellites, Telstar, the first commercial communication satellite launched in 1962.

A third type of orbit is polar, in which satellites pass above or nearly above both poles of the Earth or whatever other body they might be orbiting—such as solar research satellites—and thereby cross in the course of its orbital path virtually all of the body's surface. These polar orbits are especially useful for reconnaissance, Earth mapping, scientific observation, and some weather satellites.

These orbits about Earth—LEO, MEO, geostationary, and polar—have a large population of space objects. While it is not yet crowded in Earth orbit, there are at present approximately 25,000 human-made objects orbiting the Earth. Of these, more than 8,500 are currently satellites in orbit while the remainder are fundamentally orbital debris in the process of having their orbits decay. Both Russia and the United States have the majority of orbiting objects, more than 4,000. They also lead other nations in the orbital debris that has resulted from their space-faring activities.

Orbiting the Earth is a fundamental part of the process of leaving this planet to move outward. In more than fifty years much has been accomplished in understanding how to overcome this fundamental challenge. The pages that follow will explore this fascinating history.

This stunning image taken in 1995 by astronauts aboard the Space Shuttle Discovery, STS-70, shows the Moon setting over the Earth limb.

Getting into Orbit

The physical principles required to place an artificial satellite in Earth orbit have been understood for centuries. Isaac Newton, in his *Principia Mathematica* (1687), described hypothetical cannon able to shoot projectiles great distances. With increasing speed and distance, eventually a cannonball could encircle the entire Earth before hitting the ground. Of course, a real cannon could never "shoot around the world" due to atmospheric drag. However, above the atmosphere it would be possible for a moving object to continue on its trajectory for an unlimited time. Such objects would enter orbit, but getting into orbit requires an enormous amount of energy. Launching a satellite into low Earth orbit requires boosting it to a speed of seven kilometers per second. With the advent of capable rockets, Newton's hypothetical experiment became a real possibility.

The trajectory of a satellite in Earth orbit is determined by the momentum it receives from being accelerated by a rocket. After an object is boosted it continues to move forward in a ballistic trajectory. During its time in orbit forward momentum from the rocket boost carries the satellite forward, while gravity pulls it toward the surface. The satellite's orbital path is determined by the balance of those two vectors. A satellite in orbit has enough forward velocity to carry it continuously as the planet curves away underneath. With greater speeds, higher orbits can be reached. If an object

continues to accelerate in orbit, it eventually reaches escape velocity, or the speed necessary to leave orbit entirely. These trajectories are used by spacecraft in missions to other planets.

As stated in Kepler's third law of planetary motion, objects orbiting at higher altitudes have a longer orbital period. Satellites in low Earth orbit complete an orbit within two hours. GPS satellites, in MEO at 20,200 km altitude, require 12 hours to complete each orbit. Geosynchronous satellites at a 35,786 km altitude revolve once each 24 hours.

A satellite's orbital plane is usually not exactly aligned with the Earth's equator. Orbital planes are inclined at a certain angle determined to meet the needs of the satellite's mission. Highly inclined orbits make it possible to observe the surface of the Earth as the planet rotates under the orbiting satellite. Most satellites designed for this purpose are placed into near-polar orbits that pass over the Earth's north and south poles. For many satellites, a circular orbit is desired, but reaching a perfectly circular orbit requires careful guidance and control.

Where does space begin? There is no universally accepted definition for the altitude of where space "begins" because the atmosphere lacks a discrete boundary. About 80% of the atmospheric mass is contained within 8 miles (12 km) of the surface. Atmospheric density gradually diminishes as altitude increases. Satellites encounter atmospheric drag even in low Earth orbit, an especially serious problem

for large spacecraft. The International Space Station, for instance, must be reboosted regularly to overcome drag and maintain its orbit. All satellites in low orbit eventually reenter the atmosphere without rocket boosts. Variations in solar activity play an important role in the structure of the upper atmosphere. As the Sun's activity reaches the maximum in its 11-year sunspot cycle, extra solar radiation heats and expands the Earth's atmosphere. This atmospheric expansion creates measurable drag on satellites in low orbits, hastening their eventual reentry.

At about 62 miles (100 km) of altitude, the density of the atmosphere decreases to a point that it is impossible for a wing to produce lift to support an aircraft. This altitude, called the Kármán Line, was described by and named for astronautics pioneer Theodore von Kármän. The 100-km Kármán Line is used by the Fédération Aéronautique Internationale (FAI) to delineate the upper boundary of the atmosphere. In the early 1960s the United States Air Force defined 50 miles (about 80 km) for the altitude at which space "begins" for military pilots. The rocket-propelled X-15 aircraft exceeded that altitude several times in the 1960s, on one flight reaching 67 miles above the surface. On that basis some X-15 pilots were awarded astronaut status. NASA, and many other organizations, have refused to acknowledge this point as the appropriate place where space begins, insisting on the FAI's altitude of 62 miles (100 km).

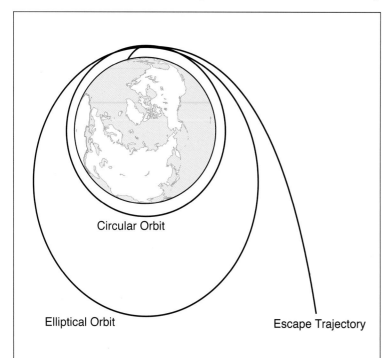

Greater velocity from a rocket boost places a satellite in higher orbit. If a spacecraft reaches escape velocity, it leaves Earth's orbit.

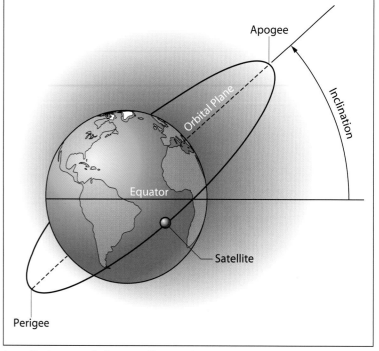

A satellite's apogee is the most distant point in its orbit, and its perigee is the closest. The inclination of the orbital plane is measured in degrees from the plane of the Earth's equator.

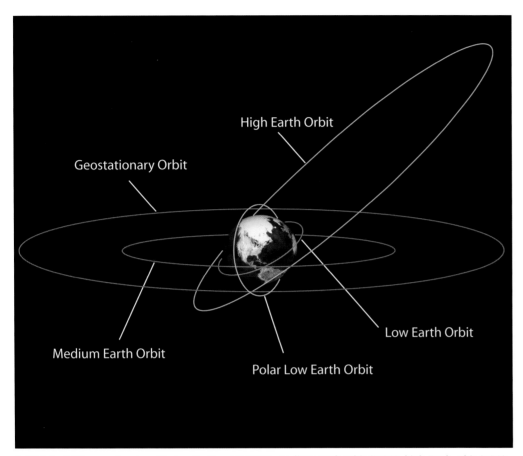

Artificial satellites can be placed in low Earth orbit (LEO), medium Earth orbit (MEO), high Earth orbit (HEO), and geosynchronous (GEO) orbits. They may also be placed in polar orbits.

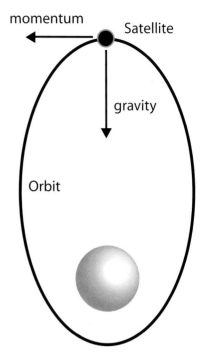

The shape of an orbit is determined by two forces: gravitational attraction and forward momentum. A body will remain in orbit if those two forces are balanced. If its forward momentum becomes greater, for instance by a rocket boost, it can reach higher orbit and escape velocity. If the forward momentum is significantly decreased, it will eventually leave orbit and strike the central planetary body.

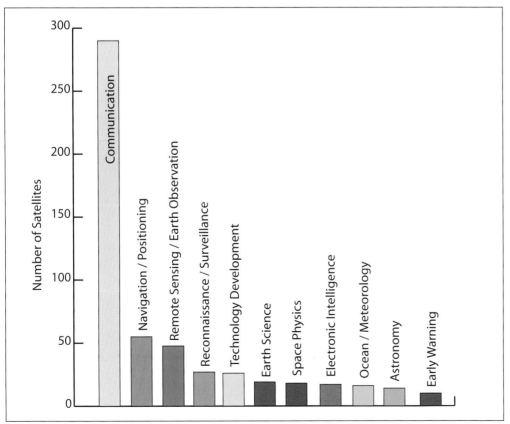

Number of satellites for a range of applications. Most orbiting satellites are used for communication purposes.

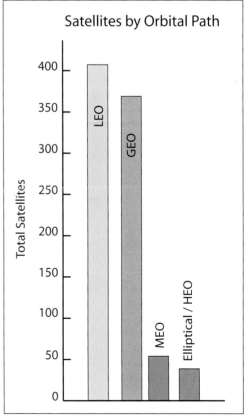

Number of satellites in each type of orbit in 2008.

The First Humans into Space

It came like a shock to the system for many in the United States when Yuri Gagarin became the first human to orbit the Earth on April 12, 1961. The flight of Vostok 1 represented one of the great success stories of the first few years of the space age. Gagarin had been chosen for cosmonaut training in 1959 and underwent a series of increasingly rigorous physical and mental exercises to prepare for spaceflight. Selected from among several other contenders for the first flight in space, Gagarin represented the Soviet ideal of the worker who rose through the ranks solely on the basis of merit. His handsome appearance, thoughtful intellectuality, and boyish charm made him an attractive figure on the world stage. The importance of these attributes was not lost on Nikita Khrushchev and other senior Soviet leaders.

The launch of this first Soviet human orbital mission proved enormously important both for Gagarin and for the Soviet Union. Vostok 1 was a three-ton ball-shaped capsule, with an attached two-ton equipment module containing (among other things) retrorockets. It was lofted into orbit atop a modified R-7 ICBM rocket. His 108-minute flight had been the direct result of Cold War competition between the United States and the Soviet Union to be the first to place a human in space, as a demonstration of technological superiority before the world. With Gagarin's success, the United States lost that challenge and the Soviet Union was recognized as a technological and scientific superpower.

Following Gagarin's triumph, on April 14, 1961, the Soviet Union held a gigantic ceremony in Red Square in Moscow honoring its first cosmonaut. The great success of the Vostok 1 flight made the gregarious Gagarin a global hero, and he was an effective spokesman for the Soviet Union on the world stage. He died in a plane crash while on a training mission for the Soviet air force on March 27, 1968. Of course, Gagarin's spaceflight energized the Soviet leadership to invest more money in space exploration during the years that followed, in part because of the international prestige that the nation gained for its spectacular missions. Subsequently the Soviets were the first to launch a woman, Valentina Tereshkova, into orbit, the first to launch two- and three-person crews, and the first to execute an extravehicular activity, or spacewalk.

The success of the Soviet Union in space in the earliest years of the space age catapulted it into the global limelight in a way never seen before. A small selection of space spectaculars would include the following:

• Sputnik 1—first human-made object in orbit, October 1957.

Yuri Gagarin was a handsome, engaging pilot who impressed all who met him. Here he speaks to a crowd of adoring Russians after his flight.

- Sputnik 2—first living thing in orbit, Laika, November 1957.
- Luna 1—first human-made object to escape the Earth's gravity, January 1959.
- Luna 2—first clear images of the Moon's surface, September 1959.
- Luna 3—first pictures of the far side of the Moon, October 1959.
- Sputnik 5—first return of living creatures from orbit, two dogs, August 1960.
- Vostok 1—first human in space, Yuri Gagarin, April 1961.
- Vostok 2—first day-long human space-flight mission, Gherman Titov, August 1961.
- Vostok 3—first long-duration spaceflight, cosmonaut Andrian Nicolayev, four days, August 1962.
- Vostok 6—first woman in space, Valentina Tereshkova, June 1963.

In a closed society such as the Soviet Union, these successful flights collectively signaled a capability that impressed the world's population.

After Gagarin's flight, therefore, it was only a salve on an open wound when Alan B. Shepard became the first American in space during a 15-minute suborbital flight on May 5, 1961, by riding a Redstone booster in the Freedom 7 Mercury spacecraft. Comparisons between the Soviet and American flights were inevitable thereafter. Gagarin had orbited the Earth; Shepard had more of a relation-ship to a cannonball shot from a gun than a space venturer. Gagarin's Vostok spacecraft had weighed 10,428 lb (4,730 kg); Freedom 7 weighed 2,100 lb (952.5 kg). Gagarin had been weightless for 89 minutes; Shepard for only 5 minutes. "Even though the United States is still the strongest military power and leads in many aspects of the space race," wrote jour-nalist Hanson Baldwin in the *New York Times* not long after Gagarin's flight, "the world—impressed by the spectacular Soviet firsts—believes we lag militarily and technologically."

Despite its outward success, Gagarin's Vostok 1 flight had several serious problems. Since the end of the Cold War, increasing amounts of information have confirmed what some analysts believed all along—namely, that Gagarin's flight had nearly been a disaster when the capsule spun dangerously out of control while beginning the reentry sequence. Gagarin told officials during a postflight debriefing, "As soon as the braking rocket shut off, there was a sharp jolt, and the craft began to rotate around its axis at a very high veloc-ity." It spun uncontrollably as the equipment

This is the classic photograph of the Mercury 7 astronauts, the first group selected for spaceflight by NASA in 1959. Front row, L-R: Walter Schirra, Deke Slayton, John Glenn, Scott Carpenter. Back Row, L-R: Alan Shepard, Gus Grissom, Gordon Cooper.

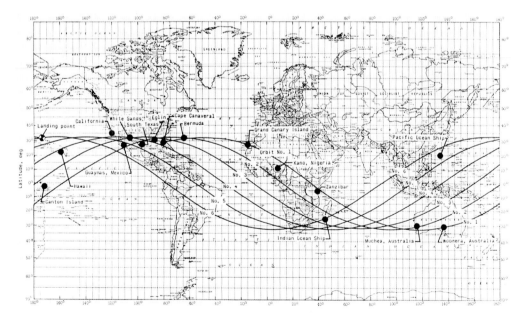

This historic map of the orbital tracks of the MA-8 mission depicts the flight of Wally Schirra's Mercury 7 flight on October 3, 1962. A near-perfect mission, Schirra flew six orbits of more than 160,000 miles (257,495 km) aboard the Sigma 7 spacecraft, which in contrast to the previous Mercury flight splashed down at its intended recovery point. It landed in the Pacific Ocean about 275 miles (442.5 km) northeast of Midway Island just 27,000 feet (8,229.6 m) from the recovery vessel. Schirra reached the recovery vessel just 37 minutes after splashdown.

module failed to separate from the cosmonaut's capsule. After ten minutes the spacecraft stabilized somewhat from its dizzying spin. Nevertheless, Gagarin ejected from the capsule and parachuted safely to Earth while the capsule came down elsewhere, dangling from its own chutes.

The United States responded by executing its own program, Mercury, of which the Shepard flight of May 5, 1961, was the first piloted mission. A second flight, another suborbital mission like Shepard's, launched on July 21, 1961, had problems. Upon landing, the capsule's hatch blew off prematurely and Liberty Bell 7 sank into the Atlantic Ocean before it could be recovered. In the process the astronaut, Virgil I. "Gus" Grissom, nearly drowned before being hoisted to safety in a helicopter. These suborbital flights, however, proved valuable for NASA technicians, who found ways to solve or work around literally thousands of obstacles to successful spaceflight.

As these issues were being resolved, NASA engineers began final preparations for the orbital aspects of Project Mercury. In this phase NASA planned to use a Mercury capsule capable of supporting a human in space not just for minutes, but eventually for as long as three days. As a launch vehicle for this Mercury capsule, NASA used the more powerful Atlas instead of the Redstone. But the decision was not without controversy. Indeed, there were technical difficulties to be overcome in mating it to the Mercury capsule, but the biggest complication was a debate among NASA engineers over its appropriateness for human spaceflight.

Most of the difficulties had been resolved by the time of the first successful orbital flight of an unoccupied Mercury-Atlas combination in September 1961. On November 29 the final test flight took place, this time with the chimpanzee Enos occupying the capsule for a two-orbit ride before being successfully recovered in an ocean landing. Not until February 20, 1962, however, could NASA accomplish an orbital flight with an astronaut. On that date John Glenn became the first American to circle the Earth, making three orbits in the Friendship 7 Mercury spacecraft.

The flight was not without problems, however; Glenn flew parts of the last two orbits manually because of an autopilot failure, and he left his retrorocket pack (which normally would be jettisoned) attached to the capsule during reentry because of a warning light showing a loose heat shield.

Glenn's flight provided a healthy boost in national pride, making up for at least some of the earlier Soviet successes. The public, more than celebrating the technological success, embraced Glenn as a personification of heroism and dignity. Hundreds of requests for personal appearances by Glenn poured into NASA headquarters, and NASA learned much about the power of the astronauts to sway public opinion. The agency leadership allowed Glenn to speak at some events, but more often it substituted other astronauts and declined many other invitations. Among other engagements, Glenn did address a joint session of Congress and participated in several ticker-tape parades around the country. NASA thereby discovered a powerful public relations tool that it has employed ever since.

The 123-foot-tall Pad 14 gantry moves back during a systems check several days before the launch of MA-9, the last flight of the Mercury program that took place on May 15–16, 1963. The gantry moved away from the Atlas about one hour from liftoff on actual flight, while the umbilical cable to the tower at left was dropped only a few minutes before liftoff.

The Launch of Freedom 7 on May 5, 1961, was the first American suborbital spaceflight of an astronaut. Aboard is Alan B. Shepard as the Mercury-Redstone (MR-3) rocket is launched from Pad 5, at what would become the Kennedy Space Center, Florida.

Three more successful Mercury flights took place during 1962 and 1963. Scott Carpenter made three orbits on May 20, 1962, and on October 3, 1962, Walter Schirra flew six orbits. The capstone of Project Mercury was the May 15-16, 1963, flight of Gordon Cooper, who circled Earth 22 times in 34 hours. The program succeeded in accomplishing its purpose: to orbit successfully a human in space, explore aspects of tracking and control, and learn about microgravity and other biomedical issues associated with spaceflight. By the end of the Mercury program in 1963, the United States had still not caught up to the Soviet Union in world opinion since a majority still believed the U.S. trailed the USSR in space accomplishments.

The result from a succession of polls asking the public "Is the Soviet Union ahead of the United States in space?" during the early 1950s usually yielded an opinion that the Soviets were outperforming the Americans. That began to change in the middle part of the decade at the time that the Gemini program began to demonstrate impressive capabilities.

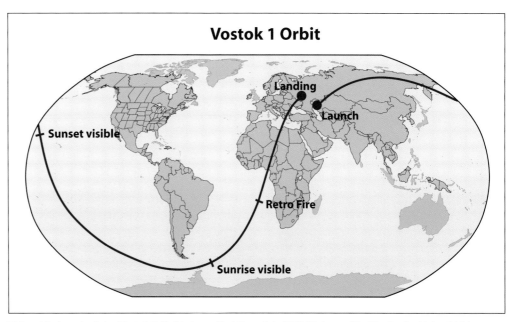

Vostok 1 Orbit

Sunset visible
Landing
Launch
Retro Fire
Sunrise visible

This orbital track of the Vostok 1 flight shows Yuri Gagarin's 1961 flight profile. The Soviet Union hid from the outside world the true track of the flight for many years. This was because he ejected from the capsule about 4 miles (7 km) above the Earth and parachuted to the ground because the capsule's parachute landing was deemed too rough for cosmonauts to survive. This violated a rule of the Fédération Aéronautique Internationale (FAI), trackers of aerospace records, which stated that a pilot must land with the spacecraft to be considered an official flight. Only many years later did the Soviet Union reveal that Gagarin had not accompanied the Vostok capsule to the ground.

Astronaut John Glenn climbing into his spacecraft for the first U.S. orbital flight on February 20, 1962.

Developing More Capabilities in Space: Long Duration, EVA, and Rendezvous and Docking

The space programs of both the United States and the Soviet Union perceived that several key capabilities had to be developed before significant exploration could take place. The U.S. specifically designed the Gemini program to gain these new techniques and capabilities. The Soviet effort was somewhat less systematic, but no less significant. They all worked to close most of the gap by experimenting and training on the ground, but four major issues required in-flight experience. The first was the building and flying of multi-person spacecraft in Earth orbit. Second, the

ability in space to locate, maneuver toward, and rendezvous and dock with another spacecraft would be central to successful long-term space operations. The third was closely related: the ability of astronauts and cosmonauts to work outside a spacecraft, undertaking extravehicular activity (EVA) space walks. The fourth involved developing the capability for extended human spaceflight with long duration missions.

The Soviets were the first to undertake a rendezvous in space. On August 12, 1962, Vostok 3 and Vostok 4 reached orbits that passed within several miles of each other, but did not actually see each other since they did not have the orbital maneuvering capability to perform a true space rendezvous. The same was true of Vostok 5 and Vostok 6 launched June 16, 1963, when they repeated the experiment. As Vasiliy Mishin, a senior official in the Soviet space program, wrote:

> The group flight . . . well, a day after the launch, the first craft was over Baikonur. If the second craft were launched now with great precision, then they would turn out to be next to each other in space. And that's what was done . . . The craft turned out to be 5 kilometers from each other! Well, since, with all of the secrecy, we didn't tell the whole truth, the Western experts, who hadn't figured it out, thought that our Vostok was already equipped with orbital approach equipment. As they say, a sleight of hand isn't any kind of fraud. It was more like our competitors deceived themselves all by their lonesome. Of course, we didn't shatter their illusions.

Moreover, in Voskhod 1, the Soviets flew the first three-person mission into space with cosmonauts Vladimir Komarov, Boris Yegorov, and Konstaning Feoktistov in October 1964.

Meantime, in the United States, to advance knowledge in the areas of rendezvous and docking, EVA, and long-duration spaceflight, NASA devised Project Gemini. Initiated in the fall of 1961 by engineers at Robert Gilruth's Space Task Group in cooperation with McDonnell Aircraft Corporation technicians (builders of the Mercury spacecraft), Gemini started out as a larger Mercury Mark II capsule but soon became a totally different proposition. It could accommodate two astronauts for extended flights of more than two weeks. It pioneered the use of fuel cells instead of batteries to power the ship, and it incorporated a series of other modifications to hardware. Its designers also

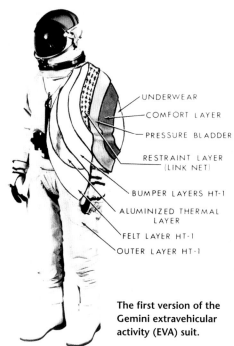

The first version of the Gemini extravehicular activity (EVA) suit.

considered using a paraglider being developed at Langley Research Center for "dry" landings instead of a "splashdown" in water and recovery by the Navy. The entire system was to be powered by the newly developed Titan II launch vehicle, another ballistic missile developed for the Air Force. A central reason for this program was to perfect techniques for rendezvous and docking, so NASA appropriated from the military some Agena rocket upper stages and fitted them with docking adapters.

Problems with the Gemini program abounded from the start. The Titan II had longitudinal oscillations, called the pogo effect because it resembled the behavior of a child on a pogo stick. Overcoming this problem required engineering imagination and long hours of overtime to stabilize fuel flow and maintain vehicle control. The fuel cells leaked and had to be redesigned, and the Agena reconfiguration also suffered costly delays. NASA engineers never did get the paraglider to work properly, and eventually they dropped it from the program in favor of a parachute system like the one used for Mercury. All these difficulties shot an estimated $350 million program to over $1 billion. The overruns were successfully justified by the space agency, however, as necessities to meet the Apollo landing commitment.

By the end of 1963 most of the difficulties with Gemini had been resolved and the program was ready for flight. Following two unoccupied orbital test flights, the first operational mission took place on March 23, 1965. Mercury astronaut Gus Grissom commanded the mission, with John W. Young, a naval avia-

Two spacecraft at different altitudes

Lower spacecraft boosted to elliptical orbit

Second boost to circularize orbit at slightly lower altitude

Lower spacecraft orbits faster

Two spacecraft rendezvous

Rendezvous between two spacecraft was critical to virtually everything the Soviet Union and the United States wanted to do in space. Maneuvering to arrive at the same orbit, make the orbital velocities the same, and bring them together had to be resolved through deliberate calculations and movement.

tor chosen as an astronaut in 1962, accompanying him. The next mission, flown in June 1965, stayed aloft for four days, and astronaut Edward H. White II performed the first American extravehicular activity (EVA), or space walk.

This failed to be the first space walk, however, because Soviet Cosmonaut Alexei Leonov beat White during the flight of Voskhod 2 on March 18, 1965, when he exited the spacecraft and floated outside the spacecraft, secured by only a safety line. He pushed away from the vehicle and drifted out to 17.5 feet (5.3 m) before returning to the spacecraft. A tense few moments ensued when Leonov found his spacesuit too rigid to reenter the airlock. He solved the problem by bleeding air out of his suit and reducing its size so that he could fit back through an inflatable airlock. As Leonov wrote about this experience:

"During my training for this mission, I did a drawing showing how I imagined myself walking in space high over the planet Earth in the outer cosmos. The dream came true, and space walking became a reality with my EVA on Voskhod 2 in March 1965. During the space walk, I was exposed to the vacuum of space for some 20 minutes, considerably longer than expected, due to problems re-entering the spaceship. The pressure difference between air in my space suit and the vacuum of the cosmos expanded my space suit and made it rigid, and I had to force some of the air out of the suit in order to close the lock's outer hatch."

The crew of Voskhod 1 is shown here at an airport in Moscow after their return from orbit. Depicted from left to right are Konstaning Feoktistove, Vladimir Komarov, and Boris Yegorov. Note their causal attire, a contrast to the bulky suits worn on the earlier Vostok flights. With the growing concern that the American project Gemini would be the first multi-astronaut spaceflight, the Soviets began to design their own three-man spacecraft, Voskhod. Achieving another space first, the Soviets launched Voskhod 1 on October 12, 1964. Yegorov, the first trained medical doctor in space, conducted several medical experiments. The mission was declared a success when the cosmonauts safely landed in Kazakhstan on October 13th.

These three stills are from the external movie camera on the Soviet Voskhod 2, which recorded Aleksei Leonov's historic space walk on March 18, 1965. Leonov's EVA made him the first human to ever walk in space, giving the Soviet Union yet another space first.

Although the Soviets trumped the Americans with the first EVA, the Gemini program soon demonstrated considerable capability. Eight more missions followed through November 1966. Despite problems great and small encountered on virtually all of them, the program achieved its goals. Additionally, as a technological learning program, Gemini had been a success, with 52 different experiments performed on the ten missions.

Also during Project Gemini rendezvous and docking gained ascendancy, and the methods developed then have been used ever since. Astronaut Buzz Aldrin became one of the key figures working on this problem, and as everyone knew without this capability the Apollo Moon landings would not be successfully completed. Aldrin's unique background among the astronauts as a Ph.D. in astronautics from Massachusetts Institute of Technology allowed him to solve one of the principal riddles of the Gemini program, how to accomplish rendezvous and docking of two spacecraft

in Earth orbit. Acquiring the nickname "Dr. Rendezvous" from his fellow astronauts, Aldrin more than other astronauts worked to develop the orbital maneuvers essential to the program's success. In 1963 and 1964, he worked hard to convince flight operations leaders that a concentric rendezvous would work. In his estimation, a target vehicle could be launched in a circular orbit with the rendezvousing spacecraft in a closer orbit to Earth. It would then take less time to circle the globe, he argued, and then catch up for rendezvous. Aldrin and others worked together to develop the trajectories and maneuvers that would allow the spacecraft to intercept a target vehicle.

What emerged was a combination system that relied on automated systems to get the Gemini spacecraft close enough to the target vehicle so that the crew could complete the rendezvous and docking process using the control handles, reading the pilot displays, and observing the optical targets through windows in the spacecraft. At some point in the approach, typically

180 feet (60 m) to 30 feet (15 m) separation, the rendezvous radar could no longer give an accurate estimate of range because of the closeness of the target. Then, visual observations of the docking targets by the crew were heavily relied upon. This approach worked flawlessly throughout the Gemini program. In all, Gemini astronauts completed successful rendezvous and dockings on Gemini VIII in March 1966, Gemini X in July 1966, Gemini XI in September 1966, leading up to the finale on Gemini XII in November 1966.

The first test of rendezvous in space occurred on the twin flights of Gemini VI and VII in December 1965. Initially intended as a rendezvous with an Agena target spacecraft, when the Agena failed during launch the mission was hastily modified to rendezvous with a piloted spacecraft. Consequently, Gemini VII, piloted by Frank Borman and James Lovell, was launched first, on December 4, 1965, to become the rendezvous target for Gemini VI. When Gemini VI was launched on December 15, piloted by Walter Schirra and Thomas Stafford, the two spacecraft rendezvoused and flew in formation for five hours. Their first test of rendezvous had been successful and proved the concept of human involvement in space rendezvous. Gemini VII remained aloft for fourteen days to study the effects of long-duration flight. The 330 hours in space had no long-term harmful effects on the crew, but the flight turned into something of an endurance test for the two pilots, confined in their hot, cramped quarters. At

This liftoff of Gemini-Titan XI (GT-11) from Complex 19 took place on September 12, 1966. The Gemini XI mission included a rendezvous with an Agena target vehicle.

The Gemini XI spacecraft is lowered onto a dolly for preflight maintenance before stacking on the Titan rocket at the Kennedy Space Center on July 21, 1966. Astronauts Dick Gordon and Pete Conrad would lift off in this spacecraft on September 12, 1966, for a mission lasting almost three days. The crew practiced docking with the Agena docking craft, and Gordon also performed two space walks during the mission.

the conclusion of the lengthy time cooped up together Lovell joked to reporters that he and Borman were happy to announce their engagement. It was astronaut humor that said quite a lot about the masculine culture of the fliers.

Buzz Aldrin flew on Gemini XII between November 11 and 15, 1966, demonstrating the success of his rendezvous and docking work for all to see; he manually recomputed all the rendezvous maneuvers after the onboard radar failed. Aldrin also engaged in a two-hour space walk that became the longest and most successful ever completed to that time. In a four-day, 59-revolution flight that successfully ended the Gemini program, he proved his theories of rendezvous of spacecraft in Earth or lunar orbit, and docking them together for spaceflight. In essence, this mission was important because it conquered the difficulties previously experienced by NASA in space rendezvous and docking. After this demonstration of capability, Gemini XII became the last Gemini to enter space, opening the way for the Apollo missions.

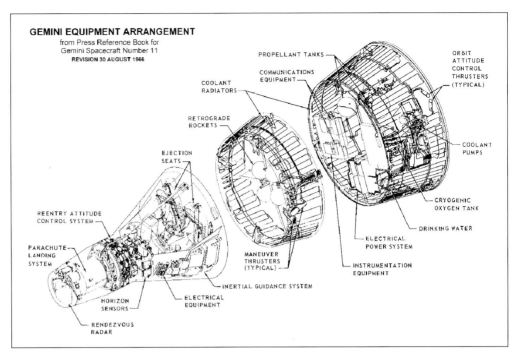

GEMINI EQUIPMENT ARRANGEMENT
from Press Reference Book for
Gemini Spacecraft Number 11
REVISION 30 AUGUST 1966

This diagram of the Gemini spacecraft dates from August 30, 1966, showing all aspects of its internal components.

The Augmented Target Docking Adapter (ATDA) as seen from the Gemini IX spacecraft in June 1966 during one of their three rendezvous in space. The ATDA and Gemini IX spacecraft are 66.5 ft. apart. Failure of the docking adapter protective cover to fully separate on the ATDA prevented the docking of the two spacecraft. The ATDA was described by the Gemini IX crew as an "angry alligator."

Swarms of Satellites

The Earth is surrounded by thousands of satellites and tons of space hardware. Since 1957 there have been about 4,600 launches that put about 6,000 satellites into orbit. About half of these satellites reentered the Earth's atmosphere by 2008, leaving more than 3,000 satellites in orbit. More than 800 were operational in 2008. The oldest satellite in orbit is Vanguard 1, launched by the United States in 1958.

Some orbits are highly concentrated with satellites and debris. These zones are where a high number of satellites are placed, especially in low Earth orbit. More than 1,100 objects, about a third of them operational satellites, form a "ring" around the Earth at the distance of geostationary orbit. The space between LEO and GEO is generally less crowded, but several constellations of satellites exist there as well.

The space around the Earth contains more than working satellites. More than 12,000 human-made objects can be found in Earth orbit, including rocket boosters, old satellites, bolts, garbage bags, and broken hardware. Most objects on low orbit eventually reenter the atmosphere. However, when satellites break apart potentially dangerous debris is left behind. Each of these explosions can create a cloud of debris that rapidly grows. While there is plenty of room in outer space, concentrations of debris are sources of serious concern to space agencies.

The total number of debris particles increases as satellites deteriorate in orbit, but decreases as particles enter the Earth's atmosphere. In high orbits, where no atmospheric drag is encountered, objects will never return to Earth unless a collision occurs. About half of all the objects in orbit are the result of explosions on satellites.

The density of objects in Earth orbit is actually low. In the densest part of low Earth orbit, there is an average of about one object per 50 million cubic kilometers, which is the volume of a cube about 370 kilometers on a side. While that sounds like a lot of space, the problem with space debris is their relative speed. The speed of objects in orbit is measured in kilometers per second. Because of their high velocity, even small objects can cause serious damage.

Each object in orbit can be tracked by ground-based radar. The U.S. Strategic Command tracks more than 8,000 objects at least 10 cm in size. This information can be used to maneuver spacecraft out of harm's way. Despite precautions, accidents do happen. A small military satellite operated by France was hit by rocket debris in July 1996. The satellite lost stability but it remained in orbit and under control.

Space Shuttles have been hit many times by orbiting debris. Small "dings" are common on Space Shuttle flights, likely caused by impacting paint flecks. Space Shuttles have performed maneuvers on several flights to avoid potential collisions.

The single largest event that contributed to orbiting space debris happened in January 2007, when Fengyun-3A, a Chinese polar-orbiting weather satellite, was deliberately impacted by a ground-launched rocket in an apparent test of an antisatellite weapon. This single event added more than 2,000 pieces of debris to low Earth orbit, about 30% of the total amount of debris at that time.

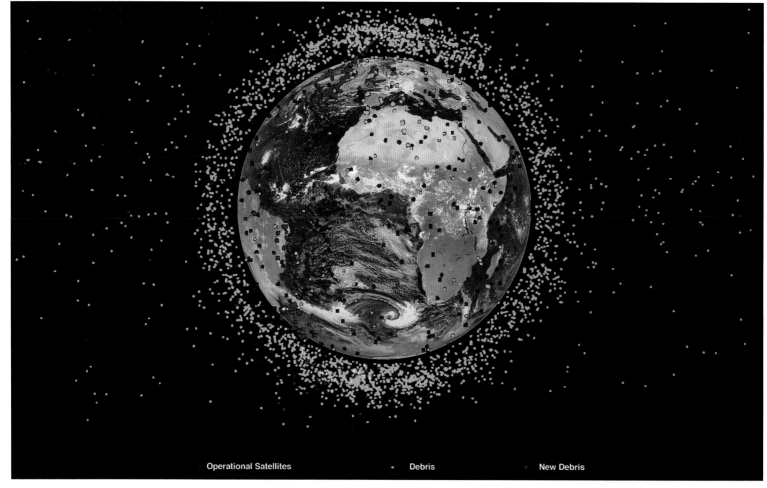

Operational Satellites   • Debris   New Debris

All orbiting objects in low Earth orbit are shown in this diagram. Operational satellites are shown with blue marks, while green marks indicate the location of disabled satellites and debris. Red marks show the volume of debris created by the destruction of the Fengyun-3A satellite in January 2007.

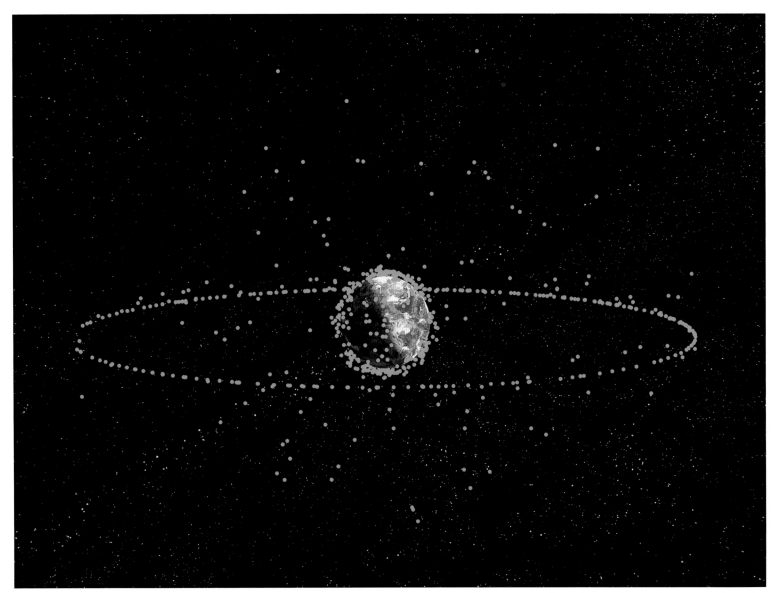

Operational satellites in orbit around the Earth in 2008. The size of each satellite has been significantly enlarged. Satellites in low Earth orbit cluster around the globe, while those in medium Earth orbit occupy the space beyond. The ring of geostationary satellites is visible outside this area.

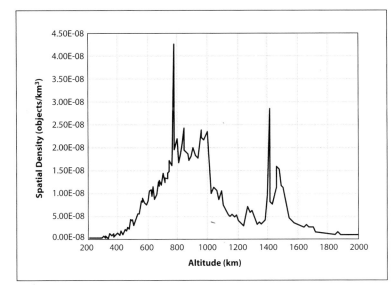

The density of orbiting objects at altitudes above the Earth's surface. The high density at 780 km altitude indicates the constellation of Iridium communications satellites.

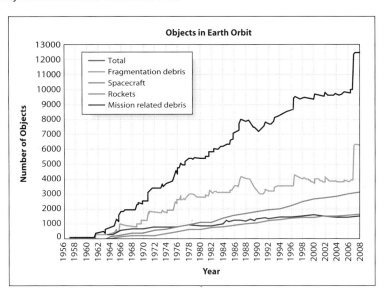

Chart showing the number of operational satellites and debris in orbit. "Mission-related" debris was intentionally left in orbit. "Fragmentation" debris is the result of explosions, collisions, or malfunctions.

The Nature of Low Earth Orbit

An equatorial orbit lies in the XY axis at a tilt of 0 degrees and this orbital tilt angle describes the inclination of the orbit relative to the Earth's equator. Low Earth orbit (LEO, 200–1,200 km), medium Earth orbit (MEO, 1,000–36,000 km) and highly elliptical orbit (HEO, 50,000–400,000 km) describe the distances a space vehicle or satellite travel. A near equatorial orbit is an orbit that lies close to the equatorial plane of the object orbited. This orbit allows for rapid revisit times (for a single orbiting spacecraft) of near equatorial ground sites.

To enter equatorial orbit, a satellite must be launched from a place on Earth close to the equator. The European Space Agency launches satellites aboard Ariane rockets into equatorial orbit from French Guiana. Additionally, the Space Shuttle's launch site is Cape Canaveral, Florida, located at 28.5 degrees North latitude. The ground track of a spacecraft in low Earth orbit resembles a sine wave varying between the launch latitude and the negative of the launch latitude. So, a vehicle launched in an orbit inclined 28.5° to the equator can never fly over latitudes above 28.5° N or below 28.5° S. In order for engineers to keep track of a vehicle in orbit, engineers use 360° to measure

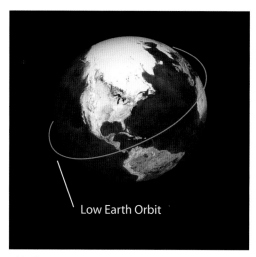

This illustration depicts the orbital planes of common lower equatorial orbits.

Low Earth Orbit

the orbit. For example, when it is first launched into orbit, a satellite moves from the perigee, the closest point to the Earth, to the apogee, the farthest point, traveling between 0° and 180°. During the second half of its orbit, the satellite travels from the apogee to the perigee in an orbit between 180° and 360°.

In relation to Kepler's Third Law, the time to complete one revolution around the Earth, or orbital period, that a satellite spends in

orbit relates to its altitude. Craft moving in lower orbits complete their revolutions more quickly than craft revolving at higher orbits, as they must travel a longer distance. The Space Shuttle, if it remains in an equatorial orbit approximately 200 miles (300 km) in altitude, can make a complete revolution in approximately 90 minutes. Whereas, a communications satellite in equatorial orbit stays further away at about 22,400 miles (35,786 km), matching the rotation period of the Earth. Hence, they maintain the same position relative to Earth at all times in a geosynchronous orbit, able to service an area as large as the visible surface of the Earth in a single field of view.

Most objects in Earth orbit are flying over the equatorial plane. This includes all of the human spaceflight vehicles of all nations. For the United States, this includes the Mercury, Gemini, Apollo, and Space Shuttle programs. For the Soviet Union/Russia, the Vostok, Voskhod, and Soyuz spacecraft all orbited in high-inclination equatorial low Earth orbits. The Chinese Shenzou spacecraft also flew on similar orbits. In terms of space stations, the American Skylab, the Soviet Almaz and Salyut series, Mir, and the International Space Station are also in equatorial low Earth orbit.

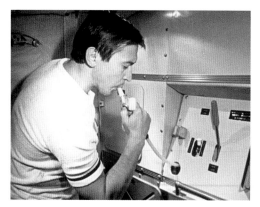

An interior view of the orbital module of a Soviet Soyuz spacecraft mock-up in 1975, located at the Cosmonaut Training Center (Star City) near Moscow. This view shows a Soviet test engineer drinking from a water dispenser. The orbital module is one of three major components of the Soyuz spacecraft. The other two components are the descent vehicle and the instrument assembly module. This photograph was made from a frame of the 35mm motion picture film entitled "Checkout of the Compatibility of Equipment in the Soyuz Spacecraft Mock-up."

The Soyuz spacecraft and launch vehicle were installed on the launch pad at the Baikonur complex in Kazakhstan in 1975. Baikonur is the world's largest space center. This launch was part of the Apollo-Soyuz Test Project (ASTP), a cooperative space mission between the United States and the USSR. The goals of ASTP were to test the ability of American and Soviet spacecraft to rendezvous and dock in space and to open the doors to possible international rescue missions and future collaboration on human spaceflights. The Soyuz and Apollo crafts launched from Baikonur and the Kennedy Space Center respectively, on July 15, 1975. The two spacecraft successfully completed the rendezvous and docking on July 17th. ASTP proved to be a significant step toward improving international cooperation in space during the Cold War.

The Salyut 7 in Earth orbit with a Soyuz T ferry craft attached in the mid-1980s.

International Space Station Layout

Solar Array
Service Module
LSM
SPP Solar Array
Solar Array
Progress
SPP
UDM
FGB
Soyuz
TCS Radiator
DC
Research
PMA 1
DSM
Node 1
Airlock
ANTENNA
PMA 3
CUPOLA
MBS
HAB
Radiators
LAB
JEM
ESA
Node 2
PMA 2
Radiators
Solar Array
Solar Array

The International Space Station is made up of modules from several nations. The first modules were launched in 1998.

Core Module
Prioda
Progress-M
Spektr
Kvant
Soyuz-TM
Kvant-2
Kristal
Docking Module

The Mir Space Station was operated by Soviet and Russian agencies beginning in 1986. The Space Shuttle later docked with the station. Mir reentered the Earth's atmosphere in 2001.

This view of Skylab in orbit was taken by the Skylab 4 (the last Skylab mission) crew, and shows the sun-shade in place. The goals of the Skylab were to enrich scientific knowledge of the Earth, the Sun, the stars, and cosmic space; to study the effects of weightlessness on living organisms, including humans; to study the effects of the processing and manufacturing of materials utilizing the absence of gravity; and to conduct Earth resource observations.

Supporting the Hubble Space Telescope in Low Earth Orbit

A space science project much in the news since 1990, both for positive and negative reasons, was the $2 billion Hubble Space Telescope (HST) that was deployed from the Space Shuttle Discovery (STS-31) into low Earth orbit in April 1990. A product of a partnership between NASA, the European Space Agency, and an international community of astronomers, it was named after Edwin P. Hubble, an American astronomer who discovered the expanding nature of the universe and was the first to realize the true nature of galaxies. The purpose of the HST was to study the cosmos from low Earth equatorial orbit. By placing the telescope in space, astronomers intended to collect data free of the Earth's atmosphere. The HST detects objects 25 times fainter than the dimmest objects seen from Earth and provided astronomers with an observable universe 250 times larger than visible from ground-based telescopes, perhaps as far away as 14 billion light-years.

The major elements of the HST were the Optical Telescope Assembly (OTA), the Support System Module (SSM), and the Scientific Instruments (SI). The HST is approximately the size of a railroad car, with two cylinders joined together and wrapped in a silvery reflective heat shield blanket. Wing-like solar arrays extend horizontally from each side of these cylinders, and dish-shaped antennas extend

above and below the body of the telescope. The Marshall Space Flight Center had responsibility for design, development, and construction of the HST. The Perkin-Elmer Corporation, in Danbury, Connecticut, developed the optical system and guidance sensors. The Lockheed Missile and Space Company of Sunnyvale, California, produced the protective outer shroud and spacecraft systems, and assembled and tested the finished telescope.

While an earlier project, the Orbiting Astronomical Observatory-1, had been launched in 1968 and placed a telescope above the Earth's obscuring atmosphere, the HST project represented a quantum leap forward in astronomical capability. After more than a decade of puritanically funded but productive research and development on the project in the 1970s and early 1980s, NASA began assembling the new space telescope. Through the telescope scientists could gaze farther into space than ever before, viewing galaxies as far away as 15 billion light-years. A key component of it was a precision-ground 94-inch primary mirror shaped to within microinches of perfection from ultra-low-expansion titanium silicate glass with an aluminum-magnesium fluoride coating.

The Hubble Space Telescope had been scheduled for launch in 1986, but had to be delayed during the Space Shuttle redesign that

followed the Challenger accident. Excitement abounded as it was finally deployed four years later and the first images began to come back to Earth. The photos provided bright, crisp images against the black background of space, much clearer than pictures of the same target taken by ground-based telescopes. Controllers then began moving the telescope's mirrors to better focus images. Although the focus sharpened slightly, the best image still had a pinpoint of light encircled by a hazy ring or "halo." NASA technicians concluded that the telescope had a "spherical aberration," a mirror defect only 1/25th the width of a human hair, that prevented Hubble from focusing all light to a single point.

At first many believed that the spherical aberration would cripple the 43-foot-long telescope, and NASA received considerable negative publicity, but soon scientists found a way with computer enhancement to work around the abnormality and engineers planned a Shuttle repair mission to fully correct it with an additional instrument. Once repaired the Hubble Space Telescope began returning impressive scientific data on a routine basis. For instance, as recently as 1980, astronomers had believed that an astronomical grouping known as R-136 was a single star, but the Hubble showed that it was made up of more than 60 of the youngest and heaviest stars ever viewed. The dense cluster, located within the Large Magellanic Cloud, was about 160,000 light-years from Earth, roughly 5.9 trillion miles away.

Because of the difficulties with the mirror of the Hubble Space Telescope, in December 1993 NASA launched the shuttle Endeavour on a repair mission to insert corrective instruments into the telescope and to service other components. During a weeklong mission, Endeavour's astronauts conducted a record five space walks and successfully completed all programmed repairs to the spacecraft. The first reports from the newly repaired HST indicated that the images being returned now were more than an order of magnitude (10 times) greater than those obtained before. The result has been enormously important to scientific understanding of the cosmos.

Because of the servicing mission, the HST dominated space science activities throughout the next several years. The results from Hubble touched on some of the most fundamental astronomical questions of the twentieth century, including the existence of black holes and the age of the universe. In addition,

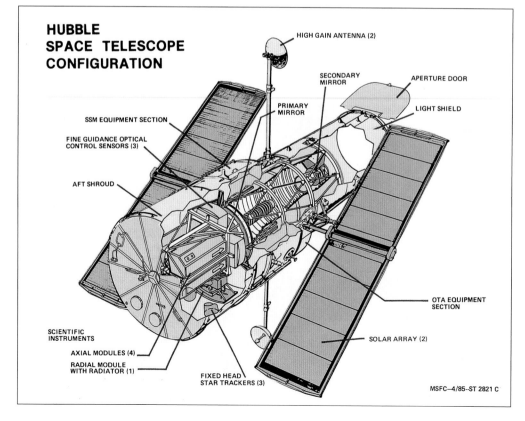

HUBBLE SPACE TELESCOPE CONFIGURATION

HIGH GAIN ANTENNA (2)

SECONDARY MIRROR

APERTURE DOOR

PRIMARY MIRROR

LIGHT SHIELD

SSM EQUIPMENT SECTION

FINE GUIDANCE OPTICAL CONTROL SENSORS (3)

AFT SHROUD

OTA EQUIPMENT SECTION

SCIENTIFIC INSTRUMENTS

AXIAL MODULES (4)

RADIAL MODULE WITH RADIATOR (1)

SOLAR ARRAY (2)

FIXED HEAD STAR TRACKERS (3)

MSFC-4/85-ST 2821 C

scientists using the HST obtained the clearest images yet of galaxies that formed when the universe was a fraction of its current age. These pictures provided the first clues to the historical development of galaxies and suggested that elliptical galaxies developed remarkably rapidly into their present shapes. However, spiral galaxies that existed in large clusters evolved over a much longer period—the majority were built and then torn apart by dynamic processes in a restless universe. The HST also discovered a new dark spot on Neptune, imaged the Eagle nebula in search of information about star formation, and observed the spectacular crash of Comet Shoemaker-Levy 9 into the planet Jupiter in 1994.

With regular maintenance visits to Hubble in a low Earth equatorial orbit using the Space Shuttle, NASA expanded the capabilities of the instrument during the more than 18 years since launch. In 2001 astronauts installed the Advanced Camera for Surveys, which captured an even wider swath of the sky and has yielded even sharper pictures than Hubble's earlier wide-field camera.

The telescope has documented in colorful detail the births and deaths of bright celestial objects. It provided visual proof that pancake-shaped dust disks around young stars are common, suggesting that the raw materials for planet formation are in place. The orbiting telescope showed for the first time that jets of material rising from embryonic stars emanate from the centers of disks of dust and gas, thus turning what was previously merely theory into an observed reality. It also monitored Supernova 1987A, the closest exploding star in four centuries, providing for the first time pictures of a collision between a wave of material ejected from the doomed star and a ring of matter surrounding it. In the next decade astronomers expect even more material to hit the ring, illuminating the surrounding material, and thereby literally throwing light on the exploding star's history. A final Hubble servicing mission is slated for 2009 to extend the instrument's service life for several more years.

To run all their systems, satellites need a way to generate power for months, even years. Like most Earth-orbiting spacecraft, the Hubble Space Telescope relies on solar arrays to recharge its onboard batteries, which must be lightweight and flexible to fit inside a relatively small launch vehicle. Consequently, they tend to be fragile, and several satellites have had to cope with damaged panels once in orbit. Fortunately, the telescope was designed for on-orbit repairs. In this image, Astronaut Kathy Thornton releases the old panel into low Earth orbit during the first Hubble Space Telescope Servicing Mission in December 1993.

The crew of Atlantis undertake repair of the Hubble Space Telescope during its first servicing mission in December 1993.

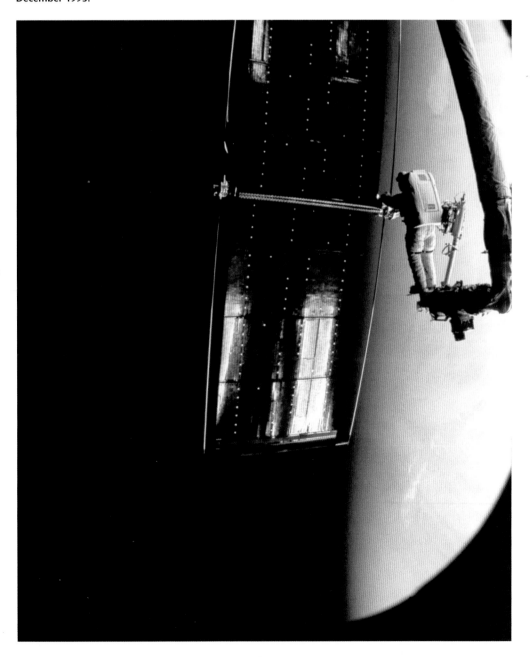

Seeking Polar Orbit

For so many reasons polar orbits are useful for remote sensing satellites. It is often low to medium altitude at an inclination that is between 45 and 90 degrees of the Earth's equator. In such an orbit a satellite passes over, or very close to, both poles of the Earth and during a single day it can observe many latitude points on the Earth. Polar orbits are especially useful for spacecraft that perform mapping or surveillance operations, such as the National Oceanic and Atmospheric Administration (NOAA) Tiros and Landsat satellites. Since the orbital plane is nominally fixed in space, the planet rotates below a polar orbit, allowing the spacecraft low-altitude access to virtually every point on the surface. It is also the orbit of choice of reconnaissance satellites so that they have a greater capability to image more parts of the globe on a regular basis. To achieve a polar orbit requires more energy, thus more propellant, than does an orbit of low inclination. A polar orbit cannot take advantage of the "free ride" provided by the Earth's rotation, and thus the launch vehicle must provide all of the energy for attaining orbital speed.

A key variation of the polar orbit is the sun-synchronous orbit providing consistent lighting of the Earth being imaged. In this orbit a satellite passes the equator and each latitude of the Earth's surface at the same local time, crossing the equator twelve times a day at the same time on the Earth's surface. The surface illumination angle will be nearly the same every time. This consistent lighting is a useful characteristic for satellites that image the Earth's surface in visible or infrared wavelengths. This results from the

This illustration depicts a generic polar orbit. With an inclination near 90 degrees to the equator, a satellite in polar orbit passes over the equator at a different longitude on each of its orbits. As a result, it provides the best coverage possible for the single satellite over virtually the entire Earth.

spacecraft's orbital plane rotating approximately one degree eastward each day to keep pace with the Earth's revolution around the sun.

The first satellites into polar orbit were weather collection spacecraft. As a result TIROS, short for Television Infrared Observation Satellite, became the world's first meteorological satellite upon launch from Cape Canaveral on April 1, 1960. It demonstrated the advantage of mapping the Earth's cloud cover, showing banded and clustered patches that required meteorologists to revise their forecasting techniques. A succession of TIROS satellites followed. It was not until 1970 that an operational system took shape with the deployment of the Improved TIROS Operational System

(ITOS), providing infrared observations of Earth cloud cover for use in weather forecasting. This series was followed by a succession of spacecraft beginning in the 1970s with the series designation NOAA-6 through NOAA-17, the last of which was launched in 2002.

A second major type of polar orbit satellite was the Landsat series, launched by NASA beginning in the 1970s. This series was a succession of increasingly advanced Earth resource mapping satellites. Landsat 1 was launched on July 23, 1972, and changed the way in which humans looked at the planet. It provided data on vegetation, insect infestations, crop growth, and associated land-use information. Two more Landsat vehicles were launched in January 1975 and March 1978, performed their missions, and exited service in the 1980s. Landsat 4, launched July 16, 1982, and Landsat 5, launched March 1, 1984, were "second generation" spacecraft, with greater capabilities to produce more detailed land-use data. Two additional Landsats have flown since, and Landsat 7 continues to provide data. The series enhanced the ability to develop a world-wide crop forecasting system. Moreover, Landsat imagery has been used to devise a strategy for deploying equipment to contain oil spills, to aid navigation, to monitor pollution, to assist in water management, to site new power plants and pipelines, and to aid in agricultural development.

Other types of polar remote sensing satellites have followed. These have taken many forms, from scientific data collection satellites seeking to understand Earth system science to

Landsat 7 was successfully launched on April 15, 1999, from Vandenberg Air Force Base, California, on a Delta-II expendable launch vehicle. It is the most recent generation of the venerable series of Landsat Earth resource monitoring satellites operated by NASA and the U.S. Geological Survey.

commercial space imaging satellites serving a variety of purposes. One of the first of those was the French SPOT-1 satellite, launched in 1986. The French space agency, CNES, developed SPOT as a government program that would be turned over to the commercial sector for operation, selling imagery of the Earth to all users. The SPOT succession of satellites, along with Landsat, successfully developed a global market for Earth observation data. These successes have led to purely commercial Earth observation satellite programs such as the Ikonos satellites by Space Imaging/GeoEye, Inc., and QuickBird by EarthWatch, Inc., and others. In addition to these ventures the governments of India (IRS) and Russia (Sovinformsputnik2) are routinely launching and operating satellites and selling optical imagery for public consumption.

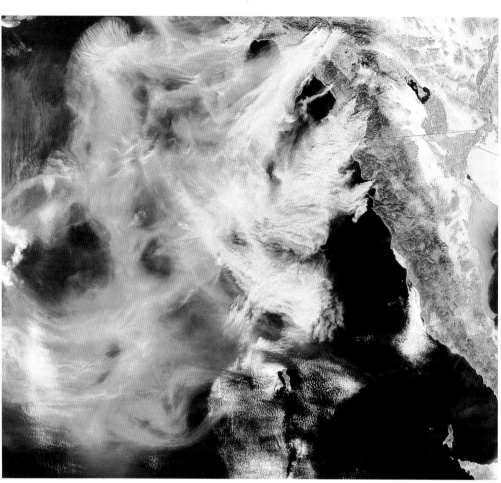

Data from remote sensing satellites can be used to track forest fires that endanger populated areas. This image of southern California was collected by the MODIS sensor on Terra satellite in October 2003. At least five groups of fires, some of the largest ever in California, are seen burning in this image.

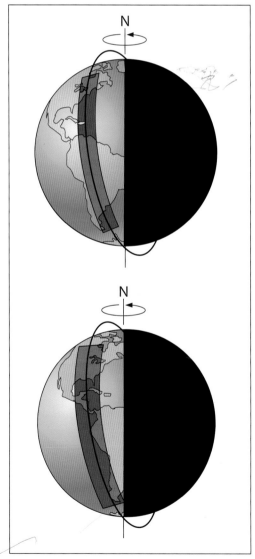

This image depicts a sun-synchronous orbit which combines altitude and inclination in such a way that an object on that orbit passes over any given point of the Earth's surface at the same local solar time.

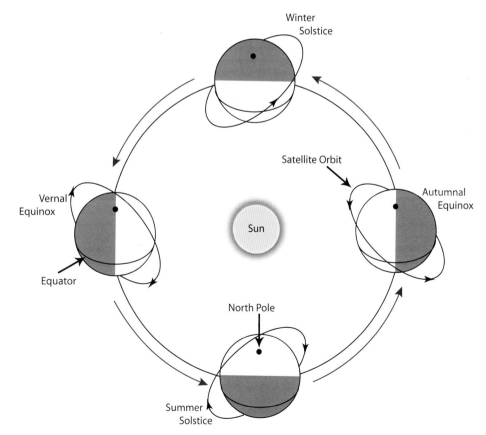

When a satellite is placed into sun-synchronous orbit, the plane of its orbit rotates at the same speed the Earth revolves around the Sun. This allows the surface of the Earth to be observed at a constant illumination angle.

Geostationary Orbit

One area where the United States made significant strides during the early years of space exploration was in application satellites. In 1945 science fiction writer and futurist Arthur C. Clarke posited that three satellites placed in geosynchronous (stationary) orbit could be used to bounce radio waves around the globe. The idea thrilled many scientists and with the dawning of the space age the U.S. moved to exploit this opportunity. The first attempt was a test program call Echo, which called for the orbiting of a 100-foot inflatable satellite covered with reflective material off of which NASA could bounce a radio beam. Difficulties abounded in trying to launch an inflatable, passive satellite, but tests were successful on August 12, 1960.

At the same time active-repeater communications satellites were being developed, the first of which was the Bell Telephone Laboratories Telstar project. Beginning in 1962, several generations of Telstars, as well as other types of communications satellites in Earth orbit, helped to make Clarke's idea of real-time global communications a reality by the mid-1960s.

Seeing the enormous commercial potential of space-based communications, the U.S. Congress passed the Communications Satellite Act of 1962, creating a Communications Satellite Corporation (COMSAT) with ownership divided fifty/fifty between the general public and the telecommunications corporations to manage global satellite communications for the United States. Near the same time U.S. leaders recognized the possibility of competition and participated

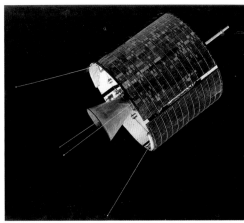

Early Bird, the world's first commercial communications satellite. Built by the Communications Satellite Corporation (COMSAT) it was launched into geosynchronous orbit on April 6, 1965. With an orbit at 22,300 miles above the equator, Early Bird provided line of sight communications between Europe and North America for telephone, television, telegraph, and facsimile transmissions.

in the establishment of the International Telecommunication Satellite Consortium (INTELSAT), with Comsat as manager, to provide an international communication satellite system. Founded by nineteen nations, with eventual membership of well over a hundred, it was initially very much an American organization, with the United States controlling 61% of the voting authority and all the technology. It oversaw the development of INTELSAT 1 in 1965, the first of the global communications satellite network. With this satellite system in orbit the world became a far different place. Within a few years telephone circuits

increased from five hundred to thousands and live television coverage of events anywhere in the world became commonplace.

Very quickly the other nations of the world moved to establish communications satellites in geosynchronous Earth orbit. Equally successful was the U.S.'s work with meteorological satellites, providing weather data from space. Project Tiros had been inherited by NASA from the DOD during the administrative consolidation between 1958 and 1960. The space agency launched Tiros 1 on April 1, 1960, and it provided valuable images of weather fronts, storms, and other atmospheric occurrences. This satellite led to a long series of weather satellites that quickly became standard weather forecasting tools in the United States and throughout the world.

The geosynchronous satellite industry, which grew significantly throughout the last third of the twentieth century, did so largely because of several related events. The use of geostationary weather satellites for imagery of weather patterns, storms, and other atmospheric occurrences soon became a staple resource for news organizations, scientists, and anyone else world wide. They are now ubiquitous in their use on television and radio weather reports, Internet sites, and newspapers. The Project Tiros weather satellite had been inherited by NASA from the Department of Defense during a consolidation of space missions between 1958 and 1960.

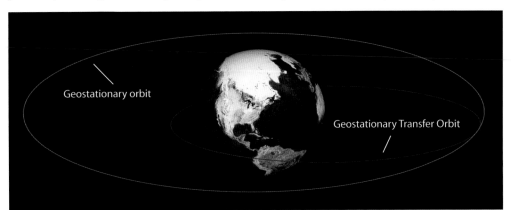

The image on the left depicts the geostationary equatorial orbit in which most communications and weather satellites are located. The image on the right depicts a full view of the Earth, taken by the Geostationary Operational Environment Satellite (GOES-8). Owned and operated by the National Oceanic and Atmospheric Administration (NOAA), GOES satellites provide the kind of continuous monitoring necessary for intensive data analysis. They circle the Earth in a geosynchronous orbit, which means they orbit the equatorial plane of the Earth at a speed matching the Earth's rotation. This allows them to hover continuously over one position on the surface. The geosynchronous plane is about 35,800 km (22,300 miles) above the Earth, high enough to allow the satellites a full-disc view of the Earth. Because they stay above a fixed spot on the surface, they provide a constant vigil for severe weather conditions such as tornadoes, flash floods, hail storms, and hurricanes. When these conditions develop, the GOES satellites are able to monitor storm development and track their movements. NASA manages the design and launch of the spacecraft. NASA launched the first GOES for NOAA in 1975 and followed it with another in 1977. Currently, the United States is operating GOES-8, positioned at 75 west longitude and the equator, and GOES-10, which is positioned at 135 west longitude and the equator. GOES-9, which malfunctioned in 1998, is being stored in orbit as an emergency backup should either GOES-8 or GOES-10 fail. GOES-11 was launched on May 3, 2000, and GOES-12 on July 23, 2001. Both are being stored in orbit as a fully functioning replacement for GOES-8 or GOES-10 on failure.

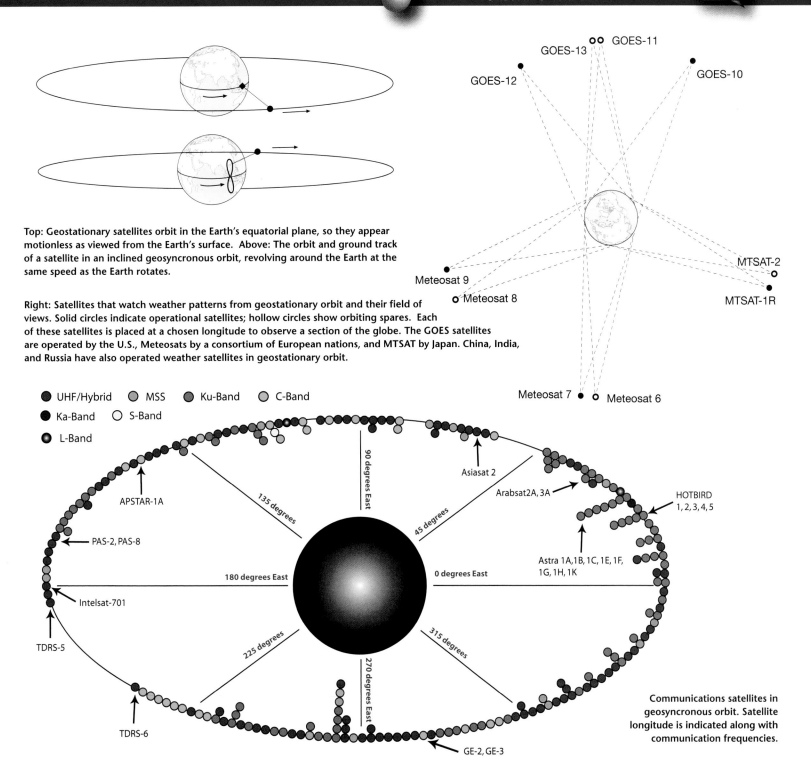

Top: Geostationary satellites orbit in the Earth's equatorial plane, so they appear motionless as viewed from the Earth's surface. Above: The orbit and ground track of a satellite in an inclined geosyncronous orbit, revolving around the Earth at the same speed as the Earth rotates.

Right: Satellites that watch weather patterns from geostationary orbit and their field of views. Solid circles indicate operational satellites; hollow circles show orbiting spares. Each of these satellites is placed at a chosen longitude to observe a section of the globe. The GOES satellites are operated by the U.S., Meteosats by a consortium of European nations, and MTSAT by Japan. China, India, and Russia have also operated weather satellites in geostationary orbit.

Communications satellites in geosyncronous orbit. Satellite longitude is indicated along with communication frequencies.

When Mt. St. Helens erupted on May 18, 1980, for example, weather satellites tracked the tons of volcanic ash that spread eastwardly, allowing meteorologists both to warn of danger and to study the effects of the explosion on the world's climate. More spectacular, and ultimately more disconcerting, Nimbus 7, in orbit since 1978, revealed that ozone levels over the Antarctic had been dropping for years and had reached record lows by October 1991. These data, combined with that from other sources, led to the 1992 decision to enact U.S. legislation banning chemicals that depleted the ozone layer. In the 1980s NASA and NOAA also began developing the Geostationary Operational Environmental Satellite (GOES) system, which viewed the entire Earth every

30 minutes, day and night, and placed seven GOES into orbit. As the 1990s began, a series of five new satellites, designated GOES-I through –M, was under development by NASA and NOAA for use beyond the year 2000.

These geosynchronous satellites have had a profound influence on human civilization. The Galveston hurricane of 1900, for instance, came from nowhere and killed one-sixth of the population when it hit on September 8. In contrast, Galveston residents evacuated over the single bridge linking it to the mainland before hurricane Rita hit in September 2005 because of warnings from geosynchronous weather satellites. (Of course, it was probably easier to convince the population to leave after the debacle in New Orleans a month earlier during

Hurricane Katrina.) In addition, weather satellites detect and track forest fires, volcanoes, and severe storms, as well as document measures of rainfall and winds. Interestingly, it is the tracking of severe weather patterns and decision making about evacuation that has benefited the most from geosynchronous weather satellites. NOAA has provided a compendium of economic statistics concerning weather disasters, noting that actions taken to overcome these efforts save in excess of $10 billion in the U.S. every year.

There will continue to be an expansion of this specific activity in the first half of the twenty-first century.

Military Satellites

A major component in the national security system of the United States was the strategic reconnaissance efforts of space satellites. Under development in the latter 1950s, Project Corona was the first successful reconnaissance satellite program of the nation. Essentially, the objective of this effort was to obtain high-quality satellite photographs of the Soviet Union and thereby ensure that the United States would never suffer another Pearl Harbor. As part of this effort, the first satellite, launched August 18, 1960, reached orbit and then correctly returned its reentry vehicle containing photographs of the ICBM base at Plesetsk and the bomber base at Mys Schmitda in the Soviet Union when it was plucked from the Pacific Ocean by Navy frogmen. After this flight, Corona became an operational mission and functioned through 1973 when it was succeeded by later-generation reconnaissance satellites.

Corona has been succeeded by a series of ever more sophisticated reconnaissance satellites and a continuous stream of data currently flows from its imagery. Overseen by the National Reconnaissance Office (NRO), this highly classified effort informs the decision making of American leaders. They view it as critical to the welfare of the United States and its continued national sovereignty. It enables the discovery of strategic weapons, military buildups, and troop movements, and provides independent verification of strategic weapons reduction efforts. Accordingly, this mission will continue indefinitely, and the United States will invest in numerous future reconnaissance satellite programs throughout the twenty-first century.

The U.S. also pursued the X-20 Dyna-Soar in the 1960s, a military spaceplane to be launched atop a newly developed launcher. The Air Force believed that the X-20 would provide long-range bombardment and reconnaissance capability by flying at the edge of space and skipping off the Earth's atmosphere to reach targets anywhere in the world. Begun on December 11, 1961, this spaceplane was always troubled by the absence of a clearly defined military mission. Accordingly, in 1963 Defense Secretary Robert S. McNamara canceled the program.

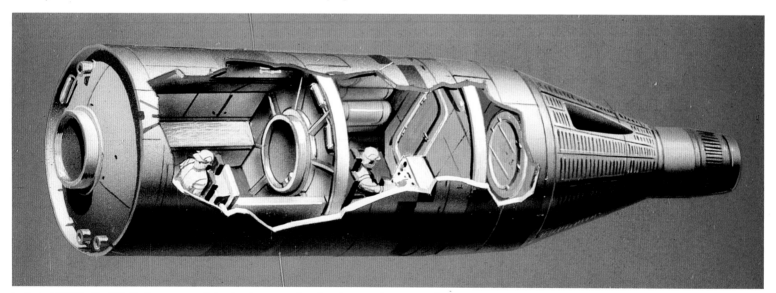

In the mid-1960s the U.S. Air Force pursued the development of a piloted reconnaissance capability in Earth orbit. The Blue Gemini spacecraft would be launched into orbit aboard a Titan IIIM vehicle. This program was terminated when costs became unsustainable.

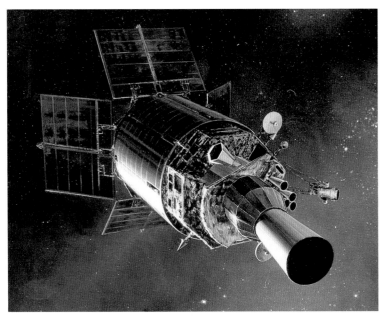

Defense Support Program (DSP) satellites provide near instantaneous detection of missile launches.

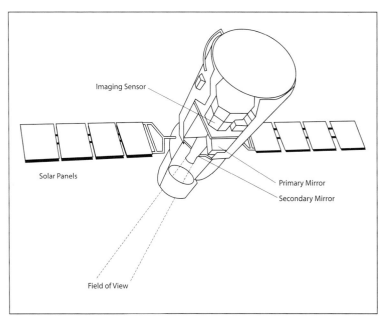

This schematic shows the components of a reconnaissance satellite postdating the Corona program.

Also continuing indefinitely into the future will be efforts to detect strategic missile launches from other nations. With the development of ballistic missiles in the 1950s, for the first time in the history of the United States, its two great oceans could not protect it from sustained attack and destruction. To warn against a Soviet ballistic missile attack, and thereby to allow time for the launch of a counterattack, the Department of Defense (DOD) sponsored the development of satellites ringing the globe that used infrared photographic technology to detect missile launches. The theory behind the system was that a heat signature from the rocket blast would be detected by satellites in space and then show up on infrared scopes at military monitoring posts. Through this process, the time and place of launch, as well as the missile trajectory, could be ascertained within seconds of launch.

It was a brilliant concept but it took years to come to fruition. The first effort, Project MIDAS, experienced numerous technical problems, but finally reached a turning point in 1963 when MIDAS 7 detected from space the first missile launch. MIDAS confirmed the concept, and the Defense Satellite Program (DSP), with its first launch in 1970, still provides early warning of missile launches. Through 2007 nearly 20 DSP satellites had been placed in orbit, not all of them operational, of course, at the same time. Beginning in 2000 the DOD began replacing DSP with a newer Space-Based Infrared Satellite (SBIRS). The United States will continue this effort with successive generations of spacecraft throughout the twenty-first century.

But strategic deterrence, satellite reconnaissance, and early warning and response capability were insufficient to guarantee the safety of the United States against a determined enemy and this prompted national security officials to seek an ultimate shield against attack. The result was the Strategic Defense Initiative (SDI), unveiled by President Ronald Reagan in March 1983. This was an expansive, technologically sophisticated, and exceptionally expensive research and development (R&D) program. SDI's aim was to create an array of space-based technologies that could track and destroy incoming missiles. The project immediately became controversial, mostly because of its technical complexity and its high price tag. Advocates of other strategic deterrence policies also opposed the effort because it would upset the balance of power between the U.S. and the U.S.S.R. that had succeeded in avoiding superpower war by holding populations hostage to nuclear forces. With the collapse of the Soviet Union in 1989 and the end of the Cold War, SDI declined in importance and survived only as a modest R&D effort within the DOD.

The military will also continue and extend the capability of a range of space-based systems that enable the United States to maintain its defense capability. These include command, control, and communications (C^3) that rely on satellites for knowledge management and movement to points where required; weather satellites for combat operations; and navigational systems such as the now famous and increasingly commercial Global Positioning System (GPS).

Indeed, with the end of the Cold War in the early 1990s the air and space defense system of the United States underwent substantial changes. The nuclear forces of the DOD have been taken off alert, some of the nuclear weapons destroyed, and SAC inactivated. The DOD component managing SDI has been reduced in size and funding. Finally, public conceptions of air and space defense, such as civil defense in its various capacities, has been minimized.

At the same time, the U.S. military began to use space for all manner of other capabilities: communications, early warning, weather, and a host of other applications. This remains a critical component of military space activities in Earth orbit to the present.

The launching of a MILSTAR military applications satellite.

Unique Constellations of Satellites

There are several types of satellites that operate as linked constellations. Global Navigation Satellite Systems (GNSS) are systems of space-based transmitters and ground equipment that allow users to determine position anywhere on the Earth. The first operational system was the U.S. Global Positioning System (GPS). Although the term "GPS" is used to refer to satellite navigation in a general way, it actually refers specifically to the U.S. system. GPS satellites are placed into 12-hour orbits. The satellites orbit in six planes inclined 55 degrees from the Earth's equator. At least four satellites in each plane are needed for global coverage. As satellites continue to operate past their planned lifetimes, more are available for service. By early 2008 there were 33 operational satellites in the GPS constellation.

Each GPS satellite transmits data that indicate its location and the current time. All GPS satellites synchronize operations so

that these repeating signals are transmitted at the same instant. The distance to the GPS satellites can be determined by estimating the amount of time it takes for their signals to reach the receiver. When the receiver estimates the distance to at least four GPS satellites, it can calculate its position in three dimensions.

Other nations have developed plans for new GNSS satellites. GLONASS, operated by the Russian Space Forces, is a deployed GNSS. Under development are Galileo, led by a European consortium, and Compass, a system being designed by China. Each system uses orbits similar, but not identical, to GPS.

In the United States, indeed in most of the world, the Global Positioning System of 24 navigation satellites interlinked in medium Earth orbit has provided precise timing, location, and velocity information since first launched in the 1990s. Combining this information with communications, comput-

ers, transponders, and a range of scientific instruments has created a remarkably versatile system that has become indispensable to a wide range of navigational uses. GPS seems limitless in its variety of uses and the number of its potential users, and since it is essentially free to users—having been built and operated by the Department of Defense—it has proven an especially important boon to terrestrial, maritime, and aviation commercial activities.

Furthermore, GPS is becoming commonplace for other uses not fully envisioned at the beginning of the program. For instance, GPS has been helpful in the navigation of satellites in Earth orbit, offering accurate position location, precise time, and spacecraft altitude determination. NASA scientists are using GPS to create a monitoring system for earthquake-prone regions by measuring the movement of the Earth. Biologists found a use for GPS in tracking wildlife movement, while climate scientists have used it to measure atmospheric conditions.

From using GPS receivers to navigate autos, boats, and airplanes, to tracking mobile telephones, the system has made a profound influence on modern society. Total growth in the market relating to GPS and satellite navigation has expanded an average of almost 25% between 1998 and 2007. Global sales of GPS units and related services exceeded $20 billion in 2007. Virtually all capabilities will expand indefinitely into the future using both GPS and future constellations.

For all of the success of GPS, the Iridium constellation of communication satellites in low Earth orbit was stillborn because of the costs involved. With a proposed constellation of 66 satellites in low Earth orbit, supporting ground stations, and cellular-sized telephone handsets, Iridium proposed revolutionizing mobile communications. Conceived by Motorola, Inc., which had been heavily involved in mobile telephone technology since the 1980s, this Iridium business venture represented a bold effort to provide wireless, digital telephone coverage over the entire planet. Iridium was intended to include 66 satellites in polar orbit at altitudes of about 400 miles. But the costs were too great, in excess of $3 billion, and less than a year after its incorporation in 1998, Iridium collapsed, and merged with another organization in 2000. Iridium later reorganized and is currently operating as a much smaller communications system at a major discount. Its largest customer now is the U.S. Department of Defense, using it as another part of its intercontinental communications system.

Artist's conception of a Global Positioning System satellite, a recently developed Block IIR, in Earth orbit.

High Earth orbits are used by some specialized communications satellites. These orbits are highly elliptical paths that allow satellites to be visible at high-latitude locations on the Earth. A Molniya orbit has a period of about 12 hours, and inclined more than 60 degrees from the equator. The altitude varies from a perigee of 500 km to an apogee of 50,000 km.

Because of slower velocity near apogee, each satellite remains visible from high latitudes on the Earth's surface for several hours. This is useful for communications at high latitudes. The first satellites to use these orbits were the Soviet Union's Molniya communications satellites. It was also used for reconnaissance satellites with an apogee over North America

or Asia for signals intelligence. A Tundra orbit is an inclined geosynchronous orbit that allows a satellite to be visible during most of its orbit over a certain continental landmass. It is similar to the Molniya orbit but with an orbital period of about 24 hours. Satellites used by the Sirius satellite radio system used this orbit to maintain coverage over North America.

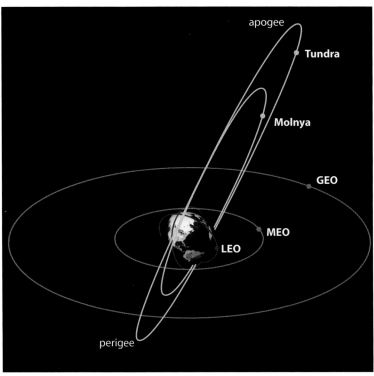

Molniya and Tundra orbits are examples of highly elliptical orbits for specialized communications systems.

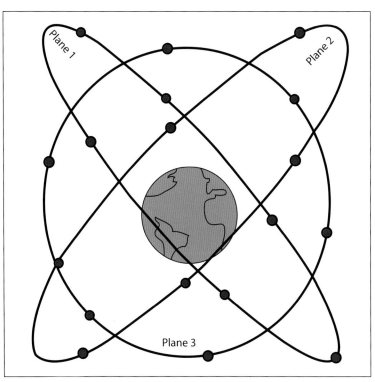

GLONASS satellites are placed into similar configuration as GPS satellites, but in three orbital planes at higher inclination and slightly lower altitude.

The Global Positioning System requires at least 24 satellites to be fully operational and provide global coverage. Satellites are placed in four orbital planes. The GPS satellites orbit at half the distance to geosynchronous orbit, thereby taking 12 hours to complete each orbit.

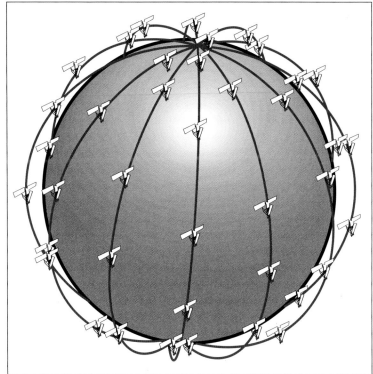

The proposed Iridium constellation of satellites in medium Earth orbit.

In 1647 a Polish astronomer named Johannes Hewelke (better known as Hevelius, 1611–1687) published *Selenographia,* containing the first true maps of the Moon made possible with the newly developed telescope. His maps were the result of ten years of work. This image depicts the famous astronomer observing the lunar surface.

part five

REACHING FOR THE MOON

Throughout history, humans have expressed a fascination with the natural universe and a desire, translated into action, to learn more about it. Ancient peoples such as the Greeks and Romans, as well as others in the non-Western tradition, have expended enormous resources to understand the places and phenomena beyond their immediate lines of sight.

There seems little doubt that both discovery and the promise of exploration and colonization were the motivating forces behind the small cadre of space program advocates in both the United States and the Soviet Union prior to the 1950s. Most American advocates of aggressive space exploration efforts invoked an extension of the popular notion of the frontier, with its positive images of territorial expansion, scientific discovery, exploration, colonization, and use.

There were many ways by which Americans and Soviets became aware that flight into space was a possibility, ranging from (1) science fiction literature and film that were becoming more closely tied to reality than ever before, to (2) speculations by science fiction writers about possibilities already being made real, to (3) serious discussions of the subject in respected popular magazines. In the United States, among the most important serious efforts were those of the handsome German emigré Wernher von Braun, who worked for the U.S. Army at Huntsville, Alabama. In addition to being a superbly effective technological entrepreneur, von Braun managed to captivate the powerful print and electronic communications media in the early 1950s; for the next two decades, no one was a more effective promoter of space exploration. In the Soviet Union, public advocates in the sciences recommended spaceflight efforts to advance the Marxist cause, the completion of a utopian order of civilization world wide.

At the same time that space exploration advocates—both buffs and scientists—were generating an image of spaceflight as a genuine possibility and no longer fantasy, and proposing how to accomplish a far-reaching program of lunar and planetary exploration, another critical element entered the picture: the role of spaceflight in national defense and international relations. Space partisans readily hitched their exploration vision to the political requirements of the Cold War—in particular, to the belief that whichever nation occupied the "high ground" of space would dominate the territories underneath it.

This led directly to an effort to reach the Moon in the 1960s, and by the end of the decade the U.S. landed its first astronauts on that most inviting and closest of all heavenly bodies.

The Cold War Space Race

In 1957 the United States and the Soviet Union, the two superpowers emerging from World War II, were locked in a Cold War rivalry that threatened both nations. Each nation viewed the other as a threat to its existence and competed between the end of World War II and the early 1990s in multiple arenas that ranged from military confrontation—though not direct conflict—to ideology, espionage, technological developments, economic and industrial capability, and several proxy wars.

For nearly four decades the Soviets and the Americans squared off in this Cold War confrontation. Virtually every place in the world was a potential flashpoint; the U.S. sought to "contain" the spread of communism outside of the areas controlled at the end of World War II. In July 1947, the quarterly journal *Foreign Affairs* published an anonymous article entitled "The Sources of Soviet Conduct," which advocated a strategy of containment in dealing with the Soviet Union. Its author, soon revealed as U.S. State Department official George Kennan, proposed active opposition to

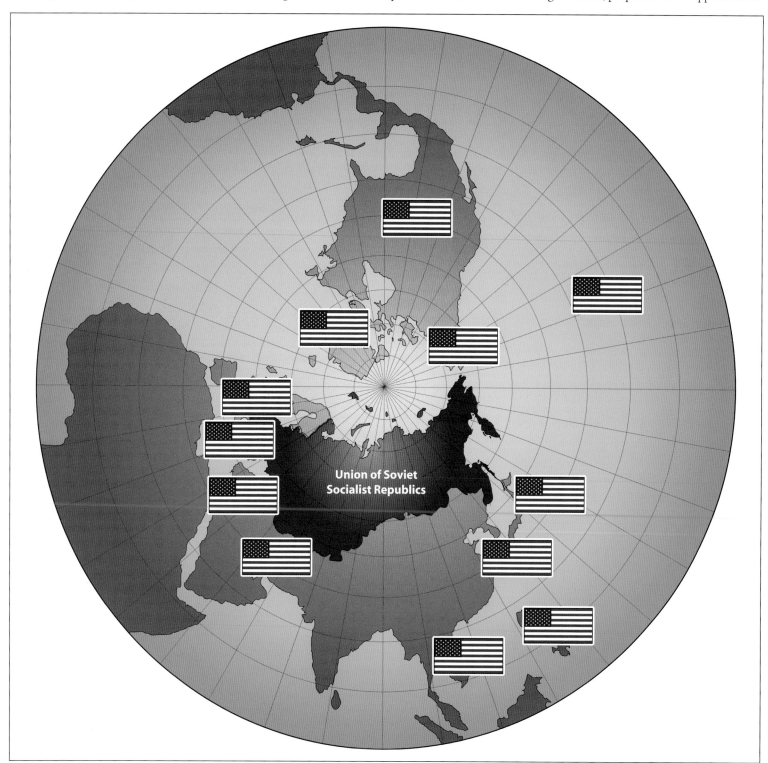

A view from above the Arctic showing the perspective of the Soviet Union as a nation surrounded by enemies.

any expansion of communist power. As Kennan wrote, "we are going to continue for a long time to find the Russians difficult to deal with. It does not mean that they should be considered as embarked upon a do-or-die program to overthrow our society." He wanted to place Stalin, leader of the Soviet Union, in a box and limit his ability to do anything internationally.

Containment became America's official strategy and in seeking to accomplish it the U.S. forged numerous alliances in Western Europe, the Middle East, and Southeast Asia. The strategy, however, engendered many controversies, some of which verged on erupting into full-scale wars between the two powers. Notably the Berlin Blockade (1948–1949), the Korean War (1950–1953), the Vietnam War (1959–1975), the Cuban Missile Crisis (1962), and the Soviet-Afghan War (1979–1989) all served to heighten tensions. In at least one instance, the Cuban Missile Crisis, nuclear holocaust almost came to pass. There were also periods when tensions declined, especially during the détente of the early 1970s, when both nations opened more amiable relations. In the end, direct military actions were deterred by the potential for mutual assured destruction (MAD)—certainly the most appropriate acronym ever dreamed up, since it referred to annihilation through the use of nuclear weapons.

By the time of the launch of the world's first artificial satellite in 1957, the U.S. and the Soviet Union each faced critical strategic challenges. Both were consumed by fears of an advance of the other into their territories. The U.S. and its allies were on the watch for Soviet advances in Europe and Asia. The Soviet Union and its allies believed it was surrounded by hostile nations led by an aggressive U.S. The Soviets, moreover, had no bases close enough to the U.S. to strike should war break out, yet it felt threatened by a plethora of U.S. allied military capabilities based in Europe and Asia. Not until the rise of ballistic missiles would this change.

These two maps, below and to the left, show differing perspectives on the geopolitics of the Cold War era. First, the map centered on the Soviet Union shows them hemmed in by hostile forces, most of whom were allies of the United States. That perspective of being boxed in proved psychologically terrifying to Soviet leaders and helped to prompt a series of aggressive responses. In the early ballistic missile era of the late 1950s, moreover, the U.S. placed nuclear weapons on Jupiter missiles in Turkey and Italy and based strategic bombers in other parts of Western Europe and in Japan and South Korea. The seeming paranoia of the Soviet leaders, especially Stalin and his successor Nikita Khrushchev, may be partially explained by this sense of being surrounded by hostile forces.

Likewise, the second map shows the world from the perspective of the United States. The lesson taken at the time from looking at this map and reviewing the belligerence of Stalin in dealing with the West was that the Soviet Union was intent on world domination. It incorporated into its sphere of influence after World War II much of Eastern Europe, including Poland, Czechoslovakia, Romania, East Germany, and other smaller nations. Struggles in Greece and other parts of Europe narrowly turned back communist takeovers. A theory of foreign relations emerged from this setting called the domino effect, asserting that if one part of a region came under the influence of communism, then surrounding areas may well follow from revolutionary efforts sparked by the neighboring communist state. President Dwight D. Eisenhower accepted this theory, stating on April 7, 1954, "You have a row of dominoes set up, you knock over the first one, and what will happen to the last one is the certainty that it will go over very quickly. So you could have a beginning of a disintegration that would have the most profound influences." Successive U.S. presidents applied this idea to Soviet relations, justifying American intervention around the world, in dealing with presumed threats from the Soviets.

Both maps offer a unique perspective on the manner in which the space race unfolded, for these strategic perspectives and ideas motivated many aspects of the competition between the U.S. and the Soviet Union in the race to the Moon.

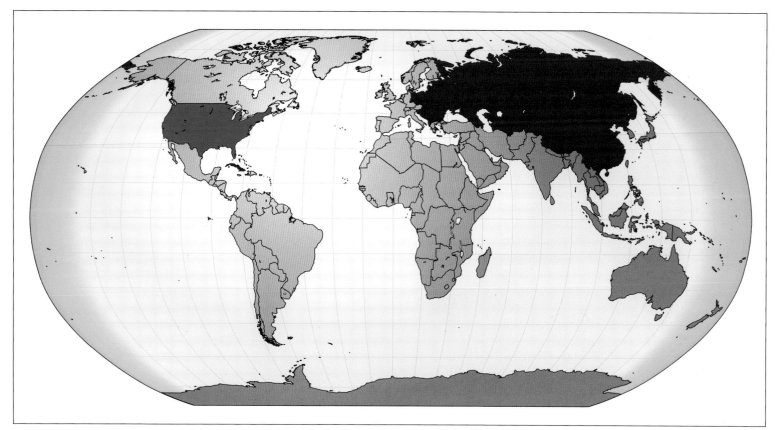

The Earth as often depicted during the Cold War in the West. The United States, in blue, is small and in a defensive posture in relation to the gigantic Soviet Union and China, in red. Moreover, many nations in Eastern Europe entered the Soviet sphere after World War II. It appeared to many Americans that the Soviet Union was marching toward world domination.

Launching NASA

The National Aeronautics and Space Administration (NASA) emerged in some measure because of the pressures of national defense during the Cold War with the Soviet Union, a broad contest over the ideologies and allegiances of the nonaligned nations of the world in which space exploration emerged as a major area of contest. From the latter 1940s the Department of Defense had pursued research in rocketry and upper atmospheric sciences as a means of assuring American leadership in technology. A major step forward came when President Dwight D. Eisenhower approved a plan to orbit a scientific satellite as part of the International Geophysical Year (IGY) for the period July 1, 1957, to December 31, 1958, a cooperative effort to gather scientific data about the Earth. The Soviet Union quickly followed suit, announcing plans to orbit its own satellite.

The Naval Research Laboratory's Project Vanguard was chosen on September 9, 1955, to realize this IGY effort, largely because it would not interfere with high-priority ballistic missile development programs—it used the nonmilitary Viking rocket as its basis—while an Army proposal to use the Redstone ballistic missile as the launch vehicle waited in the wings. Project Vanguard enjoyed exceptional publicity throughout the second half of 1955 and all of 1956, but the technological demands upon the program were too great and the funding levels too small to ensure success.

A full-scale crisis resulted on October 4, 1957, when the Soviets launched Sputnik 1, the world's first artificial satellite, as its IGY entry. This had a "Pearl Harbor" effect on American public opinion, creating an illusion of a technological gap, and provided the impetus for increased spending for space endeavors, technical and scientific educational programs, and the chartering of new federal agencies to manage air and space research and development.

Sputnik led directly to several critical efforts aimed at "catching up" to the Soviet Union's space achievements. Among these:

- A full-scale review of the civil and military space programs of the United States (scientific satellite efforts and ballistic missile development).
- Establishment of a Presidential Science Advisor in the White House who had responsibility for overseeing the activities of the federal government in science and technology.
- Creation of the Advanced Research Projects Agency in the Department of Defense, and the consolidation of several space activities under centralized management.
- Establishment of the National Aeronautics and Space Administration to manage civil space operations for the benefit "of all mankind" by means of the National Aeronautics and Space Act of 1958.
- Passage of the National Defense Education Act of 1958 to provide federal funding for education in scientific and technical disciplines.

More immediately, the United States launched its first Earth satellite on January 31, 1958, when Explorer 1 documented the existence of radiation zones encircling the Earth. Shaped by the Earth's magnetic field, what came to be called the Van Allen radiation belts partially dictate the electrical charges in the atmosphere and the solar radiation that reaches Earth. It also began a series of scientific missions to the Moon and planets in the latter 1950s and early 1960s.

NASA began operations on October 1, 1958, as a direct result of this crisis, absorbing into it the earlier National Advisory Committee for Aeronautics intact: its 8,000 employees, an annual budget of $100 million, three major research laboratories—Langley Aeronautical Laboratory, Ames Aeronautical Laboratory, and Lewis Flight Propulsion Laboratory—and two smaller test facilities. It quickly incorporated other organizations into the new agency, notably the space science group of the Naval Research Laboratory in Maryland, the Jet Propulsion Laboratory managed by the California Institute of Technology for the Army, and the Army Ballistic Missile Agency in Huntsville, Alabama, where Wernher von Braun's team of engineers were engaged in the development of large rockets. Eventually NASA created several other centers, and today has ten that are located around the country.

NASA Budget (Billions, 2007 Dollars)

This chart shows the NASA budget since the agency's founding. The high funding levels in the middle part of the 1960s show the investments that made possible the Moon landings of Project Apollo. Since the early 1970s the NASA budget has stabilized between 0.5 and 1% of the U.S. federal annual budget.

This aerial view of Johnson Space Center in Houston, Texas, was taken in 1989. The center, originally named the Manned Spacecraft Center, became home of the astronauts and the site of Mission Control for all U.S. human spaceflight missions.

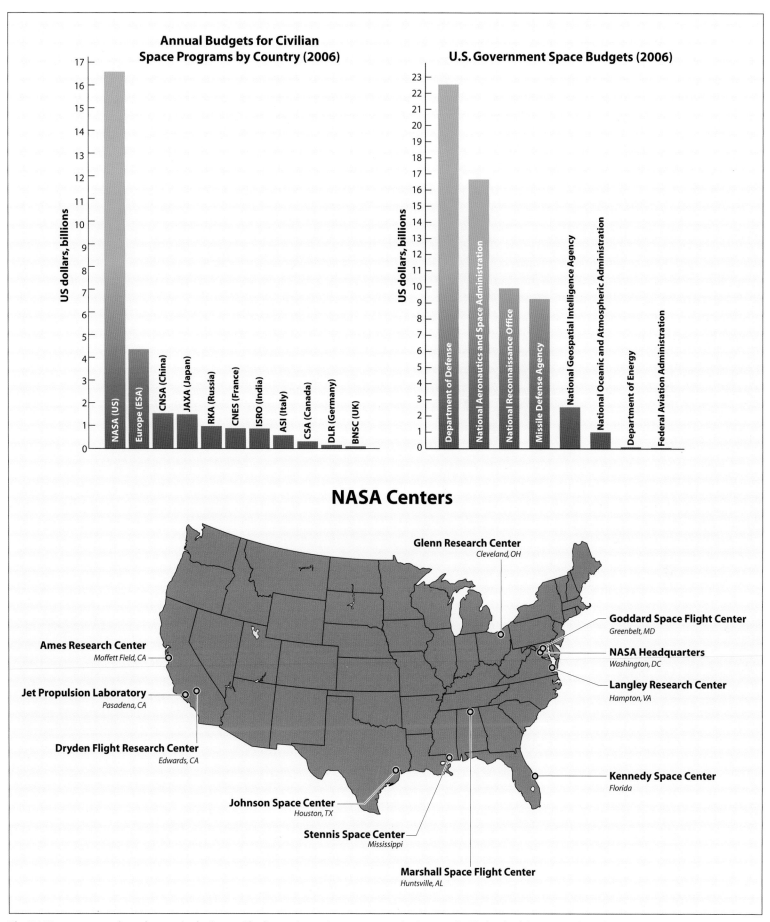

Annual Budgets for Civilian Space Programs by Country (2006)

US dollars, billions

- NASA (US)
- Europe (ESA)
- CNSA (China)
- JAXA (Japan)
- RKA (Russia)
- CNES (France)
- ISRO (India)
- ASI (Italy)
- CSA (Canada)
- DLR (Germany)
- BNSC (UK)

U.S. Government Space Budgets (2006)

US dollars, billions

- Department of Defense
- National Aeronautics and Space Administration
- National Reconnaissance Office
- Missile Defense Agency
- National Geospatial Intelligence Agency
- National Oceanic and Atmospheric Administration
- Department of Energy
- Federal Aviation Administration

NASA Centers

Glenn Research Center
Cleveland, OH

Goddard Space Flight Center
Greenbelt, MD

Ames Research Center
Moffett Field, CA

NASA Headquarters
Washington, DC

Langley Research Center
Hampton, VA

Jet Propulsion Laboratory
Pasadena, CA

Dryden Flight Research Center
Edwards, CA

Kennedy Space Center
Florida

Johnson Space Center
Houston, TX

Stennis Space Center
Mississippi

Marshall Space Flight Center
Huntsville, AL

The NASA centers arose from three major heritages. The first and most important organization was the National Advisory Committee for Aeronautics (NACA), established in 1915 and dedicated to solving the problems of flight. It brought to NASA several famous research laboratories: the Langley Research Center in Hampton, Virginia, the Lewis Research Center in Cleveland (later renamed for John Glenn), and the Ames Research Center outside San Francisco, as well as smaller facilities for rocket and aircraft testing. Second, the Army's ballistic missile organizations, especially the Jet Propulsion Laboratory in Pasadena, California, and the rocketry section of the Army Ballistic Missile Agency in Huntsville, Alabama, under the technical direction of Wernher von Braun, which became the Marshall Space Flight Center. Third, space scientists at the Naval Research Laboratory in suburban Washington, which later became the Goddard Space Flight Center.

The Geography of the Moon

The Moon, Earth's only natural satellite, is located 238,328 miles (384,400 km) away, on average, far closer than any other object in the Solar System. It is a world of its own and it has its own geography ("lunagraphy"), which has been enormously added to in the last few decades since spacecraft and humans began visiting it. Reflecting the Sun's light, it is the second brightest object in the sky. The Moon plays a prominent role in folklore, mythology, and traditional calendars from cultures around the world. The Moon is the only extrater-restrial body to be visited by humans, with 12 humans setting foot there during NASA's Apollo missions of 1969–1972.

Because the rotation and revolution period of the Moon are the same, we see the same geographic features all the time. The Moon takes exactly the same amount of time to go around the Earth as it does to rotate once. This synchronous rotation is a minimum energy configuration and is common throughout the Solar System. Relative to the Earth, the Moon makes only one rotation every 29.5 days, the exact time that it takes for the Moon to complete one revolution around the Earth. This has not always been the case, but over millions of years the effect of the Earth's gravity has slowed down the Moon's rotation until it became gravitationally locked to the Earth. Of course, it would seem logical to say that at any one time we can see 50% of the Moon's face. If the Moon were flat, that would be correct; however, because of the Moon's librations or tiny movements we actually see up to 59% of the lunar surface from Earth. To see the rest we had to go there.

The surface of the Moon can broadly be divided into two areas:

- Mare, plural maria, from the Latin word for seas: These are the dark, relatively smooth regions, roughly circular in shape, an average 2 miles (3 km) lower in elevation than the rest of surface. They are some of the most prominent features of the Moon seen from Earth. Relatively flat areas produced between 3.8 and 3.1 billion years ago, they are the basins where massive flows of lava have settled. The maria are made mostly of a rock called basalt, very similar to the rock produced in lava flows on Earth. These basaltic rocks are the youngest of the lunar rocks. Maria cover about 16% of the Moon but are not evenly distributed. The side facing Earth has large and prominent maria; not so the back side unseen from Earth.

The reason for this difference is that the Moon's center of mass is shifted toward the Earth about 1.2 miles (2 km). Regions of enhanced density known as Mascons lie beneath the maria.

- Highlands: light colored, frequently rugged or heavily cratered, the oldest lunar rocks come from highland regions. The highlands probably formed between 4.0 and 3.8 billion years ago although some highland materials recovered during Apollo date as far back as 4.3 billion years. It is dominated by a rock type known as breccia. The highlands have many high, jagged mountain peaks, as much as 3.5 miles (5 km) above the maria.

Most of the geographical features of the Moon were created billions of years ago when it was still very young. Samples returned from the Moon during the Apollo program demonstrated this beyond all doubt.

Craters on the lunar surface were caused when meteoroids or asteroids impacted the Moon. While bombardment still takes place occasionally, early in the Solar System's history the occurrences were common. The prominent rings and rays seen from the Earth are the remnants of these violent impacts. Today craters can be found everywhere on the lunar surface.

The lunar surface is covered by regolith, made of fine dust produced in meteorite impacts. The thickness of this layer varies, but it can extend tens of meters below the surface.

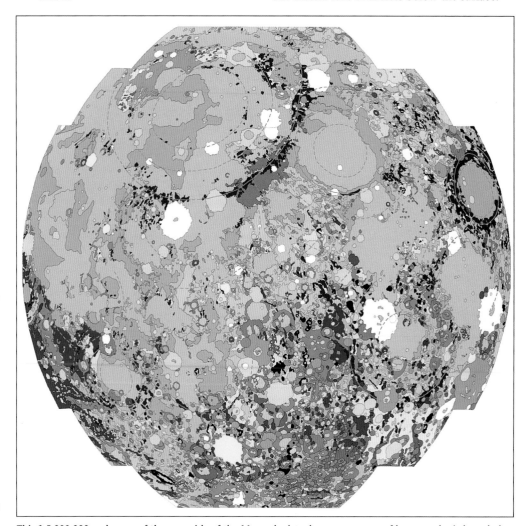

This 1:5,000,000-scale map of the near side of the Moon depicts the current state of lunar geologic knowledge arising from the robotic and human exploration of the 1960s. Published in 1971 from data obtained through Lunar Orbiter, Apollo, and ground observation, its color scheme shows the relative ages and terrain of the map, with the darker portions appearing lower and less mountainous. As on Earth, the uppermost rocks in a sequence are younger than those on which they lie; rocks cut by faults are older than the faults. Like terrestrial synoptic maps, this one provides a stratigraphic framework for determining the regional significance of surface exploration results. Systematic regional mapping shows the Moon to be a primitive body that exhibits a geologically heterogeneous surface with a long and complex history that can be only partly unraveled from existing photographic data. Maps like this sophisticated work from the U.S. Geological Survey have enabled the cataloging of the major features of the Moon during the last third of the twentieth century.

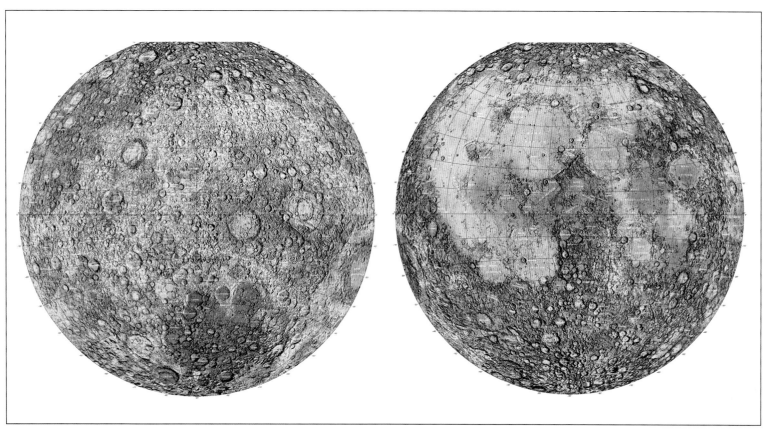

These images of the surface features of the near and far sides of the Moon could not have been prepared prior to the explorations of the body in the 1960s and 1970s.

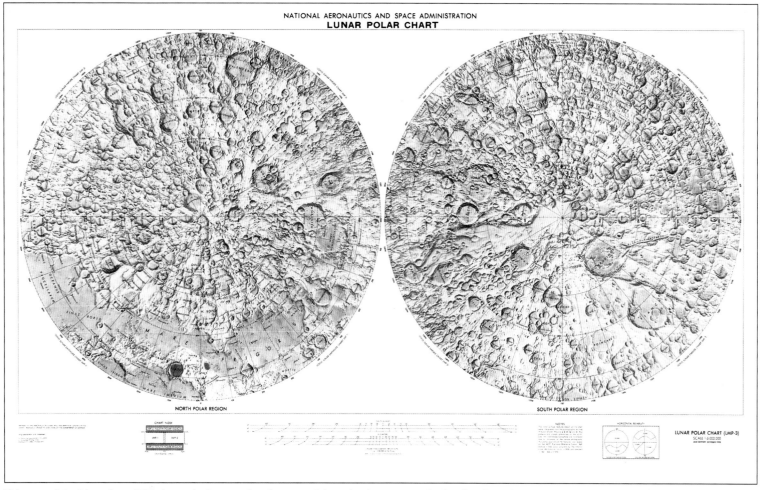

This map of the Moon from 1970 shows the lunar surface features of the poles. It was created using data from the Lunar Orbiter 1–5 missions and names major features.

Robotic Exploration of the Moon

With the dawn of the space age the United States went head-to-head with the Soviet Union in a robotic race to the Moon—and lost. The Moon was an early target for both the United States and the Soviet Union because it was comparatively close; in the context of cosmic distances it is the neighbor in the next apartment whose stereo can be heard through thin walls. There were also numerous opportunities every month for a launch from Earth to the Moon, and it would be a significant public relations coup in the international community for the nation reaching it first.

Moreover, the lure of the Moon was irresistible. In 1958, eager to demonstrate leadership in space technology, the United States started a crash effort to send a series of spacecraft named Pioneer to the Moon. The Air Force prepared three, and the Army built two Pioneer spacecraft for the Moon flights. During the winter of 1958–1959 the United States made four attempts to send a Pioneer probe in the vicinity of the Moon. None reached their destination. Indeed, none succeeded in escaping from Earth's orbit, but two produced the first information about the outer regions of the Van Allen belts.

In contrast, after some false starts in the fall of 1958, the Soviet Union succeeded in launching several successful probes. This success rested on the early capability of Soviet engineers to build large rockets with significant payload capacity, something not yet developed in the United States. In January 1959 the Soviets sent Luna 1 past the Moon and into orbit around the sun, following up with Luna 3 to transmit pictures of the far side of the Moon—thereby giving the Soviets an important "first" in lunar exploration. Meanwhile, in March 1959, Pioneer 5 finally flew past the Moon, much too late to assuage America's loss of pride and prestige. Thus ended the first phase of lunar exploration, with the Soviet Union a clear winner.

In December 1959, after the failure of the first lunar probes, the Jet Propulsion Laboratory (JPL) started the Ranger project, partly as a way to get out of the public relations mess the earlier failures had created. On August 30, 1961, NASA launched the first Ranger, but the launch vehicle placed it in the wrong orbit. Two more attempts in 1961 failed, as did two more attempts in 1962. NASA then reorganized the Ranger project and did not try to launch again until 1964. By this time the presidential decision to land Americans on the Moon had been announced, and the program was restructured to aid in acquiring the knowledge necessary about the Moon itself to ensure that the astronauts would survive. They needed to know the composition and geography of the Moon, and the nature of the lunar surface. Was it solid enough to support a lander, or was it composed of dust that would swallow up the spacecraft? Would communications systems work on the Moon? Would other factors—geology, geography, radiation, etc.—affect the astronauts?

To answer these questions three distinct satellite research programs emerged to study the Moon. The restructured Ranger program was the first of these. In this case, NASA's engineers eliminated all the scientific instruments except a television camera. Ranger's sole remaining objective was to go out in a blaze of glory as it crashed into the Moon while taking high-resolution pictures. On July 31, 1964, the

Luna 10 was the first spacecraft to enter orbit around the Moon on March 31, 1966. Its orbit was highly inclined and varied from about 350 to 1,020 km altitude. Luna 11 was a similar orbit to Luna 10. Arriving in August 1966 (the same month as the first U.S. Lunar Orbiter), it was another test of placing a spacecraft in lunar orbit. Luna 12 entered orbit on October 25, 1966. This spacecraft carried a television camera to return images of the lunar surface. Launched in April 1968, Luna 14 was the first Soviet spacecraft sent to lunar orbit in a year and a half. It was also the first to be placed in a low, almost circular orbit.

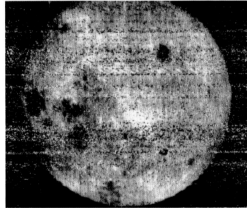

The Luna 3 spacecraft returned the first views ever of the far side of the Moon. The first image was taken at 03:30 UT on October 7, 1959, at a distance of 63,500 km after Luna 3 had passed the Moon and looked back at the sunlit far side. The last image was taken 40 minutes later from 66,700 km. A total of 29 photographs were taken, covering 70% of the far side. The photographs were very noisy and of low resolution, but many features could be recognized. This is the first image returned by Luna 3, taken by the wide-angle lens. It showed the far side of the Moon was very different from the near side, most noticeably in its lack of lunar maria (the dark areas). The right three-quarters of the disk are the far side. The dark spot at upper right is Mare Moscoviense; the dark area at lower left is Mare Smythii. The small dark circle at lower right with the white dot in the center is the crater Tsiolkovskiy and its central peak. The Moon is 3,475 km in diameter and north is up in this image.

seventh Ranger worked and transmitted 4,316 beautiful, high-resolution pictures of the lunar Sea of Clouds. The eighth and ninth Rangers also worked well. Even so, the United States seemingly lagged behind the Soviet Union in the Cold War battlefield of technological competition in space.

The second project was the Lunar Orbiter, an effort approved in 1960 to place probes in orbit around the Moon. This project, originally not intended to support Apollo, was reconfigured in 1962 and 1963 to further the Kennedy mandate more specifically by mapping the surface, photographing about 95% of the Moon's surface—more than 36 million square kilometers (14 million square miles)—to aid in the selection of landing sites for Apollo astronauts. In addition to a powerful camera that could send photographs to Earth

tracking stations, it carried three scientific experiments—selnodesy (the lunar equivalent of geodesy), meteoroid detection, and radiation measurement. While the returns from these instruments interested scientists in and of themselves, they were critical to Apollo. NASA launched five Lunar Orbiter satellites between August 10, 1966, and August 1, 1967, all successfully achieving their objectives. At the completion of the third mission, moreover, the Apollo planners announced that they had sufficient data to press on with an astronaut landing, and were able to use the last two missions for other activities.

Lunar Orbiter's bounty of images came from a unique onboard photographic system. Instead of sending television pictures back to Earth as electrical signals, Lunar Orbiter took actual photographs, developed them on board, and

then scanned them using a special photoelectric system. For this reason scientists referred to Lunar Orbiter as the "flying drugstore." Due to the possibility that radiation in space might fog photographic film, the system used a slow-speed film. To prevent blurring, the spacecraft moved slightly to compensate for the relatively long exposure times. The resulting images had exceptional quality and provided resolutions of up to 3 feet from an altitude of 30 nautical miles. After depleting their film supplies, flight controllers purposely crashed all five Lunar Orbiters onto the Moon to prevent their radio transmitters from interfering with future spacecraft.

Finally, in 1961 NASA created Project Surveyor to soft-land a satellite on the Moon. A small craft with tripod landing legs, it could take postlanding photographs and perform

This image of the Ranger spacecraft as it looked in its later configurations shows the solar panels deployed and the camera located on the fuselage.

a variety of other measurements. Surveyor 1 landed on the Moon on June 2, 1966, and transmitted more than 10,000 high-quality photographs of the surface. Although the second mission crash landed, the next flight provided photographs, measurements of the composition and surface-bearing strength of the lunar crust, and readings on the thermal and radar reflectivity of the soil. Although Surveyor 4 failed, by the time of the program's completion in 1968 the remaining three missions had yielded significant scientific data both for Apollo and for the broader lunar science community.

Meantime, the Soviet Union also visited the Moon numerous times with spacecraft. Its Luna program, sometimes called Lunik, sent 15 successful spacecraft to the Moon between 1959 and 1976, many of which represented firsts in the space race. While the Soviets had many failures, not publicly acknowledged at the time, the importance of this program should be acknowledged:

- Luna 2 mission successfully impacted upon the lunar surface, the first human-made object to do so (1959).
- Luna 3 returned the first photographs of the Moon's far side (1959).
- Luna 9 was the first probe to achieve a soft landing on another body, the Moon (1966).
- Luna 10 became the first artificial satellite of the Moon (1966).
- Luna 17 (1969) and Luna 21 (1973) deployed roving vehicles that roamed the Moon.
- Luna 16 (1970), Luna 20 (1972), and Luna 24 (1976) returned samples to the Soviet Union from the lunar surface.

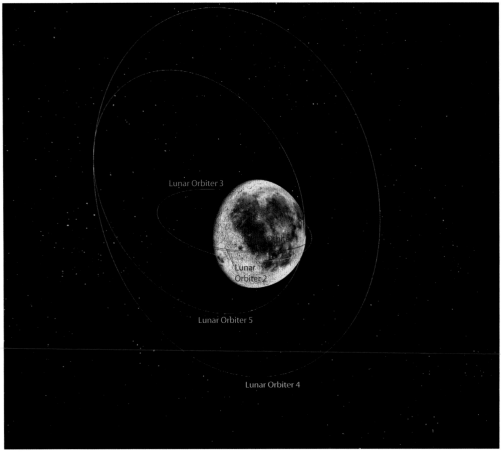

This illustration depicts the orbits of the various Lunar Orbiter probes to the Moon. The U.S. Lunar Orbiter 1 entered orbit around the Moon on August 14, 1966. Its mission was to photograph the lunar surface. Rotating around the Moon every 3.6 hours, its elliptical orbit allowed the spacecraft to obtain both close-up photos and more distant views. By the end of the mission about 2 million square miles had been photographed. In November 1966 Lunar Orbiter 2 arrived in Moon orbit. Its inital orbit was similar to Lunar Orbiter 1. Like all the spacecraft in the program, Lunar Orbiter 2 was deliberately crashed into the surface of the Moon at the end of its mission. Lunar Orbiter 3 arrived at the Moon on February 8, 1967—while Lunar Orbiter 2 was still operating. Lunar Orbiter 3 continued to provide extensive photographic coverage of the Moon, including an image of Surveyor 1 on the surface. At the end of Lunar Orbiter 3's mission high-quality imagery had been obtained for the possible Apollo landing sites. Lunar Orbiter 4 entered orbit on May 8, 1967. For the first time a spacecraft was placed into a highly inclined lunar orbit. This allowed Lunar Orbiter 4 to photograph the polar areas of the Moon. The final Lunar Orbiter arrived at the Moon in August 1967. Like Lunar Orbiter 4, it was placed into a highly inclined orbit to allow photography of the Moon's polar areas.

SURVEYOR SUCCESSFUL SOFT LANDINGS:

Surveyor 1: weight 995.2 kg (2,194 lbs), launched May 30, 1966 / 14:41:01, launch site Eastern Test Range (ETR), pad 36A, launch vehicle Atlas-Centaur / 10, operator NASA Jet Propulsion Laboratory, lunar landing June 2, 1966, 06:17:37 UT, Latitude 2.45 S, Longitude 43.21 W - Flamsteed P

Surveyor 3: 997.9 kg (2,195 lbs), launched April 17, 1967 / 07:05:01, launch site ETR, pad 36B, launch vehicle Atlas-Centaur / 12, operator NASA Jet Propulsion Laboratory, lunar landing April 20, 1967, 00:04:53 UT, Latitude 2.94 S, Longitude 23.34 W - Oceanus Procellarum (Ocean of Storms)

Surveyor 5: 1,006 kg (2,217 lbs), launched September 8, 1967 / 07:57:01, launch site ETR, pad 36B, launch vehicle Atlas-Centaur / 13, operator NASA Jet Propulsion Laboratory, lunar landing September 11, 1967, 00:46:44 UT, Latitude 1.41 N, Longitude 23.18 E - Mare Tranquillitatus (Sea of Tranquility)

Surveyor 6: 1,008.3 kg (2,222.9 lbs), launched November 7, 1967 / 07:39:01, launch site ETR, pad 36B, launch vehicle Atlas-Centaur / 14, operator NASA Jet Propulsion Laboratory, lunar landing November 10, 1967, 01:01:06 UT, Latitude 0.46 N, Longitude 1.37 W - Sinus Medii

Surveyor 7: 1,040.1 kg (2,292 lbs), launched January 7, 1968 / 06:30:00, launch site ETR / 36A, launch vehicle Atlas-Centaur / 15, operator NASA Jet Propulsion Laboratory, lunar landing January 10, 1968, 01:05:36 UT, Latitude 41.01 S, Longitude 11.41 W - Tycho North Rim

LUNA SUCCESSFUL SOFT LANDINGS:

Luna 9: 1,538 kg (3,390.7 lbs), launched January 31, 1966 / 11:41:37, launch site NIIP-5 / 31, launch vehicle Molniya-M / U103-32, operator USSR Lavochkin, lunar landing February 3, 1966, 18:44:52 UT, Latitude 7.08 N, Longitude 64.37 W - Oceanus Procellarum

Luna 13: 1,620 kg (3,571.5 lbs), launched December 21, 1966 / 10:17, launch site NIIP-5 / 1, launch vehicle Molniya-M / N103-45, operator USSR Lavochkin, lunar landing December 24, 1966, 18:01:00 UT, Latitude 18.87 N, Longitude 62.05 W - Oceanus Procellarum

Luna 16: 5,727 kg (12,626 lbs), launched September 12, 1970 / 13:25:53, launch site NIIP-5 / 81L, launch vehicle Proton-K / 248-01, operator USSR Lavochkin, lunar landing September 20, 1970, 05:18:00 UT, doc Latitude 0.68 S, Longitude 56.30 E - Mare Fecunditatis, lunar sample return launched to Earth September 21, 1970

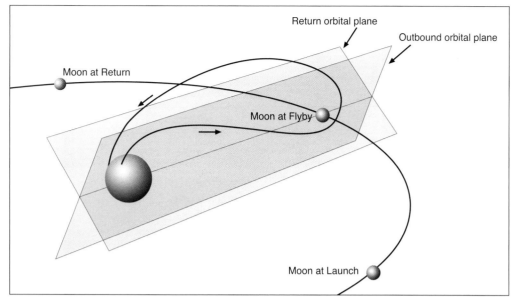

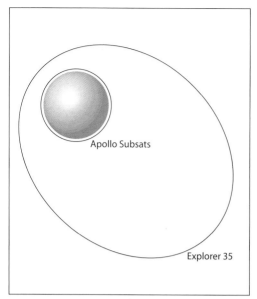

The Soviet spacecraft Zond 5 was launched on a circumlunar trajectory that took it around the Moon and returned it to Earth. It was successfully recovered after a splashdown in the Indian Ocean on September 21, 1968. This flight was a test of a manned flight around the Moon. At this time the Apollo program was nearing manned flights to the Moon. This was followed by Zond 6, which returned to land in the Soviet Union. Zond 7 followed in August 1969, but by then American astronauts had reached the Moon. In October 1970 Zond 8 was launched, taking a circumlunar trajectory and returning with a splashdown in the Indian Ocean. Another version of this trajectory was used to return the stricken Apollo 13 spacecraft to Earth in 1970.

Explorer 35 was placed into a wide elliptical lunar orbit in July 1966. Its mission was to measure the strength of the solar wind and magnetic fields. Two of the later Apollo missions placed small subsatellites in low circular orbit. Due to the variable mass of the Moon, the subsatellites encountered variable gravitational pull that decayed their low orbits.

The world's first view of Earth taken by a spacecraft from the vicinity of the Moon. The photo was transmitted to Earth by the United States Lunar Orbiter I and received at the NASA tracking station at Robledo De Chavela near Madrid, Spain. This crescent of the Earth was photographed August 23, 1966, when the spacecraft was on its 16th orbit and just about to pass behind the Moon. This image provides a footnote to perhaps the most famous image of the space age: the oft-seen "Earthrise" photograph taken by the astronauts on Apollo 8. While this is the first photograph of the Earth from the Moon, it is black and white, not color as was its more famous successor. Apollo 8's dramatic "blue Earth" captured the public imagination in a way this Lunar Orbiter image did not.

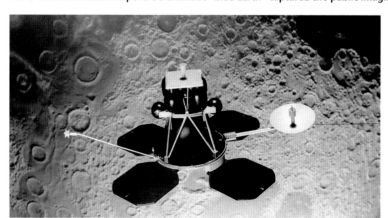

An artist's rendering in 1964 of the Lunar Orbiter, an orbital program to map the Moon in advance of human landings.

Lunar Landing Sites

Launch Date	Country of Origin	Name	Date of Impact	Latitude of Impact	Longitude of Impact	Notes
9/12/1959	Soviet Union	Luna 2	21:02 UT Sept. 13	29.1 N (26.42 N)	0 (2.08 E)	Hard Lander, first human-made object to reach Moon
9/12/1959	Soviet Union	Luna 2 3rd stage Rocket	Approx 21:32 UT Sept 13th	Approx 25 N	Approx. 70 E	Upper stage impact
4/23/1962	USA:NASA	Ranger 4	12:49 UT April 26	15.5 S	130.7 W	Hard Lander, spacecraft failed to return data
1/30/1964	USA:NASA	Ranger 6	9:25 UT February 2	9.4 N	21.5 E	Hard Lander, failed to return data, cameras failed
7/28/1964	USA:NASA	Ranger 7	13:25 UT July 31?	10.35 S	20.18 W	Hard Lander, successful
2/17/1965	USA:NASA	Ranger 8	9:57 UT February 20	2.67 N	24.65 E	Hard Lander, successful
3/21/1965	USA:NASA	Ranger 9	14:08 UT March 24	12.83 S	2.37 W	Hard Lander, successful
5/9/1965	Soviet Union	Luna 5	19:10 UT May 12	1.6 S	25 W	Soft landing attempt, spacecraft crashed
5/9/1965	Soviet Union	Luna 5 upper stage rocket	19:15 UT May 12	Approx. 32 S	Approx. 8 W	Upper stage impact
10/4/1965	Soviet Union	Luna 7	22:08 UT October 7	9.8 N	47.8 W	Hard Lander, successful in reaching Oceanus Procellarum
12/3/1965	Soviet Union	Luna 8	21:52 UT December 6	9.08 N	63.18 W	Hard Lander, successful in reaching Sea of Storms
1/31/1966	Soviet Union	Luna 9	18:45 UT February 3	7 N	64 W	First spacecraft to achieve a soft landing and transmit photographic data
3/31/1966	Soviet Union	Luna 10	Unknown	Unknown	Unknown	Batteries failed on May 30, 1966
5/30/1966	USA:NASA	Surveyor 1	6:18 UT June 2	2.57 S	43.34 W	A retrorocket was ejected approx. 14 km altitude—not tracked, but fell within a few km of landing site. Contact was kept with Surveyor until January 1967
5/30/1966	USA:NASA	Surveyor 1: retro pack	Unknown	Unknown	Unknown	Ejected at an altitude of 14 km, assumed to have landed within a few km of landing sight
8/10/1966	USA:NASA	Lunar Orbiter 1	11/29/1966	7 N	161 E	Deliberately crashed in order to avoid intereference with future flights.
8/24/1966	Soviet Union	Luna 11	Unknown	unknown	unknown	Batteries failed at 2:03 UT, October 1, 1966
9/20/1966	USA:NASA	Surveyor 2	9:35 UT September 22	4 S	11 W	Second of a series designed to achieve a soft landing on the Moon and to return lunar surface photography for determining characteristics of the lunar terrain for Apollo lunar landing missions
10/22/1966	Soviet Union	Luna 12	Unknown	unknown	unknown	Contact was lost on January 19, 1967
11/6/1966	USA:NASA	Lunar Orbiter 2	10/11/1967	3 N	119.1 E	Impacted lunar surface on command
12/21/1966	Soviet Union	Luna 13	18:01 UT December 24	19 N	62 W	Transmissions ceased on December 31, 1966
2/51967	USA:NASA	Lunar Orbiter 3	9-Oct-67	14.3 N	97.7 W	Impacted lunar surface on command
4/17/1967	USA:NASA	Surveyor 3	4:53 UT April 20	3 S	23.43 W	Touched down on the lunar surface three times before landing because the engines did not shut down as intended. It "hopped" 15–22 m from the initial landing spot, then another "hop" 11–14 m to final resting spot, then slid another 30 cm downhill.
5/4/1967	USA:NASA	Lunar Orbiter 4	No later than October 31, 1967	Probably within 30 degrees of the equator	Between 22 and 30 W	The orbit was tracked thru decay to study gravity
7/14/1967	USA:NASA	Surveyor 4	17-Jul	.43 N	1.62 W	Lat/Long is estimated due to loss of contact at 15 km altitude
8/1/1967	USA:NASA	Lunar Orbiter 5	7:58 UT January 31, 1968	2.79 S	83.04 W	Impacted lunar surface on command
9/8/1967	USA:NASA	Surveyor 5	00:47 UT September 11	1.41 N	23.18 E	Touched down on 20 degree slope of a 9 x 12 meter rimless crater in southwest Mare Tranquillitatis. Touchdown was 29 km from original target.
11/7/1967	USA:NASA	Surveyor 6	1:01 UT November 12	.47 N	1.37 W	The first launch from the lunar surface—4 m high and 2.5 m sideways. Shut down on December 2, contact was attempted on December 14 but no useful data were received in the three hours of contact
11/7/1967	USA:NASA	Surveyor 6: Centaur rocket	Unknown	Unknown	Unknown	Assumed to have crashed in lunar surface.
1/7/1968	USA:NASA	Surveyor 7	1:06 UT January 10	40.92 S	11.45 W	Shut down on January 26. Reactivated on February 12–21.
5/18/1969	USA:NASA	Apollo 10 LM descent stage	22 May, 1969	Unknown	Unknown	Jettisoned into lunar orbit, eventually impacting within a few degrees of the equator on the near side.
7/13/1969	Soviet Union	Luna 15	15:51 UT July 21	17 N	60 E	Attempted soft landing, soil sample return mission that failed.
7/16/1969	USA:NASA	Apollo 11: LM	20:18 UT July 20	.67 N	23.47 E	Equipment used included a solar wind collector, a passive seismic experiment, a laser ranging retroreflector. The PSE functioned for only 2 days. The passive LRRR is still functioning.
7/16/1969	USA:NASA	Apollo 11: LM	Separated from CSM at 0:01 UT July 22	Unknown	Unknown	Probably crashed near lunar equator within 1–4 months
11/14/1969	USA:NASA	Apollo 12: LM	6:54 UT November 19	3.01 S	23.42 W	Two EVAs: S-band antenna, solar wind collector, ALSEP, flag, etc.
11/14/1969	USA:NASA	Apollo 12: ascent stage	22:17 UT November 20	3.94 S	21.2 W	Deliberately crashed to create a seismic signal for the ALSEP seismometer.

Launch Date	Country of Origin	Name	Date of Impact	Latitude of Impact	Longitude of Impact	Notes
4/11/1970	USA:NASA	Apollo 13: SIVB upper stage	April 15	2.75 S	27.86 W	Deliberately crashed to create a seismic signal for the ALSEP seismometer. Since the ALSEP was not deployed because of the Apollo 13 mission failure no data resulted.
9/12/1970	Soviet Union	Luna 16	15:18 UT September 20	.68 S	56.3 E	Soft lander, Lunar Sample Return to Earth 9/24/1970
11/10/1970	Soviet Union	Luna 17	3:47 UT November 17	38.28 N	35 W	First successful lunar rover—Lunokhod 1
11/10/1970	Soviet Union	Lunokhod 1	6:28 UT November 17	Est. 38.287 N	Est. 35.190 W	Traveled 10.5 km from the landing site, until operations officially ended on October 4, 1971
1/31/1971	USA:NASA	Apollo 14: Upper stage SIVB	7:41 UT February 4	8.09 S	26.02 W	Deliberately crashed to create a seismic signal for the ALSEP seismometer.
1/31/1971	USA:NASA	Apollo 14: LM landing	9:18 UT February 5	3.6 S	17.5 W	Third human lunar landing—numerous experiments, including ALSEP
1/31/1971	USA:NASA	Apollo 14: EVA 2	8:11 UT February 6			Lasted approx. 4.6 hours and the crew walked 4 km. Shepard hit 2 golf balls at the end of the EVA. Mitchell threw a tool.
1/31/1971	USA:NASA	Apollo 14: LM crash	00:45 UT February 8	3.42 S	19.67 W	Intentionally crashed in order to create seismic signals for Apollo 12 and 14 seismometers.
1/31/1971	USA:NASA	Apollo 14: SIVB	6:41 UT February 4	8.02 S	26.02 W?	Deliberately crashed to create a seismic signal for seismometer monitoring.
1/31/1971	USA:NASA	LM ascent stage	2/7/1971	3.37 S	19.4 W	Deliberately crashed to create a seismic signal for seismometer monitoring.
7/26/1971	USA:NASA	Apollo 15: SIVB upper stage	20:58 UT July 29	1.51 S	11.81 W	Deliberately crashed to create a seismic signal for seismometer monitoring.
7/26/1971	USA:NASA	Apollo 15: LM	22:16 UT July 30	26.1 N	3.6 E	Third human lunar landing—numerous experiments, including ALSEP, first use of lunar rover
7/26/1971	USA:NASA	Apollo 15: LM ascent stage	3:04 UT August 4	26.36 N	.25 E	Deliberately crashed to create a seismic signal for seismometer monitoring.
7/26/1971	USA:NASA	Apollo 15: subsatellite	unknown	unknown	unknown	Ground support ended on January 1973
9/2/1971	Soviet Union	Luna 18	11-Sep	Approx. 3.34 N	Approx. 56.3 E	Lost contact right before landing
9/28/1971	Soviet Union	Luna 19	Orbited approx. 13 months	Unknown	Unknown	Its orbit evolved under the influence of the mascons
2/14/1972	Soviet Union	Luna 20	19:19 UT February 21	3.53 N	56.55 E	Soft lander, Lunar Sample Return to Earth 2/25/1972
4/16/1972	USA:NASA	Apollo 16: SIVB	21:02 UT April 19	1.3 N	23.8 W	Deliberately crashed to create a seismic signal for seismometer monitoring.
4/16/1972	USA:NASA	Apollo 16: LM	2:24 UT April 21	8.97 S	15.5 E	A total of 3 EVAs, totaling 20.25 hours and covering 27 km.
4/16/1972	USA:NASA	Apollo 16: LM crash	jettisoned at 20:54 UT April 24	Approx. 10 degrees from the equator	unknown	Remained in orbit for approx. 1 year before impacting lunar surface
4/16/1972	USA:NASA	Apollo 16: instrument boom	unknown	within 10 degrees of equator	unknown	Impacted lunar surface
4/16/1972	USA:NASA	Apollo 16: subsetellite	jettisoned 21:56 UT, lifetime of approx. 1 month. Ceased transmission (crash?) May 29.	10 N	112 E	Crash site is a guess/estimate
4/16/1972	USA:NASA	Apollo 16: Mortars fired	closest 3 fired on May 23	Unknown	Unknown	4 rounds were fired at distances of 1500 m, 900 m, 300 m and 150 m from the LM to provide seismic info.
4/16/1972	USA:NASA	Apollo 16: LM ascent stage	Unknown	Unknown, but within 10 km of the equator		Control was lost, assumed to have remained in orbit for approx. 1–2 years
12/7/1972	USA:NASA	Apollo 17: SIVB	20:33 UT December 10	4.21 S	12.31 W	Deliberately crashed to create a seismic signal for seismometer monitoring.
12/7/1972	USA:NASA	Apollo 17: LM: Landing	19:55 UT December 11	20.2 N	30.8 E	Last human lunar landing—numerous experiments, including ALSEP
12/7/1972	USA:NASA	Apollo 17: LM jettison	6:50 UT December 15	19.96 N	30.50 E	Deliberately crashed to create a seismic signal for seismometer monitoring.
12/7/1972	USA:NASA	Apollo 17: SIVB				Deliberately crashed to create a seismic signal for seismometer monitoring.
1/8/1973	Soviet Union	Luna 21/ Lunokhod 2	23:35 UT January 15	25.85 N	30.45 E	Second successful lunar rover—Lunokhod 1. Rested batteries until January 18. It is still functioning, as of 2005.
10/28/1974	Soviet Union	Luna 23	5-Nov	14 N	57 E	exact coordinates unknown
8/9/1976	Soviet Union	Luna 24	2:00 UT August 18	12.8 N	62.2 E	Lunar Sample Return, 8/19/1976
9/30/1977	USA:NASA	ALSEPs				All five were shut down
1/24/1990	Japan: ISAS	Hiten/ Hagoromo	Hiten crashed at 18:03 UT April 10, 1993	34 S	55.3 E	Hagoromo is most likely still in orbit
1/7/1998	USA:NASA	Lunar Prospector	9:52 UT July 31, 1999	87.5 S	42.35 E–60 E	Directed to crash into a crater near the south pole as part of an experiment to confirm the existence of water ice on the Moon.
9/27/2003	Europe: ESA	SMART 1	5:42 UT September 3, 2006	34.4 S	46.2 W	First ESA spacecraft to travel to and orbit around the Moon, deliberately crashed into Moon.

Lunar Impacts and Landings

NEAR SIDE

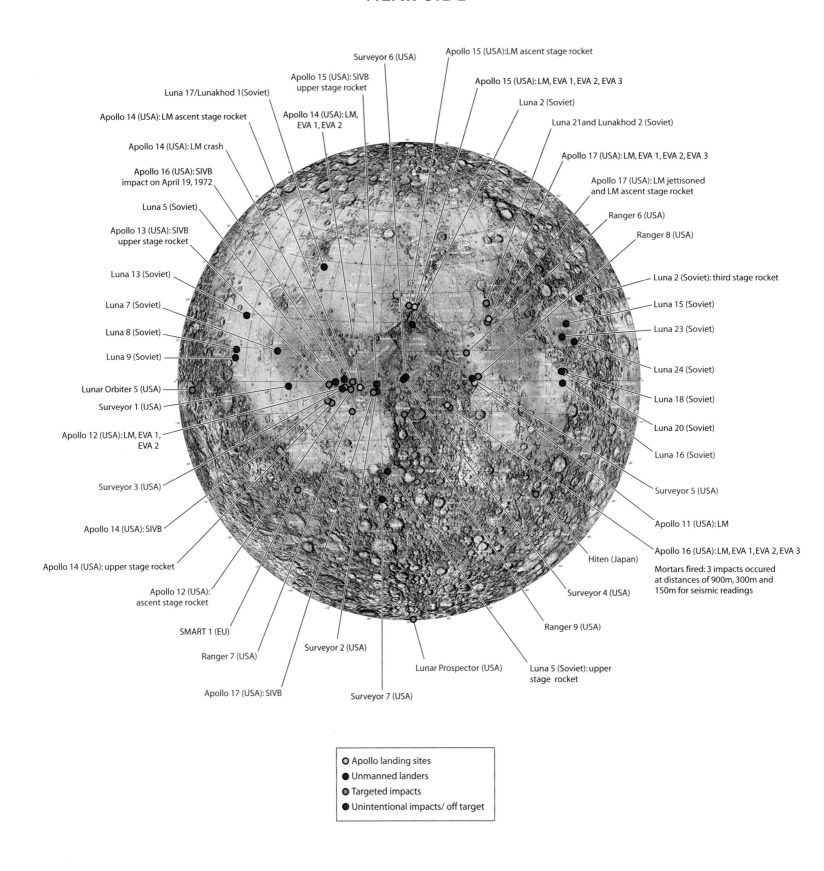

Surveyor 6 (USA)

Apollo 15 (USA):LM ascent stage rocket

Apollo 15 (USA): SIVB upper stage rocket

Apollo 15 (USA): LM, EVA 1, EVA 2, EVA 3

Luna 17/Lunakhod 1(Soviet)

Apollo 14 (USA): LM ascent stage rocket

Apollo 14 (USA): LM, EVA 1, EVA 2

Luna 2 (Soviet)

Luna 21and Lunakhod 2 (Soviet)

Apollo 14 (USA): LM crash

Apollo 17 (USA): LM, EVA 1, EVA 2, EVA 3

Apollo 16 (USA): SIVB impact on April 19, 1972

Apollo 17 (USA): LM jettisoned and LM ascent stage rocket

Luna 5 (Soviet)

Ranger 6 (USA)

Apollo 13 (USA): SIVB upper stage rocket

Ranger 8 (USA)

Luna 13 (Soviet)

Luna 2 (Soviet): third stage rocket

Luna 7 (Soviet)

Luna 15 (Soviet)

Luna 8 (Soviet)

Luna 23 (Soviet)

Luna 9 (Soviet)

Luna 24 (Soviet)

Lunar Orbiter 5 (USA)

Luna 18 (Soviet)

Surveyor 1 (USA)

Luna 20 (Soviet)

Apollo 12 (USA): LM, EVA 1, EVA 2

Luna 16 (Soviet)

Surveyor 3 (USA)

Surveyor 5 (USA)

Apollo 14 (USA): SIVB

Apollo 11 (USA): LM

Apollo 14 (USA): upper stage rocket

Apollo 16 (USA): LM, EVA 1, EVA 2, EVA 3

Apollo 12 (USA): ascent stage rocket

Hiten (Japan)

Mortars fired: 3 impacts occured at distances of 900m, 300m and 150m for seismic readings

SMART 1 (EU)

Surveyor 4 (USA)

Ranger 7 (USA)

Surveyor 2 (USA)

Ranger 9 (USA)

Apollo 17 (USA): SIVB

Lunar Prospector (USA)

Luna 5 (Soviet): upper stage rocket

Surveyor 7 (USA)

○ Apollo landing sites
● Unmanned landers
◐ Targeted impacts
● Unintentional impacts/ off target

FAR SIDE

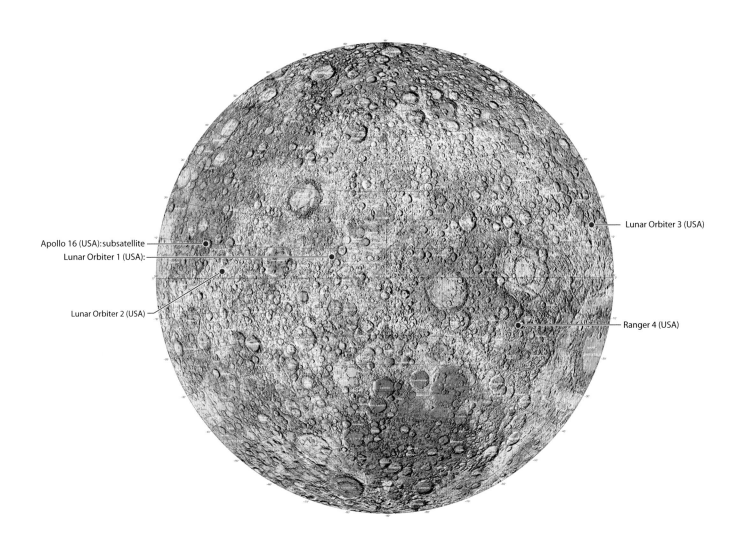

Apollo 16 (USA):subsatellite

Lunar Orbiter 1 (USA):

Lunar Orbiter 2 (USA)

Lunar Orbiter 3 (USA)

Ranger 4 (USA)

Robotic Soft Moon Lander Site Plans

Like so many other points of intersection, soft landing on the Moon with robotic probes also proved a venue for competition for the United States and the Soviet Union in the 1960s. The Soviets won that competition February 3, 1966, by sending Luna 9, which became the first spacecraft to soft land on another planetary body, to the Moon's Oceanus Procellarum region. A pole extending at the lower end of the spacecraft sensed contact with the lunar surface and triggered the ejection of an egg-shaped, 250-pound capsule. Once it came to rest on the lunar surface four spring-loaded petals opened. Equipped only with a camera and communication equipment, Luna 9 provided the first dramatic panoramic views of the surface of the Moon.

Arriving on the lunar surface on February 3, 1966, Luna 9 landed west of craters Reiner and Marius. Luna 9 was designed to release a landing pod immediately before striking the surface. A hinged arm reaching forward from the retrorocket was used to detect the surface. The pressurized pod, weighing 220 pounds on Earth, detached and rolled across the surface. After four minutes four "petals" unfolded and a 75 cm radio antenna extended. This design ensured the pod would operate "right side up." Images showed 10–20-cm rocks distributed on the surface. The television camera on Luna 9 was able to rotate 360 degrees, although imagery was not returned of the entire view because the spacecraft landed at an angle. Between the second and third transmissions from the Moon, Luna 9's inclination changed from 16.5 degrees to 27.5. It was theorized this was caused by shifting rocks beneath the lander, possibly caused by thermal expansion and contraction.

Following closely after the Soviet Union's success with Luna 9, the U.S. succeeded in soft landing Surveyor 1 on the Moon in June 1966. On reaching its final descent, it was slowed by a solid-propellant retrorocket. This was then jettisoned, removing about 60% of Surveyor's mass. Three small engines slowed the lander's velocity to about 3 miles per hour. At that point the rockets were shut off and Surveyor coasted to a gentle landing. The onboard camera on Surveyor 1 returned more than 11,000 images over six weeks. Most images showed the lunar surface to a distance of more than a mile. Observations of the Sun and Jupiter were also performed.

Landing on June 2, 1966, Surveyor 1 photographed and studied the soil of a flat area inside a 100 km crater north of Flamsteed Crater in southwest Oceanus Procellarum. The television system transmitted 10,338 photos prior to nightfall on June 14. The spacecraft also acquired data on the radar reflectivity of the lunar surface, bearing strength of the lunar surface, and spacecraft temperatures for use in the analysis of the

This mosaic of Surveyor 3 pictures in 1967 shows Block Crater just below the rim of Surveyor Crater to the right of center.

lunar surface temperatures. Surveyor 1 was able to withstand the first lunar night and after a total of 11,240 pictures had been transmitted, Surveyor 1's mission was terminated due to a dramatic drop in battery voltage.

The Soviet Union remained committed to robotic lunar exploration as well. It landed a second soft lander on the surface with Luna 13 on December 24, 1966, in the region of Oceanus Procellarum. The same petal encasement as seen on Luna 9 was opened, antennas were erected, and radio transmissions to Earth began four minutes after the landing. Unlike Luna 9 it carried new instruments mounted at the end of folding 1.5-meter arms. The first experiment tested density of the lunar soil. One end of the arm was slammed into the soil using a small explosive charge, and the seismic waves reflecting back to the surface were measured. The other arms carried radiation density meters which exposed the lunar soil to gamma rays and measured the reflected energy. On December 25 and 26, 1966, the spacecraft television system transmitted panoramas of the nearby lunar landscape at different sun angles. Each panorama required approximately 100 minutes to transmit.

After the failure of Surveyor 2 on September 22, 1966, NASA's Surveyor 3 successfully soft landed on the lunar surface on April 17, 1967, and provided imagery and soil analysis. The lander "bounced" more than once on the surface before coming to rest. Footprints from the initial impact were visible from the final landing site. Besides a camera similar to Surveyor 1, this lander also carried a mechanical scoop that dug several small trenches in the lunar soil. Over the next three weeks the camera returned more than 6,300 images showing the surrounding rocks and the movements of the scoop. Two years after landing Surveyor 3 was visited by the Apollo 12 astronauts. The television camera and other sections were removed and returned to Earth. The camera was later put on display in the Smithsonian Institution's National Air and Space Museum.

Although NASA lost contact with Surveyor 4 on July 17, 1967, it followed with Surveyors 5, 6, and 7 over the course of the next few months. While on its trajectory to the Moon, Surveyor 5 experienced serious problems with a helium pressurization system that was necessary for the retrorockets to work. Flight engineers were able to work around the problem and Surveyor 5 successfully landed on September 10, 1967. Thousands of images were returned by the television camera. Surveyor 5 also carried an alpha ray scatterer that measured composition of the lunar soil. Surveyor 6 landed on November 9, 1967. It carried similar instruments as Surveyor 5. On

Astronaut Alan Bean took this image at a 15-foot focus looking across Surveyor 3 toward the Lunar Module.

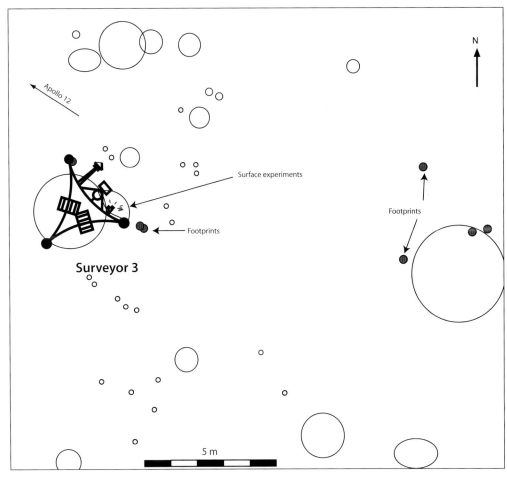

This illustration shows the features of the Surveyor 3 landing site on the Moon. The semicircular "surface experiments" zone indicates the area reachable by the robotic arm.

The Soviet Union's Luna 9 Moon landing marked the first time a spacecraft landed safely beyond Earth; the first photos from the surface of another world; and the first time humans could be sure a Moon lander would not just sink into deep dust. This first image from the surface of the Moon was taken by Luna 9 on February 2, 1966.

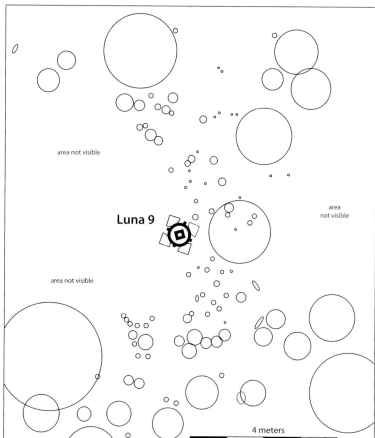

The features of the Luna 9 landing site on the Moon.

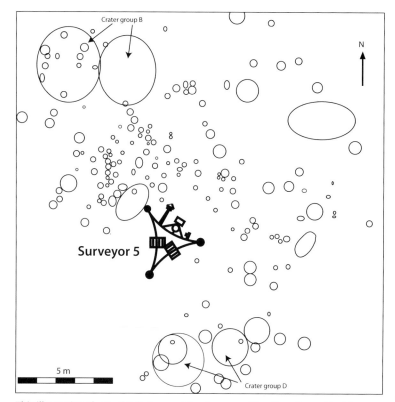

This illustration shows the features of the Surveyor 5 landing site on the Moon.

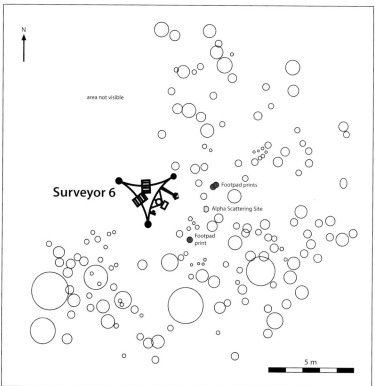

The features of the Surveyor 6 landing site on the Moon.

This Surveyor 5 image shows the footpad resting in the lunar soil. The trench at right was formed by the footpad sliding during landing. Surveyor 5 landed on the Moon on September 11, 1967, in Mare Tranquillitatis. The spacecraft landed on the inside edge of a small rimless crater at an angle of about 20 degrees, explaining the sliding. The footpad is about half a meter in diameter.

November 17 Surveyor 6 became the first spacecraft to take off from the lunar surface. Controllers noted enough fuel remained for a brief firing of the retrorockets. Surveyor 6 performed a "hop," reaching a height of about 10 feet and coming to rest about 8 feet from its first position. Both sets of footprints in the lunar soil were plainly visible in images form the television camera. Surveyor 7 landed on January 10, 1968, north of the crater Tycho. Surveyor 7 carried both a mechanical arm and an alpha scattering instrument. The arm was needed to move the latter device when it was found to be stuck. Over the next three weeks after landing, the alpha scattering sensor was lowered and then moved to test composition of soil from the surface and within trenches.

Five of the seven Surveyor spacecraft completed their missions, although the vernier rockets on Surveyor 3 did not shut down at the proper point, causing the 650-pound robot to skip twice across the lunar surface before stopping beneath a small crater rim.

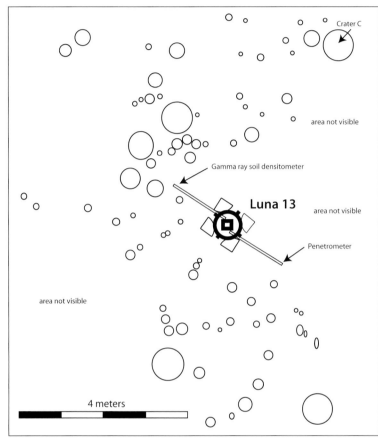

The features of the Luna 13 landing site on the Moon.

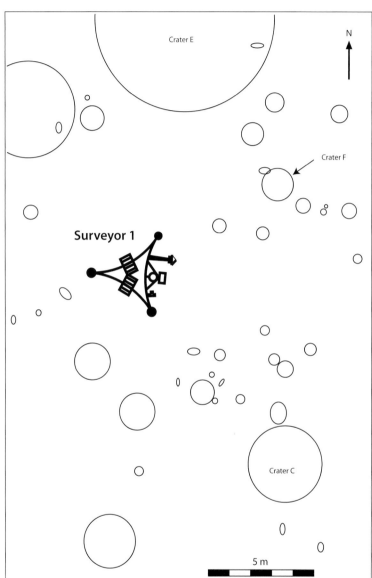

The features of the Surveyor 1 landing site on the Moon.

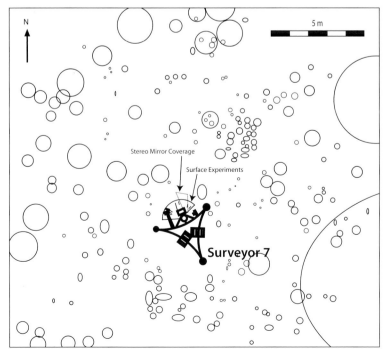

The features of the Surveyor 7 landing site on the Moon. Surveyor 7 carried a mirror that allowed the single television camera to return stereo images in a small area.

This photomosaic of lunar panorama near the Tycho crater was taken by Surveyor 7 in 1967. The hills on the center horizon are about eight miles away from the spacecraft. Since the landing site survey for the Apollo missions had been successfully completed by previous Surveyors, the landing site for Surveyor 7 was selected more for its scientific interest. It obtained images of the landing site, manipulated the soil and analyzed its composition, and obtained temperature and radar reflectivity data.

Soviet Rovers and Sample Return from the Moon

The Soviet Union never sent cosmonauts to the Moon, but landed the first robotic rovers, Lunokhods 1 and 2.

The first, Lunokhod 1, landed on November 17, 1970, when the Soviet Luna 17 spacecraft soft landed the vehicle on the lunar surface. Weighing just under one ton, this rover was intended to operate for 90 days while guided from the Soviet mission control outside Moscow. It had been launched on November 10, 1970, and flight controllers undertook two course corrections (on November 12 and 14) to bring it into lunar orbit on November 15. After landing, this eight-wheeled rover departed Luna 17 by means of ramps extending from both sides of the lander. Lunokhod 1 far exceeded its design life, and traveled around the lunar Mare Imbrium (Sea of Rains) for 11 months after landing. It ran only during the two-week-long lunar day, stopping occasionally to recharge its batteries via its solar panels. The rover's operations officially ceased on October 4, 1971, on the 14th anniversary of the launch of Sputnik 1. It was the first roving remote-controlled robot to land on another world.

Viewed initially as a scout for a landing site for Soviet cosmonauts, this rover originated in 1963 and was to carry a beacon that would be used to guide the cosmonauts to the surface. By the time that it flew, however, this mission had been overcome by events. Lunokhod 1, therefore, explored the lunar surface and returned scientific information about the geology and landscape of the Moon, imaged its surface, undertook laser ranging experiments from Earth, and measured magnetic fields. It carried a cone-shaped antenna, a highly directional helical antenna, four television cameras, and an extendable arm to test the lunar soil for soil density. Soviet scientists also included an X-ray spectrometer, an X-ray telescope, cosmic-ray detectors, and a laser ranging device.

Lunokhod 1 had a unique design: it looked like a bathtub on eight wheels. The inside of the large convex lid served as the solar array tub and the tub itself housed the instruments. Using imagery from a large panorama camera, a five-person team of controllers on Earth sent commands to the rover in real time to control its movement. By the end of its service life Lunokhod 1 had traveled 10,540 meters and had transmitted more than 20,000 TV pictures and more than 200 TV panoramas. It also conducted more than 500 lunar soil tests. The exact location of Lunokhod 1 on the lunar surface is uncertain because laser ranging experiments have been unable to detect a return signal since end of mission.

Lunokhod 2 was a virtual twin of its predecessor. Launched on the Luna 21 spacecraft on January 8, 1973, after a midcourse correction the day after launch, Luna 21 entered orbit around the Moon on January 12. Its orbital parameters were 100 x 90 kilometers at 60° inclination. The spacecraft then soft-landed on the Moon between Mare Serenitatis and the Taurus Mountains and deployed the second Soviet lunar rover (Lunokhod 2) on January 15 less than three hours after landing. The 840-kilogram Lunokhod 2 was an improved version of its predecessor and was equipped with a third TV camera, an improved eight-wheel traction system, and additional scientific instrumentation. Like its predecessor, this rover's primary objectives included imagery of the lunar surface, laser ranging experiments, solar X-ray analysis, magnetic field measure-

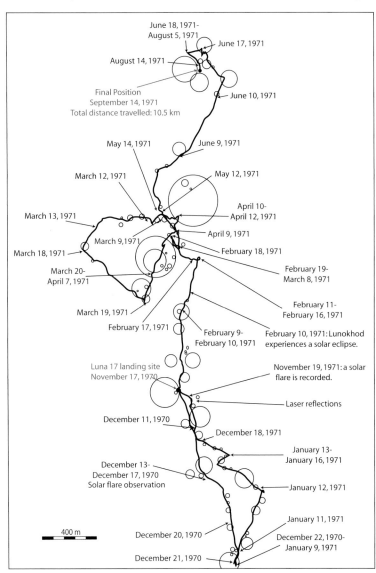

This traverse map shows the movement of Lunokhod 1 on the lunar surface.

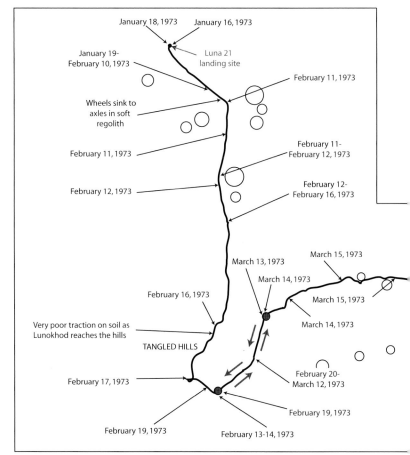

This traverse map shows the movement of the Lunokhod 2 on the lunar surface.

ments, and testing of the properties of lunar surface material. By the end of its first lunar day, Lunokhod 2 had already traveled farther than Lunokhod 1 in its entire operational life. Lunokhod 2 operated for 4 months, covered 37 km (23 miles) of terrain, including hilly upland areas and rilles, and sent back 86 panoramic images and over 80,000 TV pictures. It also completed several tests of the surface, laser ranging measurements, and other experiments. On May 9, 1973, the rover rolled into a crater and dust covered its solar panels, disrupt- ing power to the vehicle. Mission controllers attempted to salvage the rover but failed to do so. On June 3, TASS, the Soviet news agency, announced that the Lunokhod 2 mission had been terminated. It remains a target for laser ranging experiments to the present.

Interestingly, after the end of the Lunokhod 2 mission, Soviet scientists confided that an American scientist working on the Apollo program had given images of the lunar surface near the Luna 21 landing site to Soviet colleagues at a conference on planetary explo- ration in Moscow, on January 29–February 2, 1973. Those images had been taken as part of the planning for the December 1972 Apollo 17 lunar landing mission that took place in the same region. This was after the landing of the space- craft, but they proved helpful to the controllers in navigating the rover on its mission on the Moon.

In addition, the Soviet Union succeeded with two sample return missions from the Moon. After several failed attempts the first, Luna 20, was placed in an intermediate Earth park- ing orbit and from this orbit was sent toward the Moon. It entered lunar orbit on February 18, 1972. On February 21, 1972, Luna 20 soft landed on the Moon in a mountainous area known as the Apollonius highlands near Mare Foecunditatis (Sea of Fertility), 120 km. While on the lunar surface, the panoramic television system returned imagery. It also collected lunar samples by means of an extendable drilling appa- ratus. The ascent stage of Luna 20 was launched from the lunar surface on February 22, 1972, carrying 30 grams of collected lunar samples in a sealed capsule. It landed in the Soviet Union on February 25, 1972. The lunar samples were recovered the following day. A second successful sample return mission, Luna 24, landed in the area known as Mare Crisium (Sea of Crisis) on August 18, 1976. Like its predecessor, it used a sample arm and drill to collect 170.1 grams of lunar samples and deposited them into a collec- tion capsule. The capsule then returned to Earth on August 22, 1976, in western Siberia.

SPECIFICATIONS
NAMES: Lunokhod 1 and 2
OPERATOR: Deep Space Center, Lavochkin Design Bureau

LAUNCHED:
Lunokhod 1: by 8K82K + Blok D Proton launch vehicle from Baikonur Launch Complex, November 10, 1970
Lunokhod 2: by SL-12/D-1-e Proton launch vehicle from Baikonur Launch Complex, January 8, 1973

LANDING SITE:
Lunokhod 1: Mare Imbrium (Sea of Rains) at 38.17 degrees N, - 35 degrees W, landed November 17, 1970
Lunokhod 2: Le Monnier crater at 25.85 degrees N, 30.45 degrees E, landed January 15, 1973

ON-ORBIT DRY MASS:
Lunokhod 1: 5,700 kg
Lunokhod 2: 4,850 kg

CONFIGURATION: Complete spacecraft launched toward the Moon comprised an eight-wheeled rover, lander, landing rockets
ROVER DIMENSIONS: 135 cm high, 170 cm long, and 160 cm wide
ROVER MASS (for each): 840 kg
ROVER PAYLOAD: Cone-shaped antenna, directional helical antenna, four television cameras, and an extendable arm to test the lunar soil for soil density. Soviet scientists also included an X-ray spectrometer, an X-ray telescope, cosmic-ray detectors, and a laser ranging device
ROVER PROPULSION: Cleated wheels driven by individual electric motors, two speeds, ~1 km/hr and ~2 km/hr
ROVER ELECTRICAL POWER: Solar array on the inside of a round hinged lid which covered the instrument bay

HEATING ELEMENT: Polonium-210 isotopic heat source
PRIME MISSION: 90 days

LUNA 20: 5,750 kg (12,677 lbs), launched February 14, 1972 / 03:27:59, launch site NIIP-5 / 81P, launch vehicle Proton-K / 258-01, operator USSR Lavochkin, lunar sample return, landed February 21, 1972 / 19:19:00 UT, Latitude 3.57 N, Longitude 56.50 E - Mare Fecunditatis, lunar sample return launched to Earth February 25, 1972
LUNA 24: 5,800 kg (12,787 lbs), launched August 9, 1976 / 15:04:12, launch site NIIP-5 / 81L, launch vehicle Proton-K / 288-02, operator USSR Lavochkin, landed August 18, 1976 / 02:00:00 UT, Latitude 12.25 N, Longitude 62.20 E - Mare Crisium, lunar sample return launched to Earth August 19, 1976

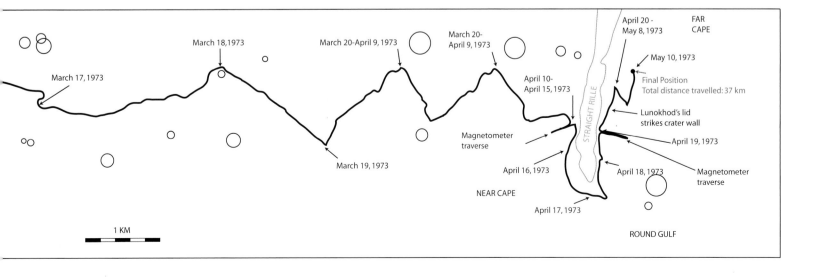

Americans to the Moon:
Developing Saturn Rocket Technology

NASA inherited the effort to develop the Saturn family of boosters used to launch Apollo to the Moon in 1960 when it acquired the rocketeers at the Army Ballistic Missile Agency in Huntsville, Alabama, under Wernher von Braun. At that time von Braun's engineers were hard at work on the first-generation Saturn launch vehicle, a cluster of eight Redstone boosters around a Jupiter fuel tank. Fueled by a combination of liquid oxygen (LOX) and RP-1 (a version of kerosene), the Saturn I could generate a thrust of 205,000 pounds. This group also worked on a second stage that used a revolutionary fuel mixture of LOX and liquid hydrogen that could generate a greater ratio of thrust to weight. The fuel choice made this second stage a difficult development effort, because the mixture was highly volatile and could not be readily handled. But the stage could produce an additional 90,000 pounds of thrust. The Saturn I was solely a research and development vehicle that would lead toward the accomplishment of Apollo, making ten flights between October 1961 and July 1965. The first four flights tested the first stage, but beginning with the fifth launch the second stage was active and these missions were used to place scientific payloads and Apollo test capsules into orbit.

The next step in Saturn development came with the maturation of the Saturn IB, an upgraded version of the earlier vehicle. With more powerful engines generating 1.6 million pounds of thrust from the first stage, the two-stage combination could place 62,000-pound payloads into Earth orbit. The first flight on February 26, 1966, tested the capability of the booster and the Apollo capsule in a suborbital flight. Two more flights followed in quick succession. Then there was a hiatus of more than a year before the January 22, 1968, launch of a Saturn IB with both an Apollo capsule and a lunar landing module aboard for orbital testing. The only astronaut-occupied flight of the Saturn IB took place between October 11 and 22, 1968, when Walter Schirra, Donn F. Eisele, and R. Walter Cunningham made 163 Earth orbits testing Apollo equipment.

The largest launch vehicle of this family, the Saturn V, represented the culmination of those earlier booster development and test programs. Standing 363 feet tall, with three stages, this was the vehicle that could take astronauts to the Moon and return them safely to Earth. The first stage generated 7.5 million pounds of thrust from five massive engines developed for the system. These engines, known as the F-1, were some of the most significant engineering accomplishments of the program, requiring the development of new alloys and different construction techniques to withstand the extreme heat and shock of firing.

The thunderous sound of the first static test of this stage, taking place at Huntsville, Alabama, on April 16, 1965, brought home to many that the Kennedy goal was within technological grasp. For others, it signaled the magic of technological effort; one engineer even characterized rocket engine technology as a "black art" without rational principles. The second stage presented enormous challenges to NASA engineers and very nearly caused the lunar landing goal to be missed. Consisting of five engines burning LOX and liquid hydrogen, this stage could deliver 1 million pounds of thrust. It was always behind schedule, and required constant attention and additional funding to ensure completion by the deadline for a lunar landing. Both the first and third stages of this Saturn vehicle development program moved forward relatively smoothly. (The third stage was an enlarged and improved version of the IB, and had few developmental complications.)

Despite all of this, the biggest problem with Saturn V lay not with the hardware, but with the clash of philosophies toward development and test. The von Braun "Rocket Team" made important technological contributions and enjoyed popular acclaim as a result of conservative engineering practices that took minutely incremental approaches toward test and verification. They tested each component of each system individually and then assembled them for a long series of ground tests. Then they would launch each stage individually before assembling the whole system for a long series of flight tests.

While this practice ensured thoroughness, it was both costly and time-consuming, and NASA had neither commodity to expend. George E. Mueller, the head of NASA's Office of Manned Space Flight, disagreed with this approach. Drawing on his experience with the Air Force and aerospace industry, and shadowed by the twin bugaboos of schedule and cost, Mueller advocated what he called the "all-up" concept in which the entire Apollo-Saturn system was tested together in flight without the laborious preliminaries.

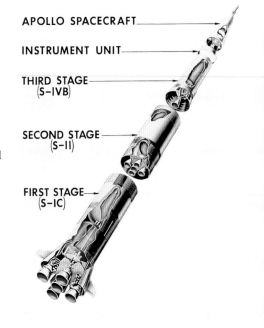

SATURN V LAUNCH VEHICLE
CHARACTERISTICS

APOLLO SPACECRAFT

INSTRUMENT UNIT

THIRD STAGE (S-IVB)

SECOND STAGE (S-II)

FIRST STAGE (S-IC)

LENGTH (VEHICLE)	281 FT
LENGTH (VEHICLE, SPACECRAFT, LES)	363 FT
WEIGHT AT LIFTOFF	6,400,000 LBS
TRANSLUNAR PAYLOAD CAPABILITY APPROX	107,350 LBS
EARTH ORBIT (2 STAGE VEHICLE)	212,000 LBS

STAGES

FIRST (S-IC)

SIZE	33 X 138 FT
ENGINES	5 F-1
THRUST	7,610,000 LBS
PROPELLANTS	LOX & RP-1

SECOND (S-II)

SIZE	33 X 81 FT
ENGINES	5 J-2
THRUST	1,150,000 LBS
PROPELLANTS	LOX & LH$_2$

THIRD (S-IVB)

SIZE	22 X 59 FT
ENGINE	1 J-2
THRUST	230,000 LBS
PROPELLANTS	LOX & LH$_2$

INSTRUMENT UNIT

SIZE	22 X 3 FT
GUIDANCE SYSTEM	INERTIAL

MSFC-71-IND 1223M

This schematic depicts the basics of the Saturn V launch stack that took the United States to the Moon.

A calculated gamble, the first Saturn V flight test launch took place on November 9, 1967, with the entire Apollo-Saturn combination. A second test followed on April 4, 1968, and even though it was only partially successful because the second stage shut off prematurely and the third stage—needed to start the Apollo payload into lunar trajectory—failed, Mueller declared that the test program had been completed and that the next launch would have astronauts aboard. The gamble paid off. In 17 tests and 15 piloted launches, the Saturn booster family scored a 100% launch reliability rate.

It was this rocket technology that took the astronauts to the Moon in the 1960s and 1970s.

The lunar orbital paths of the Apollo missions. Landing sites for all missions are indicated on the surface below each orbit. Apollo 10 and 11 remained above the equator, while later missions entered more inclined orbits.

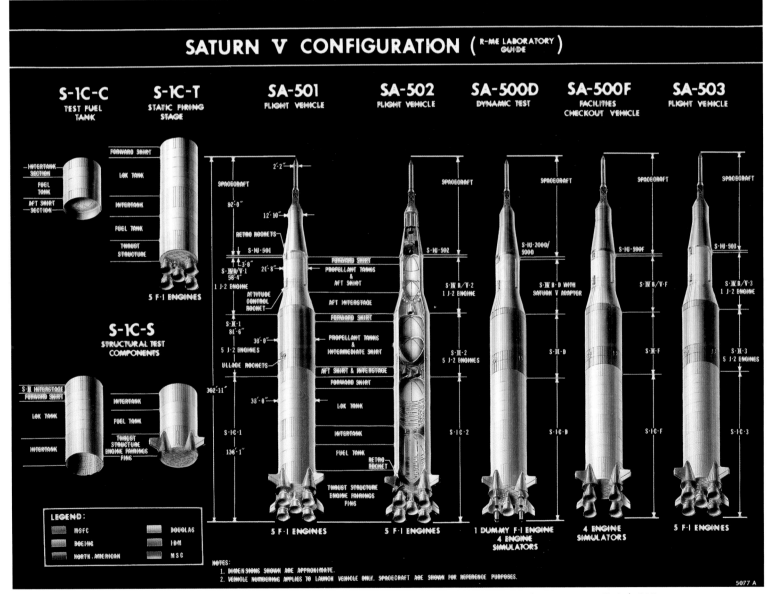

This Saturn V graphic depicts the movement of the launch vehicle from its first components through its evolution from a test to a flight vehicle.

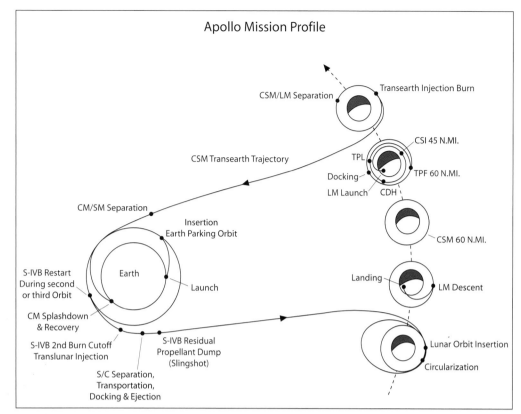

Apollo Mission Profile

This typical Apollo lunar landing mission was divided into 18 distinct parts, or phases. Each phase would normally be preceded by a Go/No Go decision from Mission Control: 1-launch, 2-Earth orbit insertion/spacecraft checkout, 3-trans-lunar injection (TLI), 4-transposition and docking of Command and Service Module (CSM) to Lunar Module (LM), 5-trans-lunar coast, 6-lunar orbit insertion (LOI), 7-mid-course correction(s), 8-LM descent and landing, 9-lunar surface operations and extravehicular activity (EVA), 10-LM liftoff, 11-LM/CSM docking, 12-LM jettison, 13-CSM trans-Earth injection (TEI), 14-trans-Earth coast, 15-midcourse correction(s), 16-trans-Earth EVA (Apollos 15, 16, 17), 17-Service Module jettison, 18-reentry, splashdown, and recovery.

This wind tunnel test of the Saturn IB stack was conducted at the Langley Research Center in Hampton, Virginia, to measure its aerodynamic integrity in 1963.

The Saturn V first stages, S-1C-10, S-1C-11, and S-1C-9, are in the horizontal assembly area for the engine (five F-1 engines) installation at Michoud Assembly Facility (MAF), New Orleans, Louisiana, in 1968.

The S-II stage of the Saturn V rocket is hoisted onto the A-2 test stand in 1967 at the Mississippi Test Facility, now the Stennis Space Center. This was the second stage of the 363-foot-tall Moon rocket.

The Apollo Spacecraft and Lunar Module

Almost with the announcement of the lunar landing commitment in 1961 NASA technicians began a crash program to develop a reasonable configuration for the trip to lunar orbit and back. What they came up with was a three-person command module capable of sustaining human life for two weeks or more in either Earth orbit or in a lunar trajectory; a service module holding oxygen, fuel, maneuvering rockets, fuel cells, and other expendable and life support equipment that could be jettisoned upon reentry to Earth; a retrorocket package attached to the service module for slowing to prepare for reentry; and finally a launch escape system that was discarded upon achieving orbit. The teardrop-shaped command module had two hatches, one on the side for entry and exit of the crew at the beginning and end of the flight and one in the nose with a docking collar for use in moving to and from the lunar landing vehicle.

Work on the Apollo spacecraft stretched from November 28, 1961, when the prime contract for its development was awarded to North American Aviation, to October 22, 1968, when the last test flight took place. In between there were various efforts to design, build, and test the spacecraft both on the

ground and in suborbital and orbital flights. For instance, on May 13, 1964, NASA tested a boilerplate model of the Apollo capsule atop a stubby Little Joe II military booster, and another Apollo capsule actually achieved orbit on September 18, 1964, when it was launched atop a Saturn I. By the end of 1966 NASA leaders declared the Apollo command module ready for human occupancy. The final flight checkout of the spacecraft prior to the lunar flight took place October 11–22, 1968, with three astronauts.

If other parts of the program offered difficult technological challenges, and they did, Lunar Module (LM) represented the most serious problem. Begun a year later than it should have been, the LM was consistently behind schedule and over budget. Much of the problem turned on the demands of devising two separate spacecraft components—one for descent to the Moon and one for ascent back to the command module—that only maneuvered outside an atmosphere. Both engines had to work perfectly or the very real possibility existed that the astronauts could not return home. Guidance, maneuverability, and spacecraft control also caused no end of headaches. The landing structure likewise presented prob-

lems: it had to be light and sturdy and shock resistant. An ungainly vehicle emerged which two astronauts could fly while standing. In November 1962 Grumman Aerospace Corp. signed a contract with NASA to produce the LM, and work on it began in earnest. With difficulty the LM was orbited on a Saturn V test launch in January 1968 and judged ready for operation.

After a piloted orbital mission to test the Apollo equipment on October 1968, on December 21, 1968, Apollo 8 took off atop a Saturn V booster from the Kennedy Space Center with three astronauts aboard for a historic mission to orbit the Moon. The advantages of this could be important, both in technical and scientific knowledge gained as well as in a public demonstration of what the U.S. could achieve. Successful on all accounts, this mission gave NASA the confidence to move forward with the program.

In all, six Apollo missions landed on the Moon between 1969 and 1972—the last three with a lunar rover that greatly expanded the reach of the astronauts on the surface—each of them increasing the time spent on the Moon and the complexity of the science conducted there. Three other missions were circumlunar

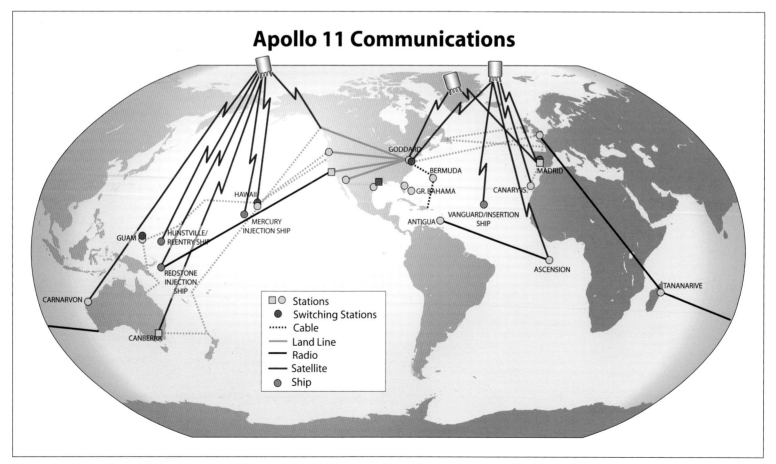

To communicate with the Apollo astronaughts NASA created a complex system of ground stations aroud the globe to transmit voice and data continuously, so that Apollo spacecraft were rarely out of contact with Earth.

flights—Apollo 8 and 10—with the Apollo 13 mission becoming an orbital mission because of the explosion in the Service Module outbound. Apollo 7 and 9 flew in Earth orbit testing Apollo hardware.

Once on the lunar surface, the astronauts engaged in a variety of scientific pursuits. They deployed the Apollo Lunar Surface Experiments Package (ALSEP) and related scientific instruments. The ALSEP included a combination of experiments taken to a site sufficiently far from the Lunar Module where it would not be destroyed or interfered with by the return to orbit by the LM ascent stage. There was a central processing station to which all of the peripheral experiments—and the

radioisotope thermoelectric generator (RTG) power source—was attached. It provided power distribution, communications with Earth, and the like. The experiments were connected to this station by cables.

With several of the packages placed on the Moon by the various Apollo crews, networks provided more information than anyone realized. For example, the seismometer network from the ALSEPs placed by Apollo 12, 14, 15, and 16 enabled the location of impacts and moonquakes. Another network of instruments enabled the study of solar wind plasma movement by detection of its contained magnetic field.

The scientific experiments placed on the

Moon and the lunar soil samples returned through Project Apollo have provided grist for scientists' investigations of the Solar System ever since. Collectively, these Apollo experiments yielded more than 10,000 scientific papers and a major reinterpretation of the origins and evolution of the Moon.

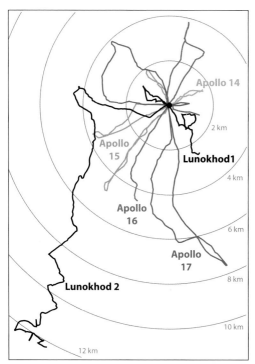

This chart compares distances covered by Apollo astronauts and the unmanned Lunokhod rovers. The Lunar Roving Vehicle (LRV) was used on Apollo 15, 16, and 17. The LRV and its astronaut drivers were able to cover large amounts of ground within days, compared to the several months required for the unmanned rovers.

This photograph from Apollo 15 shows the Lunar Roving Vehicle (LRV).

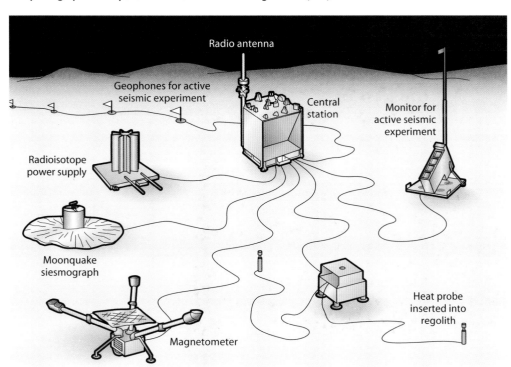

The standard deployment of the Apollo Lunar Surface Experiments Package (ALSEP) during the lunar landing program.

This cutaway of the lunar EVA spacesuit shows the layers protecting the Apollo astronaut.

1969: The Apollo 11 and 12 Landing Sites

Apollo 11 lifted off on July 16, 1969, and, after confirming that the hardware was working well, began the three-day trip to the Moon. At 4:18 P.M. EST on July 20, 1969, the LM—with astronauts Neil Armstrong and Buzz Aldrin—landed on the lunar surface while astronaut Michael Collins orbited overhead in the Apollo command module. After checkout, Armstrong set foot on the lunar surface, telling millions who saw and heard him on Earth that it was "one small step for [a] man—one giant leap for mankind." (Neil Armstrong later added "a" when referring to "one small step for a man" to clarify the first sentence delivered from the Moon's surface.) Aldrin soon followed him out, and the two plodded around the landing site in the lunar gravity (one-sixth that of Earth), planted a United States flag (but omitted claiming the land for the United States, as had been routinely done during European exploration of the Americas), collected soil and rock samples, and set up scientific experiments.

The EVA lasted approximately 2.5 hours and ended all too soon, both Armstrong and Aldrin recalled. The next day they launched back to the Apollo capsule orbiting overhead and began the return trip to Earth, splashing down in the Pacific on July 24, 1969.

This flight rekindled the excitement felt in the early 1960s with John Glenn and the Mercury astronauts. Apollo 11, in particular, met with an ecstatic reaction around the globe, as everyone shared in the success of the mission. Ticker-tape parades, speaking engagements, public relations events, and a world tour by the astronauts served to create goodwill both in the United States and abroad.

On November 14–24, 1969, Apollo 12 returned to the Moon, the second lunar landing mission. Pete Conrad, Alan Bean, and Richard Gordon undertook a remarkable mission with Apollo 12. It need not have occurred, however, if the goal had been simply to land Americans on the Moon. That had been accomplished with Apollo 11 in July 1969. The Kennedy mandate had been satisfied with that mission; the American nation could have ended the flights then. But NASA garnered the political support to continue these voyages of discovery, and what a bounty they returned.

As the second lunar landing in November 1969, Apollo 12 has not received the attention that it deserves. Although starting with prospects for disaster—it was struck by lightning twice on the launch pad—under Conrad's leadership the crew put in a textbook mission.

More than 300,000 spectators crowded into the region around the Kennedy Space Center, Florida, to watch the launch of Apollo 11. Here campers on the beach prepare for the July 16, 1969, launch.

Buzz Aldrin on the lunar surface near the landing leg of the Lunar Module on July 20, 1969.

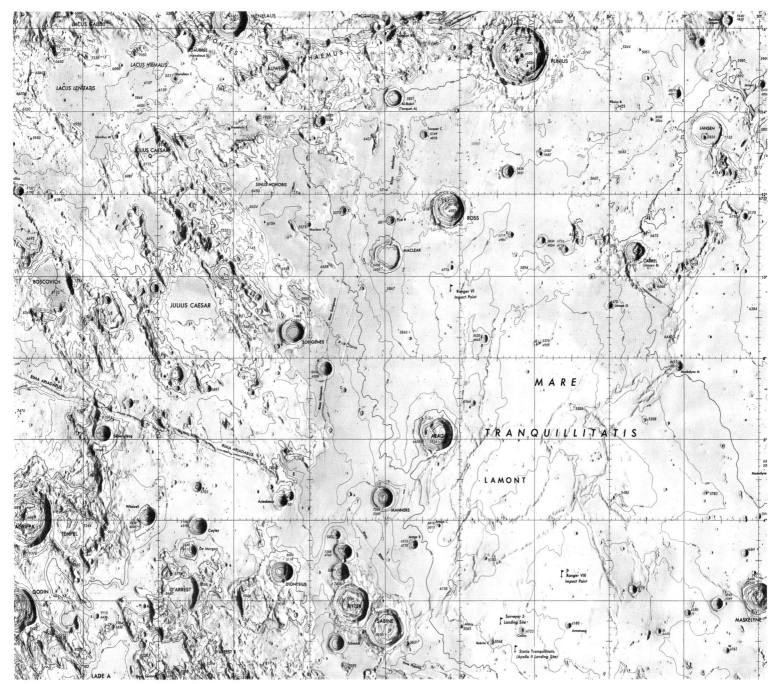

This 1978 compilation map shows the region of the Sea of Tranquillity where Apollo 11 landed in 1969. Interpreted from Apollo and Lunar Orbiter photography, this relief map was developed with an assumed morning illumination equal to the angle of slope of the features portrayed. The background tone depicts variations in reflectance of the surface at the time of full moon.

They turned it into an exercise in precision targeting, demonstrating that they could land wherever they wanted on the lunar surface. The descent was automatic, with only a few manual corrections by Conrad. The landing, in the Ocean of Storms, brought the lunar module "Intrepid" within walking distance—182.88 meters—of a robot spacecraft that had touched down there two and a half years earlier. They brought pieces of the Surveyor 3 back to Earth for analysis, and took two Moon-walks lasting just under four hours

each. Altogether they spent 7 hours and 45 minutes on the lunar surface performing a lunar traverse.

They collected rocks and set up the Apollo Lunar Surface Experiment Package that measured the Moon's seismicity, solar wind flux, and magnetic field. The data returned as a result of these scientific activities are still being analyzed by scientists and are contributing to our emerging understanding of the inner workings of our universe. Meanwhile Gordon, in the loneliest job in the space program, was

aboard the "Yankee Clipper" in lunar orbit, and took multispectral photographs of the surface. The results were so stunning that the crew stayed an extra day in lunar orbit taking photographs. When "Intrepid's" ascent stage was dropped onto the Moon after Conrad and Bean rejoined Gordon in orbit, the seismometers the astronauts had left on the lunar surface registered the vibrations for more than an hour.

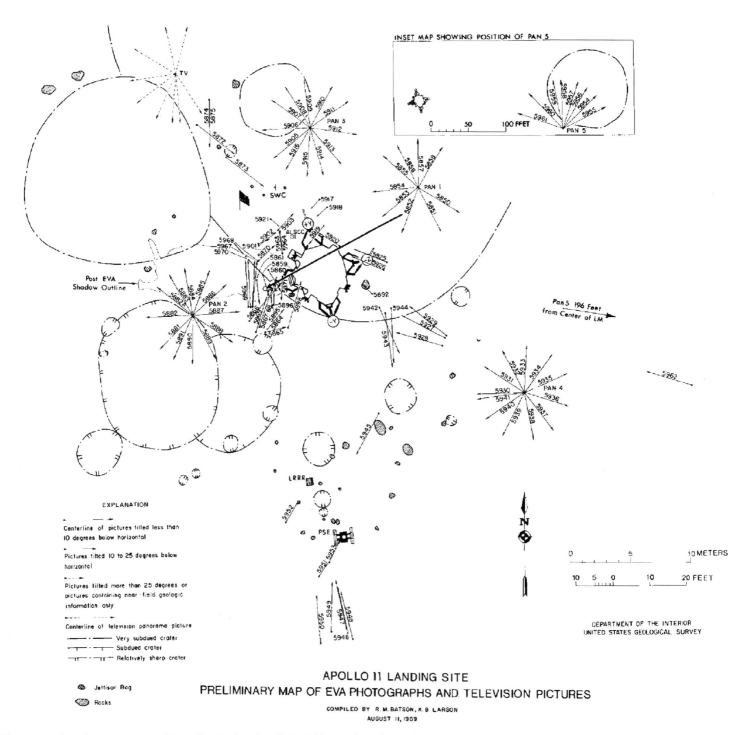

INSET MAP SHOWING POSITION OF PAN 5

PAN 3

PAN 1

PAN 5

SWC

Post EVA
Shadow Outline

PAN 2

Pan 5 196 Feet
from Center of LM

EXPLANATION

Centerline of pictures tilted less than
10 degrees below horizontal

Pictures tilted 10 to 25 degrees below
horizontal

Pictures tilted more than 25 degrees or
pictures containing near-field geologic
information only

Centerline of television panorama picture

— · — Very subdued crater

— · — Subdued crater

— · — Relatively sharp crater

Jettison Bag

Rocks

PAN 4

LRRR

PSE

N

0   5   10 METERS

10   5   0   10   20 FEET

DEPARTMENT OF THE INTERIOR
UNITED STATES GEOLOGICAL SURVEY

APOLLO 11 LANDING SITE
PRELIMINARY MAP OF EVA PHOTOGRAPHS AND TELEVISION PICTURES

COMPILED BY R. M. BATSON, K. B. LARSON
AUGUST 11, 1969

Diagrams such as these were created immediately after the mission. This map from the Apollo 11 mission shows the placement of all of the objects on the lunar surface as well as all of the pan images, keyed to their numbers on the film, taken by astronauts Neil Armstrong and Buzz Aldrin.

This color composite image of the Apollo 12 landing site was taken by Pete Conrad on November 19, 1969. It was taken near the end of the first EVA, and was assembled after return to Earth.

To train for the lunar landing NASA engineers created very accurate, high-relief maps of the lunar surface for practice on full motion training simulators.

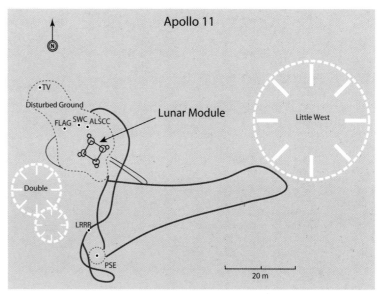

Apollo 11

These traverse maps of the Apollo 11 and 12 landing sites show the routes taken by the astronauts during their EVA, as well as the placement of the various experiments on the lunar surface. The thick lines indicate paths taken by the astronauts during the EVA (Extra-Vehicular Activity, or operations outside the spacecraft). The dotted lines outline portions of the lunar surface that were disturbed during astronaut activities. Acronyms: LM — Lunar Module, LRRR — Laser Ranging Retroreflector, PSE — Passive Seismic Experiment, SWC — Solar Wind Composition, ALSCC — Apollo Lunar Surface Closeup Camera.

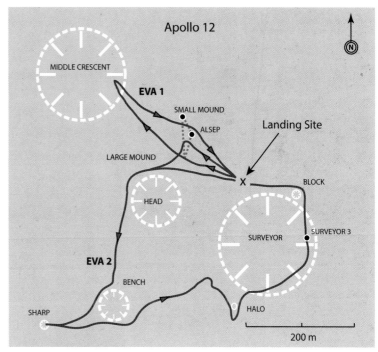

Apollo 12

Extending the Stay on the Moon: Apollos 14 and 15

Following the frightening problems of Apollo 13 in April 1970, when the crew had to abort its landing and return to Earth in a crippled spacecraft, almost ten months elapsed before the U.S. returned to the Moon with Apollo 14, January 31–February 9, 1971. This flight marked after a decade the return to flight of the first American in space, Alan B. Shepard, who had been grounded for medical reasons. Fellow astronauts Edgar D. Mitchell and Stuart A. Roosa expanded on earlier landings to sample rock and soil in the Fra Mauro region of the Moon, deploy and activate the Apollo lunar surface experiments package, extend the human capability of working in the lunar environment, and photograph specific features both on the lunar surface and from orbit.

Apollo 14 was a Type H mission, a precision piloted lunar landing demonstration along with systematic lunar exploration. It was the third successful lunar landing. They worked to return a significantly greater quantity of lunar material and to maximize scientific return. One innovation, allowing increased range for exploration, was the use of the modular equipment transporter (MET), a collapsible two-wheeled cart that could carry tools, cameras, a portable magnetometer, and lunar samples.

In two EVAs on the lunar surface the crew deployed a television camera, an S-band antenna, and a solar wind experiment; deployed and loaded the modular-ized equipment; collected samples; had some difficulty but eventually deployed the ALSEP; and photographed activities, panoramas, and equipment. During the second EVA, Shepard and Mitchell intended to visit the area of the 1,000-foot-wide Cone Crater, 0.7 miles (1.3 km) east-northeast of the landing site towing equipment with them in the MET. En route they photographed the scenery, took various samples, and made terrain descriptions. They also collected rock and soil samples at a blocky field near the rim of Cone Crater. They experienced difficulties navigating the crater's slopes, however, and fell 30 minutes behind schedule and had to scrap the remainder of the Cone Crater trip. As a result, they only reached a point within 50 feet (15 m) of the rim of the crater. They traveled about 9,800 feet (3 km) during this second EVA and collected 49.16 pounds (22.3 kg) of samples. For the mission, Shepard and Mitchell spent 9 hours, 22 minutes, and 31 seconds outside the Lunar Module, traveled more than 13,100 feet (4 km), and collected samples totaling 93.21 pounds (42.28 kg). One of the major lessons learned on this mission was when venturing beyond the line of sight of the Lunar Module navigation became a complex task because of problems in finding and recognizing small features, reduced visibility in the up-sun and down-sun directions, and the inability to judge distances.

Later in the year, July 26–August 7, 1971, Apollo 15 astronauts David R. Scott and James B. Irwin spent more than 18 hours outside their lunar module on the surface of the Moon near the foot of the Montes Apenninus (Apennine Mountains) and adjacent to Hadley Rille while Alfred M. Worden Jr. orbited overhead. Employing a lunar roving vehicle for the first time, Apollo 15 landed in the lunar highlands where the geological features were more interesting. The crew made a stunning find—the so-called Genesis rock, a piece of lunar crust that helped to define the Moon's origin.

This was the first of the Apollo "J" missions in which the astronauts remained for longer periods on the Moon, carried out more extensive and sophisticated scientific observations, and ranged across much broader territories using a battery-powered Lunar Roving Vehicle (LRV). Apollo 15 boasted a broad array of major modifications to enhance scientific activities. It added an instrument module in one of the service module bays for scientific investigations from lunar orbit, greater payload capacity on the Lunar Module, and more extensive scientific instruments to be deployed on the lunar surface. The four-wheeled, lightweight LRV weighed 462 pounds on Earth and could carry 1,080 pounds, including two astronauts and all of their equipment. The LRV was folded and stowed in Quad 1 of the LM descent stage during launch, and after landing

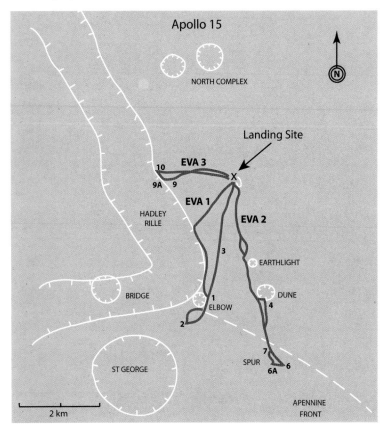

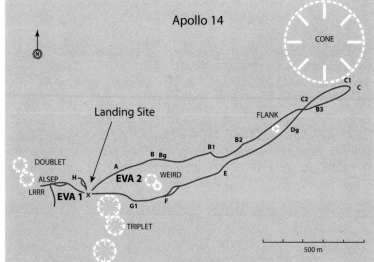

This traverse map of the Apollo 14 landing site documents the route taken by the astronauts during their EVA, as well as the placement of the various experiments on the lunar surface. The thick lines indicate paths taken by the astronauts during their two EVAs. The letters correspond to specific tasks undertaken at various points on the lunar surface.

This traverse map of the Apollo 15 landing site shows the tracks of each of the three EVAs. The Lunar Roving Vehicle was used to reach the margin of Hadley Rille, a long valley feature located west of the landing site. Numbers indicate locations of stops made during EVA activity.

the astronauts manually deployed the vehicle and could operate it for as much as 78 hours, with a cumulative distance of 35 nautical miles.

In a standup EVA and three full EVAs that followed, the Apollo 15 astronauts spent 18 hours, 34 minutes, and 46 seconds outside the spacecraft. They traveled in the lunar rover about 15.1 n mi (27.9 km), and collected 170.44 pounds (77.31 kg) of samples. The farthest point traveled from the LM was 16,470 feet.

The Apollo 15 mission was the most extensive yet, and it demonstrated the technology of the "J" missions as well as the ability of the astronauts and scientists on the ground to interact to maximize scientific results.

Furthermore, Apollo 15 demonstrated that the crew could operate to a greater degree as scientific observers and investigators and rely more on the ground support team for systems monitoring.

This image from Apollo 15 astronaut James Irwin during EVA-2 shows the Rover, the LM, and the Swann Range in the background. The lunar Apennines are the mountains that form the southeastern rim of the Imbrium Basin, extending northeast from Crater Eratosthenes to just beyond Mt. Hadley. The Swann Range was named for Apollo 15 Geology Team Leader Gordon Swann and comprises the mountains that form the eastern boundary of the landing site south of Mt. Hadley.

Astronaut James B. Irwin, Lunar Module pilot, works at the Lunar Roving Vehicle during the first Apollo 15 lunar surface extravehicular activity (EVA-1) at the Hadley-Apennine landing site. The shadow of the Lunar Module "Falcon" is in the foreground. This view is looking northeast, with Mt. Hadley in the background. This photograph was taken by Astronaut David R. Scott, Mission Commander.

Reaping a Harvest of Knowledge: Apollos 16 and 17

Apollo 16 landed on the Moon's Plain of Descartes on April 27, 1972, the second of the extended "J" missions to the lunar surface. During the first extravehicular activity (EVA), the crew of John Young, Mission Commander, and Charles Duke, Lunar Module Pilot, successfully deployed the Apollo Lunar Surface Experiments Package (ALSEP), but in the process Young accidentally tripped over and broke an electronics cable, rendering a heat flow experiment inoperative. T. K. Mattingly remained in lunar orbit with the command module during the landing. After completing deployments at the experiments site, the crew drove the Lunar Roving Vehicle (LRV) west to Flag Crater where they made visual observations, photographed items of interest, and collected lunar samples. The first extravehicular activity lasted 7 hours, 11 minutes, and 2 seconds, traveling a distance of 2.3 n mi (4.2 km).

Whereas in the first EVA the crew traveled westward, during their second EVA they headed south-southeast to a mare sampling area near the Cinco Craters on the north slope of Stone Mountain. They then drove in a northwesterly direction, making stops near Stubby and Wreck Craters. The last leg of the traverse went back north to the experiments station and the LM. That second EVA lasted 7 hours, 23 minutes, and 9 seconds and covered a distance of 6.1 n mi (11.3 km).

A final EVA by the crew found them traveling to the rim of North Ray Crater where they took photographs and gathered samples, some from House Rock, the largest single rock seen during their surface activities. They then drove southeast to a second sampling area, Shadow Rock. On completing activities there, the crew drove the vehicle back to the LM, retracing the outbound route. The third EVA lasted 5 hours, 40 minutes, and 3 seconds, and traveled 6.2 n mi (11.4 km).

Overall, the Apollo 16 crew spent 20 hours, 14 minutes, and 14 seconds on the lunar surface. They traveled a total distance of 14.5 n mi (26.9 km), operating the vehicle for 3 hours and 26 minutes. They collected lunar samples totaling 211.00 pounds (95.71 kg). The crew safely returned to Earth on April 27, 1972.

The last of the Apollo Moon landings, Apollo 17, proved to be one of the most propitious of all of them. For one, it included as a crew member the only academically credentialed geologist, Harrison H. Schmitt, to fly as an astronaut. Schmitt is the only geologist ever to undertake field work on the Moon, or any other body of the Solar System. The mission also proved uniquely productive, as the crew explored areas far removed from the landing site and with results that proved critical to establishing the origins of the Moon.

Launched on December 7, 1972, the crew of Apollo 17, Eugene Cernan and Harrison Schmitt, reached the lunar surface on December 11, 1972, while Ronald Evans remained in orbit with the Command Module. Their landing site was in a seven-mile-wide valley in the Taurus Mountains at the outer, southeastern rim of the Mare Serenitatis. A specific target was the Littrow Crater, located 17 miles north of the selected landing spot. Scientists chose this landing area because they had discovered a recent landslide there and believed that this would bring lunar material from the heights of the nearby Taurus Mountains close. It also had apparent volcanic activity and the promise of learning about the evolution of the Moon from these activities was enticing.

Cernan and Schmitt undertook their first EVA by completing ceremonial activities of planting the U.S. flag, in this case one that had hung in the Mission Control Center since Apollo 11, and photographing the obligatory salute. They also deployed the Advanced Lunar Science Experiment Package (ALSEP); this was a more capable version of the ALSEP than used in previous Apollo missions. They then unfurled the LRV and drove south to Steno Crater. During this EVA a wheel fender extension came off and lunar dust showered the

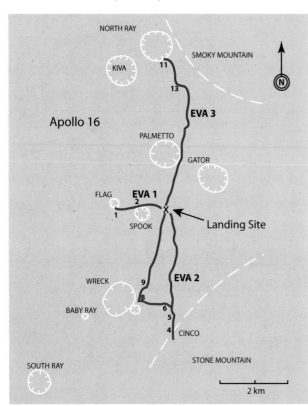

This map shows EVAs during Apollo 16 surface activity. Numbers indicate locations where astronauts stopped for sample collection or photography.

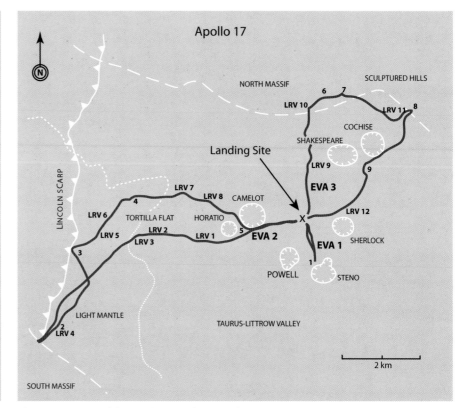

This traverse map of the Apollo 17 landing site documents the route taken by the astronauts during their three EVAs, as well as the placement of the various experiments on the lunar surface. The thick lines indicate paths taken by the astronauts during their EVAs. On their second EVA, astronauts reached Lincoln Scarp, a topographic feature to the west.

crew and the LRV. They also traveled to deploy a surface electrical properties experiment and a seismic profiling explosive charge. They intended to explode these charges and measure the shock waves with the Seismic Profiler, thereby determining the depth and composition of the valley floor. While driving south toward Steno Crater the astronauts realized that they were unable to pinpoint their position. Visual distances were difficult to discern because of the strange lighting and the lack of surface features that could be identified and approximate sizes understood. This was something earlier crews had experienced, but the far-ranging Apollo 17 mission compounded the problem.

At the start of the second EVA the astronauts repaired the fender on the LRV with a rig of four maps, taped together and held in position by two clamps from portable utility lights. The astronauts later remarked this made an excellent substitute for the extension. During their travels the crew deployed three explosive packages for the seismic profiling experiment, made seven traverse gravimeter measurements, gathered numerous samples, and completed their panoramic photographic tasks. The trip to the South Massif, five miles distant, was the longest

journey away from the LM undertaken by any Apollo crew. In this trip they found the oldest rock of any collected on the lunar surface, dating from 4.5 billion years ago. On the way back they discovered a yellow-colored material, which proved to be of volcanic origin, at Shorty Crater. This coloring implied that the soil had been oxidized by volcanism. Scientists later found that the material was the result of very early volcanic action contemporary with lava flows that had formed the valley floor. Meteor impacts had later turned the valley floor and exposed the "yellow" substrata.

During a third EVA the Apollo 17 crew undertook additional sampling objectives, finished nine traverse gravimeter measurements, and completed additional panoramic and other photography. They returned to the LM for the last time after an EVA of 7 hours, 15 minutes, and 8 seconds. Overall, astronauts Cernan and Schmitt had spent 22 hours, 3 minutes, and 57 seconds in three EVAs. They had traveled a total distance in the lunar rover vehicle of 19.3 n mi (35.7 km). They collected samples totaling 243.65 pounds (110.52 kg). It was an auspicious ending to the Apollo program, with scientific analyses to follow for decades thereafter.

Astronaut John W. Young, commander of the Apollo 16 lunar landing mission, jumps up from the lunar surface as he salutes the U.S. Flag at the Descartes landing site during the first Apollo 16 extravehicular activity (EVA-1). Astronaut Charles M. Duke Jr., lunar module pilot, took this picture. The Lunar Module (LM) "Orion" is on the left. The Lunar Roving Vehicle is parked beside the LM. The object behind Young in the shade of the LM is the Far Ultraviolet Camera/Spectrograph built by George Carruthers. Stone Mountain dominates the background in this lunar scene.

This extraordinary lunar panorama shows Apollo 17 astronaut-geologist Harrison (Jack) Schmitt at Station 4 (Shorty Crater) with the Lunar Roving Vehicle (LRV) during the crew's second extravehicular activity (EVA-2) at the Taurus-Littrow landing site. Shorty Crater is to the right. The peak in the center background is Family Mountain. A portion of South Massif is on the horizon at the left edge.

Post-Apollo Lunar Exploration

At the end of the space race of the 1960s and early 1970s between the United States and the Soviet Union, both nations abandoned their efforts to explore the Moon. The Americans ceased with the flight of Apollo 17 in December 1972 and the Soviets with the return of Luna 24 in August 1976.

Scientists worldwide shared data and samples from both nations' missions, comparing results and geological details. Data from these explorations led to the rise of a consensus on the origins of the Moon. Indeed, if there is one dramatic moment—as opposed to myriad important but mundane events—in the history of lunar science it is the 1984 conference in Kona, Hawaii, in which scientists around the world presented papers on the sole topic of how the Moon originated. So contentious had the question of lunar origins been prior to the American and Soviet Moon exploration efforts that many scientists just threw up their hands in frustration at ever being able to develop a reasonable hypothesis. Confusion ruled among scientists about the Moon's origin as competing schools battled among themselves for dominance

of their particular viewpoint in the textbooks. Indeed, some expressed concern that determining the Moon's origins should be the single most significant scientific objective of Project Apollo, thinking of it as a hopeless objective.

Their concern was legitimate based on what had gone before. Prior to the 1960s the origin of the Moon had been a subject of considerable scientific debate and careers had risen and fallen on championing one of three principal theories:

1. Co-accretion—a theory that the Moon and the Earth formed at the same time from the Solar Nebula.
2. Fission—a theory that the Moon split off from the Earth.
3. Capture—a theory that the Moon formed elsewhere and was subsequently drawn into orbit around the Earth.

The data supporting these various theories had been developed to an amazingly fine point over time but none of these theories actually answered enough open questions to convince a majority of planetary scientists.

The new and detailed information from the Moon explorations pointed toward an impact theory—which suggested that the Earth had collided with a very large object (as big as Mars and named "Theia")—and that the Moon had formed from the ejected material. This proved to be a theory that fit the fact that although the Earth has a large iron core the Moon does not, because the debris blown out of both the Earth and the impactor would have come from iron-depleted, rocky mantles. Also lending credence to this theory, although the Earth has a mean density of 5.5 grams/cubic centimeter the Moon's density is only 3.3 g/cc, which would be the case were it to lack iron, as it does. The Moon has exactly the same oxygen isotope composition as the Earth, whereas Mars rocks and meteorites from other parts of the Solar System have different oxygen isotope compositions. While there were some details to this theory that remained to be worked out, the impact theory came out as the scientific consensus and is now widely accepted.

This seemed to settle the most contentious of the outstanding scientific debates about the Moon, that is until 1994 when a new mission suggested the possibilities of ice buried deep in craters on the lunar south pole. It came as a result of the United States's return to the Moon for the first time since Apollo. Clementine was a joint robotic mission to the Moon flown in 1994 by the Department of Defense's (DOD) Strategic Defense Initiative Organization and NASA. Its objective was to test sensors and spacecraft components under extended exposure to the space environment and to make scientific observations of the Moon. The observations included imaging at various wavelengths, including ultraviolet and infrared, laser ranging altimetry, and charged particle measurements.

Operated on a shoestring budget, the Clementine spacecraft was launched on January 25, 1994, from the West Coast launch complex at Vandenburg Air Force Base, and achieved lunar insertion on February 21. Lunar mapping took approximately two months, but as the mission was beginning a new phase in May 1994, the spacecraft malfunctioned. In spite of this, Clementine mapped more than 90% of the lunar surface. The late 1996 revelation from scientists that data returned by Clementine suggested that ice existed from an asteroid crash at the Moon's Shackleton Crater at the South Pole reenergized lunar science. The temperature there never rises above about −170 degrees C, and any ice there could remain frozen for extremely long periods of time.

Excitement over this discovery spurred the team developing Lunar Prospector, a small, spin-

This map shows post-Apollo orbital tracks. The polar orbits allowed these spacecraft to observe most of the lunar surface.

stabilized craft that would "prospect" the lunar crust and atmosphere for minerals, water ice, and certain gases; map the Moon's gravitational and magnetic fields; and learn more about the size and content of the Moon's core. Launched on January 6, 1998, Lunar Prospector began its short-term mission to globally map the Moon.

Lunar Prospector's most significant discovery, announced on March 5, 1998, was confirmation that somewhere between 10 to 300 million tons of water ice may be scattered inside the craters of the lunar poles. Not only was ice found—as expected—in the Aitken Basin of the lunar South Pole, but also in the craters of the North. To many scientists' surprise, Lunar Prospector detected nearly 50% more water ice in the North than in the South. From these data, mission scientists also inferred that the ice crystals must be dispersed over a large surface area: 5,000 to 20,000 square kilometers at the South Pole and 10,000 to 50,000 square kilometers at the North Pole. Based on these data, some lunar scientists have estimated that the total quantity of water ice may be close to one cubic kilometer. To help determine how much, in July 1999, at the end of its mission, NASA deliberately crashed Lunar Prospector into a crater near the Moon's South Pole, in the hope that detectable quantities of water would be liberated. Spectroscopic observations from ground-based telescopes did not reveal anything.

Should it prove true, the discovery of ice on the Moon portends enormous consequences. From ice, humans could create water, oxygen, and hydrogen. The latter could be used to produce rocket fuel and generate electricity. Solar rays would provide an additional source of energy for the half-month that the Sun faces that section of the Moon. If it proves out, this finding makes human research stations on the Moon more possible than ever before.

There are some scientists, among them geologist Bruce Campbell of the National Air and Space Museum's Center for Earth and Planetary Studies, who question that the data from Clementine and Lunar Prospector should be interpreted as evidence of lunar ice. Observations from the Arecibo radar observatory in Puerto Rico in 2006 suggest that the purported evidence of lunar ice may actually be a false positive associated with rocks containing hydrogen ejected from young craters. If true, this does not prohibit the possibility that there might be water ice in permanently shadowed craters, but it calls into question the evidence thus far supporting that conclusion.

The Lunar Reconnaissance Orbiter (LRO), set to launch in 2009, is specifically designed to help resolve this debate. It has an impactor aboard, LCROSS (Lunar Crater Observation and Sensing Satellite), that will directly impact one of the permanently shadowed regions near the Moon's pole to create a crater, throwing tons of debris and potentially water ice and vapor above the lunar surface. As it does so, the LRO will fly through taking measurements of hydrated minerals which would tell researchers if there is water or not.

At the same time, the Japanese Space Exploration Agency (JAXA) has undertaken the Kaguya mission, an orbiter at 62 miles (100 km) altitude and two small satellites (Relay Satellite and VRAD Satellite) in polar orbit. Launched on September 14, 2007, from the Tanegashima Space Center in Japan, its mission is to explore the evolution of the Moon. Scientific instruments will undertake a global map of the lunar surface, magnetic field measurements, and gravity field measurement.

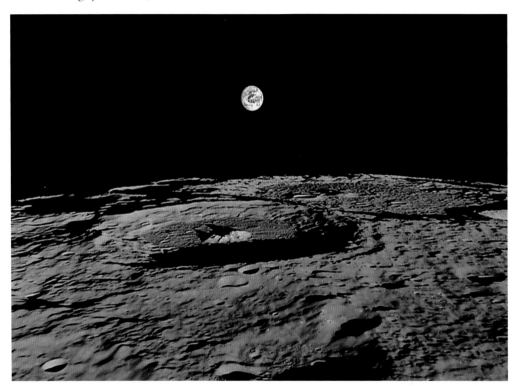

This image from the Japanese lunar probe Kaguya taken on November 19, 2007, shows the Earth in the background.

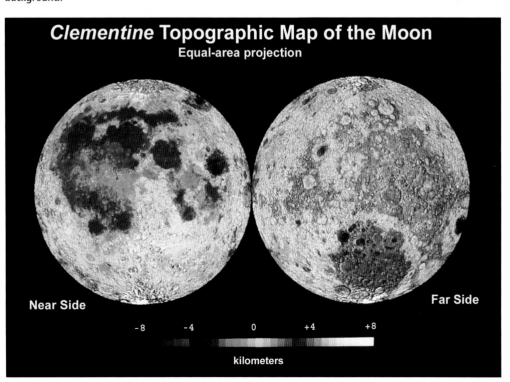

This Clementine topographic map of the Moon, showing both near and far side, was compiled from more than 5,000 images taken during the Clementine mission in 1994. It shows laser altimetry (red = high; purple = low). Most of the near side is low, while the far side is high and mountainous. Note also the large (2,500-km-diameter) South Pole-Aitken basin that can be readily seen on the far side of the Moon.

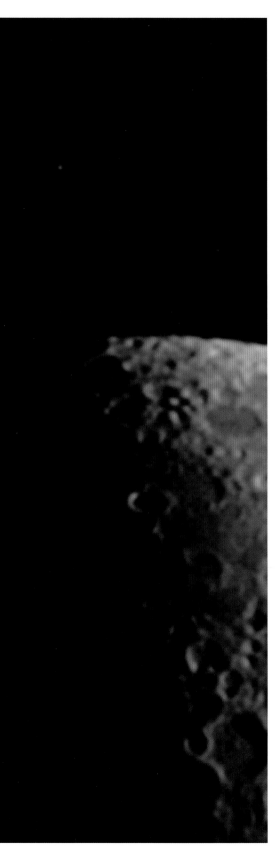

part six
OTHER TERRESTRIAL WORLDS

During the 1960s, both the United States and the Soviet Union began an impressive effort to gather information about the planets of the inner Solar System by using a combination of ground-, air-, and space-based instruments. Especially important was the creation of two types of spacecraft: one a probe that was sent toward another body in the Solar System, and the second an Earth-orbiting observatory that could gain the clearest resolution available in telescopes because it did not have to contend with the atmosphere. Once again, the compilation of these new data revolutionized human understanding of Earth's immediate planetary neighbors. Although the most significant findings of this investigation would not come until the 1970s, studies of the planets captured the imagination of people from all backgrounds like nothing else except the Apollo lunar missions. For all the genuine importance of magnetospheric physics and solar studies, it was photographs of the planets and theories about the origins of the Solar System that appealed to a broad cross-section of the public. As a result, NASA had little difficulty in capturing and holding a widespread interest in this aspect of the space science program.

The National Aeronautics and Space Administration (NASA), as well as other organizations elsewhere in the world, have aggressively pursued knowledge about the inner Solar System—the four terrestrial planets of Mercury, Venus, Earth, and Mars—through a succession of flight projects that enabled spacecraft to visit each since the beginning of the space age. Through this process of planetary exploration knowledge about the origins and evolution of the Solar System, as well as the myriad attributes of the bodies making it up, has expanded enormously.

Without question, the Solar System exploration program has become the stuff of legend and myth in some measure because of its rich harvest of knowledge about Earth's neighboring planets, a transformation of our understanding of the Solar System's origin and evolution, and a demonstration of what might be accomplished using limited resources when focusing on scientific goals rather than large human spaceflight programs aimed at buttressing American prestige.

This effort did not take place by magic. It required considerable effort. The foundation for this was laid in the 1950s, when space science first became a major field of study. During the decade of the 1960s both the United States and the Soviet Union began an impressive effort to gather information on the planets of the inner Solar System.

While successes in planetary science have been very real all was not rosy with the politics of planetary exploration. In many respects the 1960s proved a training ground for how to envision, develop, and gain approval for planetary science missions. These political realities were played out thereafter. The labyrinth of modern science policy ensures that those engaged in government-funded science must play a savvy game of bureaucratic politics that is at once both insightful and extreme. A variety of strategies arose to succeed at this game. These included keeping individual projects small so as to avoid serious scrutiny, bringing aboard the project as many scientific disciplines as possible to ensure that everyone has a stake in the effort, developing large partnerships with multifaceted research and educational institutions in numerous congressional districts, and creating international coalitions, to name only a few.

Since those first years, robotic exploration of the terrestrial planets have proceeded with numerous missions, especially to Venus and Mars, and yielded treasure in the form of knowledge about the universe. We have both placed spacecraft in orbit around and landed on the terrestrial planets of Venus and Mars. The missions to explore the inner Solar System have stunned all who consider those efforts.

The Clementine lunar probe's Startracker imaged this spectacular shot of the sunrise, planets, and Moon. This color-enhanced image shows, from right to left, the Moon lit by the Earth, the terminator—or boundary between light and dark—into the dark side with the solar corona just rising over the limb, and the bright planets Saturn, Mars, and Mercury. Several dimmer stars may also be seen.

The Inner Solar System

The Solar System consists of the sun and all other objects bound to it by gravity—especially the eight formal planets and their 166 known moons, four dwarf planets, and billions of smaller bodies. Among those smaller bodies are asteroids, icy Kuiper belt objects in the outer Solar System, comets, meteoroids, and interplanetary dust.

The Sun, of course, is the most prominent feature in our Solar System, and the entity containing approximately 98% of the total mass in the system. Over 1.3 million Earths could fit inside the Sun. Every second it releases 5 million tons of pure energy, and as time progresses the Sun becomes lighter. It provides the heat, light, energy, and gravity that maintains the Solar System's integrity.

The Sun has been active for approximately 4.6 billion years, and will continue to burn for about another 5 billion years. Then, with its fuel nearly expended it, will fuse helium into heavier elements and swell up into a red giant, engulfing many other bodies of the Solar System including the Earth. At the end of its life it will collapse into a tiny white dwarf star, burning the last of its fuel.

The territory closest to the Sun, the inner Solar System, is dominated by the so-called terrestrial planets—Mercury, Venus, Earth, and Mars as well as the asteroid belt. Rocky bodies all, these planets are composed of silicates and metals. They cluster close to their star with a radius between the Sun and Mars less than the distance between Jupiter and Saturn. These four terrestrial planets have dense, rocky compositions, no ring systems, and few moons. They possess crusts and mantles, with cores of metals such as iron and nickel. The planets Venus, Earth, and Mars have significant atmospheres, but Mercury has virtually none. In part because of this, these are the places where most believe life might exist, or once existed, in the Solar System.

The orbits of the terrestrial planets are ellipses with the Sun at one focus, and all except Mercury are very nearly circular. Most of the Solar System's large bodies orbit the sun on a plane close to that of the Earth's orbit, called an ecliptic orbit because of its close relation to Earth's orbital plane. Any ecliptic orbit is inclined 7 degrees or less from the plane of the Sun's equator. While the planets have apogees and perigees of relative consistency, comets, asteroids, and Kuiper belt objects are often at significantly greater angles. All of these objects orbit in the same direction (counterclockwise from above the Sun's north pole).

This artist's conception shows a system where a rocky Earth-like planet might be formed. The brown ring of material circling closest to the central star depicts a huge belt of dusty material, more than 100 times as much as in our asteroid belt, or enough to build a Mars-size planet or larger. The rocky material in the belt represents the early stages of planet formation, when dust grains clump together to form rocks, and rocks collide to form even more massive rocky bodies called planetesimals. The belt is located in the middle of the system's terrestrial habitable zone, or the region around a star where liquid water could exist on any rocky planets that might form. Earth is located in the middle of our Sun's terrestrial habitable zone.

This illustration shows the relative sizes of the terrestrial planets and Earth's Moon. Earth and Venus, almost the same size, appear in the upper left and right. The surface of Venus is shown here using radar data from the Magellan mission. Mars is in the lower row in the center and Mercury in the lower right. The Moon appears below the Earth in the lower left. Terrestrial planetary bodies all share a metallic and rocky composition. Evidence for an active molten interior has only been found for the Earth, but signs of volcanic activity can be found on all of these bodies.

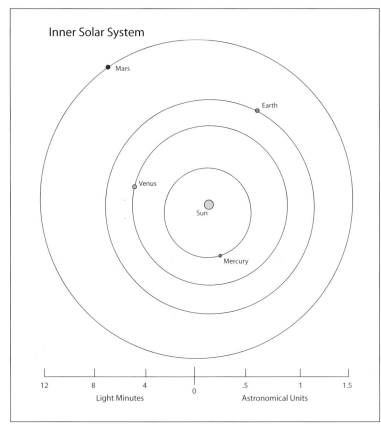

This illustration depicts the orbits of the terrestrial planets of the inner Solar System.

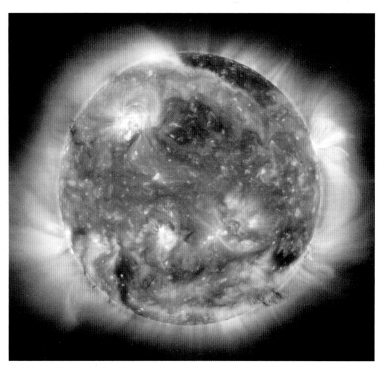

At the center of the Solar System is our Sun, the dominant astronomical object in our sky. This composite image of May 1998 from the Solar and Heliospheric Observatory (SOHO) spacecraft combines images from three wavelengths (171, 195 and 284 angstrom) into one that reveals solar features unique to each wavelength. Since the EIT images come to us from the spacecraft in black and white, they are color coded for easy identification and merged into a single photograph.

The Geology of Mars

How did Mars become the planet we see today? Why is Mars the dry, lifeless place humans have found? Where did the processes that shaped the surface of Mars originate? What accounts for the differences and similarities between Earth and Mars? These questions, and others, may be considered through the science of geology as applied to the red planet. In essence, geology is the science of investigating and understanding the relative roles of wind, water, volcanism, tectonics, magnetism, cratering, cataclysmic events, and other processes that have interacted over eons to form and transform the Martian surface.

The Martian surface consists mostly of sand and rock, and is dominated by a cold, dry desert landscape. While many features on the planet's surface, especially volcanoes, canyons, and valleys, look remarkably like desolate regions on Earth, the appearance is misleading. First, the atmosphere is very thin, with mean surface level pressure of 600 Pa (0.6 kPa), compared to Earth's 101.3 kPa. What atmosphere is present on Mars consists of 95% carbon dioxide, 3% nitrogen, and 1.6% argon, with traces of oxygen, water, and methane also present. With this low pressure, water on the surface of Mars would instantly vaporize. The possibility that Mars was once a watery planet now motivates much scientific thought about the planet. The Martian surface is littered with features that appear to have been eroded by liquid water, but why the planet lost it is a puzzle planetary scientists are investigating. Large amounts of water would have required a much thicker atmosphere. But where did all that air and water go? Evidence suggests that much of the Martian atmosphere was blown away millions of years ago by the solar wind. This is a question still to be resolved. In part because of this the average surface temperature is –63 degrees C (–81 degrees F), and nighttime temperatures on Mars can plunge to –110 degrees C (–170 degrees F). By comparison, the lowest temperature ever recorded on Earth was –89 degrees C (–130 degrees F) at Vostok, Antarctica, in July 1983.

Second, the planet is much smaller than Earth and has a far less strong gravitational field. The gravitational constant on Mars is .08 of Earth, and something weighing 100 pounds on Earth would only weigh 40 pounds on Mars. Indeed, the planet is one of the tiniest planets in the Solar System, similar in size to Mercury, with a diameter of 4,217 miles (6,786 km). For comparison, it is only about half the size of Earth. Its daily rotation is similar to Earth's at 24 hours, 37 min, but it has an orbit of 687 Earth days around the sun because it has a distance from the sun of 142 million miles (228 million km).

The forces that have affected the planet Mars are many and varied. It is the home to incredi-

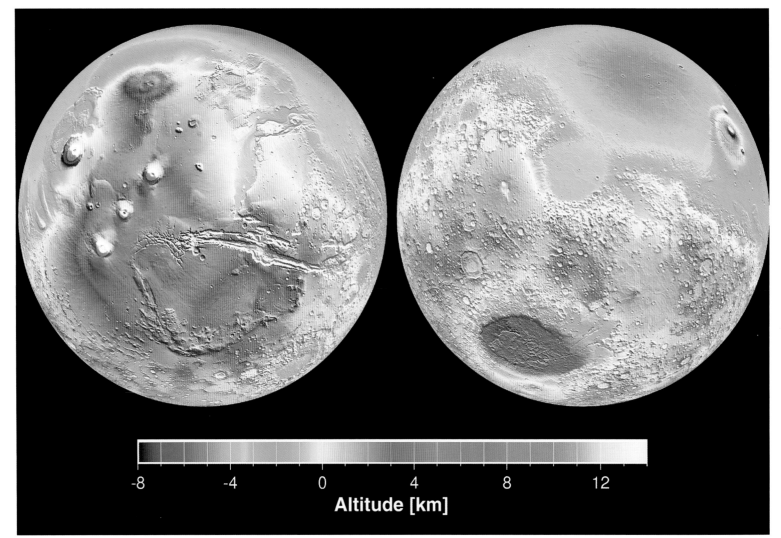

These maps are global false-color topographic views of Mars at different orientations from the Mars Orbiter Laser Altimeter (MOLA). The right-hand image features the Hellas impact basin (in purple, with red annulus of high standing material). The left hand features the Tharsis topographic rise (in red and white). Note also the subtle textures associated with the resurfacing of the northern hemisphere lowlands.

This mosaic of Mars is composed of 104 Viking Orbiter images acquired in February 1980. At that time, it was early northern summer on Mars. The center of the image is at latitude 3 degrees, longitude 185 degrees. A major geologic boundary extends across this mosaic, with the lower third of the image showing ancient cratered highlands; north of this boundary are the lowland northern plains. Other prominent features in this image include the large dark area left of the image center (named Cerberus), and the Elysium volcanic region. Thin white clouds are dispersed over the northern hemisphere, and the opaque cloud in the upper right overlies the Olympus Mons Aureole. The arcuate markings west of the Aureole are thought to be extended drift of windblown material.

This mosaic of Mars shows the planet at a distance of 2,500 kilometers. The mosaic is composed of 102 Viking Orbiter images of Mars. The center of the scene (lat -8, long 78) shows the entire Valles Marineris canyon system, over 2,000 kilometers long and up to 8 kilometers deep, extending form Noctis Labyrinthus, the arcuate system of graben to the west, to the chaotic terrain to the east. Many huge ancient river channels begin from the chaotic terrain from north-central canyons and run north. The three Tharsis volcanoes (dark red spots), each about 25 kilometers high, are visible to the west. South of Valles Marineris is very ancient terrain covered by many impact craters.

ble volcanoes, as much as 100 times larger than those on Earth. In part this is because of the lower gravity of the planet, enabling the total volume of lava to pile up into one, very large volcano on the surface.

Consequently, there are huge uplifts or domes on the planet, especially in the Tharsis and Elysium regions of Mars. The Tharsis dome is 2,500 miles (4,000 km) across and rises to 6.2 miles (10 km) in height. Located on its northwest flank are three large shield volcanoes: Ascraeus Mons, Pavonis Mons, and Arsia Mons. Beyond the dome's northwest edge is Olympus Mons, the largest volcano in the Solar System, some 15 miles (24 km) high and 340 miles (550 km) in diameter. As a comparison, the largest volcano on Earth is Mauna Loa, a paltry 6 miles (9 km) high. Elysium Planitia

is the second largest volcanic region on Mars, with a broad dome that is 1,060 by 1,490 miles (1,700 by 2,400 km) in size.

While the magnetic field of Mars is virtually nonexistent at present, in the planet's ancient past there was a magnetic field much like Earth possesses today. Because magnetic fields in general act to shield planets from many forms of cosmic radiation, this discovery has important implications for the prospects for finding evidence of past life on the Martian surface. Study of the ancient magnetic field also provides important information about the interior structure, temperature, and composition of Mars in the past. The presence of magnetic fields also suggests that Mars was once more of a dynamic Earth-like planet than it is today.

Numerous missions to Mars have been

completed since the beginning of the space age. Scientists are pursing knowledge about the origins, age, composition, and possibility of life on the planet by examining remotely the different types of rocks and formations. Geologists use these studies to determine the sequence of events in a planet's history. Composition information tells them what happened over time. Particularly important is the identification of rocks and minerals formed in the presence of water. Water is one of the keys to whether life might have started on Mars. Critical to this process are Mars meteorites discovered on Earth that help give clues about the planet.

Early Missions to Mars

Robotic exploration of Mars has been one of the persistent efforts of the space age. It began, just as lunar exploration had, in a race between the United States and the Soviet Union to see who would be the first to place some sort of spacecraft near Mars. After four unsuccessful launches of what were believed to be Mars probes in 1960 and 1962, the Soviets successfully flew a spacecraft within 120,000 miles of Mars on June 19, 1964. Unfortunately, a communications failure several months before the flyby prevented the spacecraft from sending any data to Earth. The Americans were more successful.

This endeavor was not just an opportunity to best the rival in the Cold War: scientists in both the United States and the Soviet Union recognized the attraction of Mars for the furtherance of planetary studies. Smaller than Earth, but observed by astronomers for centuries and seen to have what appeared as climate changes on its surfaces, Mars had long been viewed as an abode of life. These observations brought myriad speculations about the nature of Mars and the possibility of life existing there in some form.

Of the two U.S. spacecraft launched to Mars in 1964, only one successfully found its way to its intended target. On July 15, 1965, Mariner 4 flew within 6,118 miles of Mars. The spacecraft returned 21 close-up photographs that showed lunar-style craters on the surface. Data returned also included measurements of the planet's ionosphere and atmosphere, as well as surface temperature readings. These photographs dashed the hopes of many that life might be present on Mars, for the first close-up images showed a cratered, lunarlike surface. They depicted a planet without structures and canals, nothing that even remotely resembled a pattern that intelligent life might produce.

Mariner 6 and Mariner 7, launched in February and March 1969, each passed Mars in August 1969, studying its atmosphere and surface to lay the groundwork for an eventual landing on the planet. Their pictures verified the Moon-like appearance of Mars and gave no hint that Mars had ever been able to support

Dr. William H. Pickering (left), Director of NASA's Jet Propulsion Laboratory, presents Mariner spacecraft photos to President Lyndon B. Johnson in July 1965. The presence of craters on the Martian surface dashed many scientists' hopes of finding a planet conducive to life.

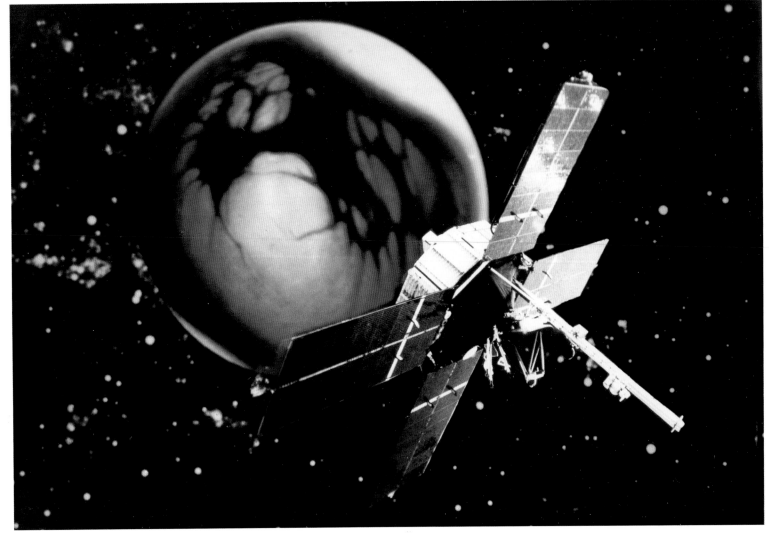

This image of Mariner 4 superimposed on an image of Mars was used to advertise the 1965 mission.

life. Among other discoveries from these probes, they found that volcanoes had once been active on the planet, that the frost observed seasonally on the poles was made of carbon dioxide, and that huge plates indicated considerable tectonic activity in the planet's history. There was still hope, however, that we might yet find signs of life. NASA administrator James C. Fletcher, for example, commented on this possibility in 1975: "It is hard to imagine anything more important than making contact with another intelligent race. It could be the most significant achievement of this millennium, perhaps the key to our survival as a species."

Between 1965 and 1969, NASA sent three Mariner probes on initial investigations of Mars. All of these were flyby missions that returned important scientific data about the planet:

- Mariner 4 - USA Mars Flyby - 260 kg - (28 November 1964 - 20 December 1967): Mariner 4 arrived at Mars on 14 July 1965 and passed within 6,118 miles of the planet's surface after an eight-month journey. This mission provided the first close-up images of the red planet. It returned 22 close-up photos showing a cratered surface. The thin atmosphere was confirmed to be composed

of carbon dioxide in the range of 5–10 mbar. A small intrinsic magnetic field was detected. Mariner 4 is now in a solar orbit. (Successful)

- Mariner 6 - USA Mars Flyby - 412 kg - (24 February 1969): Mariner 6 arrived at Mars on 24 February 1969, and passed within 3,437 kilometers of the planet's equatorial region. Mariner 6 and 7 took measurements of the surface and atmospheric temperature, surface molecular composition, and pressure of the atmosphere. In addition, over 200 pictures were taken. Mariner 6 is now in a solar orbit. (Successful)

- Mariner 7 - USA Mars Flyby - 412 kg - (27 March 1969): Mariner 7 arrived at Mars on 5 August 1969, and passed within 3,551 kilometers of the planet's south pole region. Mariner 6 and 7 took measurements of the surface and atmospheric temperature, surface molecular composition, and pressure of the atmosphere. In addition, over 200 pictures were taken. Mariner 7 is now in a solar orbit. (Successful)

In addition there were several unsuccessful missions that attempted to fly by Mars in the early era:

- Mars 1960A - USSR Mars Probe - (10 October 1960): Failed to reach Earth orbit. (Unsuccessful)
- Mars 1960B - USSR Mars Probe - (14 October 1960): Failed to reach Earth orbit. (Unsuccessful)
- Mars 1962A - USSR Mars Flyby - (24 October 1962): Spacecraft failed to leave Earth orbit after the final rocket stage exploded. (Unsuccessful)
- Mars 1 - USSR Mars Flyby - 893 kg - (1 November 1962): Communications failed en route. (Unsuccessful)
- Mars 1962B - USSR Mars lander - (4 November 1962): Failed to leave Earth orbit. (Unsuccessful)
- Mariner 3 - USA Mars Flyby - 260 kg - (5 November 1964): Mars flyby attempt. Solar panels did not open, preventing flyby. Mariner 3 is now in a solar orbit. (Unsuccessful)
- Zond 2 - USSR Mars Flyby - (30 November 1964): Contact was lost en route. (Unsuccessful)
- Mariner 8 - USA Mars Flyby - (8 May 1971): Failed to reach Earth orbit. (Unsuccessful)
- Kosmos 419 - USSR Mars Probe - (10 May 1971): Failed to leave Earth orbit. (Unsuccessful)

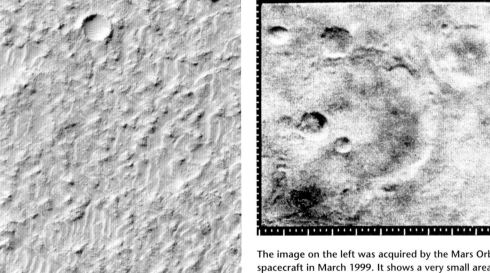

This Mariner 4 image shows the 96-mile-diameter Mariner crater at 35 S, 164 W, on Mars. Running from the lower left corner of the frame through the bottom of the crater is a linear ridge which is part of Sirenum Fossae. The image was taken from 12,600 km and covers 250 km by 254 km. North is up. Mariner 4 was the first spacecraft to get a close look at Mars. Flying as close as 9,846 kilometers (6,118 miles), Mariner 4 revealed Mars to have a cratered, rust-colored surface, with signs on some parts of the planet that liquid water had once etched its way into the soil. Mariner 4 was launched on November 28, 1964, and arrived at Mars on July 14, 1965. After completing its mission, Mariner 4 continued past Mars to the far side of the Sun.

The image on the left was acquired by the Mars Orbiter Camera (MOC) on the Mars Global Surveyor spacecraft in March 1999. It shows a very small area within the crater seen in the Mariner 4 image above. While detail is limited in Mariner 4 images, features as small as about 10 feet are visible in the MOC image. This crater was named "Mariner" in 1967 to recognize its discovery by Mariner 4.

Orbiting Mars

The United States, the Soviet Union/Russia, Japan, and the European Space Agency have each sent orbiters to Mars since the 1970s. The Soviet Union achieved partial successes early on with its Mars 2 and 3 in 1971, by inserting orbiters into Martian orbit. This was following in the later part of the year with Mariner 9 from the United States. Mariner 9, entering Martian orbit in November 1971, detected a chilling dust storm spreading across Mars; by mid-October dust obscured almost all of Mars. Mariner 9's first pictures showed a featureless disk, marred only by a group of black spots in a region known as Nix Olympia (Snows of Olympus). As the dust storm subsided, however, the spots emerged from the dust cloud to become recognizable as the remains of giant extinct volcanoes dwarfing anything on the Earth.

The discovery of Mons Olympus by Mariner 9 was a stunning result of the mission. It dwarfed anything on Earth and in time scientists would discover it to be the largest in the Solar System. It is 300 miles across at the base with a crater in the top 45 miles wide. Rising 20 miles from the surrounding plane, Mons Olympus is three times the height of Mt. Everest. In addition, other pictures showed a canyon, Valles Marineris, 2,500 miles long and 3.5 miles deep. Later, as the dust settled, meandering "rivers" appeared indicating that, at some time in the past, fluid had flowed on Mars. Suddenly, Mars fascinated scientists, reporters, and the public.

The most exciting discovery on Mars is the now well accepted consensus that it was once a watery planet that held the building blocks of life. Mars remains an inviting target, however, all the more so because of extraordinary findings from Mars Global Surveyor, which has been orbiting and mapping the Martian surface since March 1998. It imaged gullies on Martian cliffs and crater walls, suggesting that liquid water has seeped onto the surface in the geologically recent past. This was confirmed by Mars Odyssey 2001, another NASA orbiter, which found that hydrogen-rich regions are located in areas known to be very cold and where ice should be stable. This relationship between high hydrogen content with regions of predicted ice stability led scientists to conclude that the hydrogen is, in fact, in the form of ice. The ice-rich layer is about two feet beneath the surface at 60 degrees south latitude, and gets to within about one foot of the surface at 75 degrees south latitude. This evidence suggests that the planet was once significantly more habitable than it is today. Of course, it remains unknown if living creatures ever existed there. Only time and more research will tell if these findings will prove out. If they do, then human opportunities for colonization of Mars expand exponentially. With water, either in its liquid or solid form, humans might be able to make many other necessary compounds necessary to live and work on Mars.

During the period between 1971 and the present a total of 19 missions have undertaken orbital flights of Mars, some of them with landers attempting to reach the surface. Not all of them were successful, and predictably several of the early orbiters failed. While the prospects have improved over time, Mars has long proven a difficult challenge for robotic spacecraft and as recently as 1999 NASA lost its Mars Climate Orbiter and Mars Polar Lander without receiving any useful scientific data. The following is a synopsis of each of these missions and the results coming from them:

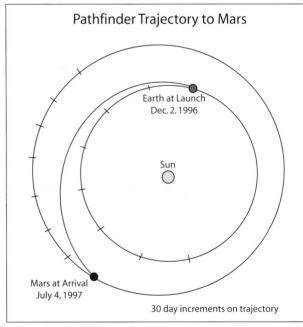

Pathfinder Trajectory to Mars

Earth at Launch
Dec. 2. 1996

Sun

Mars at Arrival
July 4, 1997

30 day increments on trajectory

The trajectory from Earth to Mars is similar for most missions. This diagram shows the trajectory of the Mars Pathfinder mission in 1996–1997. A mission to Mars must leave Earth orbit with added acceleration to move into a solar orbit. This second orbit is calculated to intersect with that of Mars. The two planets must be in the correct relative position for the trajectory to work with minimum amount of thrust required. It is possible to use this type of trajectory about every 26 months.

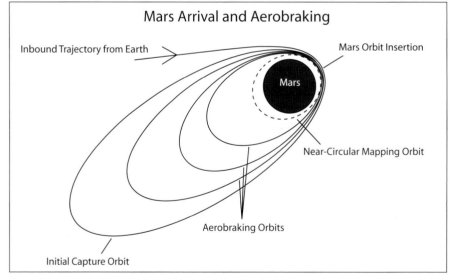

Mars Arrival and Aerobraking

Inbound Trajectory from Earth

Mars Orbit Insertion

Mars

Near-Circular Mapping Orbit

Aerobraking Orbits

Initial Capture Orbit

One of the principal means of reaching an orbit around Mars is aerobraking, a maneuver that reduces the high point of an elliptical orbit by flying the vehicle through the upper part of the atmosphere, thereby using atmospheric drag to slow the spacecraft. This has become the primary method enabling something more than flybys of the red planet. First experimented with during the Magellan mission at Venus, aerobraking is a low-cost procedure for lowering and circularizing an orbit. All the post-Viking missions arrived at Mars by entering elliptical orbits. These orbits require the least amount of thrust to achieve. During the aerobraking phase of a mission, the spacecraft is intentionally "dipped" into the upper reaches of the atmosphere. A small amount of atmospheric drag slows the spacecraft. After many months, a circular orbit can be achieved with the use of very little propellant. Without aerobraking, the spacecraft would have to carry much more fuel and therefore be larger.

During aerobraking the density of the upper atmosphere must be estimated. High levels of solar activity can heat and expand the upper atmosphere, causing more atmospheric drag. Performing this maneuver can be tricky; it is often unknown exactly how long the procedure will take. Aerobraking itself would not be possible without precise navigation that allows a spacecraft to be positioned in the upper edge of the atmosphere without getting too low.

- Kosmos 419 – USSR Mars Probe – (10 May 1971): Failed to leave Earth orbit. (Unsuccessful)
- Mars 2 – USSR Mars Orbiter/Soft Lander – 4,650 kg – (19 May 1971): The Mars 2 lander was released from the orbiter on 27 November 1971. It crash-landed because its breaking rockets failed – no data were returned and the first human artifact was created on Mars. The orbiter returned data until 1972. (Partial Success)
- Mars 3 – USSR Mars Orbiter/Soft Lander – 4,643 kg – (28 May 1971): Mars 3 arrived at Mars on 2 December 1971. The lander was released and became the first successful landing on Mars. It failed after relaying 20 seconds of video data to the orbiter. The Mars 3 orbiter returned data until August 1972. It made measurements of surface temperature and atmospheric composition. (Partial Success)
- Mariner 9 – USA Mars Orbiter – 974 kg – (30 May 1971 – 1972): Mariner 9 arrived at Mars on 3 November 1971 and was placed into orbit on 24 November. This was the first U.S. spacecraft to enter an orbit around a planet other than the Moon. At the time of its arrival a huge dust storm was in progress on the planet. Many of the scientific experiments were delayed until the storm had subsided. The first high-resolution images of the moons Phobos and Deimos were taken. River- and channel-like features were discovered. Mariner 9 is still in Martian orbit. (Successful)
- Mars 4 – USSR Mars Orbiter – 4,650 kg – (21 July 1973): Mars 4 arrived at Mars on February 1974, but failed to go into orbit due to a malfunction of its breaking engine. It flew past the planet within 2,200 kilometers of the surface. It returned some images and data. (Unsuccessful)
- Mars 5 – USSR Mars Orbiter – 4,650 kg – (25 July 1973): Mars 5 entered into orbit around Mars on 12 February 1974. It acquired imaging data for the Mars 6 and 7 missions. (Successful)
- Mars 6 – USSR Mars Orbiter/Soft Lander – 4,650 kg – (5 August 1973): On 12 March 1974, Mars 6 entered into orbit and launched its lander. The lander returned atmospheric descent data, but failed on its way down. (Partial Success)
- Mars 7 – USSR Mars Orbiter/Soft Lander – 4,650 kg – (9 August 1973): On 6 March 1974, Mars 7 failed to go into orbit about Mars and the lander missed the planet. Carrier and lander are now in a solar orbit. (Unsuccessful)
- Viking 1 – USA Mars Orbiter/Lander – 3,399 kg – (20 August 1975 – 7 August 1980): Viking 1 was launched from the Kennedy Space Center, on 20 August 1975, for the trip to Mars and went into orbit about the planet on 19 June 1976. The lander touched down on 20 July 1976 on the western slopes of Chryse Planitia (Golden Plains). The lander conducted experiments to search for Martian micro-organisms. The results of these experiments are still being debated. The lander provided detailed color panoramic views of the Martian terrain. It also monitored the Martian weather. The orbiter mapped the planet's surface. The orbiter weighed 900 kg and the lander 600 kg. The Viking 1 orbiter was deactivated on 7 August 1980, when it ran out of altitude-controlled propellant. Viking 1 lander was accidentally shut down on 13 November 1982, and communication was never regained. Its last transmission reached Earth on 11 November 1982. Controllers at NASA's Jet Propulsion Laboratory tried unsuccess-

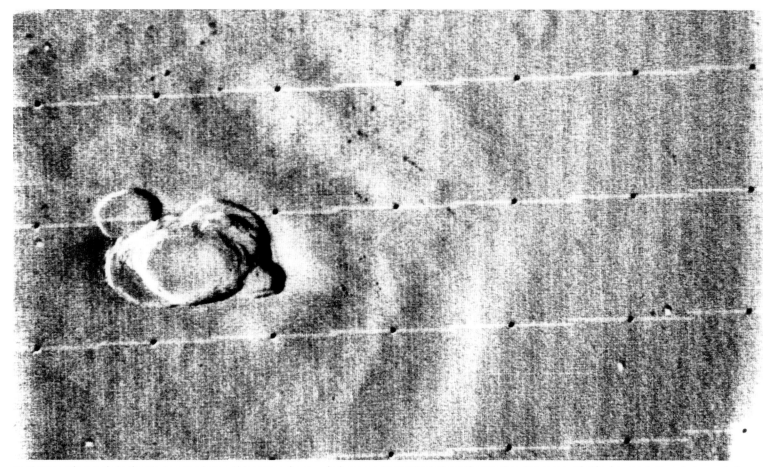

In pictures taken early in the Mariner 9 mission, this region shows a dark mountain standing above the Martian dust storm. This higher resolution photograph shows that the area contains a complex crater, called Olympus Mons (Nix Olympica or Snows of Olympus), nearly 64 kilometers (40 miles) in diameter. The multiple crater form with scalloped margins is characteristic of calderas—volcanic collapse depressions on Earth. In the Mariner 6 and 7 flights in 1969, an outer ring, 1600 kilometers (1,000 miles) in diameter, was seen. It is hidden by the dust in the oblique picture. Earth-based radar observations show that this is a high region on Mars and is usually covered by a white cloud when observed telescopically. This picture was taken on November 27, 1971.

fully for another six and one half months to regain contact with the lander, but finally closed down the overall mission on 21 May 1983. (Successful)

- Viking 2 - USA Mars Orbiter/Lander - 3,399 kg - (9 September 1975 - 25 July 1978): Viking 2 was launched for Mars on 9 November 1975, and landed on 3 September 1976. The Viking project's primary mission ended on 15 November 1976, eleven days before Mars's superior conjunction (its passage behind the Sun), although the Viking spacecraft continued to operate for six years after first reaching Mars. (Successful)

- Phobos 1 - USSR Mars Orbiter/Lander - 5,000 kg - (7 July 1988): Phobos 1 was sent to investigate the Martian moon Phobos. It was lost en route to Mars through a command error on 2 September 1988. (Unsuccessful)

- Mars Observer - USA Mars Orbiter – 2,573 kg - (25 September 1992): Communication was lost with Mars Observer on 21 August 1993, just before it was to be inserted into orbit. (Unsuccessful)

- Mars Global Surveyor - USA Mars Orbiter – 1,062.1 kg - (7 November 1996): The Mars Global Surveyor began America's return to Mars after a 20-year absence by launching this spacecraft. This mission opened a new and exciting era of scientific missions to study the red planet. For more than a year the Surveyor will return an unprecedented amount of data regarding Mars's surface features, atmosphere, and magnetic properties. Scientists will use the data gathered from this mission both to learn about the Earth by comparing it to Mars, and to build a comprehensive data set to aid in planning future missions. (Successful)

- Mars 8 - Russia Orbiter & Lander – 6,200 kg - (16 November 1996): Mars '96 consisted of an orbiter, two landers, and two soil penetrators that were to reach the planet in September 1997. The rocket carrying Mars 96 lifted off successfully, but as it entered orbit the rocket's fourth stage ignited prematurely and sent the probe into a wild tumble. It crashed into the ocean somewhere between the Chilean coast and Easter Island. The spacecraft sank, carrying with it 270 grams of plutonium-238. (Unsuccessful)

- Nozomi (Planet B) – Japan Mars Orbiter – 536 kg - (4 July 1998): Japan's Institute of Space and Astronautical Science (ISAS) launched this probe to study the Martian environment. Launch of the Planet-B spacecraft took place from Kagoshima

Space Center on an M-V vehicle on Saturday, 4 July at 3:12 AM local time (Friday at 2:12 PM EDT). Planet-B was renamed Nozomi, or "hope," after lift-off. Flight operations are handled by Sagamihara Spacecraft Operations Center, and Martian orbit insertion will take place in October 1999, followed immediately by data collection. The two-year mission objective is to study the structure and dynamics of the atmosphere and iono-sphere of Mars, including any interactions with the solar wind. The results obtained will be compared with those obtained from the Pioneer Venus Orbiter mission to better understand the direct interactions between the planetary atmosphere and ionosphere and the solar wind. (Unsuccessful)

- Mars Climate Orbiter - USA Orbiter

– 639 kg - (11 December 1998): Mars Climate Orbiter, a mission to study the Martian weather, climate, and water and carbon dioxide was launched on a Delta II from Pad A of Launch Complex 17 at Cape Canaveral Air Station, Florida. After a brief cruise in Earth orbit, the Delta II 3rd stage put the spacecraft into trans-Mars trajectory and about 15 days after launch the largest trajectory correction maneuver (TCM) was executed using the hydrazine thrusters. During cruise to Mars, three additional TCM's using the hydra-zine thrusters were performed on 4 Mar., 25 Jul., and 15 Sept. 1999. The spacecraft reached Mars and executed a 16-minute, 23-second orbit insertion main engine burn on 23 Sep. 1999. The spacecraft passed behind Mars and was to reemerge

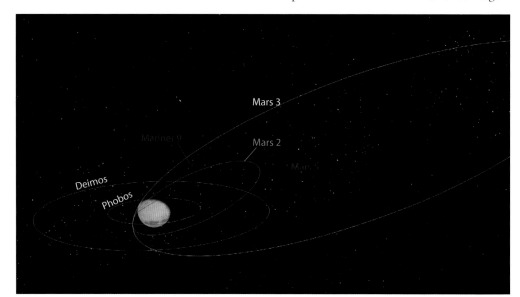

The U.S. Mariner 9 and the Soviet Mars 2, 3, and 5 missions. Mars orbiters occupied wide elliptical orbits. Mariner 9 was the first probe to return images of a significant amount of the surface. All these spacecraft were placed into elliptical orbits that allowed them to observe one side of Mars during the part of their orbits close to the planet.

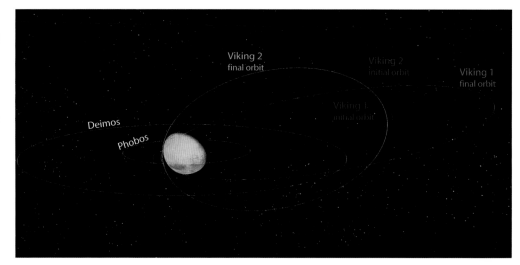

In 1976 the two Viking orbiters arrived in Mars orbit. One of their first tasks was releasing the Viking landers, both of which arrived successfully on the surface. Unlike previous missions, the Viking orbiters had the ability to alter their orbits using thrusters. This allowed them to change the apogee and perigee after the primary mission was completed. The orbits were changed several times to allow flybys of Phobos and Deimos, the two natural satellites of Mars. Data revealed these to be asteroids captured by the gravity of Mars.

and establish radio contact with Earth, however contact was never reestablished and no signal was ever received from the spacecraft. Findings of the failure review board indicate that a navigation error resulted from some spacecraft commands being sent in English units instead of being converted to metric. This caused the spacecraft to miss its intended 140–150 km altitude above Mars during orbit insertion, instead entering the Martian atmosphere at about 57 km. Atmospheric stresses and friction at this low altitude would have destroyed the spacecraft. (Unsuccessful)

- 2001 Mars Odyssey - USA Mars Probe - 376.3 kg - (7 April 2001): The Mars lander/rover aspect of the project has been canceled. The 2001 Mars Odyssey is the remaining part of the Mars Surveyor 2001 Project, which originally consisted of two separately launched missions, the Mars Surveyor 2001 Orbiter and the Mars Surveyor 2001 Lander. The lander space-craft was canceled as part of the reorgani-zation of the Mars Exploration Program at NASA. The orbiter, renamed the 2001 Mars Odyssey, will nominally orbit Mars for three years, with the objective of conducting a detailed mineralogical analy-sis of the planet's surface from orbit and measuring the radiation environment. The

mission has as its primary science goals to gather data to help determine whether the environment on Mars was ever conducive to life, to characterize the climate and geology of Mars, and to study poten-tial radiation hazards to possible future astronaut missions. After a seven-month cruise the spacecraft reached Mars on 24 October 2001. The spacecraft used a 19.7-minute main-engine propulsive maneuver to transfer into an 18.6-hour elliptical capture orbit and used aerobraking until 11 January 2002, when the spacecraft pulled out of the aerobraking orbit into a 201 x 500 km orbit. This orbit was trimmed over the next few weeks until it became a 2-hour, approximately 400 x 400 km polar science orbit on 30 January 2002. The Orbiter will act as a communications relay for the Mars 2003 Rovers, scheduled to arrive in January 2004, and possibly other future missions. Data will be collected from orbit until the end of the 917-day nominal mission in July 2004. The spacecraft will continue to act as a communications relay until October 2005. (Successful)

- Mars Express - European Space Agency (ESA) Mars orbiter and lander - 1123 kg – (2 June 2003): This Mars probe consisted of an orbiter, the Mars Express Orbiter, and a lander, Beagle 2. The scientific objec-tives of the Mars Express Orbiter were

to obtain global high-resolution photo-geology (10 m resolution), mineralogical mapping (100 m resolution), and mapping of the atmospheric composition; and study the subsurface structure, the global atmo-spheric circulation, and the interaction between the atmosphere and the subsur-face, and the atmosphere and the inter-planetary medium. The Beagle 2 lander objectives were to characterize the landing site geology, mineralogy, and geochemistry, the physical properties of the atmosphere and surface layers, collect data on Martian meteorology and climatology, and search for possible signatures of life. After launch on a Soyuz/Fregat rocket from Baikonur Cosmodrome, the orbiter released Beagle 2 on 19 December 2003. It coasted for five days after release and entered the Martian atmosphere on the morning of 25 December. Landing was expected to occur at about 02:54 UT on 25 December (9:54 p.m. EST 24 December). No signals have been received and the lander was declared lost. The orbiter continued to operate in Mars orbit for more than a year thereaf-ter and returned scientific data. (Partially Successful)

- Mars Reconnaissance Orbiter (MRO) - USA Mars Probe - 2180 kg – (12 August 2005): This probe was designed to orbit Mars over a full Martian year and gather data with six scientific instruments, includ-ing a high-resolution imager. The science objectives of the mission were to: char-acterize the present climate of Mars and its physical mechanisms of seasonal and interannual climate change; determine the nature of complex layered terrain on Mars and identify water-related landforms; search for sites showing evidence of aque-ous and/or hydrothermal activity; identify and characterize sites with the highest potential for landed science and sample return by future Mars missions; and return scientific data from Mars-landed craft during a relay phase. MRO will return high-resolution images, study surface composition, search for subsurface water, trace dust and water in the atmosphere, and monitor weather. It went into orbit around Mars on 10 March 2006. Aerobraking was used over the next six months to lower the orbit to a projected 255 x 320 km polar orbit. Science operations begun at the end of solar conjunction in November 2006 were intended to continue until the next solar conjunction in November 2008, roughly one Martian year. (Successful)

After Viking, spacecraft sent to Mars were placed into more precise orbits. Better navigation and control techniques allowed spacecraft to be placed into lower orbits without risking the safety of the spacecraft. All of these orbiters have also employed aerobraking to arrive at their final orbits. The low circular orbits of Mars Global Surveyor, Mars Odyssey, and Mars Reconnaissance Orbiter were required to allow accurate mapping of the surface.

Follow the Water

The robotic probes first sent to Mars found a planet far different from that envisioned in Western popular culture. Humanity had envisioned a world filled with some type of life, perhaps only plants, but it found a desert, rocky surface. Planetary scientist and JPL director Bruce Murray noted that public expectations to find evidence of life on the red planet devastated any desire to return to Mars for more than two decades. While there were plan-

ning exercises for missions to Mars, none from the U.S. actually flew until the 1990s.

One important change in the interest registered about Mars came in August 1996 when a team of NASA and Stanford University scientists announced that a Mars meteorite found in Antarctica contained possible evidence of ancient Martian life. When the 4.2-pound, potato-sized rock (identified as ALH84001) was formed as an igneous rock

about 4.5 billion years ago, the scientists believed that Mars was much warmer and probably contained oceans hospitable to life. Then, about 15 million years ago, a large asteroid hit the red planet and jettisoned the rock into space, where it remained until it crashed into Antarctica around 11,000 B.C.E. Scientists presented three suggestive, but far from conclusive, pieces of evidence suggesting that fossil-like remains of Martian microorgan-

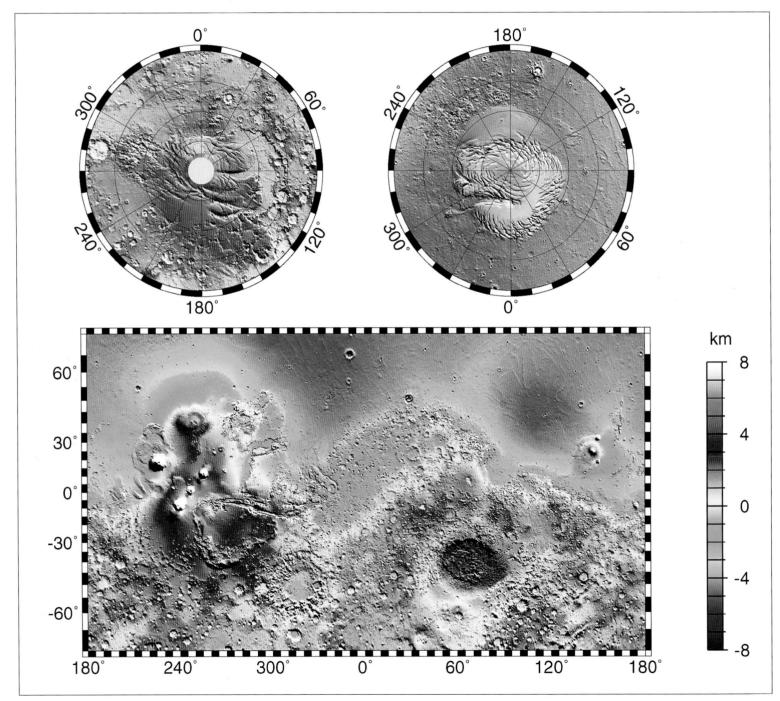

These maps of Mars's global topography show the red planet as revealed from orbit. The projections are Mercator to 70° latitude and stereographic at the poles with the south pole at left and north pole at right. Note the elevation difference between the northern and southern hemispheres. The Tharsis volcano-tectonic province is centered near the equator in the longitude range 220° E to 300° E and contains the vast east-west trending Valles Marineris canyon system and several major volcanic shields including Olympus Mons (18° N, 225° E), Pavonis Mons (0°, 247° E), and Arsia Mons (9° S, 239° E). Major impact basins include Hellas (45° S, 70° E), Argyre (50° S, 320° E), Isidis (12° N, 88° E), and Utopia (45° N, 110° E).

isms, which date back 3.6 billion years, might be present in ALH84001. Scientific consensus is now that the formation of the features found in this asteroid did not, in fact, require biological activity. However, when the possibility was suggested it added support for an aggressive set of missions to Mars.

Thereafter the strategy for much of Mars exploration has been built upon the motto, "Follow the Water." In essence, this approach noted that life on Earth is built upon liquid water and that any life elsewhere would probably have chemistries built upon these same

elements. Accordingly, to search for life on Mars, past or present, NASA's strategy must be to follow the water. If scientists could find any liquid water on Mars, probably only deep beneath the surface, the potential for life to exist was also present.

The Mars of today, without any evidence of water whatsoever on the surface, probably had water flowing freely in its ancient history. Evidence of changes to the planet's surface from fast-flowing water has been collected by many space probes orbiting the planet since the latter 1990s. The spacecraft to open this

possibility was Mars Global Surveyor, opening the planet in 1998 to a new and exciting era of scientific missions to study the red planet. Its recent discoveries offer titillating hints for learning about the possibility of life on Mars, at least in the distant past. In an exciting press conference in June 2000, astronomer Michael Malin discussed his analysis of imagery from Mars Global Surveyor, a stunningly successful NASA probe. He showed more than 150 geographic features all over Mars probably created by fast-flowing water. He suggested that there might actually be water in the substrata of Mars, and our experience on Earth has indicated that where water exists life as we understand it exists as well.

Operating for several years, Mars Global Surveyor continued to send back views of the Martian surface that seemed to show evidence of dry riverbeds, flood plains, gullies on Martian cliffs and crater walls, and sedimentary deposits that suggested the presence of water flowing on the surface at some point in the history of Mars. This led scientists to theorize that billions of years ago, Earth and Mars might have been very similar places. Of course, Mars lost its water and the question of why that might have been the case has also motivated many Mars missions to the present. At that point, a consensus emerged that on any mission to Mars we should "follow the water" and seek the answer to the ultimate question: "Are we alone in the universe?" Mars may well provide a definite answer.

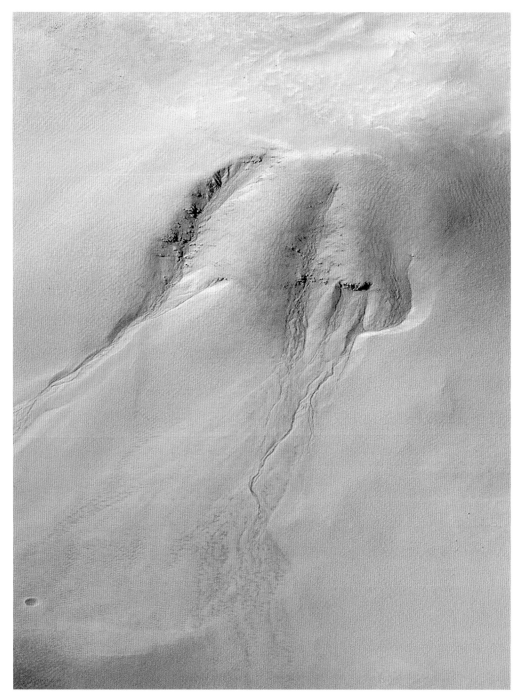

Taken in September 1999 by the Mars Global Surveyor, this image of the surface of Mars shows a 3-km-wide area of an impact crater's south-facing wall located at 54.8°S, 342.5°W. The photograph excited both scientists and the public as it appears to have been formed by groundwater seepage and surface runoff. Furthermore, some theorized that the location and young age of the gullies suggest the possibility of subsurface liquid water still on Mars. It was one of the first and most dramatic images suggesting that the "follow the water" strategy represented the best way to pursue Mars exploration.

At present, most scientists believe the odds are almost nonexistent that complex life forms could have evolved on Mars because of its extremely hostile environment. The stories of "advanced civilizations," as proposed by Percival Lowell, or "little green men" are just that: stories. But many scientists believe there is sufficient evidence to think that microscopic organisms might once have evolved on the planet when it was much warmer and wetter billions of years ago. There are even a few scientists who would go somewhat further and theorize that perhaps some water is still present deep inside the planet. In that case simple life forms might still be living beneath Mars's polar caps or in subterranean hot springs warmed by vents from the Martian core. These might be Martian equivalents of single-celled microbes that dwell in Earth's bedrock. Scientists are quick to add, however, that these are unproven theories for which evidence has not yet been discovered.

This strategy of "follow the water" has dominated all planning for Mars science missions for more than a decade and results thus far have been promising. Scientists continue to plan an integrated set of missions to continue this strategy.

Geologic Mapping of Mars

The dynamic Martian climate has been the subject of scientific research using data from spacecraft in orbit and on the ground. The environment of Mars may have been more similar to conditions of Earth long ago. Many signs of a warmer, moister planet can be found across Mars, unlike the cold and dry planet we see today. Mars contains many features that appear to have been carved by liquid water. If Mars indeed did have significant amounts of liquid water, it would also have had a denser and warmer atmosphere, good conditions for life to develop. Images from the Viking orbiters showed eroded terrain and networks of stream valleys. Subsequent missions to Mars have attempted to discover more about the role of water in shaping the planet.

Scientists attempting to understand the history of a planet often observe the number and distribution of impact craters. Images of Mars show a great number of large impact features. On Earth a thick atmosphere and active geological processes obscure impact craters. Mars, Venus, Mercury, and the Moon do not have plate tectonics that would recycle any signs of past impacts. The southern hemisphere of Mars contains significantly more craters than the north, evidence for the older age of the northern part of the planet.

While ancient craters cover most of the southern hemisphere on Mars, the north is very flat and smooth. For this reason the southern hemisphere is recognized as an older surface than the north. Billions of years in the past, both hemispheres may have had a similar appearance. At some point the majority of the north was resurfaced. The mechanism behind this massive process, and the length of time it required, is the subject of scientific research.

The amount of water that existed on Mars in the past has been a subject of debate among planetary scientists. In previous decades many scientists thought that an ocean of water covered much of the northern hemisphere in the past. A major piece of evidence for this was the unusually flat topography for that part of the planet. More recent evidence has shown

that there was likely no large northern ocean, but other structures exist that appear to be related to flowing water. On the surface, some evidence has been found for small pools of standing water.

Large features on Mars that appear to have been created by running water include outflow channels and valley networks. Outflow channels are massive areas that appear to be left behind after huge flooding events. Most of them are oriented such that flooding water would have emptied into the northern hemisphere. Valley networks consist of long

connected channels, and have been theorized to have been produced by water running downhill.

The volume of water required to produce some of the features seen on Mars is staggering. Some outflow channels northeast of Vallis Marineris are wider than 100 kilometers. Although the features appear to have been carved by a moving liquid, a likely source for this volume of water has not been identified. Other perplexing details include the lack of large sediment deposits associated with many outflow channels. Also, valley networks on

Mars Odyssey, which arrived at the red planet on October 24, 2001, is an orbiter carrying science experiments designed to make global observations of Mars to improve our understanding of the planet's climate and geologic history, including the search for water and evidence of life-sustaining environments. Odyssey used a technique called "aerobraking" that gradually brought the spacecraft closer to Mars with each orbit. By using the atmosphere of Mars to slow down the spacecraft in its orbit rather than firing its engine or thrusters, the spacecraft saved fuel for later maneuvers.

Mars are much less dense than similar features on Earth. Are these channels the result of flowing water or forms of volcanism? Scientists continue to investigate using data from new missions to Mars.

The Mars Reconnaissance Orbiter (MRO) was specifically designed to pursue the "follow the water" strategy at Mars. Its science instruments monitor the present water cycle in the Mars atmosphere and the associated deposition and sublimation of water ice on the surface, while probing the subsurface to see how deep is the water ice reservoir detected by earlier missions. At the same time, MRO searched for carbonates and sulfates that may signal the extended presence of liquid water on the planet's surface earlier in its history. The instruments involved are the shallow radar SHARAD, the CRISM spectrometer, the MARCI weather camera, the HiRISE high-resolution camera, the CTX context camera, and the Mars Climate Sounder (MCS). In addition to surface imagery in a variety of resolutions, these instruments are critical to analyzing the current climate and surface of Mars, recording variations in temperature, humidity, ice clouds, dust clouds and hazes, and ozone distribution, producing daily global maps in multiple colors to monitor daily weather and seasonal changes.

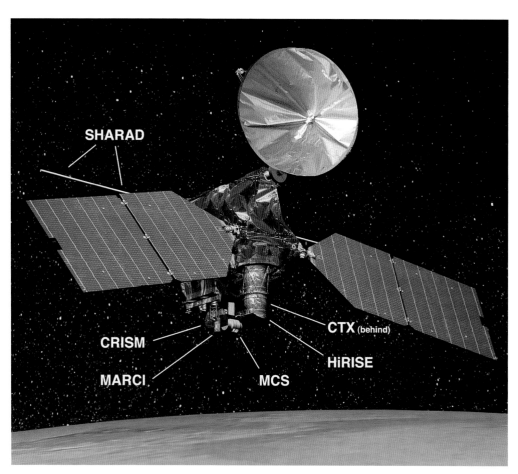

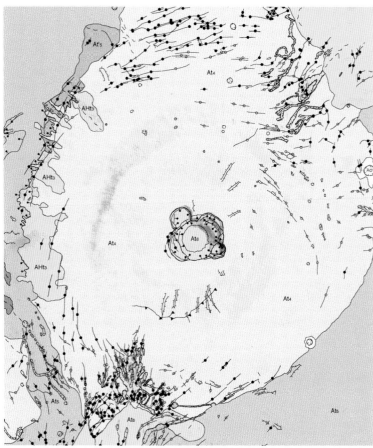

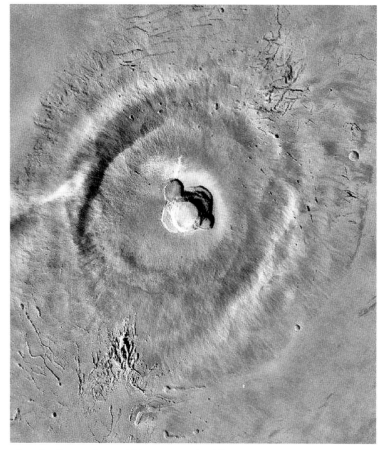

Planetary geologists attempt to reconstruct the history of an alien world. This is done by using images from orbiting spacecraft. Different sections of the surface are interpreted to determine their likely origin. For instance, lava flows on the slopes of volcanoes can be compared to determine their relative age. Using images, a geologist can deduce how different features were made and when. The map shown here describes the geology of Ascreaeus Mons, one of the large volcanoes in the Tharsis bulge. It was produced using imagery from the Viking orbiters. Map colors indicate different geological units, or ages of material. Structures such as faults are indicated with black symbols.

Mars Landing Sites

Since the beginning of the space age there have been 14 landings on the surface of Mars, some of which were not successful. Initially the Soviet Union carried out two attempted landings in 1971, Mars 2 and 3, but the first lander crashed and the second returned only 20 seconds of data before failing on the Martian surface. Regardless, these became the first human-built artifacts to reach the surface of Mars. Another landing attempt took place in 1973 when the Soviet Union dispatched Mars 7 to the red planet. It failed to rendezvous with Mars and went into a solar orbit without accomplishing its mission. A major contribution came in 1976 with the successful landings of Viking 1 and 2 by the United States.

After the Vikings, despite other attempts, no other landers were successful in reaching the Martian surface until 1997 when Mars

On July 20, 1976, the Viking 1 lander captured this first ever photograph from the surface of Mars. The photo shows one of three footpads of the spacecraft resting on Mars's surface.

Pathfinder opened the modern age of Martian exploration. Thereafter, three additional landers have successfully made it to the surface of the red planet and have reshaped humanity's understanding of this intriguing planet. Mars

has proven a difficult place on which to land successfully. The box score for the record of landings is six successes, eight failures. While it might be expected that landing failures would have been common early in the space age, greater success should come with time, experience, and more sophisticated technology. This is the case, certainly, but unfortunately in the last decade two of five Mars landing missions have failed. Successfully reaching the surface of this planet has proven a task not without difficulties, yet the prize of scientific knowledge continues to spur significant efforts. There is no dearth of plans for continued exploration using landers, rovers, and flying machines that might operate in the thin Martian atmosphere. The following is a chronological list of all landing missions on Mars, along with their basic activities.

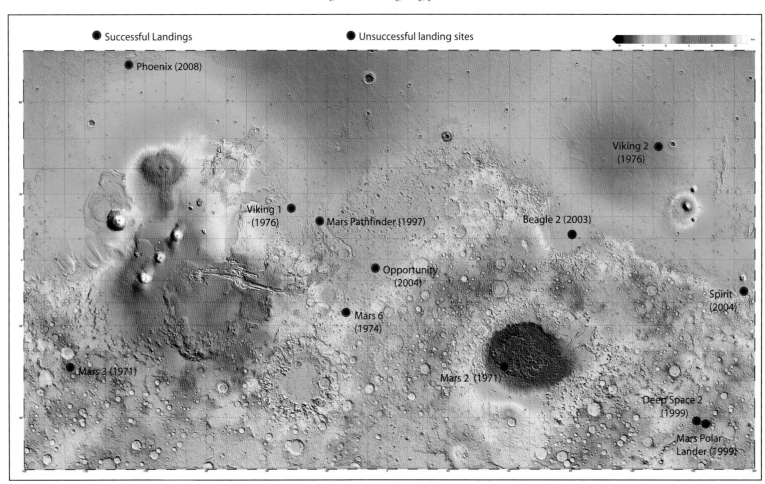

This map shows the location of landings attempted on the surface of Mars. The Soviet Mars landers, none of which returned useful data despite arriving to the surface, are shown. Also shown is the Mars Polar Lander that also failed to reach the south polar region. Phoenix, a similar mission in 2008, successfully landed in the north polar region.

1. **Mars 2** - USSR Mars Orbiter/Soft Lander - 4,650 kg - (19 May 1971): The Mars 2 lander was released from the orbiter on 27 November 1971. It crash-landed because its breaking rockets failed—no data were returned and the first human artifact was created on Mars. (Lander unsuccessful)

2. **Mars 3** - USSR Mars Orbiter/ Soft Lander - 4,643 kg - (28 May 1971): Mars 3 arrived at Mars on 2 December 1971. The lander was released and became the first successful landing on Mars. It failed after relaying 20 seconds of video data to the orbiter. (Lander unsuccessful)

3. **Mars 7** - USSR Mars Orbiter/Soft Lander - 4,650 kg - (9 August 1973): On 6 March 1974, Mars 7 failed to go into orbit about Mars and the lander missed the planet. Carrier and lander are now in a solar orbit. (Unsuccessful)

4. **Viking 1** - USA Mars Orbiter/ Lander - 3,399 kg - (20 August 1975 - 7 August 1980): Viking 1 was launched from the Kennedy Space Center, on 20 August 1975, for the trip to Mars and went into orbit about the planet on 19 June 1976. The lander touched down on 20 July 1976 on the western slopes of Chryse Planitia (Golden Plains). The lander conducted experiments to search for Martian microorganisms. The results of these experiments are still being debated. The lander provided detailed color panoramic views of the Martian terrain. It also monitored the Martian weather. The orbiter mapped the planet's surface. The orbiter weighed 900 kg and the lander 600 kg. The Viking project's primary mission ended on 15 November 1976, eleven days before Mars's superior conjunction (its passage behind the Sun), although the Viking spacecraft continued to operate for six years after first reaching Mars. Viking 1 lander was accidentally shut down on 13 November 1982, and communication was never regained. Its last transmission reached Earth on 11 November 1982. Controllers at NASA's Jet Propulsion Laboratory tried unsuccessfully for another six and one half months to regain contact with the lander, but finally closed down the overall mission on 21 May 1983. (Lander successful)

5. **Viking 2** - USA Mars Orbiter/ Lander - 3,399 kg - (9 September 1975 - 25 July 1978): Viking 2 was launched for Mars on 9 November 1975, and landed on 3 September 1976. The orbiter weighed 900 kg and the lander 600 kg. The lander conducted experiments to search for Martian microorganisms. The results of these experiments are still being debated. The lander provided detailed color panoramic views of the Martian terrain. It also monitored the Martian weather. The orbiter mapped the planet's surface, and, with its Viking 1 orbiter, acquired over 52,000 images. The Viking project's primary mission ended on 15 November 1976, eleven days before Mars's superior conjunction (its passage behind the Sun), although the Viking spacecraft continued to operate for six years after first reaching Mars. (Lander successful)

6. **Phobos 1** - USSR Mars Orbiter/ Lander - 5,000 kg - (7 July 1988): Phobos 1 was sent to investigate the Martian moon Phobos. It was lost en route to Mars through a command error on 2 September 1988. (Unsuccessful)

7. **Phobos 2** - USSR Phobos Flyby/ Lander - 5,000 kg - (12 July 1988): Phobos 2 arrived at Mars and was inserted into orbit on 30 January 1989. The orbiter moved within 800 kilometers of Phobos and then failed. The lander never made it to Phobos. (Lander Unsuccessful)

8. **Mars 8** - Russia Orbiter & Lander – 6,200 kg - (16 November 1996): Mars '96 consisted of an orbiter, two landers, and two soil penetrators that were to reach the planet in September 1997. The rocket carrying Mars 96 lifted off successfully, but as it entered orbit the rocket's fourth stage ignited prematurely and sent the probe into a wild tumble. It crashed into the ocean somewhere between the Chilean coast and Easter Island. The spacecraft sank, carrying with it 270 grams of plutonium-238. (Unsuccessful)

9. **Mars Pathfinder** - USA Lander & Surface Rover - 870 kg - (4 December 1996): The inexpensive Mars Pathfinder (costing only $267 million) landed on Mars on 4 July 1996, after its launch in December 1996. A small, 23-pound, six-wheeled robotic rover named Sojourner departed the main lander and began to record weather patterns, atmospheric opacity, and the chemical composition of rocks washed down into the Ares Vallis flood plain, an ancient outflow channel in Mars's northern hemisphere. This vehicle completed its projected milestone 30-day mission on 3 August 1997, capturing far more data on the atmosphere, weather, and geology of Mars than scientists had expected. In all, the Pathfinder mission returned more than 1.2 gigabits (1.2 billion bits) of data and over 10,000 tantalizing pictures of the Martian landscape. The images from both craft were posted to the Internet, to which individuals turned for information about the mission more than 500 million times through the end of July. The mission's primary objective was to demonstrate the feasibility of low-cost landings on the Martian surface. This was the second mission in NASA's low-cost Discovery series. (Successful)

10. **Mars Polar Lander** - USA lander - 538 kg - (3 January 1999): The Mars Polar Lander and its attached Deep Space 2 probes were launched on a Delta II rocket which placed them into a low Earth parking orbit. The third stage fired for 88 seconds to put the spacecraft into a Mars transfer trajectory. Trajectory correction maneuvers were performed on 21 January, 15 March, 1 September, 30 October, and 30 November 1999. After an 11-month hyperbolic transfer cruise, the Mars Polar Lander reached Mars on 3 December 1999. The lander was to make a direct entry into Mars's atmosphere at 6.8 km/s but was lost during the landing sequence. JPL lost contact with the spacecraft and due to lack of communication, it is not known whether the probe followed the descent plan or was lost in some other manner. (Unsuccessful)

11. **Mars Express** - European Space Agency (ESA) Mars orbiter and lander - 1123 kg – (2 June 2003): This Mars probe consisted of an orbiter, the Mars Express Orbiter, and a lander, Beagle 2. The scientific objectives of the Mars Express Orbiter were to obtain global high-resolution photo-geology (10 m resolution), mineralogical mapping (100 m resolution) and mapping of the atmospheric composition; and to study the subsurface structure, the global atmospheric circulation, and the interaction between the atmosphere and the subsurface, and the atmosphere and the interplanetary medium. The Beagle 2 lander objectives were to characterize the landing site geology, mineralogy, and geochemistry, the physical properties of the atmosphere and surface layers, collect data on Martian meteorology and climatology, and search for possible signatures of life. After launch on a Soyuz/Fregat rocket from Baikonur Cosmodrome, the orbiter released Beagle 2 on 19 December 2003. It coasted for five days after release and entered the Martian atmosphere on the morning of 25 December. Landing was expected to occur at about 02:54 UT on 25 December (9:54 p.m. EST 24 December). No signals have been received and the lander was declared lost. (Lander unsuccessful)

12. **Mars Exploration Rover A** - USA Mars Rover - 827 kg – (10 June 2003): Named "Spirit" upon landing on the Martian surface on 4 January 2004 this rover was one of a pair launched to Mars in mid-2003. Equipped with a battery of scientific instruments it was intended to operate for 90 days, until April 2004, and to traverse about 100 meters a day. The scientific goals of the rover missions are to gather data to help determine if life ever arose on Mars, characterize the climate of Mars, characterize the geology of Mars, and prepare for human exploration of Mars. It has performed exceptionally well and is still operating in November 2007. A primary mission objective was to search for geological clues to the environmental conditions that existed when liquid water was present and assess whether those environments were conducive to life. It landed in Gusev Crater because it had the appearance of a crater lakebed. The rover's scientific data suggest that Gusev may have at one time been filled with water. (Successful)

13. **Mars Exploration Rover B** - USA Mars Rover - 827 kg – (7 July 2003): Named "Opportunity" upon landing on the Martian surface on 25 January 2004 this rover was the second of a pair launched to Mars in mid-2003. It carried identical instruments to "Spirit" and landed at Terra Meridiani, also known as the "Hematite Site" because it displays evidence of coarse-grained hematite, an iron-rich mineral that typically forms in water. This mission has also continued into November 2007. (Successful)

14. **Phoenix Mars Lander** - USA Mars Lander - 350 kg – (4 August 2007): The Phoenix Mars Lander was designed to study the surface and near-surface environment of a landing site in the high northern area of Mars. The primary science objectives for Phoenix are to: determine polar climate and weather, interaction with the surface, and composition of the lower atmosphere around 70 degrees north for at least 90 sols; determine the atmospheric characteristics during descent through the atmosphere; characterize the geomorphology and active processes shaping the northern plains and the physical properties of the near-surface regolith focusing on the role of water; determine the aqueous mineralogy and chemistry as well as the adsorbed gases and organic content of the regolith; characterize the history of water, ice, and the polar climate and determine the past and present biological potential of the surface and subsurface environments. Phoenix was launched on 4 August 2007 on a Delta II 7925 from Cape Canaveral Air Force Station, Florida. The 681 million km heliocentric cruise to Mars took approximately 10 months, with landing on Mars on 25 May 2008. (Successful)

Landers on Mars

The first truly successful landings on Mars took place in 1976 when the Viking mission used two identical spacecraft, each consisting of a lander and an orbiter. Launched on August 20, 1975, from the Kennedy Space Center in Florida, Viking 1 spent nearly a year cruising to Mars, placed an orbiter in operation around the planet, and landed on July 20, 1976, on the Chryse Planitia (Golden Plains). Viking 2 was launched on September 9, 1975, and landed on September 3, 1976. The Viking project's primary mission ended on November 15, 1976, 11 days before Mars's superior conjunction (its passage behind the sun), although the Viking spacecraft continued to operate for six years after first reaching Mars. The last transmission from the planet reached Earth on November 11, 1982.

One of the most important scientific activities of this project involved an attempt to determine whether there was life on Mars. Although the three biology experiments discovered unexpected and enigmatic chemical activity in the Martian soil, they provided no clear evidence for the presence of living microorganisms in soil near the landing sites. According to mission biologists, Mars was self-sterilizing. They concluded that the combination of solar ultraviolet radiation that saturates the surface, the extreme dryness of the soil, and the oxidizing nature of the soil chemistry had prevented the formation of living organisms in the Martian soil. However, the question of life on Mars at some time in the distant past remains open.

The exploration received new life on July 4, 1997, when Mars Pathfinder successfully landed on Mars, the first return to the red planet since 1976. Its small, 23-pound robotic rover, named Sojourner, departed the main lander and began to record weather patterns, atmospheric opacity, and the chemical composition of rocks washed down into the Ares Vallis flood plain, an ancient outflow channel in Mars's northern hemisphere. This vehicle completed its projected milestone 30-day mission on August 3, 1997, capturing far more data on the atmosphere, weather, and geology of Mars than scientists had expected. In all, the Pathfinder mission returned more than 1.2 gigabits (1.2 billion bits) of data and

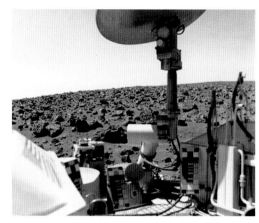

The boulder-strewn field of red rocks reaches to the horizon nearly two miles from Viking 2 on Mars's Utopian Plain. Scientists believe the colors of the Martian surface and sky in this photo represent their true colors. Fine particles of red dust have settled on the spacecraft surfaces. The salmon color of the sky is caused by dust particles suspended in the atmosphere. Color calibration charts for the cameras are mounted at three locations on the spacecraft. Note the blue star field and red stripes of the flag. The circular structure at top is the high-gain antenna, pointed toward Earth. Viking 2 landed September 3, 1976, some 4,600 miles from its twin, Viking 1, which touched down on July 20.

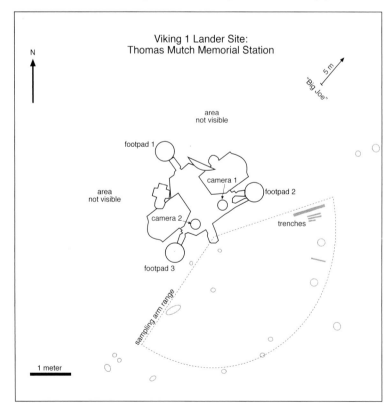

The Viking 1 lander was the first successful arrival on the surface of Mars. Viking 1 transmitted images and meteorological data to Earth for longer than six years. The Viking landers also carried seismometers and a sampling arm. The arm could reach to the surface to scoop soil and return it to a miniaturized laboratory on the lander. This map shows the Viking 1 landing site. Prominent rocks are shown on the surface, along with trenches dug by the sampling arm. In 1981 ownership of the Viking 1 lander was transferred to the Smithsonian National Air and Space Museum. Renamed the Thomas A. Mutch Memorial Station, it is the most distant piece in the museum's collection. It was named after Thomas Mutch, the former lead scientist of the Viking lander imaging experiment.

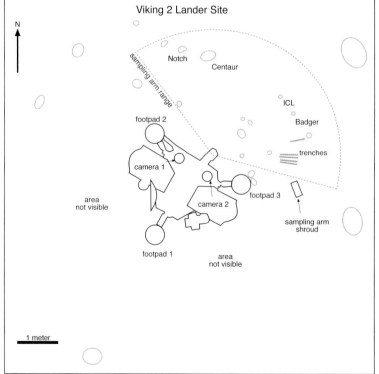

Viking 2 landed on September 3, 1976. Identical to the Viking 1 lander, it operated on the surface for three years and seven months. Both Viking landers utilized a radioisotope power supply. Powered by the radioactive decay of plutonium, these power supplies allowed the landers to operate for many years without relying on solar panels.

Near the Viking 1 Lander on the Chryse Plains of Mars, "Big Joe" stands a silent vigil. This large, often-photographed dark rock has a topping of reddish fine-grained silt that spills down its sides. It is about 2 meters (6.6 feet) long and lies about 8 meters (26 feet) from the spacecraft. The rough texture of the sides shows it to be coarse grained. Big Joe appears to be part of a field of large blocks that has a roughly circular alignment and that may be part of the rim of an ancient degraded crater. Some of the other blocks of the field can be seen to the left, extending out toward the horizon, perhaps 1.5 kilometers (1 mile) away. Drifts of fine-grained material cover the surface to the right and left of Big Joe. The part of the Lander that is visible in the lower left is the cover of the nuclear power supply.

This "glamor" photograph of the Viking lander from 1976 displays its major features, including its scoop and chemistry instruments.

over 10,000 tantalizing pictures of the Martian landscape.

A new portrait of the Martian environment began to emerge in the months after Pathfinder because of the new data that were collected in this mission. The rover's alpha proton X-ray spectrometer team analyzed the first ever in situ measurements of Mars rocks. Similarly, atmospheric-surface interactions, measured by a meteorology package onboard the lander, confirmed some conditions observed by the Viking landers in the later 1970s, while raising questions about other aspects of the planet's global system of transporting volatiles such as water vapor, clouds, and dust. The meteorology mast on the lander observed a rapid drop-off in temperature just a few feet above the surface, and one detailed 24-hour measurement set

This panoramic image shows the Mars Pathfinder landing site. The Sojourner rover has driven down the ramp and is visible on the right near the large rock nicknamed "Yogi." Rocks and other features near landing sites are often given nicknames by mission teams as shorthand to identify sites of interest.

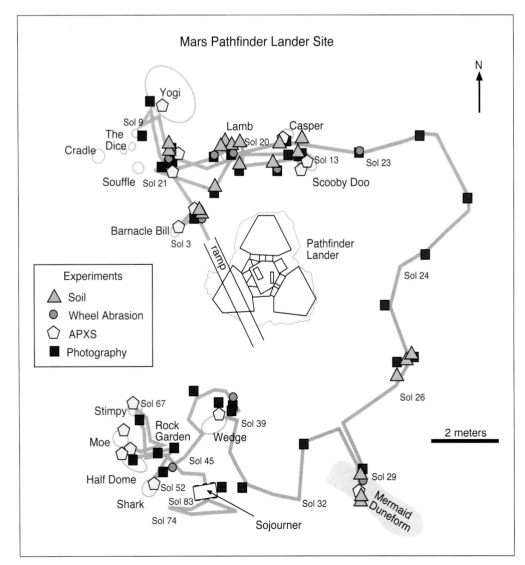

LEFT: Mars Pathfinder carried a small rover, known as Sojourner, to the surface of Mars. For 82 Martian days Sojourner moved about in the immediate vicinity of the main lander. On board the rover were several instruments. The location of experiments are shown on the map. The rover transmitted data to the main spacecraft, which in turn transmitted results to Earth. The range for this rover on the Martian surface was limited by a short communications link to the main lander.

RIGHT: This image was returned from the surface of Mars by the Phoenix Lander on June 10, 2008. It shows the robotic arm holding a sample above one of the lander's solar panels. The arm delivered several samples to instruments designed to analyze soil composition and detect water ice. INSET: Map of the immediate surroundings of the Phoenix Lander site. The robotic arm was able to extend about two meters on the northeastern side of the lander. Trenches dug by the arm up to October 2008 are shown as solid gray rectangles, along with their informal names. The landing site in the north polar region was chosen to learn more about the nature of water ice on Mars. Phoenix landed on May 25, 2008, and operated on the surface for more than five months.

revealed temperature fluctuations of 30–40 degrees Fahrenheit in a matter of minutes.

Moreover, Sojourner, a robust rover capable of semiautonomous "behaviors," captured the imagination of the public, which followed the mission with great interest via the World Wide Web. Twenty Pathfinder mirror sites recorded 565 million hits worldwide during the period of July 1 and August 4, 1997. The highest volume of hits in one day occurred on July 8, when a record 47 million hits were logged, which was more than twice the volume of hits received on any one day during the 1996 Olympic Games in Atlanta. The data from the mission are still being analyzed and will help to answer some of the age-old questions associated with the origins of the Solar System.

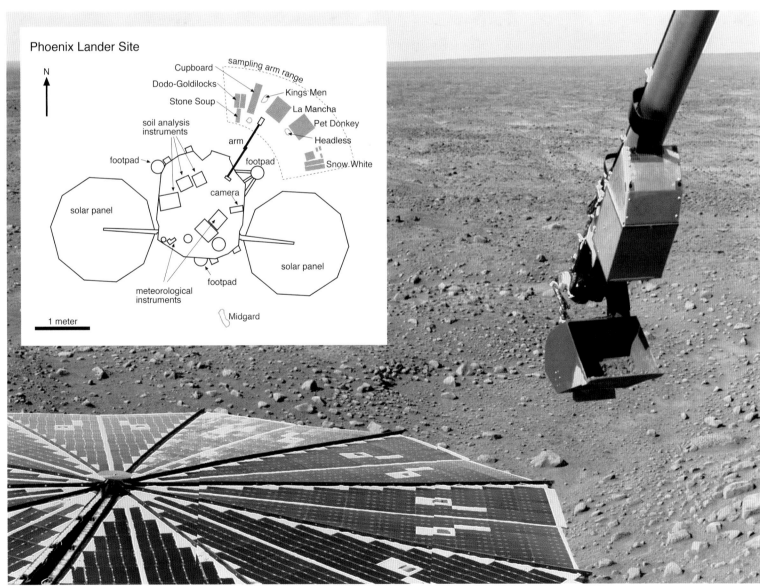

Mars Exploration Rover A: Spirit

Since the beginning of the space age in 1957 robotic exploration flights to Mars has remade it into a unique world of remarkable variety and complexity. The Mars Exploration Rovers (MER), two extraordinary robots named Spirit and Opportunity, displayed a noteworthy toughness and flexibility even as they amazed everyone with their sophisticated capacity for decision making on the Martian surface. Designed for 90-day missions to search for evidence of the effects of water in shaping Martian geology, Spirit and Opportunity remained operational more than four years after they first reached different parts of the planet in January 2004. During that time, they drove more than seven times as far as the distance originally set as the criterion for a successful mission. Spirit covered 3.4 miles by February 6, 2007; Opportunity became the first spacecraft to traverse 10,000 meters—or 6.2 miles—on the surface of Mars. Both contended with hills and craters and escaped sandtraps, and overcame numerous technical problems.

Spirit and Opportunity are twins, each with five scientific instruments: a panoramic camera, a miniature thermal emission spectrometer, a Mössbauer spectrometer, an alpha particle X-ray spectrometer, and a microscopic imager. They also have a rock abrasion tool for grinding weathered rock surfaces to expose the interior. Each rover weighs nearly 180 kilograms (about 400 pounds). A robotic arm, modeled on a human elbow and wrist, makes it possible to manipulate rocks. In the mechanical "fist" of the arm is a microscopic camera that serves the same purpose as a geologist's magnifying lens.

Spirit explored the Gusev Crater and revealed a basaltic setting, one not greatly suggestive of past water on Mars. It traveled to "Columbia Hills" and found a variety of rocks indicating that early Mars was characterized by impacts, explosive volcanism, and abundant subsurface water. Unusual-looking bright patches of soil turned out to be extremely salty and were probably affected by past water. At "Home Plate," a circular feature in the "Inner Basin" of the "Columbia Hills" region, Spirit discovered finely layered rocks that are as geologically compelling as those found by Opportunity. Spirit even turned its attention away from the surface to observe the Martian moons Phobos and Deimos.

SPECIFICATIONS

Country: United States
Operator: NASA Jet Propulsion Laboratory
Launched: June 10, 2003 on Delta II 7925 rocket from Cape Canaveral, Florida
Landed: January 3, 2004, Gusev Crater, Mars
Configuration: Complete spacecraft launched toward Mars comprised a six-wheeled rover, lander, backshell with parachute, heatshield, and cruise stage
Total Launch Mass: 1,063 kg (2,343 lb)

ROVER

Dimensions: 1.6 m (5.2 ft) long, 1.5 m (4.9 ft) tall
Mass: 185 kg (408 lb)
Payload: Panoramic camera, miniature thermal emission spectrometer, Mössbauer spectrometer, alpha particle X-ray spectrometer, magnets, microscopic imager, rock abrasion tool
Power: Max 140W from solar array
Primary Mission: 90 days/1.2 km (0.75 mi)
Status: Still operational

On May 19, 2005, NASA's Mars Exploration Rover Spirit captured this stunning view as the Sun sank below the rim of Gusev Crater on Mars. This panoramic camera (Pancam) mosaic was taken around 6:07 in the evening of the rover's 489th martian day, or sol. Spirit was commanded to stay awake briefly after sending that sol's data to the Mars Odyssey orbiter just before sunset. This small panorama of the western sky was obtained using Pancam's 750-nanometer, 530-nanometers and 430-nanometer color filters. This filter combination allows false color images to be generated that are similar to what a human would see, but with the colors slightly exaggerated. In this image, the bluish glow in the sky above the Sun would be visible to us if we were there, but an artifact of the Pancam's infrared imaging capabilities is that with this filter combination the redness of the sky farther from the sunset is exaggerated compared to the daytime colors of the Martian sky. Because Mars is farther from the Sun than the Earth is, the Sun appears only about two-thirds the size that it appears in a sunset seen from Earth. The terrain in the foreground is the rock outcrop "Jibsheet," a feature that Spirit had been investigating for several weeks (rover tracks are dimly visible leading up to "Jibsheet"). The floor of Gusev Crater is visible in the distance, and the Sun is setting behind the wall of Gusev some 80 km (50 miles) in the distance.

Spirit Traverse

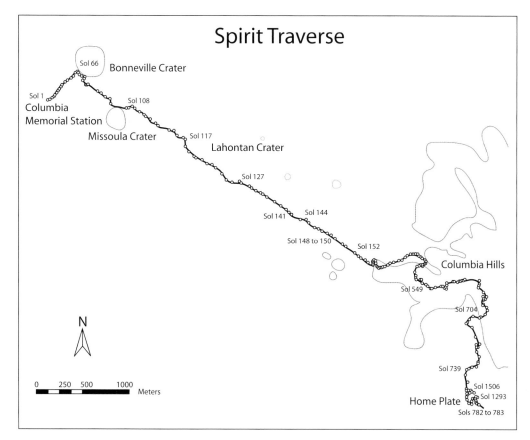

Sol 66 Bonneville Crater

Sol 1
Columbia
Memorial Station

Sol 108

Missoula Crater

Sol 117

Lahontan Crater

Sol 127

Sol 144
Sol 141
Sol 148 to 150
Sol 152

Columbia Hills

Sol 549

Sol 704

N

0 250 500 1000 Meters

Sol 739
Sol 1506
Sol 1293
Home Plate
Sols 782 to 783

After the success of the Mars Pathfinder and the Sojourner rover, missions for larger rovers were proposed. The two Mars Exploration Rovers were often described by their designers as remote field geologists. They carried instruments similar to the ones that would be used by a human geologists on Earth: cameras, microscope, and an instrument for measuring composition of rocks. Even the rovers' wheels could be used to dig small trenches.

The Mars Exploration Rover Spirit landed in Gusev Crater on January 4, 2004. After landing it traveled several kilometers across the surface. Gusev Crater, more than 160 kilometers wide, was theorized to have been filled by a large flood in the past. However, Spirit found few conclusive signs of past water on the surface.

An artist's concept portrays a NASA Mars Exploration Rover on the surface of Mars. Two rovers undertook 2003 launches and a January 2004 arrival at two sites on Mars. Each rover has the mobility and toolkit to function as a robotic geologist.

Mars Exploration Rover B: Opportunity

As with Spirit, Opportunity was sent to Mars in 2003 and reached the red planet the next January. Designed for 90-day missions to search for evidence of the effects of water in shaping Martian geology, Spirit and Opportunity have remained operational through 2008. On February 6, 2007, Opportunity became the first spacecraft to traverse 10,000 meters (6.2 miles) on the surface of Mars. It contended with hills and craters and escaped sandtraps, and overcame numerous technical problems.

Both the Spirit and Opportunity rovers were named through a student essay competition. The winning entry was by Sofi Collis, in 2004 a third-grade Russian-American student from Arizona. As she wrote, "I used to live in an Orphanage. It was dark and cold and lonely. At night, I looked up at the sparkly sky and felt better. I dreamed I could fly there. In America, I can make all my dreams come true. . . . Thank-you for the 'Spirit' and the 'Opportunity.'" Prior to this, during the development and building of the rovers, they were known only as MER-1 and MER-2.

After an airbag-protected landing, Opportunity settled onto the Martian surface and opened petal-like doors before the vehicles rolled out to take panoramic images. Those first images gave scientists the information they needed to select promising geological targets that would tell part of the story of water in Mars's past. Then, the rovers drove to those locations to perform on-site scientific investigations over the course of their mission. Scientists, literally around the world, had the capability to control both rovers, sending in their turn commands to direct their actions.

Opportunity had early success by landing close to a thin outcrop of rocks that lent itself to an analysis confirming that a body of salty water once flowed gently over the area. Opportunity found sands that were reworked by water and wind, solidified into rock, and soaked by groundwater. It continues to examine more sedimentary bedrock exposures along its route depicted in the map, where an even broader, deeper section of layered rock revealed new aspects of Martian geologic history. Scientific analysis on Earth pointed to a past environment that could have been hospitable to life and also could have fossil evidence preserved in it.

As twins, both Spirit and Opportunity have five scientific instruments: a panoramic camera, a miniature thermal emission spectrometer, a Mössbauer spectrometer, an alpha particle X-ray spectrometer, and a microscopic imager. They also have a rock abrasion tool for grinding weathered rock surfaces to expose the interior. Each rover weighs nearly 180 kilograms (about 400 pounds).

By grinding, photographing, and analyzing rock samples, they achieved their primary mission of proving beyond doubt that the Martian surface had once featured large bodies of water. Each rover represented the mechanical equivalent of a geologist walking the surface of Mars. Their mast-mounted cameras are mounted 5 feet high and provide 360-degree, stereoscopic, humanlike views of the terrain. A robotic arm, modeled on a human elbow and wrist, makes it possible to manipulate and analyze rocks.

The Mars Exploration Rover Opportunity landed in the Meridiani Planum region. After landing it traveled more than 10 kilometers across the surface. It arrived in the middle of a small crater on a flat plain. It first traveled east to Endurance Crater, then south to Erebus and Victoria Craters. The area selected for landing contained evidence from orbit of hematite, a mineral that on Earth is largely formed in the presence of water. Signs of past water were found by Opportunity, including small areas containing salts on the surface. These salts were possibly left behind as small pools of water evaporated.

Opportunity made this curving, 15.8-meter (52-foot) drive during its 1,160th Martian day, or sol (April 29, 2007). It was testing a navigational capability called "Field D-star," which enabled the rover to plan optimal long-range drives around any obstacles in order to travel the most direct safe route to the drive's designated destination. Opportunity and its twin, Spirit, did not have this capability until the third year after their January 2004 landings on Mars. Earlier, they could recognize hazards when they approached them closely, then back away and try another angle, but could not always find a safe route away from hazards. Field D-Star and several other upgrades were part of new onboard software uploaded from Earth in 2006. The Sol 1,160 drive by Opportunity was a Martian field test of Field D-Star and also used several other features of autonomy, including visual odometry to track the rover's actual position after each segment of the drive, avoidance of designated keep-out zones, and combining information from two sets of stereo images to consider a wide swath of terrain in analyzing the route.

SPECIFICATIONS

NAMES: Spirit and Opportunity (Mars Exploration Rovers)

OPERATOR: NASA Jet Propulsion Laboratory

LAUNCHED: Rover B (Opportunity): by Delta II 7925H from Cape Canaveral, July 7, 2003

LANDING SITE:

Rover B (Opportunity): Meridiani Planum, landed January 24, 2004

CONFIGURATION: Complete spacecraft launched toward Mars comprised a six-wheeled rover, lander, backshell with parachute, heatshield, and cruise stage

ROVER DIMENSIONS: 5.2 ft (1.6 m) long, 4.9 ft (1.5 m) tall

TOTAL LAUNCH MASS: 2,343 lb (1,063 kg)

ROVER MASS: 408 lb (185 kg)

ROVER PAYLOAD: Panoramic camera, miniature thermal emission spectrometer, Mössbauer spectrometer, alpha particle X-ray spectrometer, magnets, microscopic imager, rock abrasion tool

ROVER PROPULSION: Cleated wheels driven by individual electric motors

ROVER ELECTRICAL POWER: Max 140W from solar array

HEATING ELEMENT: Radioisotope Heating Units

PRIME MISSION: 90 days/0.75 miles (1 km)

This computer-generated diagram shows the elements of the two Mars Exploration Rovers.

The Geography of Venus

One of the most stunning astronomical sites in the evenings and the early mornings is Venus, the nearest planet to Earth, and the one that is closest to this planet in size, density, and mass. Covered with a dense cloud covering, little is known about its surface and for many years this fueled all manner of speculation about what might lie beneath. For instance, early in the twentieth century a popular theory held that the sun had gradually been cooling for millennia and that as it did so, each planet in the Solar System had a turn as a haven for life of various types. Although it was now Earth's turn to harbor life, the theory suggested that Mars had once been habitable and that life on Venus was now just beginning to evolve.

Not until the first space probes reached there in the 1960s did a portrait of Venus emerge that demonstrated it was a very inhospitable place. It has a dense atmosphere more than 100 times that of Earth's. Scientists also learned that Venus's atmosphere consists of approximately 97% carbon dioxide. And while it was very rocky, it had no water whatsoever, and temperatures on the surface of more than 450 degrees Celsius regardless of whether it was night or day, summer or winter. Finally, the pressure on the surface of Venus is 90 times what may be found on the Earth. Based upon knowledge gained about the climatology of Venus, scientists led by Carl Sagan theorized about the possibility of cloud density and its contributions to the creation of the scorched greenhouselike world of Venus.

For centuries Earth-bound astronomers had been observing the upper reaches of Venus's cloud cover, only about 45 miles (70 km) above the surface. Analyzing these clouds using instruments that measured its various elements, scientists determined that it primarily consisted of sulfuric acid as well as other trace materials. They also found above it at about 74 miles (90 km) a layer of ice crystals forming a haze around the planet.

Beyond the cloud covering, space probes have returned data suggesting that Venus has high peaks and low valleys, much greater than seen on Earth. These range from elevations of 6 miles (10.6 km) to one mile (1.5 km), but they are located on only 8% of the planet. Radar mapping missions have also found that much of the surface is quite smooth, the result of considerable volcanic activity; about 65% of Venus consists of rolling, gently sloping plains. Another 27% consists of lowlands, basins, and valleys, some reaching the depth of 1.3 miles (2.5 km).

Because of data returned from robotic probes, scientists believe that Venus's interior is similar to that of Earth, holding an iron core about 1,900 miles (3,000 km) in radius and a molten rocky mantle making up the majority of the planet.

These same robotic analyses of Venus have determined that igneous rocks—basalts—predominate on its surface. Additionally, in imagery from the Venusian surface scientists identified numerous sharp-edged rocks, indicating that the planet is geologically active and is still forming surface features.

From analyses of scientific data returned from robotic probes, scientists have determined that the oldest terrain on Venus appears to be about 800 million years old but much is quite a bit younger. Scientists theorize that extensive volcanism on Venus shaped the planet at that time, engulfing the earlier impact craters that had shaped the planet at the Solar System's formation. Since Venus did not display the same features of plate tectonics as on Earth, geologists believe that volcanism on the planet has been more regional and less systematic. But there are still over 1,600 major volcanoes or volcanic features identified on Venus, and this is more than on any other celestial body of the Solar System thus far explored.

Although Venus has no rainfall, oceans, or strong winds, there appears to be some weathering and erosion. These are probably the result of intense volcanism since there was strong "Canali," lava-carved channels similar to the sinuous rilles found on the Moon. Canali may extend more than 3,000 miles (5,000 km), longer than on any other planet. Geologists believe that these were probably formed when very hot, fluid lava erupted onto the surface.

Venus slowly rotates on its axis once every 243 Earth days, while orbiting the Sun every 225 days. The periods of Venus's rotation and of its orbit are synchronized so that it always presents the same facade toward Earth when the two planets are at their closest approach. Finally, Venus is the only planet in our Solar System that rotates "backward"—from its surface, to an observer of Venus the Sun would seem to rise in the west and set in the east.

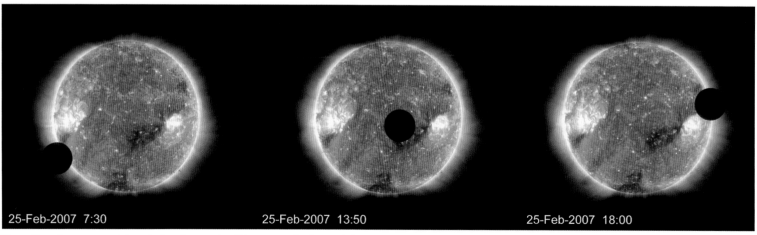

25-Feb-2007 7:30   25-Feb-2007 13:50   25-Feb-2007 18:00

These three images were taken during the transit of Venus past the Sun on February 25, 2007.

Planetary Radius (km)
6048 6050 6052 6054 6056 6058 6060 6062

The Magellan spacecraft produced these global maps of Venus. The dense atmosphere of Venus contains clouds that completely obscure the surface. Therefore it is necessary to use radar to "see" the surface. Using radar, a pulse of energy is transmitted toward the surface. The reflection back upward is received back on the orbiter. Two types of information can be obtained: topography and a measure of surface roughness.

A very rough surface scatters the radio energy in all directions, while a smooth surface reflects mostly in one direction. This difference can allow the roughness to be interpreted. The size of rocks that lie on the surface naturally varies. If the landscape is dominated by certain rock size, that will become apparent in the radar data.

Topography can be mapped from radar data by measuring the amount of time needed for radio transmissions to reach the surface and return to the spacecraft. These maps show the altitude as a color range.

Near the equator of Venus is the Aphrodite Terra, an area of high mountainous topography. The highest mountain on the planet, Maxwell Montes, is visible to the north.

Venus has many large impact features. Planetary scientists used Magellan data to count the number of craters as a way to estimate the age of different landscapes. On Venus they discovered that all the impact features are evenly spread across the entire planet. This implies that the whole planet has a surface of approximately the same age. How this situation developed is the subject of continuing research.

Venus also has large features known as coronae (plural of *corona*). These structures are hundreds of kilometers across and circular in shape. It is not completely understood how they form, but theories have been proposed that describe volcanic upwelling in the planet's interior. Venus is the only planet where coronae have been found.

Planetary Radius (km)
6048 6050 6052 6054 6056 6058 6060 6062

Reaching for Venus

Regarded as both the evening and the morning star, Venus had long enchanted humans—and all the more so since astronomers had realized that it was shrouded in a mysterious cloak of clouds permanently hiding the surface from view. It was also the closest planet to Earth, and a near twin to this planet in terms of size, mass, and gravitation.

After carrying out ground-based efforts in 1961 to view the planet using radar, which could "see" through the clouds, and learning among other things that Venus rotated in a retrograde motion opposite from the direction of orbital motion, both the Soviet Union and the United States began a race to the planet with robotic spacecraft. The Soviets tried first, launching Venera 1 on 12 February 1961. Unlike lunar exploration, however, the Soviets did not win the race to Venus; their spacecraft broke down on the way. The United States claimed the first success in planetary exploration during the summer of 1962 when Mariner 1 and Mariner 2 were launched toward Venus. Although Mariner 1 was lost during a launch failure, Mariner 2 flew by Venus on December 14, 1962, at a distance of 21,641 miles. It probed the clouds, estimated planetary temperatures,

This image from the Pioneer Venus Orbiter in 1979 shows a mysterious cloud covered planet that had been earlier revealed to be a greenhouse run amok.

measured the charged particle environment, and looked for a magnetic field similar to Earth's magnetosphere (but found none). Most important, it found that the planet's surface was a fairly uniform 800 degrees Fahrenheit, thereby making unlikely the theory that life—at least as humans understood it—existed on Venus.

Mariner 10 was the seventh successful launch in the Mariner series, and the first spacecraft to use the gravitational pull of one planet (Venus) to reach another (Mercury). It was also the first probe to visit two planets. Launched on November 3, 1973, it reached Venus on February 5, 1974. Using a gravity assist from this planet, Mariner 10 first crossed the orbit of Mercury on March 29, 1974, and did so a second time on September 21, 1974. A third and last Mercury encounter took place on March 16, 1975. It measured the environments of both Venus and Mercury. It then undertook experiments in the interplanetary medium. Mariner 10 showed that Venus had at best a weak magnetic field, and the ionosphere interacted with the solar wind to form a bow shock. At Mercury, it confirmed that Mercury had no atmosphere and a cratered, dormant, Moon-like surface.

Because of Venus's thick cloud cover, scientists early on advocated sending a probe with radar to map Venus. Pioneer 12 had made a start toward realizing this goal, orbiting the planet for more than a decade to complete a low-resolution radar topographic map. Likewise, the Soviets' Venera 15 and 16 missions in 1983 provided high-resolution

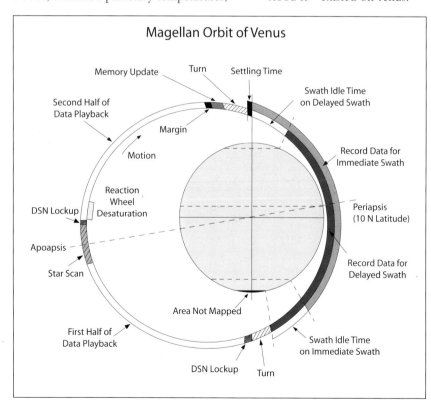

When orbiting Venus, the Magellan spacecraft spent half its time collecting radar data and the remainder transmitting those data to Earth. This required turning the entire spacecraft every orbit, because the same antenna was used for the radar imaging and data transmissions. Thrusters were used to point the antenna in the correct directions.

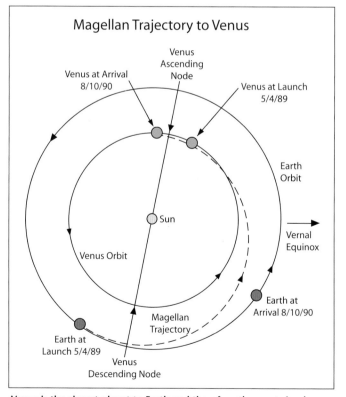

Venus is the closest planet to Earth and therefore the most simple to visit with a spacecraft. The trajectory of Magellan is shown here, but most Venus missions have used a similar trajectory. During a mission to Venus, the spacecraft must be placed into solar orbit with decreased velocity to intersect Venus.

coverage over the northern reaches of the planet.

The most significant mission to Venus took place when the Magellan orbiter mapped Venus with imaging radar. This mission followed a Pioneer Venus 1 spacecraft that had orbited the planet throughout the 1980s, completing a low-resolution radar topographic map, and Pioneer Venus 2, which dispatched heat-resisting probes to penetrate the planet's dense clouds. It also built on the work of the Soviet Union, which had compiled radar images of the northern part of Venus and had deployed balloons into the Venusian atmosphere. Magellan arrived at Venus in September 1990 and mapped 98% of the surface at high resolution, parts of it in stereo. This data betrayed some surprises, among them the discovery that plate tectonics was at work on Venus and that lava flows showed clearly the evidence of volcanic activity. In 1993, at the end of its mission, scientists turned their attention to a detailed analysis of Magellan's data. Although years of research await Venus explorers from the data returned by these probes, collectively they fundamentally altered most of the beliefs held as recently as a generation ago about Venus as a tropical, protoorganic planet.

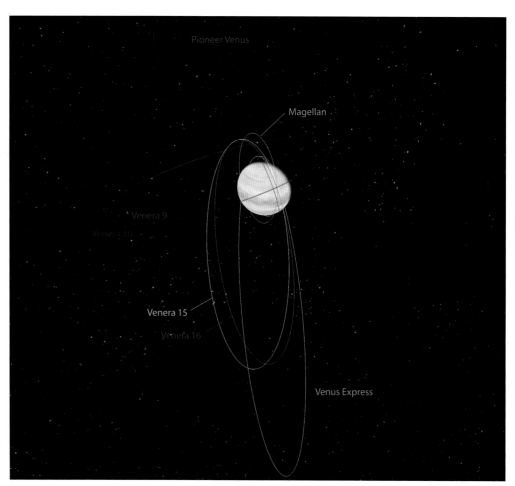

The early Venera spacecraft were placed into elliptical paths around the planet. Magellan used a lower orbit to perform mapping of the surface. Venus Express orbits in an elliptical polar orbit.

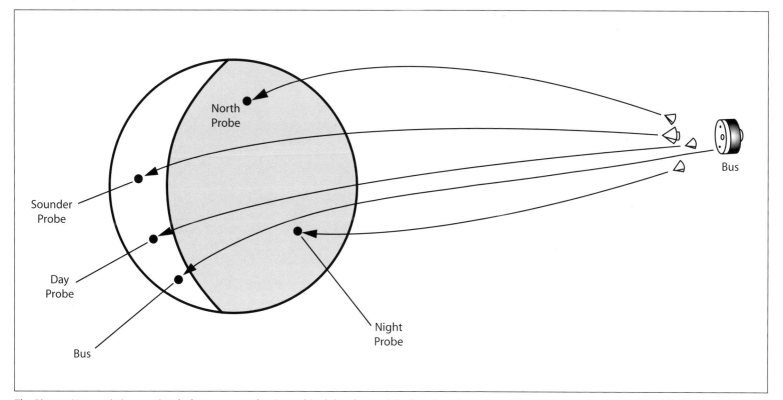

The Pioneer Venus mission consisted of two spacecrafts. One orbited the planet while the other, shown here, released four probes that entered the atmosphere. One probe was larger than the other three. All four were intended to study the atmosphere instead of the surface. The small probes were not even equipped with parachutes. The probes were dispersed to enter the atmosphere at different locations. The three small probes were named the Day, Night, and North probes according to these locations. The Day probe survived impact and continued to transmit data for moore than an hour from the surface.

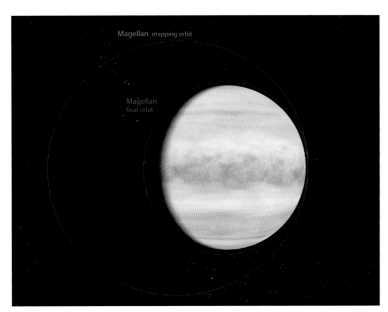

During the mapping phase of the Magellan mission, it maintained an elliptical orbit. Mapping was performed when it was closer to Venus. After the mapping was completed, mission planners desired to lower the orbit of Magellan to perform mapping of the planet's gravitational field. Not enough propellant was available to enter a low circular orbit. The answer was found by using the atmosphere. For the first time a planetary spacecraft was placed into the upper reaches of an atmosphere. The added atmospheric drag slowed orbital velocity, enabling Magellan to enter a circular orbit. At the end of the mission Magellan was lowered still more until it finally burned up during entry in the atmosphere.

Mariner 2 was the world's first successful interplanetary spacecraft. Launched August 27, 1962, on an Atlas-Agena rocket, Mariner 2 passed within about 34,000 kilometers (21,000 miles) of Venus, sending back valuable new information about interplanetary space and the Venusian atmosphere.

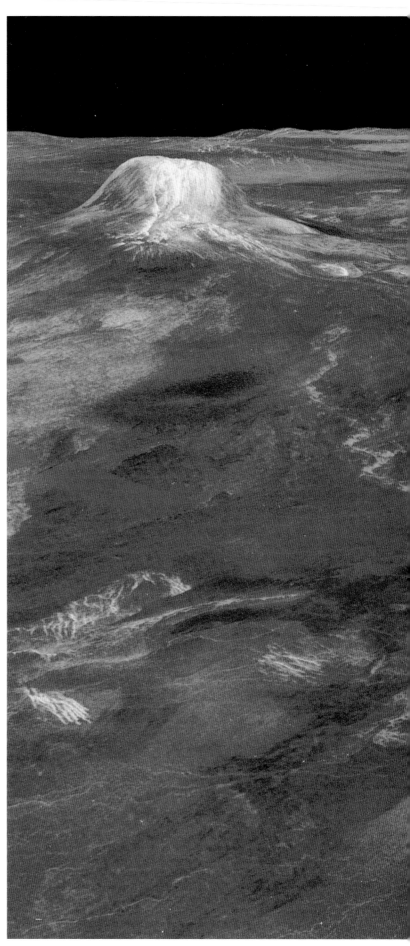

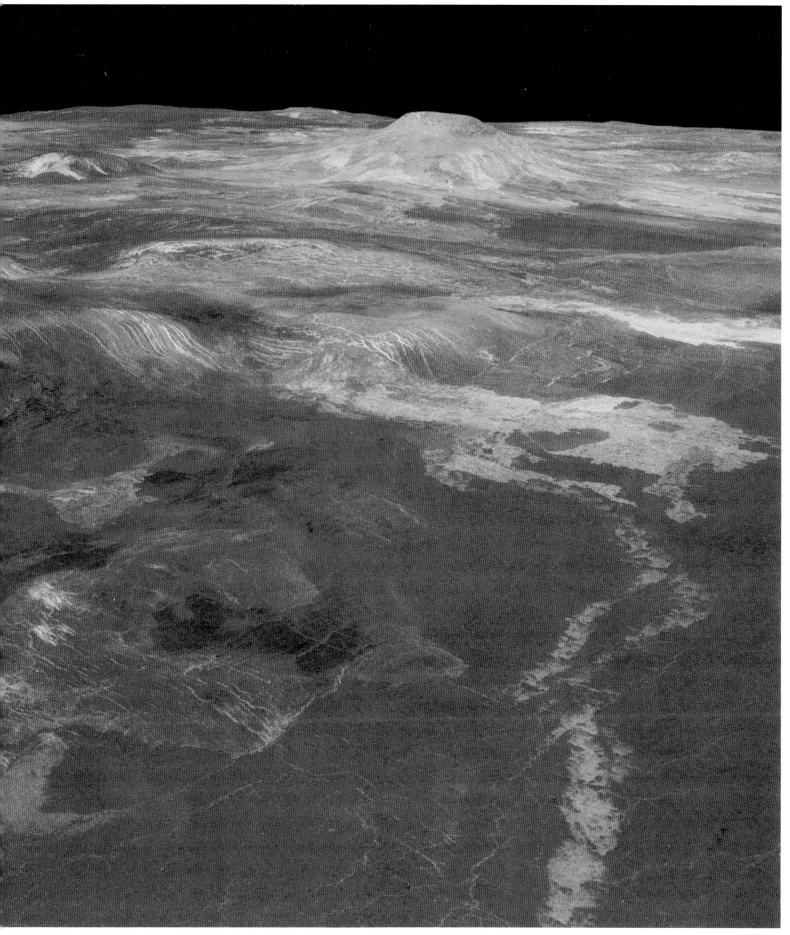

Lava flows in the Western Eistla Regio extend for hundreds of kilometers to Gula Mons, a 3-km-high volcano (upper left), and to 2-km-high volcano Sif Mons (upper right), which has a diameter of 300 km (180 miles).

Landings on Venus

Although the Soviet Union made several attempts to reach Venus, only in 1965 was it successful in reaching the surface when Venera 3 crashed there without returning any scientific data. In 1967 the Soviets sent Venera 4, which successfully deployed a probe into the atmosphere and returned information about the makeup of the planet's surface. Both spacecrafts demonstrated that Venus was a very inhospitable place for life to exist. Collectively, these and subsequent planetary probes revealed that Venus was superheated because of the greenhouse effect of the cloud layer and that

the pressure on the surface was about 90 atmospheres, far greater than even in the depths of the oceans on Earth.

Through the late 1960s, the Soviets continued to send probes to Venus to obtain data from the inhospitable surface, but none succeeded until Venera 7 returned the first information from the surface in December 1970. For 23 minutes, the lander transmitted data about conditions on the ground before succumbing to the extreme heat and pressure. It was the first time that any probe had returned information from the surface of another planet.

Two Soviet probes launched in 1975, Venera 9 and Venera 10, returned the first photographs from the surface of Venus. These images showed flat rocks spread around the landing area. Two new probes, Venera 11 and Venera 12, landed on the planet in 1978 (although they were unable to return photographs). In 1982, another pair, Venera 13 and Venera 14, sent the first color photographs of the surface. Probes such as Venera 15 and Venera 16 also mapped the Venusian surface from orbit using high-powered radars. Perhaps the most ambitious Soviet mission to Venus was the success-

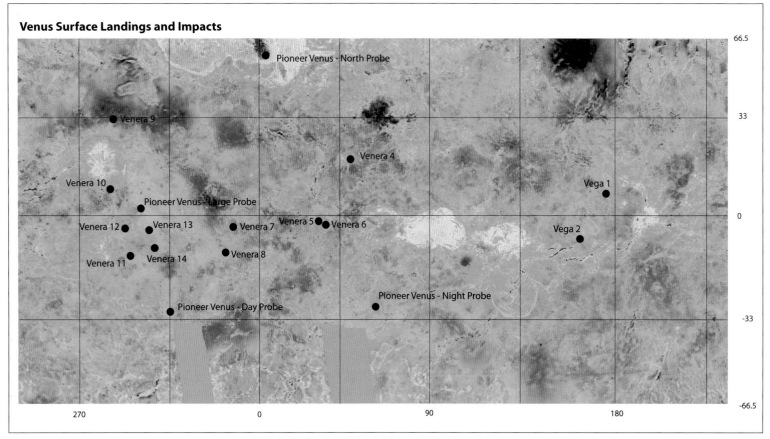

Venus Surface Landings and Impacts

The spacecraft that have landed or impacted on Venus are shown here. Most of these are Soviet Venera and Vega missions. The four U.S. Pioneer Venus probes also arrived at the surface. The two Vega probes landed near Aphrodite Terra, the high-altitude area on the right of this map. Only four probes, Venera 9, 10, 13, and 14, returned images of the surface of Venus.

Image from the Venera 13 lander on Venus. This image from camera 2 shows a surface covered by flat rocks with little evidence of weathering. The small rocks near the lander were probably the results of the landing itself. The cover of the camera's aperture was dropped and is visible near the center. A color bar, used to calibrate imagery, is visible on the right. The horizon is visible at the upper left and right corners of the image.

ful Vega 1 and Vega 2, launched in 1984. The two spaceships were each made up of landers, atmospheric balloons, and flyby probes for encounters with Halley's Comet. The French-made balloons, each weighing about 46 pounds (21 kilograms), transmitted important data about the atmosphere as they drifted slowly through the Venusian skies.

Most recently in the twenty-first century the Messenger spacecraft has encountered Venus, but will not land on the surface of the planet.

Four Venera landers returned images from the surface of Venus. Due to the high temperature and pressure, it was necessary to encase each camera within the lander pressure container. The cameras scanned from left to right. Each camera was tilted 50 degrees down toward the surface. This provided a view of the surface directly in front the lander, and also allowed the distant horizon to be seen in the corners of the images. Venera 9 and 10 carried one camera each, while Venera 13 and 14 carried two. The diagram illustrates the field of view for the cameras on Venera 13 and 14. At the extreme left and right ends of the scans the field of view extends to the horizon. The scanning motion of the cameras was necessary because of the short duration of the mission. Each lander to Venus must perform tasks before it is overcome by the extreme heat. Although this proved to be a simple solution to the complex problem of getting images from the surface of Venus, it resulted in a complex image geometry.

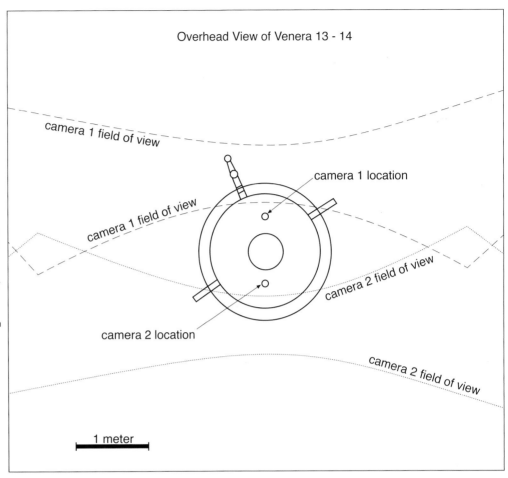

Overhead View of Venera 13 - 14

camera 1 field of view

camera 1 location

camera 1 field of view

camera 2 location

camera 2 field of view

camera 2 field of view

1 meter

These black-and-white images show the surface of Venus at the Venera 14 landing site. The image from camera 1 (top) shows the extended arm holding a device to measure surface density. Unfortunately the arm is resting on the ejected camera cover, which prevented the experiment from functioning.

Exploring Mercury

While it resembles Earth's Moon in outward appearance, studies of Mercury have revealed many surprises. Among these are the Caloris Basin, the largest structure visible on the surface. The Caloris Basin was formed as an enormous impact feature. So much energy was contained in the impact that small hills were created at the opposite point on the globe where seismic waves were focused.

Images from the 2008 MESSENGER flyby also showed evidence of past volcanic activity.

Instruments on Mariner 10 detected a magnetic field strong enough to deflect the solar wind. This was not expected before the mission because Earth's Moon has an extremely small magnetic field.

Mercury is distinctive in the solar system because it shows evidence of its changing size. Mercury's core contracted as it cooled during an early period in the history of the Solar System. The planet's diameter shrunk by more than 1 kilometer. As a result, the surface buckled and folded. This caused crevaces in the crust known as lobate scarps, features that have been identified across Mercury in images from Mariner 10 and MESSENGER.

Mariner 10 Trajectory

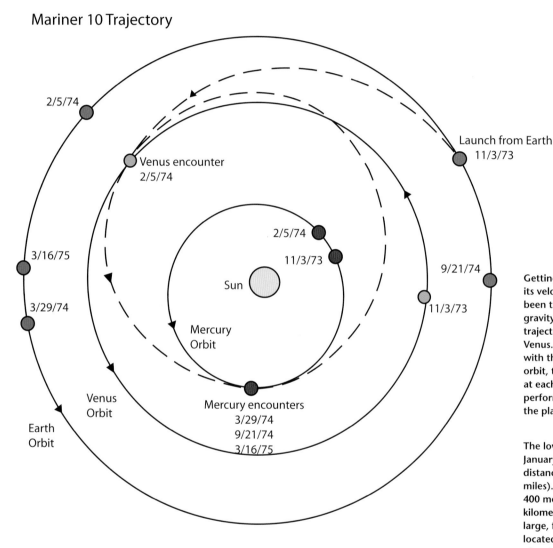

Getting to Mercury requires a spacecraft to decrease its velocity around the Sun. Only two missions have been targeted to Mercury, and both have used gravity assists to arrive there. Mariner 10, using the trajectory shown here, first performed a flyby of Venus. It then entered a solar orbit that intersected with that of Mercury. Due to the nature of Mercury's orbit, the same side of the planet was facing the Sun at each Mariner 10 flyby. The result was that despite performing three flybys of Mercury, only one side of the planet was seen.

The lower image was taken by MESSENGER on January 14, 2008, and shows Mercury from a distance of about 5,000 kilometers (about 3,100 miles). The image shows features as small as 400 meters (0.25 miles) in size and is about 370 kilometers (230 miles) across. It shows part of a large, fresh crater with secondary crater chains located near Mercury's equator on the side of the planet newly imaged by MESSENGER. Large, flat-floored craters often have terraced rims from post-impact collapse of their newly formed walls. The hundreds of secondary impactors that are excavated from the planet's surface by the incoming object create long, linear crater chains radial to the main crater. These chains, in addition to the rest of the ejecta blanket, create the complicated, hilly terrain surrounding the primary crater. By counting craters on the ejecta blanket that have formed since the impact event, the age of the crater can be estimated. This count can then be compared with a similar count for the crater floor to determine whether any material has partially filled the crater since its formation. With their large size and production of abundant secondary craters, these flat-floored craters both illuminate and confound the study of the geological history of Mercury.

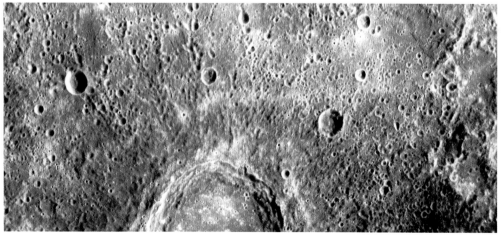

After passing on the dark side of the planet, Mariner 10 photographed the other, somewhat more illuminated hemisphere of Mercury. The north pole is at the top.

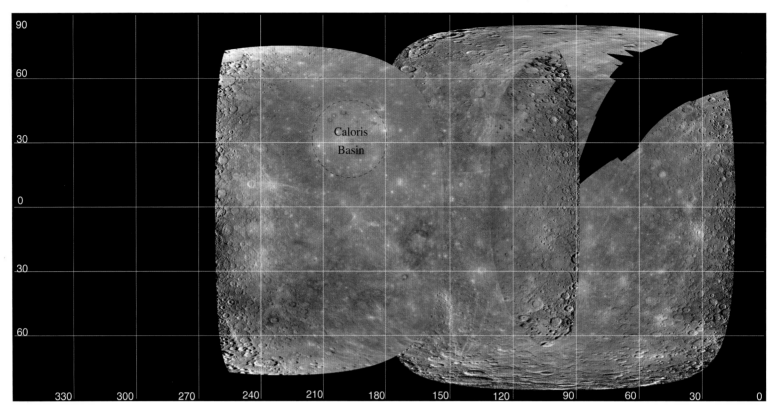

This map of Mercury was produced from data returned from Mariner 10 and the first MESSENGER flyby in January 2008. The two spacecraft provided different views of features such as the Caloris Basin due to changes in sun angle. The entire planet will be mapped when MESSENGER enters orbit around Mercury in 2011.

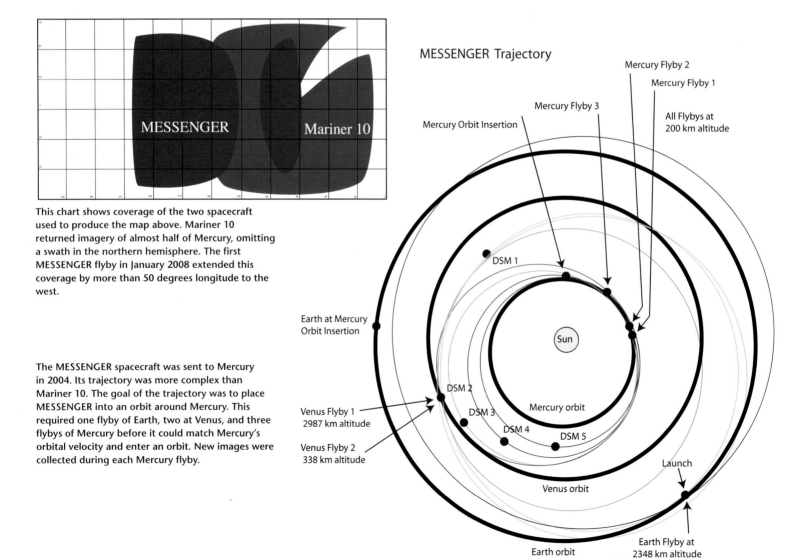

This chart shows coverage of the two spacecraft used to produce the map above. Mariner 10 returned imagery of almost half of Mercury, omitting a swath in the northern hemisphere. The first MESSENGER flyby in January 2008 extended this coverage by more than 50 degrees longitude to the west.

The MESSENGER spacecraft was sent to Mercury in 2004. Its trajectory was more complex than Mariner 10. The goal of the trajectory was to place MESSENGER into an orbit around Mercury. This required one flyby of Earth, two at Venus, and three flybys of Mercury before it could match Mercury's orbital velocity and enter an orbit. New images were collected during each Mercury flyby.

MESSENGER Trajectory

This image was acquired by MESSENGER on October 6, 2008, during its second flyby of Mercury. The majority of this area was newly imaged by MESSENGER on this flyby. Kuiper Crater appears near the left side of the image. Rays of bright material were ejected from an impact crater off the upper edge of this image.

part seven

ACROSS THE SOLAR SYSTEM

What have we learned about the outer Solar System since the beginning of the space age in 1957? The answer is quite a lot. This region, known for the Jovian planets—Jupiter, Saturn, Uranus, and Neptune, as well as their planet-sized satellites—have proven endlessly fascinating. These objects, along with others that may best be characterized as comets, meteors, and asteroids, collectively account for 99% of the mass in orbit around the Sun. While Jupiter and Saturn are largely made up of hydrogen and helium, Uranus and Neptune have considerable icy features. Each of these gas giants has rings of dust and other particles, although only that of Saturn is easily discernible without special instruments. Beyond the gas giants are two other regions of the Solar System. These are known as the Kuiper Belt, populated by icy minor bodies with highly eccentric orbits, and the Oort Cloud consisting of objects composed largely of frozen elements. The outer Solar System is also home to five dwarf planets: Ceres, in the asteroid belt between Mars and Jupiter, as well as Pluto (classified before 2006 as the ninth planet), Haumea, Makemake, and Eris, all located in the Kuiper Belt.

During the decade of the 1960s the U.S. space program began an impressive effort to gather information on the outer Solar System using a variety of equipment. Especially important in this project was the use of two types of spacecraft, one a probe sent toward a body in the Solar System, and the second an Earth-orbiting observatory that could gain the clearest resolution available in telescopes because it did not have to contend with the Earth's atmosphere. The analysis of these new data revolutionized humanity's understanding of Earth's neighbors beyond Mars.

The satellite exploration of the outer Solar System gained steam in the 1970s, leading some to refer to the decade as the "golden age" of planetary science. Studies of the outer Solar System—especially Jupiter, Saturn, Uranus, Neptune, Pluto, and other Kuiper Belt objects—captured the imagination of many people from all types of backgrounds like nothing else save the Apollo lunar missions. For all the genuine importance of magnetospheric physics and solar studies, meteorology and plate tectonics, it was photographs of the planets and theories about the origins of the Solar System that appealed to a much broader cross-section of the public. While observation of the planets from Earth-bound instruments had been going on for centuries, with the beginning of the space age investigations using radio, radar, and optical astronomy entered a new era. This capability, coupled with visits to the planets beyond Mars, rewrote the science textbooks of the world.

Since the first missions to the outer planets in the 1970s with Pioneer 10 and 11 and Voyagers 1 and 2, a host of spacecraft have been dispatched to explore these strange new worlds. If the 1970s brought the first results of probes to the outer Solar System, the 1990s saw the first sustained efforts to learn about them. The Galileo probe to Jupiter, the Cassini mission to Saturn, and New Horizons to Pluto and the Kuiper Belt all represented enormously significant developments in the exploration of the outer Solar System.

This montage of the planets and four large moons of Jupiter in this solar system are set against a false-color view of the Rosette Nebula. The light emitted from the Rosette Nebula results from the presence of hydrogen (red), oxygen (green), and sulfur (blue). Most of the planetary images in this montage were obtained by NASA's planetary missions, which have dramatically changed the human understanding of the Solar System in the past 50 years.

Three Zones of the Solar System

The solar system consists of the Sun and the objects bound to it through gravity. This includes the Sun, eight planets (since in 2006 Pluto was redesignated a dwarf planet), their 158 currently known moons, and a large number of asteroids, meteoroids, planetoids, comets, and interplanetary dust. These may be conveniently divided into three distinct zones, each with its own characteristics. The inner zone closest to the Sun contains rocky planets, known as terrestrial planets because of their comparative relationship to Earth. The second part contains the four gas giant planets—Jupiter, Saturn, Uranus, and Neptune. The third

zone includes the Kuiper Belt, of which Pluto is the most famous (but not largest) body, and the Oort Cloud of distant long-period comets.

Each of these zones has its own challenges and opportunities. The terrestrial planets in this Solar System occupy a habitable zone, defined as the region around a star that has conditions conducive to life as we understand it. Fundamentally, this means that the region has at least some planets with temperatures high enough to maintain liquid water. Of course, Earth is seemingly the only object in our Solar System in this category but evidence supported the theory that Mars once had liquid water as

well. Accordingly, the planets in this zone have long been viewed as possible abodes of life and were early targets for exploration because of this and because of their relative closeness to Earth. All have been visited, some of them many times, and the findings from the scientific investigations have both dashed hopes of finding life and excited other possibilities for exploration.

Beyond the orbit of Mars but inside the orbit of Jupiter lies the main asteroid belt, consisting of thousands of rocky and metallic bodies. The total mass of this material is small.

The second zone, the Jovian planets or gas

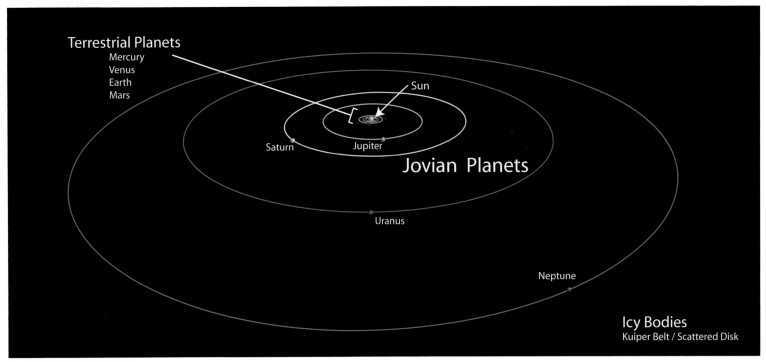

The three zones of the Solar System.

This artist's concept depicts a hypothetical Solar System similar to this one. As we look from the outer fringes of the system, a ring of dusty debris can be seen, and within it, planets circling a star the size of our Sun. This debris is all that remains of the planet-forming disk from which the planets evolved. Planets are formed when dusty material in a large disk surrounding a young star clumps together. Leftover material is eventually blown out by solar wind or pushed out by gravitational interactions with planets. Billions of years later, only an outer disk of debris remains. These outer debris disks are too faint to be viewed by visible-light telescopes. They are washed out by the glare of the Sun.

giants, have enamored all astronomers from the time that Galileo turned the first telescope on them. Little wonder that as soon as the opportunity permitted, spacecraft began to visit these. The most stunning of these missions was the Voyager 1 and 2 probes to the outer Solar System. Launched in 1977, these spacecraft visited their primary targets of Jupiter and Saturn and then went on to all the giant outer planets. The two Voyagers took well over 100,000 images of the outer planets, rings, and satellites, as well as millions of magnetic, chemical spectra, and radiation measurements. The Voyagers' windshield tour of the Jovian

planets in the second zone returned information to Earth that revolutionized the science of planetary astronomy.

The Kuiper Belt comprising the third zone is perhaps the most mysterious of those parts of the Solar System since it is as yet unexplored by spacecraft. There are more icy dwarf planets than in the other two zones, and this led the National Academy of Sciences to assign priority to missions to visit this third zone—especially the Pluto–Charon system—and the New Horizons mission was launched in 2006 to help fulfill this objective.

In the Kuiper Belt, icy dwarf planets represent

a fascinating puzzle. Are they planetary embryos, whose growth was stunted? Are they relics of the origin of the Solar System? Most scientists believe they are both, dating back more than 4 billion years. If they are the bodies out of which the larger planets accumulated, they promise new understandings of the origins and evolution of the Solar System. With these efforts to explore the farthest zone of the Solar System, humanity will complete the first stage of the reconnaissance of the Solar System. What is learned in the process will inform the direction of future explorations.

This image from Cassini shows four moons huddled near Saturn's multi-hued disk. The coloration of the planet's northern hemisphere has changed noticeably since the Cassini spacecraft's arrival in orbit in mid-2004. Giant Titan (5,150 kilometers, or 3,200 miles across), with its darker winter hemisphere, dominates the smaller moons in the scene. Beneath and left of Titan is Janus (181 kilometers, or 113 miles across). Mimas (397 kilometers, or 247 miles across) appears as a bright dot close to the planet and beneath the rings. Prometheus (102 kilometers, or 63 miles across) is a faint speck hugging the rings between the two small moons. This view looks toward the unilluminated side of the rings from less than a degree above the ringplane. This image was taken by Cassini's wide-angle camera on October 26, 2007, at a distance of approximately 1.5 million kilometers (920,000 miles) from Saturn and 2.7 million kilometers (1.7 million miles) from Titan.

Studying the Sun

Throughout the globe astronomers and other scientists, as well as many amateurs, turn their telescopes toward the Sun to learn about the Earth's nearest star. In addition, since the beginning of the space age scientists have dispatched numerous probes to investigate the features and effects of the Sun on Earth. The explosions (flares and coronal mass ejections) on the Sun fascinate us, and the highly energetic particles and millions of tons of very hot, electrified material expelled holds important ramifications for life on this planet. Indeed, sometimes this material takes a collision course with Earth and affects our orbiting satellites and electronics. As humanity becomes more dependent upon satellites in space we will increasingly feel the effects of space weather and need to predict it.

The magnetic emissions from the Sun are also critical to this planet, and how it interacts with the Earth's magnetosphere has a profound influence on us. The most famous effect from this interaction is the Aurora in the polar latitudes when the upper atmosphere becomes excited by energetic electrons from storms on the Sun. Additionally, when the Earth's environment is affected by activity from the Sun it causes geomagnetic storms and variations in the Earth's magnetic field.

Moreover, scientists who study the Sun have helped to chart the history of the Solar System, its origin and evolution, and are capable of predicting in a general sense what will happen to the Sun and the planets that orbit it in the distant future. With the Sun as a test subject, scientists have been able to resolve features and study physical processes in a way that is impossible with more distant stars and other astrophysical objects. Their work has determined that other stars also have spots and hot coronae. They also have learned how energy is released and particles are accelerated in the universe by studying these same processes on the Sun. Existing theories of particle physics are in part the result of these investigations.

Beginning at the start of the space age an extensive constellation of satellites has been dispatched toward the Sun to study solar properties and especially the Sun/Earth connection. Some of the satellites and observatories have made it their special mission to study the Sun at the height of the solar maximum, an 11-year cycle of activity. Some of the major satellites involved in this effort include:

• Orbiting Solar Observatory (OSO): this series of eight NASA satellites built to study the Sun was launched between 1962 and 1975. Their primary mission was to observe an 11-year sunspot cycle in ultraviolet and X-ray spectra.

• Helios I and II: launched in 1974 and 1976 these probes, a joint project of NASA and the Federal Republic of Germany, entered a heliocentric orbit to study solar processes.

• Solar Maximum Mission: this satellite was a pioneering mission in the field of solar science. It was launched in 1980 to study solar activity during the solar maximum and collected images and data for nine years.

• Geotail: launched in 1992 by Japan's Institute of Space and Astronautical Science (ISAS) and NASA, Geotail studied the magnetosphere to see how the solar wind and Earth interact.

• Yohkah: a Japanese satellite launched in 1992, Yohkah used X-ray instruments to collect data about the Sun.

• Ulysses: undertaking a polar orbit around the Sun, Ulysses completed its first orbit in 1994–1995 and continued thereafter to study high-altitude solar wind during solar maximum.

• Wind: launched on November 1, 1994, by NASA, Wind explored the solar wind to help decipher its physical and chemical properties.

• The Solar and Heliospheric Observatory (SOHO): launched in 1995 SOHO studied the Sun from its position 1.5 million kilometers out in space.

• Polar: launched on February 24, 1996, by NASA, this satellite makes daily passes over Earth's north and south poles to measure the energy and particles flowing into and out of the magnetosphere and producing the aurora.

• ACE (Advanced Composition Explorer): launched on August 25, 1997, the primary purpose of ACE was to determine and compare the isotopic and elemental composition of several distinct samples of matter, including the solar corona, the interplanetary medium, the local interstellar medium, and Galactic matter.

• Transition Region and Coronal Explorer (TRACE): launched in April 1998 this satellite gave scientists valuable information on magnetic field conditions in the photosphere, the transition region, and the corona during the upcoming solar maximum.

Launched in December 1995, the Solar and Heliospheric Observatory (SOHO) flew an eccentric orbit to L1, entering a halo orbit around the point and delivering data about the Sun/Earth connection. From that vantage point it observed solar activity. The halo orbit allowed for uninterrupted observations of the Sun in ultraviolet and other wavelengths. Since April 1996 it has kept the Sun under almost constant observation, enabling the early warning of solar coronal mass ejections that could potentially disrupt communications.

- Genesis: launched in 1999 this spacecraft collected solar wind samples and returned them to Earth, but the recovery was faulty with the failure of the parachute system. Nonetheless, scientists recovered much of the data from the probe.
- Cluster II: two satellites launched July 16, 2000, these satellites measured the Earth's magnetic field by making simultaneous measurements. They enabled a three-dimensional study of the changes and processes taking place in near-Earth space.
- IMAGE (Imager for Magnetopause-to-Aurora Global Exploration): launched in early 2000 this satellite used neutral atom, ultraviolet, and radio imaging techniques to collect data about the magnetosphere during substorms and magnetic storms in the solar maximum.
- Reuven Ramaty High-Energy Solar Spectroscopic Imager (HESSI): launched on February 5, 2002, HESSI measured the energy released during a solar flare through a combination of high-resolution imaging in X-rays and gamma rays along with high-resolution spectroscopy. This approach enabled researchers to find out where these particles were accelerated and to what energies. Such information was intended to advance understanding of the fundamental high-energy processes at the core of the solar flare problem.
- Solar TErrestrial RElations Observatory (STEREO): launched on September 18, 2006, this spacecraft used two observatories—one ahead of Earth in its orbit and the other trailing behind—to study the structure and evolution of solar storms as they blast from the Sun and move out through space.
- Hinode (SOLAR-B): launched on September 23, 2006, this was Japan's third solar observation satellite. It contained three onboard telescopes to study the Sun's eruptive phenomena and space weather, helping to predict the Sun's influence on the Earth.
- Time History of Events and Macroscale Interactions during Substorms mission (THEMIS): launched in February 2007, five identical satellites line up once every four days along the equator and take observations synchronized with ground observatories of aurora phenomena.

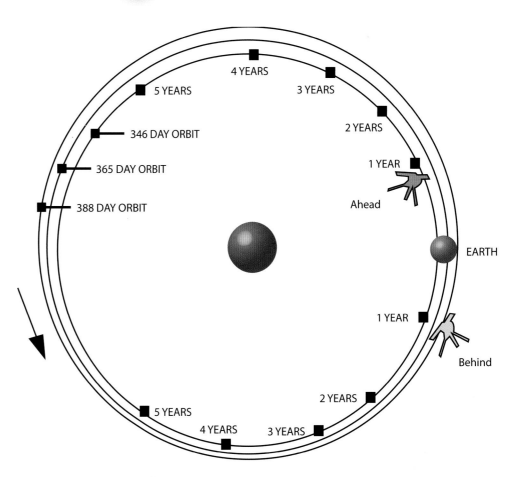

The twin Solar-Terrestrial Relations Observatory (STEREO) spacecraft were launched in October 2006 to study the three-dimensional structure of solar emissions. One probe was placed into solar orbit with a period of 388 days, the other with a period of 346 days. In those two orbits, one STEREO spacecraft slowly moves ahead of the Earth while the other slowly loses ground. By 2010 the two probes will be located at nearly opposite points from each other within Earth's path around the Sun. Using two identical sets of instruments, it is possible to observe the movement of material ejected from the Sun toward the Earth.

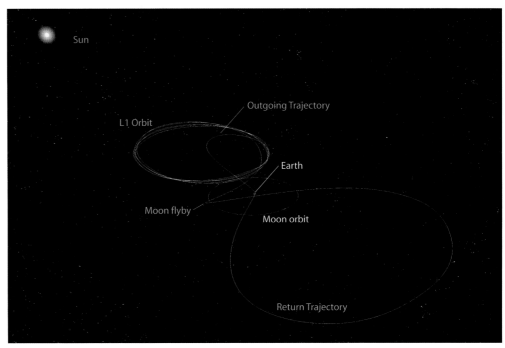

The goal of the Genesis mission was to collect particles from the solar wind and return them to Earth for laboratory study. Launched in August 2001, it first entered a halo orbit around the L1 libration point between the Earth and Sun. After two and a half years of collecting solar particles, it left the L1 halo orbit in April 2004. After a flyby of the Moon, Genesis released its return capsule and returned to L1 halo orbit. The return capsule entered the Earth's atmosphere on September 8, 2004. The parachute failed to deploy, causing the capsule to impact the ground at high velocity. However, the majority of the science goals were later met.

This image from SOHO shows the Sun as it appeared on October 17, 2008.

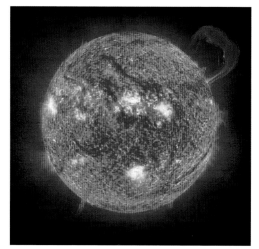

This Extreme Ultraviolet Imaging Telescope (EIT) aboard SOHO image of a huge, handle-shaped prominence was taken on September 14, 1999, showing prominences of huge clouds of relatively cool dense plasma suspended in the Sun's hot, thin corona. The hottest areas appear almost white, approximately 60,000 degrees K, while the darker red areas indicate cooler temperatures.

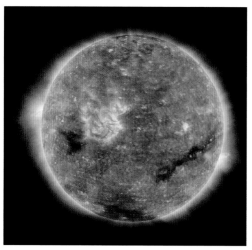

On March 26, 2007, this image was taken by the SECCHI Extreme UltraViolet Imager (EUVI) mounted on the STEREO-B spacecraft. STEREO-B is located behind the Earth, and follows the Earth in orbit around the Sun. This location enables us to view the Sun from the position of a virtual left eye in space.

Helios Orbits

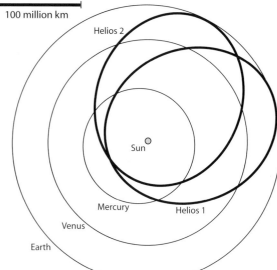

Helios I was launched on December 10, 1974, and Helios II was launched on January 15, 1976. This illustration depicts the highly heliocentric orbits of the spacecraft ranging from the orbit of Earth to inside the orbit of Mercury around the Sun. The purpose of the mission was to make pioneering measurements of the interplanetary medium from the vicinity of the Earth's orbit to 0.3 Astronomical Units (AU). Helios I ended its mission in 1982 after several years of successful operation, while Helios II was less successful and ended its mission on April 17, 1976. The two Helios probes were designed to study the environment near the Sun. They carried instruments to measure solar magnetic fields and charged particles.

This illustration depicts the extensive orbital trajectory of the Ulysses spacecraft on its journey around the Solar System, noting its Jupiter flyby en route to its polar orbit over the Sun. Launched in October 1990, the spacecraft's six-year orbits over the Sun's poles allowed scientists to observe it from an unprecedented angle during both calm and turbulent periods. Initially directed toward Jupiter, it swung by that planet to enter a polar orbit around the Sun, the only spacecraft to do so. During passes over the north and south poles of the Sun, Ulysses collected data on the solar wind, magnetic fields, and X-rays. Ulysses made the first direct measurements of interstellar dust particles and interstellar helium atoms in the Solar System and the discovery that the magnetic field leaving the Sun is balanced across latitudes. The observations redefined the way scientists thought about space weather.

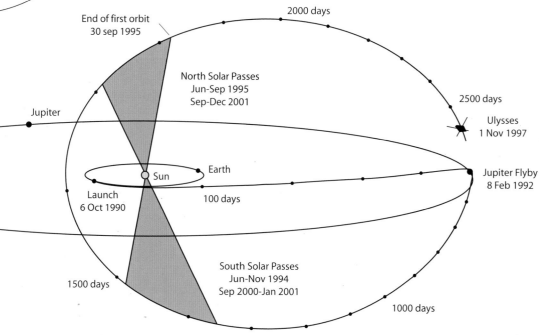

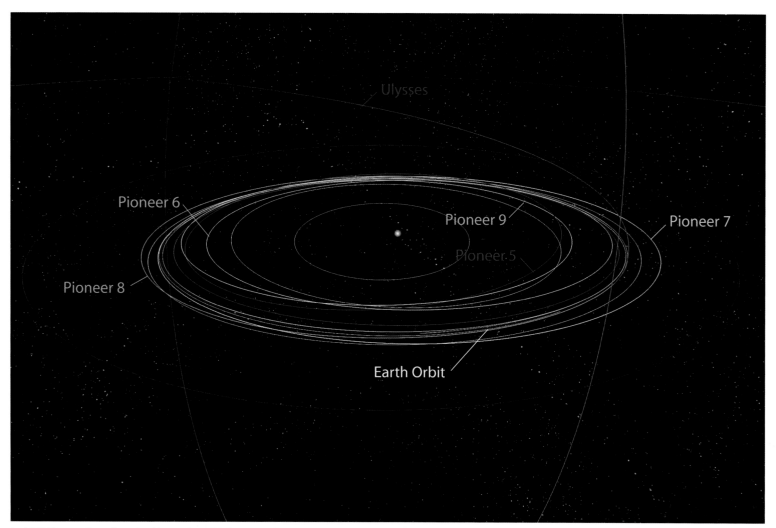

In 1960 Pioneer 5 was launched into solar orbit between the Earth and Venus. It was followed by Pioneers 6–9 from 1965 to 1968. The Pioneer spacecraft were equipped with instruments to study the Sun. Pioneer 6 was the longest-surviving spacecraft. Data were received from Pioneer 6 in December 2000, 35 years after launch. This chart shows the distribution of Pioneers 5–9 across the inner Solar System. All those probes remain in solar orbit near Earth's path around the Sun. Also shown is the trajectory of the later Ulysses spacecraft.

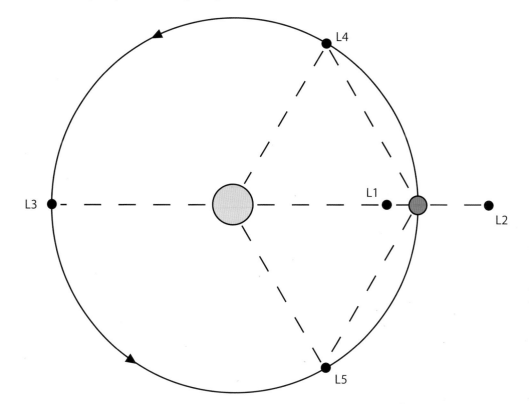

In a system when one body orbits another, there are certain points when the gravitational attraction is equal. At these libration points, also called Lagrange points, a spacecraft can maintain a stable position with little use of propellant. Italian-French mathematician Josef Lagrange discovered these five serene points at locations where the gravitational pull of the two larger bodies precisely cancel each other out. There are three Lagrange points—labeled L1, L2, and L3—resting along an invisible line between the two larger bodies. The L1 point of the Earth-Sun system affords an uninterrupted view of the Sun and is currently home to SOHO. L2 is located at a more distant point. The other two Lagrange points—labeled L4 and L5—form the apex of two equilateral triangles that have the large masses at equidistant angles. Spacecraft can also be placed in a "halo" orbit around each of these points. Libration points have been especially useful for missions to study the Sun.

Chasing Comets

Comets are some of the most exciting astronomical objects to view. As small Solar System bodies that often fly close to the Sun they sometimes exhibit a visible tail resulting from interactions with solar radiation. It is the presence of this tail, more properly called a coma, that largely distinguishes comets from asteroids. Overall, comets are loose collections of ice, dust, and rocks that rarely measure more than a few miles in diameter.

Most comets of the Solar System are believed to have originated in the Kuiper Belt or the associated scattered disc beyond the orbit of Neptune. They sometimes come to the inner Solar System by gravitational disturbances from the gas giants or because of collisions with other objects. There are some famous comets that fly near Earth regularly. These include the Perseid meteor showers that occur every year between August 9 and 13 when the Earth passes through the orbit of the Comet Swift-Tuttle. Comet Halley, furthermore, makes a visit to the region of Earth every 75–76 years and always presents a dramatic image in the nighttime sky. Scientists have found 3,535 comets as of June 2008 but this number is steadily increasing and some speculate that there may appropriately be as many as one trillion such bodies in the outer Solar System.

Since the dawn of the space age, humanity has sought to visit various comets and in 1986 the periodic visit of Comet Halley presented an opportunity to do so. Several nations sent an armada of spacecraft to take measurements of the object. The Soviet Vega 1 began returning images of Halley on March 4, 1986, and the first ever of its nucleus, and made its flyby on March 6, followed by Vega 2 on March 9. The Giotto probe from the European Space Agency also made its closest pass on March 14, and two Japanese spacecraft, Sakigake and Suisei, followed. Notable by its absence was any spacecraft sent by NASA.

The following is a brief list of various missions to comets since Comet Halley in 1986.

- Halley Armada: encountered Comet Halley in 1986. It consisted of probes from the European Space Agency (ESA), two from the Soviet Union and France, and two from Japan. These were Giotto, the first space probe to get close-up color images of the nucleus of a comet (ESA);

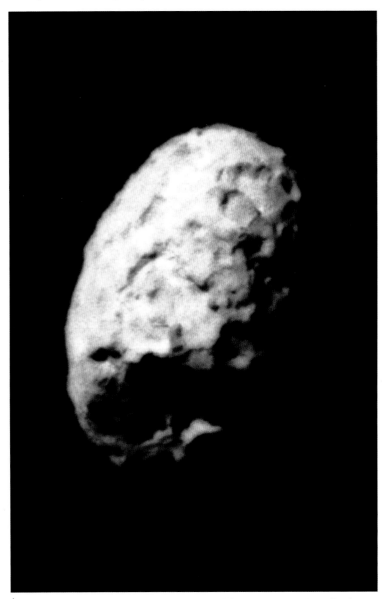

The Stardust spacecraft arrived at the comet Wild 2 in January 2004, collecting material from the comet's tail and returning images. This view from Stardust shows the 2-kilometer-wide nucleus of Wild 2.

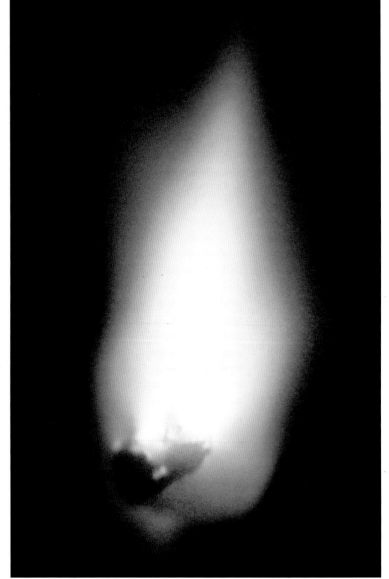

The first clear images of a comet nucleus were returned by the Giotto spacecraft during its flyby of Halley's Comet on March 13, 1986. This image shows the plume of material being released by the nucleus, which is approximately 15x8 kilometers. The Sun is in the direction toward the lower margin as seen here.

Vega 1 and Vega 2, which dropped a balloon probe and lander on Venus before going on to Comet Halley (USSR/France); and Suisei and Sakigake, Japan's first probes to leave Earth's orbit.

- International Sun-Earth Explorer (ISEE) 3/International Cometary Explorer (ICE): launched August 12, 1978, by NASA, this was the first U.S. spacecraft to fly past a comet. It flew through the tail of comet Giacobini-Zinner, further confirming theories that comets are "dirty snowballs" of ice and rock. The spacecraft is on a trajectory that will bring it close to Earth in August 2014. It could possibly be recaptured and returned to Earth, and ultimately end up on display at the Smithsonian Institution's National Air and Space Museum.
- Galileo: while not intended as a comet explorer, the Galileo probe to Jupiter launched in 1989 provided the only direct observations of comet Shoemaker-Levy 9's spectacular impact with Jupiter on July 16–22, 1994. Earth-based astronomers had to wait to see the impact sites as they rotated into view. Galileo's images, while fuzzy, revealed the shocking power of the collision.
- Ulysses: also not intended as a comet hunter, Ullysses made unplanned studies of comets Hale-Bopp and Hyakutake in May 1996 when it unexpectedly encountered Hyakutake's tail as its nucleus approached the Sun. This tail extended half a billion kilometers (more than 300 million miles)—more than three times the distance from the Earth to the Sun.
- Deep Space 1: launched by NASA in 1998 this probe flew within 10 miles (16 kilometers) of Asteroid 1992 KD Braille on July 28, 1999. A test of new propulsion and navigation technology, it also flew by two other comets, Wilson-Harrington and Borrelly.
- Stardust: launched by NASA in 1999, it flew past comet Wild 2 and captured dust grains blown from the comet's surface. These were returned to Earth for analysis in January 2006. The return capsule is now on display at the Smithsonian Institution's National Air and Space Museum.
- COmet Nucleus Tour (CONTOUR): launched by NASA on July 3, 2002, this mission was designed to make a detailed study of the interior of at least two comets, especially Encke, Schwassmann-Wachmann 3 SW3, and d'Arrest. NASA lost contact with the spacecraft after an August 15, 2002, engine burn intended to propel it out of Earth orbit.
- Rosetta: launched by the European Space Agency on March 2, 2004, this space-

craft began a 10-year mission to explore comet 67P/Churyumov-Gerasimenko, making orbits of the comet and observing it for two years as it approached the Sun. Rosetta will also release a small lander to the surface of the comet.

- Deep Impact-EPOXI: a NASA/University of Maryland mission was launched on January 12, 2005, to deliver a special impactor spacecraft into the path of comet Tempel 1. The spacecraft successfully accomplished this task in July 2005 and observed a fine, powdery material, not the expected water, ice, and dirt emanating from the comet. It is now on an extended mission to observe a second comet, Hartley 2, making its closest approach in 2010.

This image was taken from NASA's Kuiper Airborne Observatory, on April 8/9, 1986, during its New Zealand Expedition to image Comet Halley as it crossed the Milky Way.

This artist's rendering of the Stardust spacecraft shows it encountering Comet Wild 2. The spacecraft was launched on February 7, 1999, from Cape Canaveral Air Station, Florida, aboard a Delta II rocket. It delivered samples from the comet to Earth in January 2006.

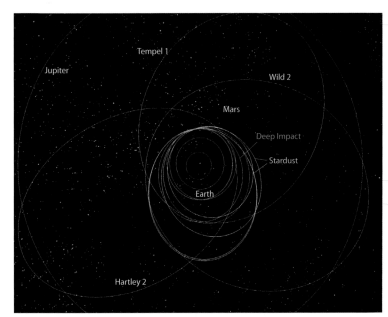

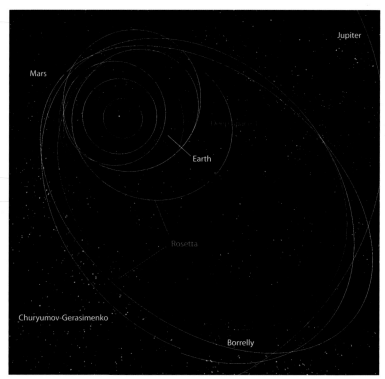

The Stardust mission collected particles from a comet and returned samples to Earth. After entering an elliptical solar orbit it encountered comet Wild 2 on January 2, 2004. The samples were returned to Earth on January 15, 2006. The main spacecraft remained in its elliptical solar orbit, and a flyby of comet Tempel 1 was planned for February 2011. Stardust would visit Tempel 1 almost six years after the Deep Impact mission. The Deep Impact mission was to visit a comet and send a small probe to impact a comet at high velocity, while the main spacecraft returned images and other data from a relatively safe distance. Deep Impact was launched on January 12, 2005, into an elliptical solar orbit. It arrived at the comet Tempel 1 on July 4, 2005. The impactor hit the surface at a relative velocity of more than 10 kilometers per second, releasing enough energy to vaporize a large amount of material. Instruments on the main spacecraft recorded the composition of this material. After the main mission was completed, three Earth flybys were planned to allow Deep Impact to rendezvous with comet Hartley 2 in October 2010.

Deep Space 1 was launched in October 1998 to demonstrate technology necessary to visit small bodies in the inner solar system. It performed a flyby of the comet Borrelly in September 2001, returning images and other data. Rosetta was launched in March 2004 to perform close observation of comet Churyumov-Gerasimenko beginning in 2014. It carries a small lander, Philae, which will land on the comet after achieving orbit. To match the comet's orbit, Rosetta performed maneuvers to make its orbit more elliptical. On February 25, 2007, Rosetta flew by Mars to achieve the orbit necessary to reach Churyumov-Gerasimenko. On September 5, 2008, during another one of its preliminary orbits, Rosetta flew by the asteroid 2867 Steins.

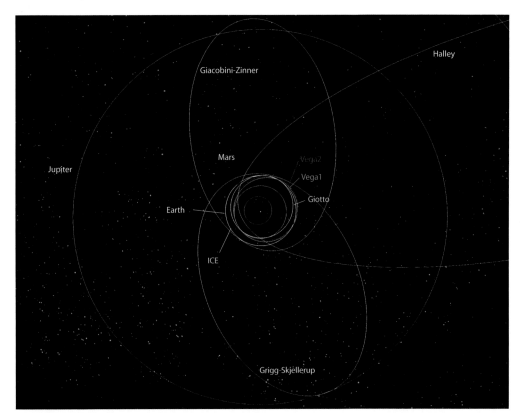

This illustration depicts the path of the Halley Armada as it encountered Comet Halley in 1986. Intense interest followed the return of Halley's Comet in 1986–1987, encouraging several missions to visit the famous object. At the same time the ICEE 3 spacecraft was renamed ICE and targeted to another comet, Giacobini-Zinner. The Soviet Union sent the Vega 1 and 2 probes to intercept Halley. Both were launched in December 1984 and performed flybys of Venus before reaching Halley. At Venus, Vega 1 and 2 released decent modules containing atmospheric balloons. These balloons carried instruments for measuring atmospheric conditions and composition. Vega 1 arrived at Halley on March 6, 1986. Vega 2 followed three days later. In 1985 the European Giotto spacecraft was launched into solar orbit to intercept Halley. It returned images and other data during a close flyby on March 13, 1986. Impacting dust particles damaged some instruments, including the camera. After the Halley encounter, Giotto became the first spacecraft from deep space to fly by the Earth, receiving a gravitational boost. This altered its orbit to allow for a flyby of the comet Grigg-Skjellerup on July 10, 1992. Also sent to Halley were the twin Japanese Suisei and Sakigake spacecraft. Suisei entered elliptical solar orbit and encountered Halley on March 8, 1986. Sakigake followed on March 11. In 1992 Sakigake flew by the Earth, followed by two more Earth flybys.

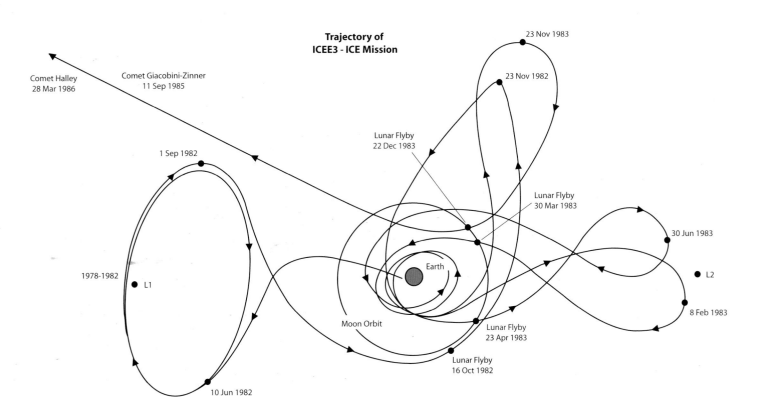

Trajectory of ICEE3 - ICE Mission

The International Sun-Earth Explorer (ICEE) 3 spacecraft was placed in an elliptical halo L1 orbit in 1978 as part of a three-spacecraft mission to study Sun-Earth interactions. ICEE 3 was later renamed the International Cometary Explorer (ICE) when it was decided to send it to intercept comet Giacobini-Zinner. ICEE 3 left its L1 halo orbit in September 1982, performed five flybys of the Moon, arrived at the vicinity of the L2 libration point twice, and swung by the Earth several times. This very complex trajectory allowed ICE to visit comet Giacobini-Zinner in September 1985. It also made distant observations of Halley's comet in March 1986. It was the first spacecraft to fly by a comet.

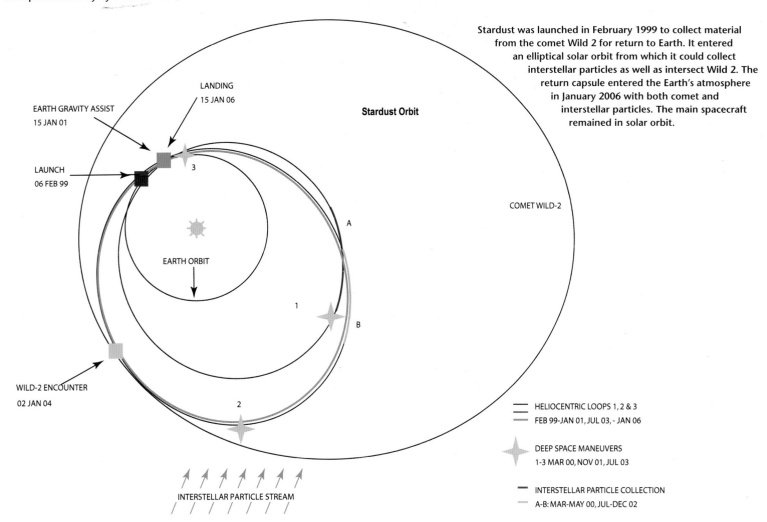

Stardust was launched in February 1999 to collect material from the comet Wild 2 for return to Earth. It entered an elliptical solar orbit from which it could collect interstellar particles as well as intersect Wild 2. The return capsule entered the Earth's atmosphere in January 2006 with both comet and interstellar particles. The main spacecraft remained in solar orbit.

Asteroids and Other Objects

Since humans first began charting the heavens, several hundred thousand asteroids have been discovered and given designations, and there seems no end in sight to the perhaps millions more that might yet be discovered. They range in size from tiny particles, some streaking into the Earth's atmosphere and burning up from the friction, to larger objects as much as 164 miles (200 km) in diameter. There are in 2008 a total of 26 known asteroids larger than 164 miles in diameter. Scientists believe they have identified 99% of those asteroids ranging larger than 62 miles (100 km) in diameter, but of those smaller, in the 10 to 100 km range, only about half have been catalogued.

The largest asteroid by far is 1 Ceres, an object approaching 974 km in diameter and containing about 25% of the mass of all other known asteroids combined. The next largest are 2 Pallas, 4 Vesta, and 10 Hygiea, which are between 400 and 525 km in diameter. All other known asteroids are less than 340 km across.

It is important to track these objects, because even a small asteroid impact could have disastrous consequences for Earth should a large one strike the planet. A sky survey to identify and track these objects is under way but much works remains.

Several asteroids have been explored, if only in a cursory fashion. Not intended as an asteroid hunter, the Galileo spacecraft sent to Jupiter in 1989 encountered two asteroids en route to the Solar System's largest planet. It passed by asteroid 951 Gaspra at a distance of 1,000 miles (1,600 km) in 1991. The knowledge gained there—noting that Gaspra is an irregular object (19 x 12 x 11 kilometers) lacking the large craters common on many planetary satellites—excited scientists for the next encounter with asteroid 243 Ida, at a distance of 1,500 miles (2,400 kilometers). Surprisingly, Galileo showed a tiny moon orbiting Ida—the first known moon of an asteroid. Dactyl, about 1 mile (1.5 km) in diameter, orbits about 62 miles (100 km) from Ida's center.

Since that time there have been several additional encounters with asteroids, some of the missions specifically designed for asteroid-only activities. A list of major programs follow:

- Near-Earth Asteroid Rendezvous (NEAR) Shoemaker: launched by NASA in 1996, NEAR flew within 753 miles (1,212 kilometers) of Asteroid Mathilde in June 1997. It rendezvoused with and landed on the asteroid Eros in February 12, 2001.
- Deep Space 1: launched in 1998, Deep Space 1 flew past asteroid 9969 Braille in July 1999. During a flyby at a range of only 16 miles (26 km), Deep Space 1's instruments found intriguing similarities between Braille and asteroid Vesta, one of the largest asteroids in the Solar System.
- Stardust: built for a comet rendezvous and sample return, it also encountered asteroid Annefrank in 2002, passing within 2,050 miles (3,300 km) of the asteroid, finding it irregularly shaped, cratered, and about 5 miles (8 km) in diameter.
- Hayabusa (MUSES-C): launched on May 9, 2003, this was a Japanese sample return mission to the asteroid Itokawa. In November 2005 it successfully landed on Itokawa. In April 2007, Hayabusa started full cruising operation to return to Earth.
- Dawn: launched in 2007, Dawn began an

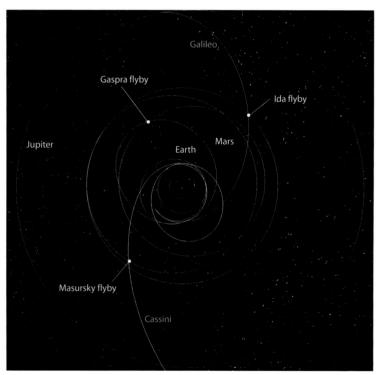

Missions to the outer planets must pass through the main asteroid belt between the orbits of Mars and Jupiter. They can include encounters with asteroids before their arrival at Jupiter or Saturn. The Galileo spacecraft performed two loops through the asteroid belt on its way to Jupiter. During the first, it became the first spacecraft to visit an asteroid. On October 29, 1991, Galileo flew by the asteroid 951 Gaspra. On August 28, 1993, during its final orbit toward Jupiter, Galileo performed a flyby of the asteroid Ida. Images revealed the presence of the small satellite orbiting the asteroid, which was later named Dactyl. The Cassini mission to Saturn also performed several orbits to achieve the necessary velocity to reach its destination. On January 23, 2000, Cassini encountered the asteroid Masursky during its passage through the asteroid belt.

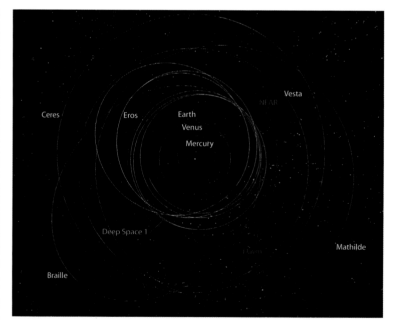

The Near Earth Asteroid Rendezvous (NEAR) - Shoemaker spacecraft was the first to orbit and land on an asteroid. NEAR-Shoemaker encountered the asteroid Mathilde on June 27, 1997. It arrived at the asteroid Eros in January 2000. On February 14, it entered orbit around Eros and later landed on the surface. The Dawn mission was planned to visit the two largest asteroids, Ceres and Vesta. Launched in September 2007, it will arrive at Vesta in 2011 and orbit for about seven months. Dawn will then return to solar orbit and encounter Ceres in 2015. Deep Space 1 flew by the Earth-crossing asteroid Braille on July 29, 1999. This mission was planned to test new technologies. The asteroid flyby was performed while Deep Space 1 was on its way for a comet flyby.

eight-year, 3-billion-mile (4.9 billion km) mission. Beginning in August 2011, Dawn will make the first of two rendezvous with the asteroid Vesta and dwarf planet Ceres (in 2015), two of the largest objects that lie within the asteroid belt between Mars and Jupiter.

Dawn is using small thrusters to achieve the trajectory needed to visit the two largest asteroids. For most of the time between asteroid encounters, it uses an electrically powered thruster to slowly change its velocity. After arriving at Ceres it will remain in orbit around that asteroid.

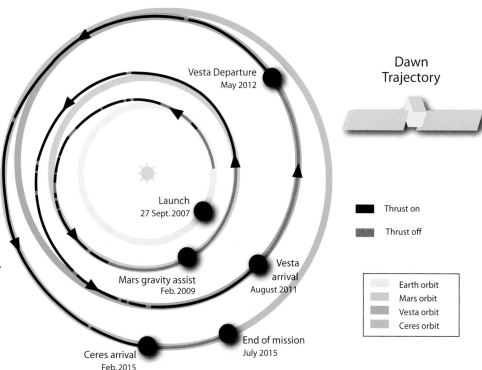

Vesta Departure
May 2012

Launch
27 Sept. 2007

Mars gravity assist
Feb. 2009

Vesta arrival
August 2011

Ceres arrival
Feb. 2015

End of mission
July 2015

Dawn Trajectory

■ Thrust on
▬ Thrust off

Earth orbit
Mars orbit
Vesta orbit
Ceres orbit

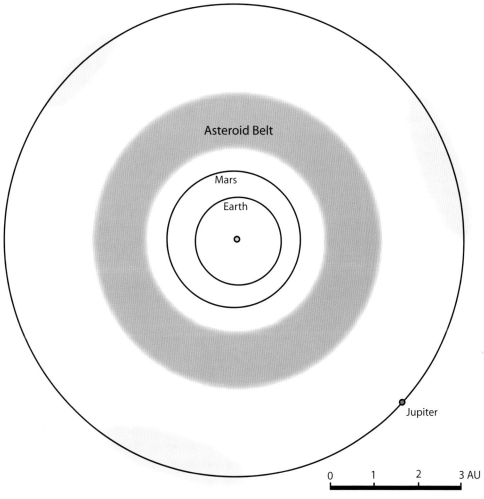

Asteroid Belt

Mars

Earth

Jupiter

0   1   2   3 AU

Most asteroids are in the main asteroid belt, a zone between the orbits of Mars and Jupiter. Only a small number of these asteroids have diameters larger than 100 km, but they contain the majority of the total mass in the main asteroid belt.

Three other distinct groups of asteroids orbit the Sun at the same distance as Jupiter. Trojan asteroids orbit at the libration points between Jupiter and the Sun. They orbit in the same path as Jupiter in leading and trailing positions. The two groups are often known as the "Trojan" and "Greek" asteroids. "Hilda" asteroids orbit at the libration point opposite from Jupiter. The areas shown on this chart contain the vast majority of asteroids, but these zones do not have discrete boundaries. Asteroids can be found across the inner Solar System.

Dawn Spacecraft with Hartmann artistic background.

The European Space Agency's Rosetta spacecraft captured this first image of an unusually bright object in the asteroid belt between Mars and Jupiter, in a flyby on September 7, 2008, that got it as close as 800 km from it. The object was asteroid Steins, Rosetta's first nominal scientific target in its 11½-year mission to explore the nucleus of Comet 67P/Churyumov-Gerasimenko, ESA revealed.

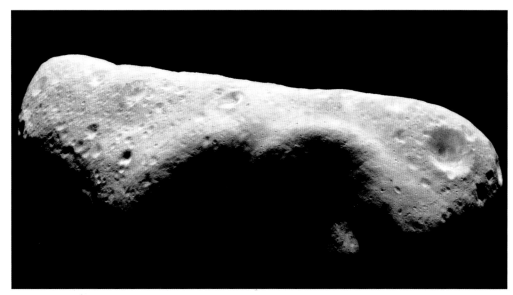

This image mosaic of Eros's southern hemisphere, taken by NEAR-Shoemaker on November 30, 2000, offers a long-distance look at the cratered terrain south of where the spacecraft touched down on February 12, 2001. In this view, south is to the top and the landing site itself is just into the shadows, slightly left of center. The length of the asteroid is 33 kilometers (21 miles).

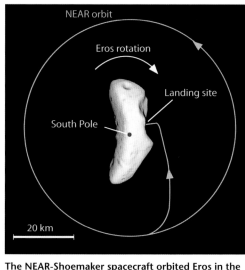

The NEAR-Shoemaker spacecraft orbited Eros in the opposite direction of the asteroid's rotation. This chart shows NEAR in its lower final orbit and the path it took to reach the surface.

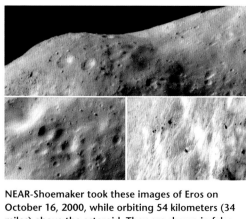

NEAR Trajectory

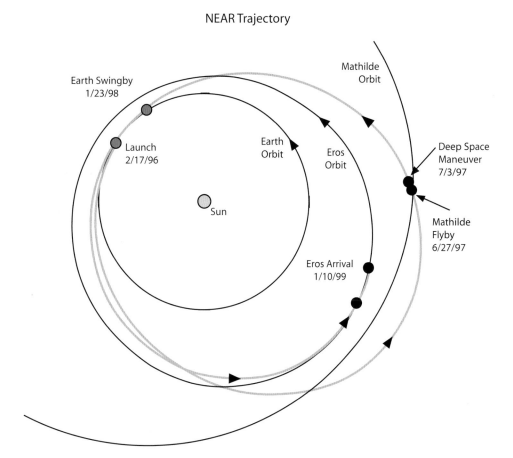

Earth Swingby
1/23/98

Launch
2/17/96

Sun

Earth Orbit

Eros Orbit

Mathilde Orbit

Deep Space Maneuver
7/3/97

Mathilde Flyby
6/27/97

Eros Arrival
1/10/99

NEAR was launched in February 1996. After flying by the asteroid Mathilde and a deep space maneuver, it flew by Earth to receive a gravitational boost to achieve an orbit that matched the asteroid Eros.

NEAR-Shoemaker took these images of Eros on October 16, 2000, while orbiting 54 kilometers (34 miles) above the asteroid. They are shown in false color, constructed from images taken in green light and two different wavelengths of infrared light. Surface materials that have been darkened and reddened by the solar wind and micrometeorite impacts appear as pale brown, whereas fresher materials exposed from the subsurface on steep slopes appear in bright whites or blues. Compared with Gaspra and Ida, similar asteroids imaged in color from the Galileo spacecraft, Eros exhibits large brightness variations but only subtle color variations. The top panorama shows the rounded rim of the saddle-shaped feature Himeros. The fresh, bright materials appear in localized patches set on a background of older fragmental debris, or regolith. In most regions of Eros, such as in the panorama and the view at lower left, the bright patches are strongly concentrated on the inner wall's craters. However, on the inner wall of Himeros (lower right), steep slopes are extensive and the bright material appears as pervasive, scattered patches.

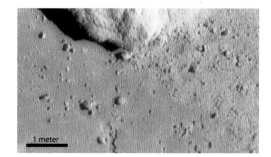

The last image returned by NEAR-Shoemaker before it settled on the surface of Eros. The spacecraft was not designed to survive landing, but it briefly continued to transmit data from the surface.

The small size and minimal gravitational attraction of the asteroid Itokawa allowed the Hayabusa spacecraft to approach the surface and withdraw using only small thrusters.

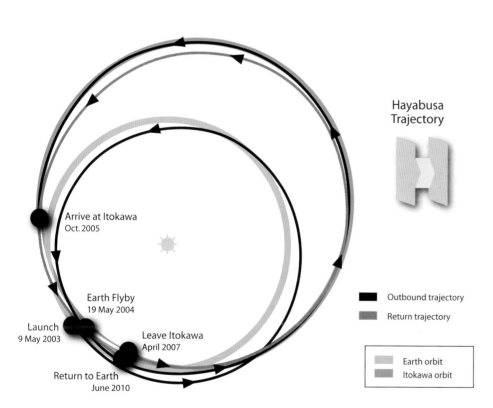

Hayabusa
Trajectory

Artist's conception of the Hayabusa spacecraft and the Minerva surface hopper. Courtesy of JAXA/MEF/ISAS.

Arrive at Itokawa
Oct. 2005

Earth Flyby
19 May 2004

Launch
9 May 2003

Leave Itokawa
April 2007

Return to Earth
June 2010

Outbound trajectory

Return trajectory

Earth orbit
Itokawa orbit

The Hayabusa (originally called MUSES-C) mission was planned to encounter the asteroid Itokawa and approach the surface. A small pellet was to be shot at the surface and a small amount of material collected and returned to Earth. Hayabusa arrived at Itokawa in October 2005. The sample collection was not successful, but the spacecraft continued to operate. Still in solar orbit, it will return to the vicinity of Earth in June 2010.

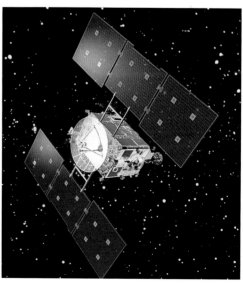

Artist's conception of the Hayabusa spacecraft deploying one of the surface target markers that will be used to guide the spacecraft's descent to the surface of asteroid Itokawa. Courtesy of JAXA/MEF/ISAS.

In Search of Jupiter

Jupiter, the largest planet in the Solar System, is also one of its most intriguing places. With a diameter of 88,846 miles (142,984 km), more than 11 times that of Earth, and a dense atmosphere, it has long been an attractive target for astronomical observation. From Earth, Jupiter also appears brighter than most stars, and is routinely the second brightest planet, after Venus, in the nighttime sky. Located 483,780,000 miles (778,570,000 km) from the Sun, it is more than five times farther than Earth from the Sun. It has also been visited by six spacecraft since the 1970s, including the extended mission of Galileo between 1995 and 2002.

Visitation of Jupiter commenced when NASA scientists realized that once every 176 years, the giant planets on the outer reaches of the Solar System all gathered on one side of the Sun, and such a configuration was due to occur in the late 1970s. This geometric lineup made possible close-up observation of all the planets in the outer Solar System (with the exception of Pluto) in a single flight, the so-called Grand Tour. The flyby of each planet would bend the spacecraft's flight path and increase its velocity enough to deliver it to the next destination. This would occur through a complicated process known as "gravity assist," something like a slingshot effect, whereby the flight time to Neptune could be reduced from 30 to 12 years.

To prepare the way for the Grand Tour, in 1964 NASA conceived Pioneer 10 and 11 as outer Solar System probes. Although severe budgetary constraints prevented starting the project until the fall of 1968 and forced a somewhat less ambitious effort, Pioneer 10 was launched on 3 March 1972. It arrived at Jupiter on the night of 3 December 1973,

This image was acquired by the New Horizons spacecraft during a February 2007 Jupiter flyby on its way to Pluto and the Kuiper Belt. The great Red Spot appears light blue in this infrared view. Jupiter's satellite Io appears in the foreground. Visible near Io's north pole, the volcano Tvashtar is in the midst of an eruption.

and although many were concerned that the spacecraft might be damaged by intense radiation discovered in Jupiter's orbital plane, the spacecraft survived, transmitted data about the planet, and continued on its way out of the Solar System, away from the center of the Milky Way galaxy.

In 1973 NASA launched Pioneer 11, providing scientists with their first close-up view of Jupiter. The close approach and the spacecraft's speed of 107,373 mph, by far the fastest ever reached by an object launched from Earth, hurled Pioneer 11 1.5 billion miles across the Solar System toward Jupiter, encountering the

planet's south pole within 26,600 miles of its cloud tops in December 1974. In 1990 Pioneer 11 officially departed the Solar System by passing beyond Pluto and headed into interstellar space toward the center of the Milky Way galaxy. Pioneer 11 ended its mission September 30, 1995, when the last transmission from the spacecraft was received.

Earth received Pioneer 10's last, very weak signal on January 22, 2003. The last time a Pioneer 10 contact actually returned telemetry data was April 27, 2002. At last contact, Pioneer 10 was 7.6 billion miles from Earth, or eighty-two times the nominal distance between the Sun and Earth. At that distance, it takes more than eleven hours and twenty minutes for the radio signal, traveling at the speed of light, to reach the Earth. It will continue to coast silently as a ghost ship into interstellar space, heading generally for the red star Aldebaran, which forms the eye of the constellation Taurus (The Bull). Aldebaran is about sixty-eight light-years away. It will take Pioneer 10 more than two million years to reach it. "From Ames Research Center and the Pioneer Project, we send our thanks to the many people at the Deep Space Network (DSN) and the Jet Propulsion Laboratory (JPL), who made it possible to hear the spacecraft signal for this long," said Pioneer 10 Flight Director David Lozier at the time of the last contact.

Both Pioneer 10 and 11 were remarkable space probes, stretching from a 30-month design life cycle into a mission of more than 20 years and returning useful data not just about the Jovian planets of the Solar System but also about some of the mysteries of the interstellar universe.

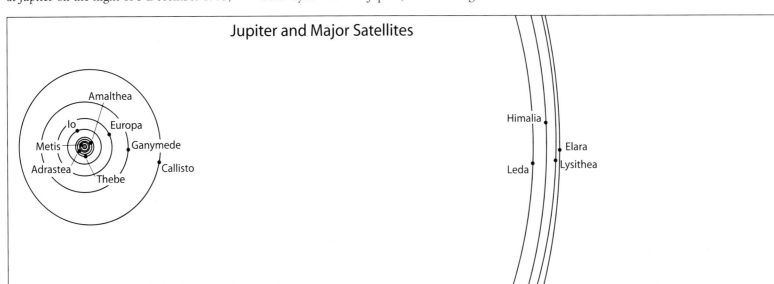

Jupiter and Major Satellites

Jupiter, as the largest planet of the Solar System and a powerful gravitational system in its own right, has 16 moons circling it at various orbits. The four largest satellites of Jupiter, known as the Galilean satellites, are Io, Europa, Ganymede, and Callisto. Smaller satellites orbit within the distance of Io. Eight other relatively large satellites form two bands at a greater distance. Dozens more satellites, all of them much smaller, are not shown here for clarity.

Meanwhile, NASA technicians prepared to launch what became known as Voyager. Even though the four-planet mission was known to be possible, it soon became too expensive to build a spacecraft that could go the distance, carry the instruments needed, and last long enough to accomplish such an extended mission. Thus, the two Voyager spacecraft were funded to conduct intensive flyby studies only of Jupiter and Saturn, in effect repeating on a more elaborate scale the flights of the two Pioneers. Nonetheless, the engineers designed as much longevity into the two Voyagers as the $865 million budget would allow. NASA launched them from the Kennedy Space Center, Florida: Voyager 2 lifted off on August 20, 1977, and Voyager 1 entered space on a faster, shorter trajectory on September 5, 1977.

As the mission progressed, having successfully accomplished all its objectives at Jupiter and Saturn in December 1980, additional flybys of the two outermost giant planets, Uranus and Neptune, proved possible—and irresistible—to mission scientists. Accordingly, as the two spacecraft flew across the Solar System, remote-control reprogramming was used to redirect the Voyagers for the greater mission. Eventually Voyager 1 and Voyager 2 explored all the giant outer planets, 48 of their moons, and the unique systems of rings and magnetic fields those planets possess.

The two spacecraft returned information to Earth that has revolutionized Solar System science, helping resolve some key questions while raising intriguing new ones about the origin and evolution of the planets. The two Voyagers took well over 100,000 images of the outer planets, rings, and satellites, as well as millions of magnetic, chemical spectra, and radiation measurements. They discovered rings around Jupiter, volcanoes on Io, shepherding satellites in Saturn's rings, new moons around Uranus and Neptune, and geysers on Triton. The last imaging sequence was Voyager 1's portrait of most of the Solar System, showing Earth and six other planets as sparks in a dark sky lit by a single bright star, the Sun.

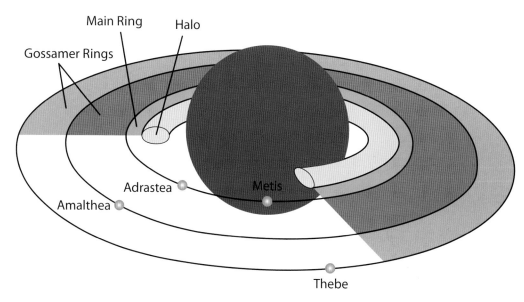

Three groups of rings surround Jupiter, all made of small ice and dust particles. Closest to the planet is the halo ring. The main ring orbits just outside this distance. At greater distance are the gossamer rings, named for their tenuous appearance. The small satellites shown here maintain the rings with their gravitational attraction.

Pioneer 10–11 Trajectories at Jupiter

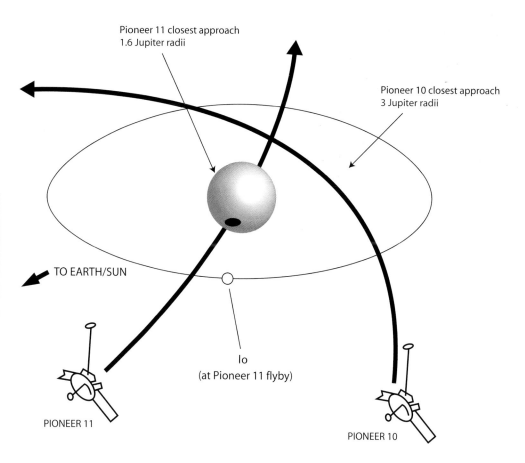

The Pioneer 10 and 11 spacecraft flew by Jupiter with very different trajectories. Pioneer 10 passed Jupiter close to the equatorial plane, while Pioneer 11 was directed over Jupiter's poles. This allowed it to be targeted for a later encounter with Saturn.

The Moons of Jupiter

Since the visitations of the Jovian system by Pioneers 10 and 11, Voyagers 1 and 2, and Galileo, humanity has learned much about the moons that circle Jupiter. In all 16 moons have been identified from the large and complex Callisto, Ganymede, Europa, and Io, to the much smaller and less inviting outer moons, some of which are little more than a part of an asteroid captured in Jupiter's orbit.

For example, one of the truly exciting missions under consideration for the future is a probe to Europa. In searching for life elsewhere in the Solar System one likely site is Europa. Somewhat smaller than the Earth's Moon, Europa is covered with a crust of water ice, frozen by a bone-chilling surface temperature of -260 degrees Fahrenheit. The tidal tug-of-war created by the gravitational pull of Jupiter and the Jupiter's other moons creates an internal source of heat. (The same heating mechanism creates spectacular volcanoes on Io, another one of Jupiter's large moons.) The heat may have created a subterranean ocean and a favorable environment for the development of life.

No sunlight falls on the subterranean seas of Europa. What little sunlight arrives is blocked by the surface ice. The absence of sunlight, however, need not have retarded the evolution of life. In the 1990s, marine scientists on the Earth began to discover dense populations of sea creatures at the bottom of the ocean. Tubeworm, clams, and mussels lived well below the sunlight zone under conditions of amazing hostility. The creatures cluster around hydrothermal vents, cracks in the ocean floor that provide a source of heat and nourishing

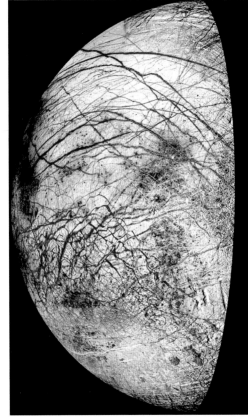

This view of Europa was produced by combining Galileo data collected in 1995–1998. The colors, which have been strongly enhanced, show differences in visible and infrared reflectance.

chemicals. These animals draw energy not from sunlight but from sulfur and carbon dioxide emitted by the vents.

The existence of creatures thriving under conditions that resembled a toxic waste dump startled scientists. They widened their assump-

tions about the range of conditions under which life evolves. Scientists now believe that the so-called habitable zone of the Solar System includes hostile sites as far away as the moons of Jupiter and Saturn. If life can maintain itself at the bottom of the Earth's seas, it may have appeared under similar conditions on Europa.

As planetary scientist Wesley T. Huntress remarked in 1998: "If our robotic missions find an ocean below the ice on Europa, and if our aquabots find things swimming in the European ocean, then the temptation to send humans will be unbearable. Right now we know of no way to shield humans from a swift death in the radiation environment of Europa, even inside a spacecraft, but perhaps they can be enclosed in a magnetically shielded cocoon of some kind until they are well underneath the natural ice shield of Europa's surface. Who can predict what we will find as we proceed over the next years to investigate our Solar System and the stars beyond? Who could have predicted in 1990 all that we have learned since then about water on Mars, potential early life on Mars, oceans beneath the ice of Europa, planets around other stars, and the robustness and early origin of life on Earth? So in the coming years, as my 17-year-old son would put it, other stuff might happen. When it does, let's be ready."

The results of the exploration of the Jovian system has led to the unveiling of a series of remarkable worlds that invite further exploration. At this time NASA is planning an Outer Planetary Flagship mission that may return to the Jupiter system in the coming decade. Should this mission take place, further discoveries will result.

This shows the relative sizes of the four largest moons of Jupiter. From left to right they are Callisto, Ganymede, Io, and Europa.

NASA's Galileo spacecraft acquired its highest resolution images of Jupiter's moon Io on July 3, 1999, during its closest pass to Io since orbit insertion in late 1995. This color mosaic uses the near-infrared, green and violet filters (slightly more than the visible range) of the spacecraft's camera and approximates what the human eye would see. Most of Io's surface has pastel colors, punctuated by black, brown, green, orange, and red units near the active volcanic centers. A false color version of the mosaic has been created to enhance the contrast of the color variations. The improved resolution reveals small-scale color units that had not been recognized previously and that suggest that the lavas and sulfurous deposits are composed of complex mixtures. Some of the bright (whitish), high-latitude (near the top and bottom) deposits have an ethereal quality like a transparent covering of frost. Bright red areas were seen previously only as diffuse deposits. However, they are now seen to exist as both diffuse deposits and sharp linear features like fissures. Some volcanic centers have bright and colorful flows, perhaps due to flows of sulfur rather than silicate lava. In this region bright, white material can also be seen to emanate from linear rifts and cliffs. Comparison of this image to previous Galileo images reveals many changes due to the ongoing volcanic activity. North is toward the top of the picture and the Sun illuminates the surface from almost directly behind the spacecraft. This illumination geometry is good for imaging color variations, but poor for imaging topographic shading. However, some topographic shading can be seen here due to the combination of relatively high resolution (1.3 kilometers or 0.8 miles per picture element) and the rugged topography over parts of Io. The image is centered at 0.3 degrees north latitude and 137.5 degrees west longitude. The resolution is 1.3 kilometers (0.8 miles) per picture element. The images were taken at a range of about 130,000 kilometers (81,000 miles) by the Solid State Imaging (SSI) system on NASA's Galileo spacecraft during its twenty-first orbit.

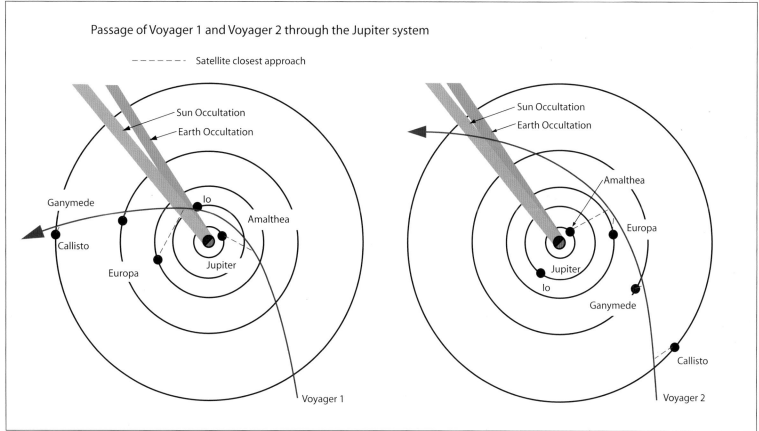

Passage of Voyager 1 and Voyager 2 through the Jupiter system

The Voyager 1 and 2 missions at Jupiter were targeted to allow observation of the maximum number of satellites. Each closest approach is indicated. During Sun occultation, the spacecraft was in Jupiter's shadow. Communications were blocked during Earth occultation.

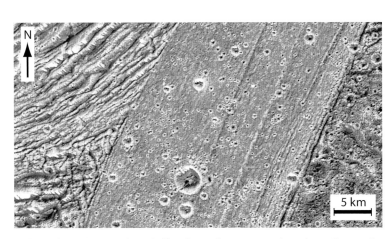

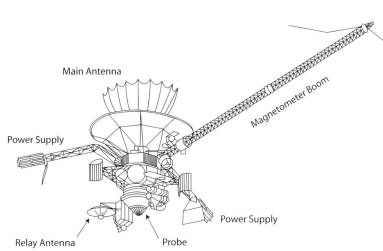

High-resolution imagery from Galileo shows diverse types of terrain on Ganymede. The icy surface has been repeatedly altered and resurfaced. The banded landforms visible in the center represent the youngest terrain.

The Galileo spacecraft carried a suite of instruments, an atmospheric entry probe, and a small antenna to collect data from the probe during its descent. The main antenna, designed to open like an umbrella, failed to correctly deploy. This limited the amount of data that could be returned from Jupiter orbit.

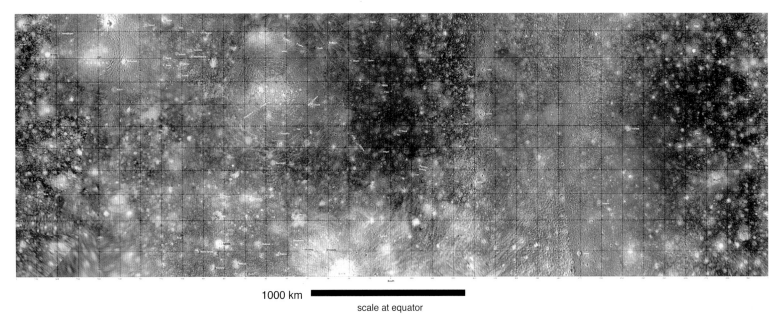

1000 km ▬▬▬▬▬▬▬
scale at equator

Callisto has the oldest and most cratered surface of the Galilean satellites. Unlike the others, tidal forces have played a minimal role in reshaping the surface of Callisto. This has limited the amount of interior heating. Several very large impact basins have remained largely unmodified.

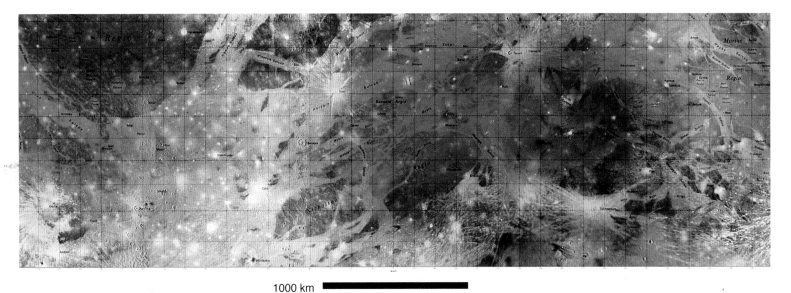

1000 km ▬▬▬▬▬▬▬
scale at equator

Ganymede is the largest satellite in the Solar System. The surface is a combination of ice and dust. Darker areas are highly cratered and are the older sections of the surface. Light-toned areas have been resurfaced more recently. Very bright spots are fresh impact craters and surrounding ejecta.

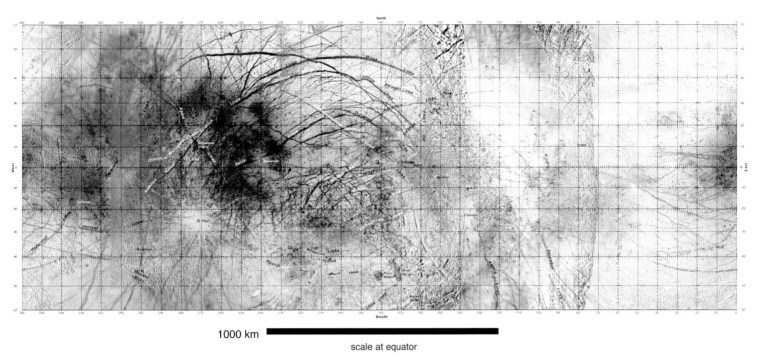

1000 km

scale at equator

Europa is covered by a reflective icy surface crossed by dark-colored linear features. These are breaks or cracks where slightly warmer material is closer to the icy surface. Beneath the icy surface of Europa is a layer of liquid water, kept warm from within. The gravitational pull of Jupiter and its large moons causes tidal forces that pull at Europa, stretching and twisting the satellite enough to create a small amount of heat in the interior. This global map of Europa was created using images from Galileo, with some areas using data from the Voyager encounters.

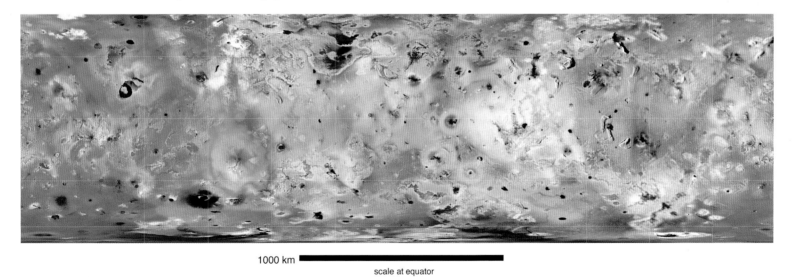

1000 km

scale at equator

Io is the only body in the Solar System besides the Earth where active volcanoes spewing molten rock have been observed. This color global map produced from Galileo and Voyager 1 data shows large volcanoes across the surface of Io. Large volcanoes can be identified as dark patches surrounded by light-colored rings of recently ejected material.

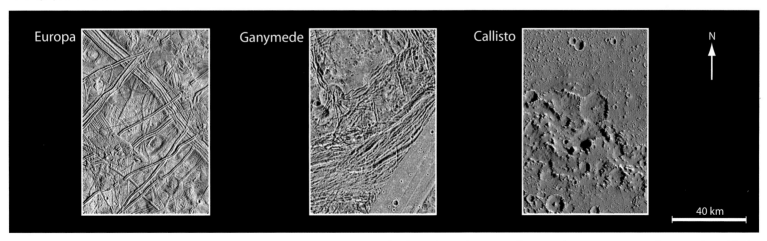

Galileo images of Europa, Ganymede, and Callisto are compared here at the same scale. The surfaces of Europa and Ganymede contain numerous linear cracks and folds, while the surface of Callisto shows less activity.

Galileo to Jupiter

A sustained exploration of Jupiter commenced on October 18, 1989, when NASA deployed the Galileo spacecraft from a space shuttle mission, STS-34, and set it on a gravity-assisted journey to Jupiter, arriving in December 1995. The first spacecraft to orbit the giant planet, 32 times in all, Galileo had to fly by both Venus and the Earth and made the first close flyby of asteroid Gaspra in 1991, providing scientific data on all. This began a two-year encounter with the planet in which Galileo sent back to Earth scientific data about the density and chemical makeup of the giant planet's cloud cover.

Prior to reaching its destination in 1995, Galileo had become a source of great concern by both NASA and public officials because not all of its systems were working properly (i.e., its large high-gain telecommunications antenna

failed to unfurl as intended), but once it arrived at Jupiter and carried on its mission through 2003, it returned enormously significant scientific data including evidence of subcrustal oceans on Europa, Jupiter's large ice-rock moon.

Among Galileo's other successes was capturing imagery of comet Shoemaker-Levy 9's collision with Jupiter in July 1994, discovering a turbulent Jovian atmosphere, complete

with lightning and thunderstorms a thousand times the size of those on Earth, and conducting close-up inspections of the Jovian moons Ganymede, Callisto, and Io. While passing by the latter moon, Galileo observed eruptions of Io's Loki volcano, the largest and most powerful in the Solar System. Galileo also sent a probe into Jupiter's atmosphere, whose findings writes historian Michael Melzer "made

In the summer of 1994 the comet Shoemaker-Levy 9 slammed into Jupiter with spectacularly destructive result. This succession of images from Galileo depicts the comet as it approached the Jovian system.

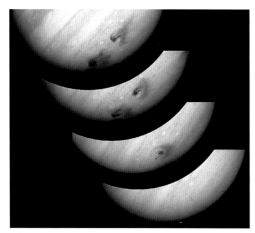

This succession of images from Galileo show the impact of Comet Shoemaker-Levy 9 on Jupiter in 1994. This impact site as the comet entered Jupiter's atmosphere is clearly visible in each of these images, along with the impact plume in the bottom right photograph.

The Galileo probe was targeted for entry into Jupiter's atmosphere just north of the equator. This target was chosen to allow a communications link with Galileo and to enable a safe atmospheric entry.

Galileo Trajectory to Jupiter

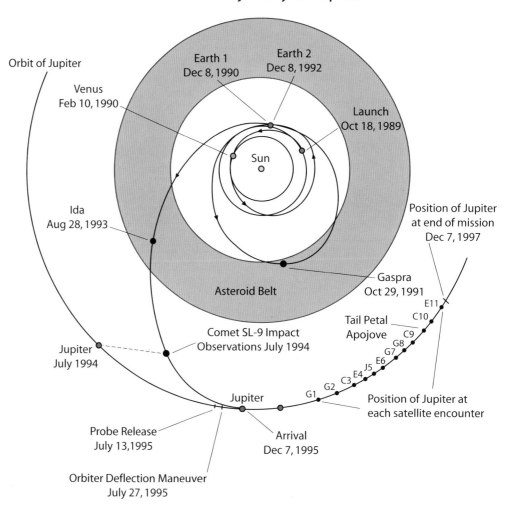

Orbit of Jupiter

Venus
Feb 10, 1990

Earth 1
Dec 8, 1990

Earth 2
Dec 8, 1992

Launch
Oct 18, 1989

Sun

Ida
Aug 28, 1993

Position of Jupiter
at end of mission
Dec 7, 1997

Asteroid Belt

Gaspra
Oct 29, 1991

E11

Tail Petal   C10
Apojove   C9
G8
G7
E6
J5
E4
C3
G2
G1

Comet SL-9 Impact
Observations July 1994

Jupiter
July 1994

Position of Jupiter at
each satellite encounter

Jupiter

Probe Release
July 13, 1995

Arrival
Dec 7, 1995

Orbiter Deflection Maneuver
July 27, 1995

Galileo performed two flybys of Earth and one of Venus after being launched. Each flyby was planned to acquire greater velocity. A path aimed directly at Jupiter would have required a much larger rocket boost, making it necessary to plan a complex trajectory.

it necessary for scientists to revisit many of their beliefs about the formation and evolution of our solar system's giant gaseous planets. Measurements of atmospheric composition, wind velocities, temperatures, cloud characteristics, electrical storms and elemental and molecular abundances painted a very different picture of Jupiter from what was expected."

In mid-1995 Galileo deployed the probe that would parachute into Jupiter's dense atmosphere. The two spacecraft then flew in formation the rest of the way to Jupiter; while the probe began its descent into the planet's atmosphere, the main spacecraft went into a trajectory that placed it in a near-circular orbit. On December 7, 1995, the probe began its descent. Its instruments began relaying data back to the orbiter on the chemical composition of the atmosphere, the nature of the cloud particles and structure of the cloud layers, the atmosphere's radiative heat balance and pressure and dynamics, and the ionosphere. The probe lasted for about 45 minutes before the atmosphere and the pressure of the planet destroyed it. During that time the orbiter stored the returned data. With the high-gain antenna being inoperative, for months thereafter scientists and technicians coaxed the data back to Earth for analysis.

In 1996 data from Galileo revealed that Jupiter's moon, Europa, may harbor "warm ice" or even liquid water—key elements in life-sustaining environments. Many scientists and science fiction writers have speculated that Europa—in addition to Mars and Saturn's moon Titan—is one of the three planetary bodies in this Solar System that might possess, or may have possessed, an environment where primitive life could exist. This proved one of

the astounding scientific discoveries of the 1990s and prompted scientists to advocate sending a lander to explore Europa.

Galileo's mission has led to a reinterpretation of understanding about Jupiter, its moons, and the outer Solar System. A short list of Galileo's most important discoveries include the following:

- Evidence for liquid water ocean under Europa's surface, one of the moons of Jupiter.
- The discovery of a satellite (Dactyl) circling the asteroid Ida.
- Discovery of an intense interplanetary dust storm (the most intense ever observed).
- Discovery of an intense new radiation belt approximately 31,000 miles above Jupiter's cloud tops.
- Detection of Jovian wind speeds in excess of 400 mph.
- Far less water was detected in Jupiter's atmosphere than estimated from earlier Voyager observations and from models of the Comet Shoemaker-Levy 9 impact.
- Far less lightning activity (about 10% of that found in an equal area on Earth) than anticipated. The individual lightning events, however, are about ten times stronger on Jupiter than the Earth.
- Helium abundance in Jupiter is very nearly the same as its abundance in the Sun (24% compared to 25%).
- Extensive resurfacing of Io's surface due to continuing volcanic activity since the Voyagers flew by in 1979.
- Preliminary data support the tentative identification of intrinsic magnetic fields for Jupiter's moons, Io and Ganymede.

The flight team for Galileo ceased operations on February 28, 2003, after a final playback of scientific data from the robotic explorer's tape recorder. The team prepared commands for the spacecraft's onboard computer to manage the remainder of its life. Galileo coasted for the next seven months before taking a September 21, 2003, plunge into Jupiter's atmosphere, thereby ending what had been a remarkably successful mission.

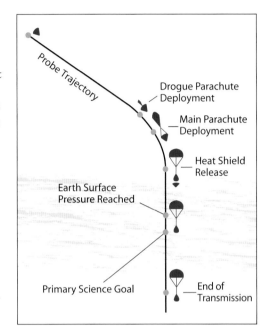

The Galileo probe was equipped with a heat shield to slow its velocity as it encountered Jupiter's atmosphere. While still above the main cloud layers, a small parachute was released, followed rapidly by the main parachute. It then drifted down into the atmosphere. The probe continued to transmit data for about an hour, reaching about 200 kilometers into the atmosphere. At this point it finally succumbed to the intense pressure, about 22 times that at sea level on Earth.

Galileo at Jupiter

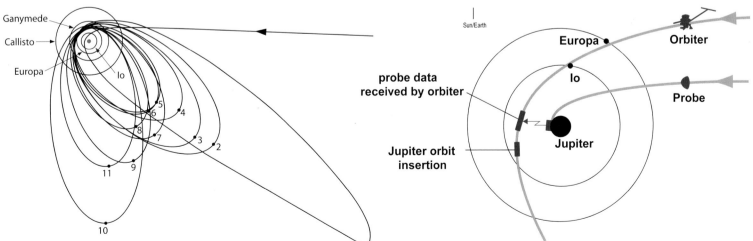

After being captured by Jupiter's gravity, Galileo looped around the planet, used its thruster to perform a maneuver, and then entered orbit. On each subsequent orbit a close flyby of a different satellite was planned. This chart shows the initial 11 orbits after arrival at Jupiter. Galileo eventually completed 32 orbits before being deliberately targeted for entry into Jupiter's atmosphere.

Galileo released its entry probe five months before arriving at Jupiter. The probe coasted to Jupiter while the main spacecraft performed a maneuver to enter Jupiter's orbit. On December 7, 1995, the probe entered the atmosphere, with the main spacecraft relaying data to Earth during descent.

Exploring Saturn

Like Jupiter, Saturn was visited first by the Pioneer 10 and 11 spacecraft as they sped to the outer reaches of the Solar System. Also like Jupiter, this was followed by a more thorough reconnaissance of Saturn by the Voyager 1 and 2 spacecraft. Saturn had also long been a target of exploration. The second largest of the bodies of the Solar System, Saturn also boasted spectacular rings that were analyzed by these efforts.

To learn more about Saturn, their encounters in the Jovian system and a boost from Jupiter's gravitational field, the Voyagers set course for distant, ringed Saturn, where Voyager 1 arrived in November 1980 and

Voyager 2 arrived in August 1981. Pioneer 2 had recently completed its work at Saturn in September 1979, discovering faint rings outside those discernible from Earth and demonstrating a safe flight path for the Voyager to follow.

Beginning with a course correction 2 hours after its closest approach to Jupiter, Voyager 2 sped on to Saturn. It began its encounter with the second largest planet in the Solar System on August 22, 1981, two years after leaving the Jovian system. It first took pictures of Saturn's moon, Iapetus. A flyby that did not linger at Saturn, Voyager 2 came within 63,000 miles (101,000 km) on August 26, 1981. Stunning

images of the rings, a newly discovered F-ring, and its shepherding moons proved most exciting. It also imaged the moons Hyperion, Enceladus, Tethys, and Phoebe.

Voyager 1 soon followed its twin into the Saturnian system, arriving there on November 12, 1979, in another flyby. It passed within 2,500 miles (4,000 km) of the planet. A special target was Saturn's moon Titan, and its encounter with this inviting moon revealed it as a place of complexity, having an atmosphere, thick clouds, and water ice. The spacecraft also found that Titan's atmosphere was composed of 90% nitrogen, and that the pressure and

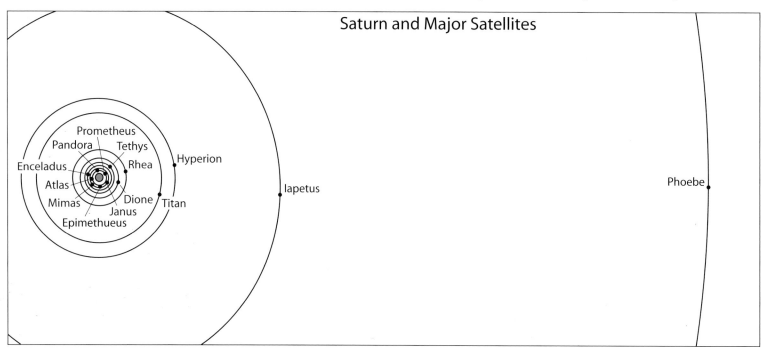

Saturn and Major Satellites

Titan is the largest satellite of Saturn. At greater distances lie Iapetus and Phoebe, but all the other large satellites orbit closer to Saturn.

This view of Saturn was returned by the Cassini spacecraft on January 19, 2007. The planet itself was deliberately overexposed to show details in the rings.

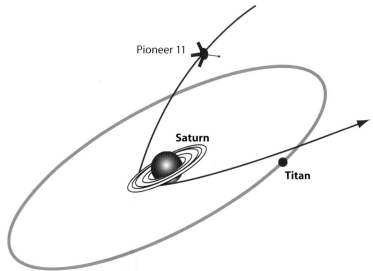

Pioneer 11 encountered Saturn on September 1, 1979. The trajectory was planned to allow observation of Titan after close approach to Saturn.

temperature at the surface was 1.6 atmospheres and −180° C. This made it a place that scientists wanted to learn more about and this played into mission planning for a sustained investigation of the Saturn system that came at the dawn of the twenty-first century.

Overall, Voyager 1 found five new moons and a ring system consisting of thousands of bands, discovered a new ring (the "G-ring"), and found "shepherding" satellites on either side of the F-ring satellites that kept the rings well defined. In addition to Titan, Voyager 1 also photographed the moons, Mimas, Enceladus, Tethys, Dione, and Rhea.

Flying over the unlit side of Saturn's rings, the Cassini spacecraft captured Saturn's glow in this stunning neonlike image. Containing brilliant shades of electric blue, sapphire, and mint green as the planet's shadow casts a wide net on the rings, this image is a false-color mosaic created from 25 images taken by Cassini's visual and infrared mapping spectrometer over a period of 13 hours on February 24, 2007, while the spacecraft was 1.58 million kilometers (1 million miles) from the planet and 34.6 degrees above the ring plane. In this view, Cassini was looking down on the northern, unlit side of the rings, which are rendered visible by sunlight filtering through from the sunlit, southern face.

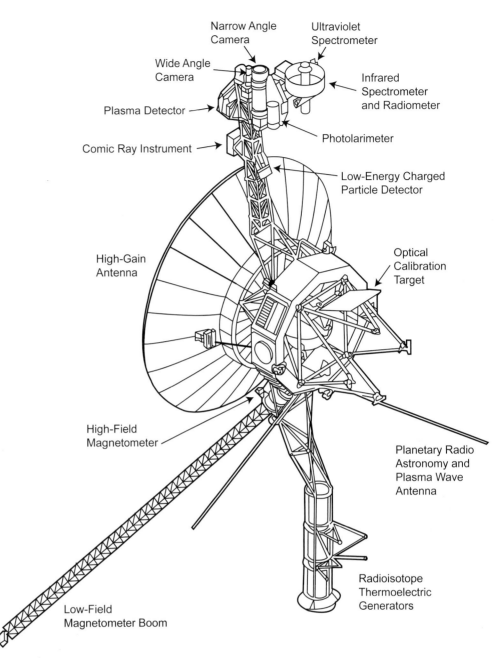

The two Voyager spacecraft carried a range of instruments for measuring the environment of the outer planets. Imaging instruments were mounted on the moveable scan platform located at the top of this diagram.

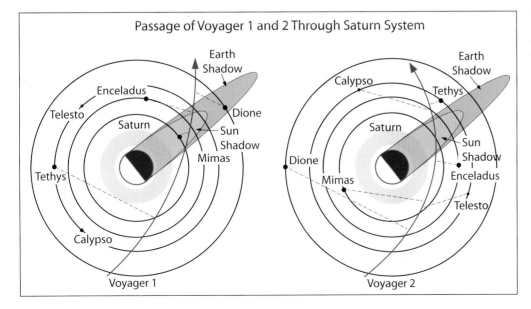

The Voyager 1 and 2 trajectories at Saturn are shown here with the inner satellites. Voyager 1 was also targeted for a close encounter with Titan, which orbits outside the satellites shown here.

Cassini-Huygens Goes to Saturn

Representing the international character of many NASA planetary missions since Voyager, Cassini-Huygens, a joint effort of NASA, the European Space Agency, and Italian Space Agency, has also proved to be an incredible success. Cassini is the first spacecraft to orbit Saturn. Launched in 1997 it arrived at Saturn and began orbiting the planet on July 1, 2004. It also sent a probe (Huygens) to the surface of Saturn's moon Titan on January 15, 2005. Huygens was a product of the European Space Agency, and the first outer planetary mission by that organization.

But even before its Saturnian encounter, the Cassini mission advanced science by finding individual storm cells of upwelling bright-white clouds in dark "belts" in Jupiter's atmosphere, and by conducting a radio signal experiment on October 10, 2003, that supported Einstein's theory of general relativity.

At Saturn, Cassini has discovered three new moons (Methone, Pallene, and Polydeuces), observed water ice geysers erupting from the south pole of the moon Enceladus, obtained images appearing to show lakes of liquid hydrocarbon (such as methane and ethane) in Titan's northern latitudes, and discovered a storm at the south pole of Saturn with a distinct eye wall. Cassini, like Galileo at Jupiter, has demonstrated that icy moons orbiting gas giant planets are potential refuges of life, and attractive destinations for a new era of robotic planetary exploration.

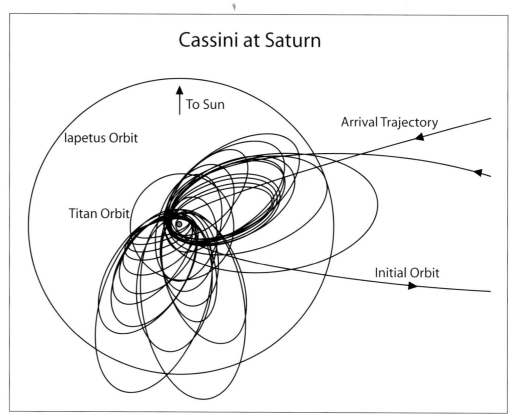

Cassini's initial orbit around Saturn was very elliptical. Flybys of satellites were performed while lowering the orbit to within the distance of Iapetus. For clarity this chart shows only half of the orbits during the initial phase of the mission.

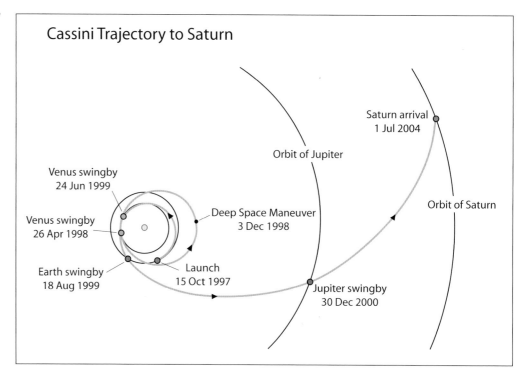

Cassini performed two flybys of Venus and one of Earth to obtain the velocity needed to leave the inner Solar System. It then flew by Jupiter before finally arriving at Saturn in July 2004, more than six years after launch.

Titan

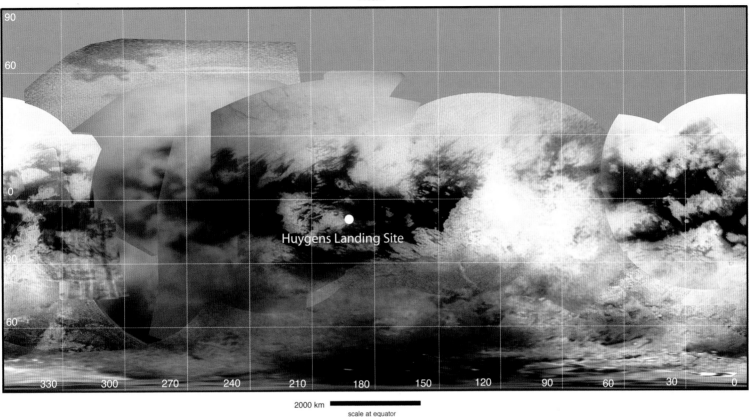

2000 km

scale at equator

This global surface map of Titan was made from radar data from the Cassini spacecraft. Dark areas are covered by material that absorbs radar, possibly layers of liquid hydrocarbons on the surface. The hazy atmosphere of Titan is opaque to visible light, requiring sensors that use infrared or radar to observe the surface from above.

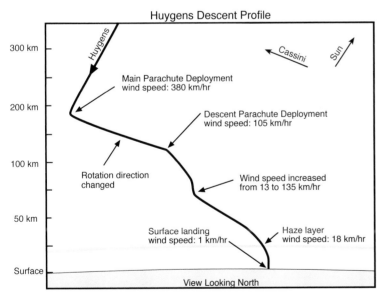

Huygens Descent Profile

Huygens

Cassini

Sun

Main Parachute Deployment
wind speed: 380 km/hr

Descent Parachute Deployment
wind speed: 105 km/hr

Rotation direction changed

Wind speed increased from 13 to 135 km/hr

Surface landing
wind speed: 1 km/hr

Haze layer
wind speed: 18 km/hr

View Looking North

As the Huygens probe entered the dense atmosphere of Titan on January 14, 2005, its velocity was slowed by its heat shield. A large parachute was deployed just below 200 kilometers altitude. The heat shield was released and the probe drifted with the wind. Later the large parachute was jettisoned and replaced by a smaller one to speed descent. Huygens was intended to rotate as it descended to allow observations from different points of view. Between the two parachute deployments, the rotation rate slowed and then reversed. At an altitude of about 65 kilometers, the probe encountered strong winds as it descended. At 21 kilometers altitude it passed through a layer of atmospheric haze.

185°   azimuth   200°

20 cm   2 meters

20 cm   1 meter

20 cm   50 cm

approximate scale   approximate distance

The Huygens probe survived landing on the surface of Titan and continued to transmit data. Huygens included an image sensor designed to collect images during descent. This sensor also recorded the view from the surface shown here. The color is the result of atmospheric scattering of sunlight. The objects in the foreground are 10–15 centimeters wide. A few larger objects are visible in the background.

Saturn's Moons

Saturn has officially 60 moons with confirmed orbits, of which 52 have been named. The vast majority of these are quite small. Some, like Titan, are fascinating because of their atmosphere and landscape containing hydrocarbon lakes and river networks. Additionally, Enceladus may have liquid water beneath its frozen surface. Most, however, are rocky bodies without atmospheres or regular orbits, and possessing inhospitable conditions.

Dione

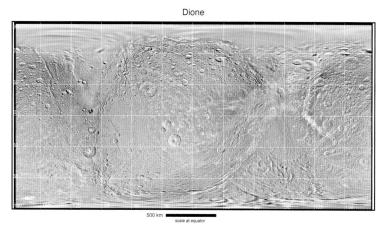

The leading hemisphere of Dione, on the left side of this map, is heavily cratered. The trailing hemisphere contains long linear features known as lineae. These features are the result of tectonic forces fracturing the icy surface, creating long cliffs of exposed reflective water ice.

Enceladus

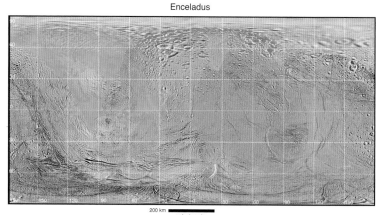

Enceledus is covered by an icy surface fractured by long cracks. New material containing ice and dust flowed over the surface from these cracks. Older cratered terrain dominates much of the northern hemisphere. Enceledus remains an active place, with geysers releasing ice and dust from the southern polar region. These emissions are the source of material in the E ring around Saturn.

Iapatus

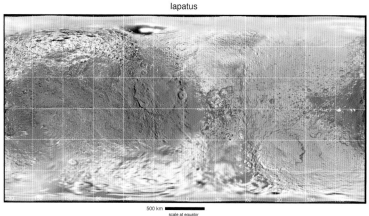

The eastern and western hemispheres of Iapatus are starkly different. Like most satellites of the outer planets, one side of Iapatus faces forward as it orbits around Saturn. Most of this hemisphere is covered by dark material. The other hemisphere, however, is very bright.

Mimas

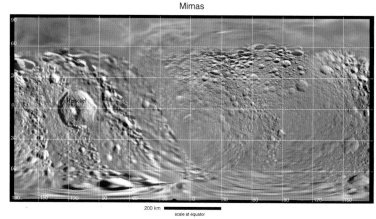

Dominating the leading hemisphere of Mimas is the impact crater Herschel. The impact was so large it probably came close to completely shattering Mimas.

Tethys

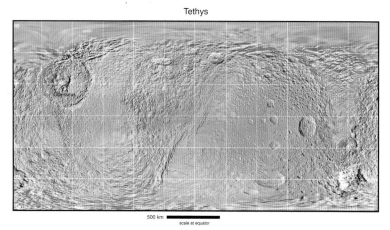

The surface of Tethys is mostly water ice. Large canyons stretch across the side of Tethys that faces Saturn, in the center of the map. The large impact crater Odysseus is in the western hemisphere.

Rhea

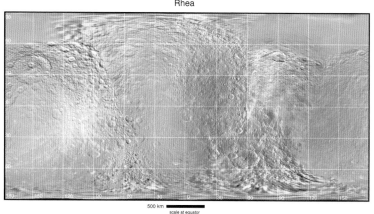

Rhea, like Dione, contains very different features between its leading and trailing hemispheres. It is larger than Dione but similar in composition.

This Cassini image of Iapatus from September 10, 2007, was created using infrared, visible, and ultraviolet data. It shows the bright trailing hemisphere.

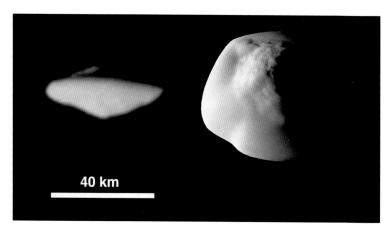

This Cassini image shows Atlas, a small satellite of Saturn. Along the equator of this body is a layer of icy material that has settled on the surface, giving Atlas a distinctive appearance. More than one quarter of the mass of Atlas is found in this ring of material.

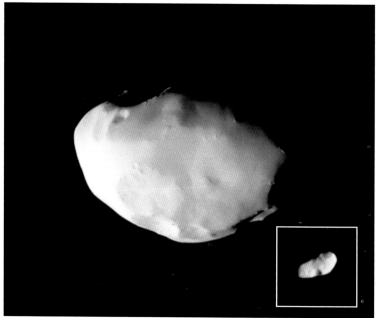

Calypso (inset) and Telesto are small Trojan satellites of Tethys, meaning they orbit in the same path as Tethys at leading and trailing positions. Ultraviolet, visible, and infrared data have been combined to discern differences in rock types. Telesto appears to be covered by material masking craters and other features.

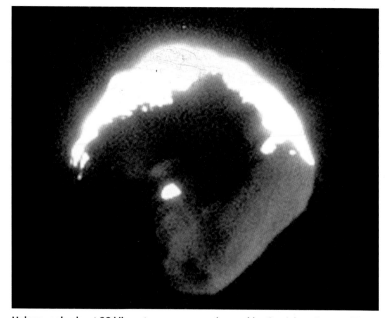

Helene, only about 32 kilometers across, was imaged by Cassini on August 17, 2006.

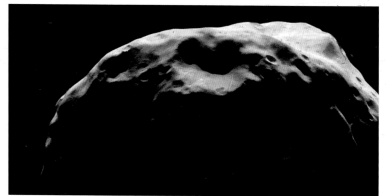

Cassini acquired images of Janus, about 180 kilometers across, on June 30, 2008.

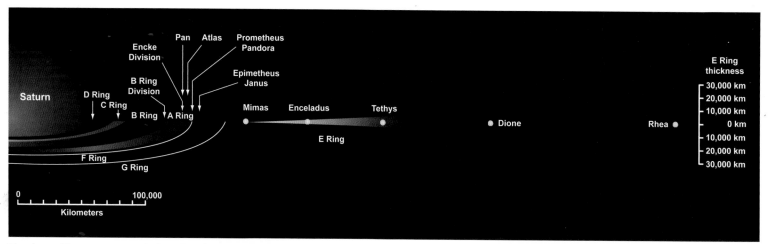

The rings of Saturn, composed of ice particles, are easily visible in Earth-based telescopes. The size of the particles varies from about 4 meters across to specks of dust. Although they extend for more than 120,000 kilometers from Saturn, the rings are only about 20 meters thick. Several of the rings are maintained by the gravitational attraction from large satellites. The ring divisions appear dark when viewed in reflected sunlight in Earth-based telescopes, but they in fact contain a significant amount of material. Long ago, astronomers identified three rings, labeled A, B, and C, with various gaps between them. The rings are lettered roughly in order of discovery. The main A, B, and C rings are shown in this chart along with the inner D ring. The thin F and G rings are maintained by gravitational pull of small satellites. The E ring is composed of material ejected from Enceladus. Giovanni Cassini discovered the first gap in the rings, splitting them into an A and B division in 1675. A second division, in the A ring, was discovered in 1837 by astronomer Johann Encke. All of these rings were created, scientists learned during the space age, from a large number of narrow ringlets that contain a significant amount of water. Building on centuries of observation, during the space age scientists have identified 31 moons circling Saturn.

Images from Cassini show Phoebe, in a distant orbit of Saturn, to be similar to bodies that exist in the Kuiper Belt beyond Neptune.

Hyperion has been battered by impacts in its past. The irregular shape is the result of energetic impacts that have removed large amounts of material. This Cassini image was acquired on September 26, 2005.

Voyager 2 at Uranus

The seventh planet from the sun, Uranus is also the third largest in the Solar System. It is a gas giant with a dense atmosphere of "ices" made from liquids such as water, ammonia, and methane. It also, curiously, has traces of hydrocarbons. It contains the coldest planetary atmosphere in the Solar System, with a minimum temperature of 49 K (−224° C). Its atmosphere is quite complex, having a layered cloud structure, with water thought to make up the lowest clouds, and methane thought to make up the uppermost layer of clouds. With 17 known satellites, it has only been visited by Voyager 2 in 1986. It was discovered by Sir William Herschel on March 13, 1781, the first discovery of a planet made using a telescope.

Voyager 2, launched in 1977, made its closest approach to Uranus on January 24, 1986, flying by at breakneck speed some 81,500 kilometers from the planet's cloud tops. Without lingering in the Uranus system, Voyager 2 took structural and chemical composition readings of the atmosphere and weather patterns, and discovered 10 new moons. It determined that Uranus had a near horizontal tilt of its planetary axis, at 97.77°, and confirmed that a faint ring system existed there. Finally, Uranus has a powerful magnetic field with an irregular structure, with a tilt and unique corkscrew magnetotail resulting from Uranus's sideways orientation.

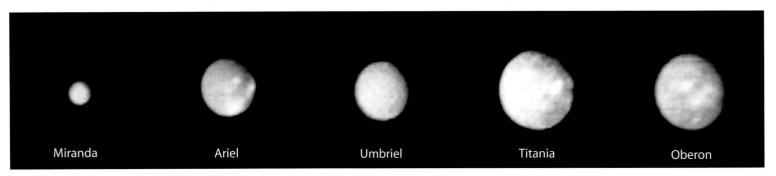

| Miranda | Ariel | Umbriel | Titania | Oberon |

This "family portrait" of Uranus's five largest moons was compiled from images sent back January 20, 1986, by the Voyager 2 spacecraft. The pictures were taken through a clear filter from distances of 5.0 to 6.1 million kilometers (3.1 to 3.8 million miles). In this comparison, we see the relative sizes and relativities of the satellites. From left, in order of increasing distance from the planet, they are Miranda, Ariel, Umbriel, Titania, and Oberon. The two largest, Oberon and Titania, are about half the size of Earth's Moon, or roughly 1,600 kilometers (1,000 miles) in diameter. Miranda, smallest of the five, has about one-quarter to one-third the diameter. Even in these distant views, the satellites exhibit distinct differences in appearance. On average, Oberon and Titania reflect about 20% of the sunlight, Umbriel about 12%, Ariel and Miranda about 30%. Ariel shows the largest contrast on its surface, with the brightest areas about 25%. All five satellites show only slight color variations on their surfaces, with their average color being very nearly gray.

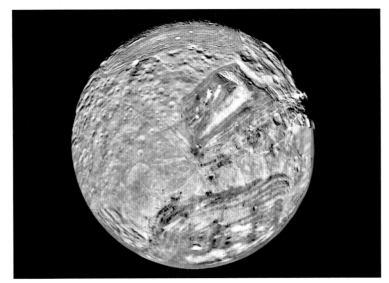

This color composite of Uranus's satellite Miranda was taken by Voyager 2 on January 24, 1986, from a distance of 147,000 kilometers (91,000 miles). This picture was constructed from images taken through the narrow-angle camera's green, violet, and ultraviolet filters. It is the best view of Miranda returned by Voyager. Miranda, just 480 km (300 mi) across, is the smallest of Uranus's five major satellites. Miranda's regional geologic provinces show very well in this view of the southern hemisphere, imaged at a resolution of 2.7 km (1.7 mi). The dark- and bright-banded region with its curvilinear traces covers about half of the image. Higher-resolution pictures taken later show many fault valleys and ridges parallel to these bands. Near the terminator (at right), another system of ridges and valleys abuts the banded terrain; many impact craters pockmark the surface in this region. The largest of these are about 30 km (20 mi) in diameter; many more lie in the range of 5 to 10 km (3 to 6 mi) in diameter.

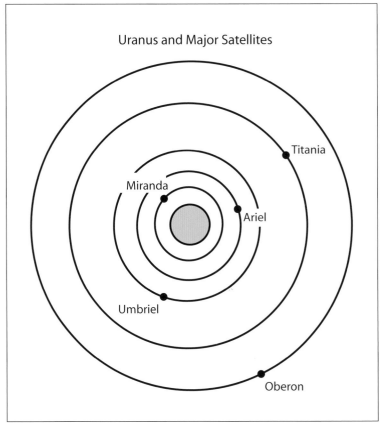

Uranus and Major Satellites

Uranus has five large satellites: Miranda, Ariel, Umbrial, Titania, and Oberon. Several smaller satellites orbit closer to Uranus within the planet's ring system.

This image was acquired by Voyager 2 on January 10, 1986, before its closest approach to Uranus. This view approximates the colors visible to the eyes. Most of Uranus is usually covered by bluish haze. More details in the atmsophere are visible using ultraviolet wavelengths.

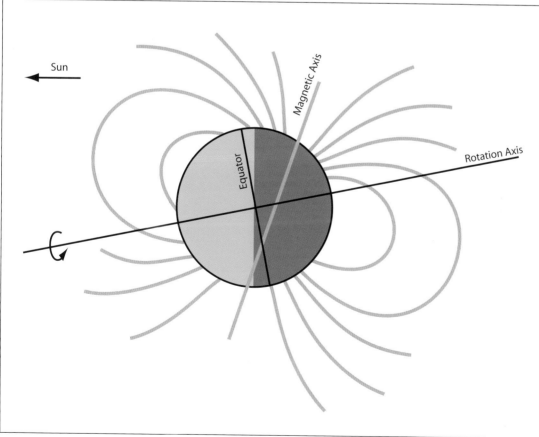

The magnetosphere of Uranus, like the planet's axis of rotation, is greatly tilted from the ecliptic. The north pole of Uranus points toward the Sun.

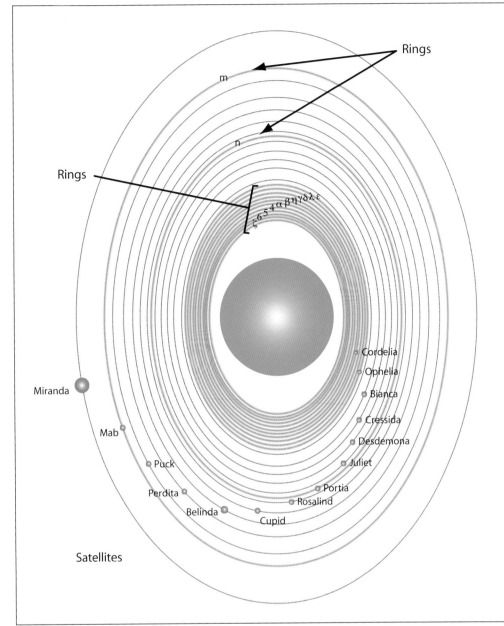

Rings

Rings

ζ 6 5 4 α β η γ δ λ ϵ

m

n

Cordelia
Ophelia
Bianca
Cressida
Desdemona
Juliet
Portia
Rosalind
Cupid

Miranda
Mab
Puck
Perdita
Belinda

Satellites

The ring particles in orbit around Uranus are ice and dust, but unlike the rings of Saturn they are much darker and not visible in reflected sunlight. The first nine rings were detected by measuring the light of a star passing behind the rings. Two others were detected by Voyager 2. Two outer rings, corresponding to the orbits of the satellites Portia and Mab, were later found using data from the Hubble Space Telescope.

Voyager 2 returned detailed images of Ariel. This image shows the lower reaches of wide canyons that had been filled in with new material.

The surface of Titania, the largest satellite of Uranus, was revealed by Voyager 2 to contain at least two massive canyons and a large impact basin.

Near the center of this Voyager 2 image of Oberon, two large impact basins are visible surrounded by bright layers of ejecta.

This view of Verona Rupes, a cliff on the surface of Miranda, was returned by Voyager 2 on January 24, 1986. About 20 kilometers high, it may be the highest near-vertical cliff in the Solar System.

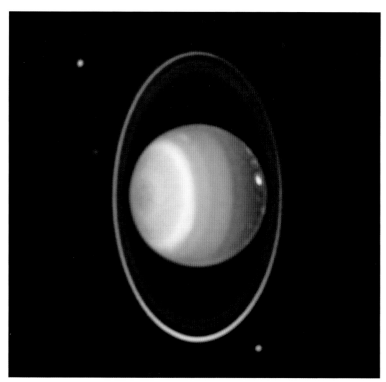

This recent image from the Hubble Space Telescope reveals Uranus surrounded by its four major rings and by 10 of its 17 known satellites. This false-color image was generated by Erich Karkoschka using data taken on August 8, 1998, with Hubble's Near Infrared Camera and Multi-Object Spectrometer. Hubble recently found about 20 clouds—nearly as many clouds on Uranus as the previous total in the history of modern observations.

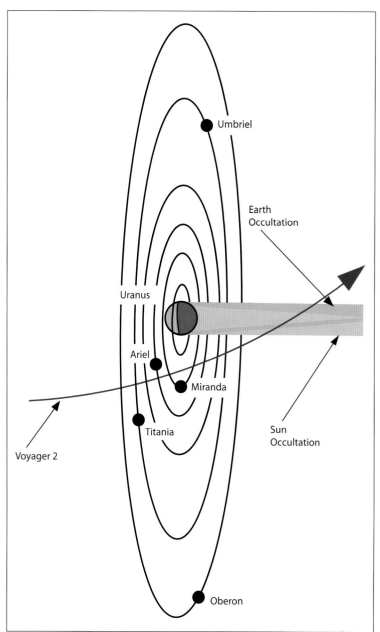

Uranus and its satellites have a unique configuration in the Solar System. The axis of rotation of Uranus is tilted more than 90 degrees from the ecliptic, so the poles of Uranus and its satellites point toward the Sun. This required an unusual trajectory for the Voyager 2 mission. The spacecraft was targeted for a flyby of the planet near the inner satellite Miranda. The other satellites were all viewed, but from greater distances.

Voyager 2 images showed Umbriel with a generally dark surface. One exception was a reflective region in the north polar area.

The Eighth Planet: Neptune

Neptune, the eighth planet from the Sun, was discovered in a unique way from all others identified from Earth. Scientists undertook mathematical predictions rather than regular observations of the sky and determined that a body the size, shape, and orbit of Neptune had to exist. Although Galileo had seen it in 1612 in his small telescope, he believed it was a fixed star and did not realize its planetary status. The rest of the story about its true nature emerged when observers noted that Uranus did not travel exactly as astronomers expected were it the last planet in the Solar System, and French mathematician, Urbain Joseph Le Verrier, proposed the position and mass of another as yet unknown planet that could cause the observed changes to Uranus's orbit. This deduction was confirmed by Johann Gottfried Galle at the Berlin Observatory in 1846, when he found Neptune in the orbit that Le Verrier predicted on his first night of searching for it. Only 17 days later, its largest moon, Triton, was also discovered.

This image from Voyager 2 shows Neptune's south pole as the spacecraft sped away on a southward trajectory in 1989.

Neptune is nearly 4.5 billion kilometers (2.8 billion miles) from the Sun, and only orbits the Sun once every 165 years. It is invisible to the naked eye as a small pinpoint of light because of its extreme distance from Earth and is easily confused with stars.

Only one spacecraft, Voyager 2, has visited Neptune since the beginning of the space age. The "little spacecraft that could" took advantage of a rare planetary alignment to visit the four giant outer planets Jupiter, Saturn, Uranus, and Neptune over the course of 12 years between 1977 and 1989. Voyager 2 skimmed the north pole of Neptune by a mere 4,800 kilometers (3,000 miles), and determined basic characteristics of Neptune and its largest moon Triton. Voyager 2 also discovered six new Neptunian moons and three new rings plus a broad sheet of ring material. Unexpectedly, geysers of gaseous nitrogen were found on the largest moon, Triton. Neptune's magnetic field also tilted 47 degrees with respect to the rotational axis, and offset from the center of the planet by half the planet's radius. Voyager 2's flight path past Neptune sent the spacecraft diving below the ecliptic plane, where it journeyed on to the heliopause (the boundary between the Sun's influence and interstellar space).

This chart shows the relationship between Triton, Neried, and Proteus, the largest inner satellite of Neptune.

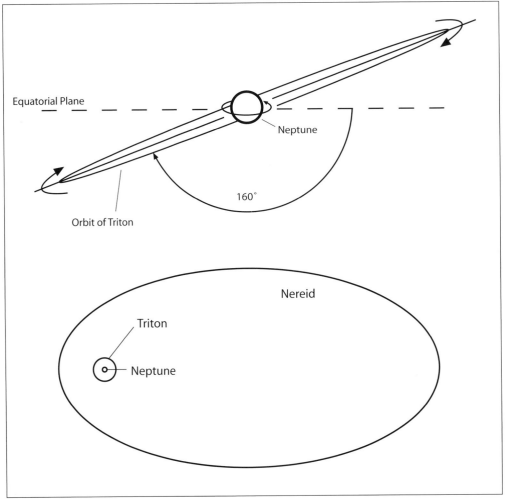

Triton is by far the largest satellite of Neptune. Triton is unique for a large satellite in that it revolves around its parent planet in a retrograde orbit, moving in the opposite direction as the planet's rotation. Along with its highly inclined orbit, these clues point to the origin of Triton as possibly being a captured object from the Kuiper Belt. Nereid, much smaller than Triton, orbits at a greater distance.

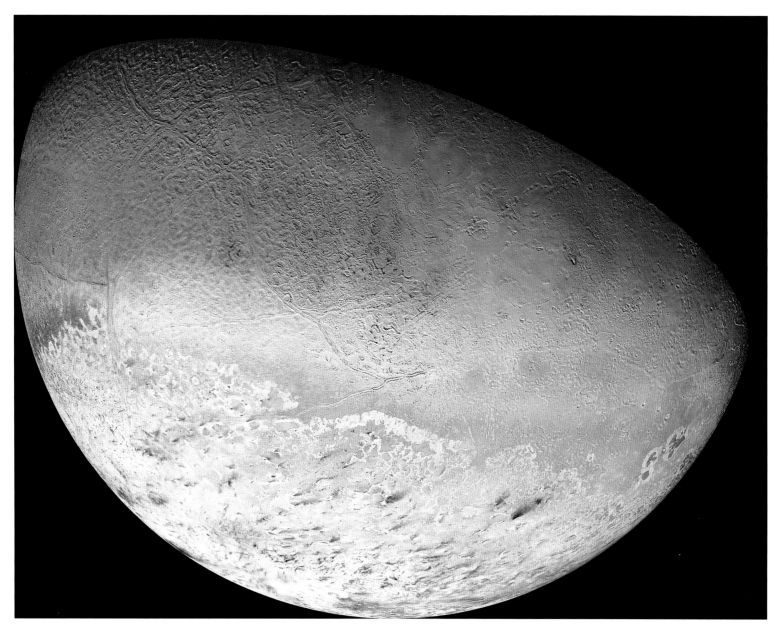

This color view of Triton was acquired by Voyager 2 using visible and ultraviolet wavelengths. The surface is covered in frozen nitrogen. Dark spots are composed of material flowing upward through structures similar to geysers. Active geyser plumes were detected in other Voyager images.

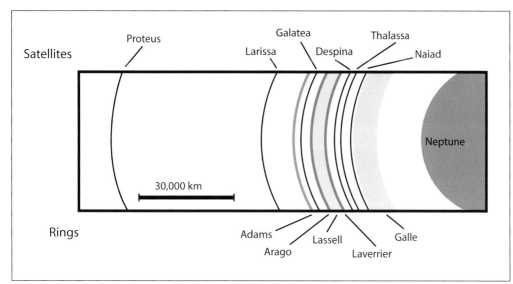

The rings of Neptune circle the planet within the orbits of the small inner satellites. Five rings have been identified. Like the rings of Uranus, the material is darker than at Saturn. At Neptune the Lassell ring extends between the Arago and Laverrier rings. The Adams ring consists of five arc sections instead of forming a complete disk.

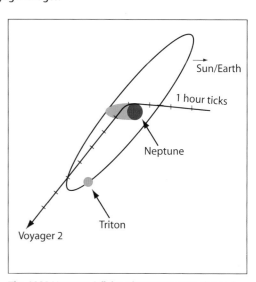

The 1989 Voyager 2 flyby of Neptune was planned to provide a close encounter with Triton after closest approach to Neptune. Voyager passed within 5,000 kilometers of Neptune's north pole. This was closer than any other planetary flyby to that point.

The Kuiper Belt

The Kuiper Belt is often referred to as the Solar System's "final frontier" because of its location far beyond the eight planets making up this system. It is a disk-shaped region of icy debris located about 4.5 to 7.5 billion km (2.8 billion to 4.6 billion miles), or 30 to 50 Astronomical Units (AU) from the Sun. Scientists only reached consensus about its existence in the 1990s; before that time they were uncertain of this region. The Kuiper Belt and its collection of icy objects—KBOs— are an emerging area of research in planetary science.

What is now known as the Kuiper Belt, named for astrophysicist Gerard Kuiper, was first theorized in 1950 by Dutch astronomer Jan Oort, who believed that the outer Solar System had captured thousands of icy bodies at the far reaches of the Sun's gravitational field. Gerard Kuiper made the case the next year that this material was debris left over from the formation of the Solar System. Since that time other scientists, including Jan Oort, have discovered that the majority of comets

that make their way into the terrestrial zone of the Solar System are from the Kuiper Belt. Indeed, the Kuiper Belt is the major source of cometary impacts on Earth. Many Kuiper Belt objects are heavily endowed with organic (carbon-bearing) molecules and water ice—the raw materials from which life evolves.

Kuiper's ideas about this part of the Solar System gained momentum with the advent of computer modeling that found that ancient formation of the system predicated that a disk of debris should naturally form around its edge. Accordingly, planets would have coalesced quickly in the inner-region stellar disk, gravitationally sweeping up residual debris. But beyond Neptune scientists learned that there was a debris field of icy objects that never agglomerated into planets.

The Kuiper Belt remained theory until the 1992 detection of a 150-mile-wide body, called 1992QB1 and located at the distance of the suspected belt. Several similar-sized objects were discovered thereafter, confirming that the belt of icy objects Kuiper had predicted

did indeed exist. The planet Pluto, discovered in 1930 by Clyde Tombaugh, is only the largest member of the Kuiper Belt. Moreover, Pluto's largest moon, Charon, is half the size of Pluto and the two form a binary planet, whose gravitational balance point is between the two bodies. Other named objects soon joined Pluto, including 1992 QB_1, Orcus, Quaoar, Ixion, 90377 Sedna, and Varuna.

The discovery of these many objects, nearly as large as Pluto and occupying a broad range in the outer Solar System, led the International Astronomical Union (IAU) in 2006 to redesignate Pluto from a planet—there would henceforth be eight of them in the Solar System—and call it by the new designation of "dwarf planet." The first members of the "dwarf planet" category were Ceres, Pluto, and 2003 UB_{313}. They deliberated on this long and hard before reaching a definition of planets that included the following criteria: (a) it is in orbit around the Sun, (b) it has sufficient mass for its self-gravity to overcome rigid body forces so that it assumes

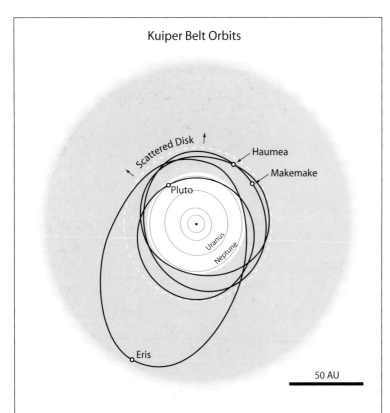

The Kuiper Belt and the individual orbits of the four largest objects beyond Neptune are shown on this chart. Beyond Neptune, thousands of icy bodies orbit the Sun. The gravitational attraction of Neptune plays a central role in determining the distribution of these bodies. Most bodies within about 40 Astronomical Units, or 40 times the Sun-Earth distance, are linked to the movements of Neptune. Beyond this distance most objects have more complex orbits. Many scientists refer to this distant zone as the Scattered Disk, which may represent a separate group of objects.

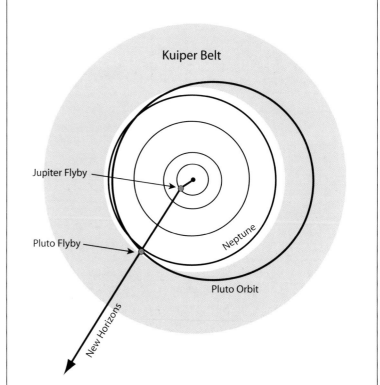

The New Horizons spacecraft launched in 2006 was targeted for a gravity assist flyby of Jupiter, after which it was directed toward a flyby of Pluto in 2015. It will then pass through the Kuiper Belt on its way out of the Solar System.

a hydrostatic equilibrium (nearly round) shape, and (c) it has cleared the neighborhood around its orbit. Its members also specifically commented that "dwarf planet" status of Pluto would hereafter be recognized as a critical prototype of this new class of trans-Neptunian objects. While this decision remains controversial, it represents an important recent step in understanding the origins and evolution of the Solar System.

Since no planetary spacecraft had been sent to Pluto or the Kuiper Belt, upon its launch New Horizons will be the first to visit this region of the outer Solar System. It was launched aboard an Atlas V rocket from Cape Canaveral Air Force Base, Florida, on January 19, 2006, and conducted a Jupiter flyby 13 months later to gain further acceleration. New Horizons will make its closest approach to Pluto on July 14, 2015. The half-ton spacecraft

contains scientific instruments to map the surface geology and composition of Pluto and its three moons, investigate Pluto's atmosphere, measure the solar wind, and assess interplanetary dust and other particles. After it passes Pluto, controllers plan to fly the spacecraft by one or two Kuiper Belt objects. New Horizons carries several souvenirs from Earth, including some of the remains of Clyde Tombaugh (1906–1997), discoverer of Pluto.

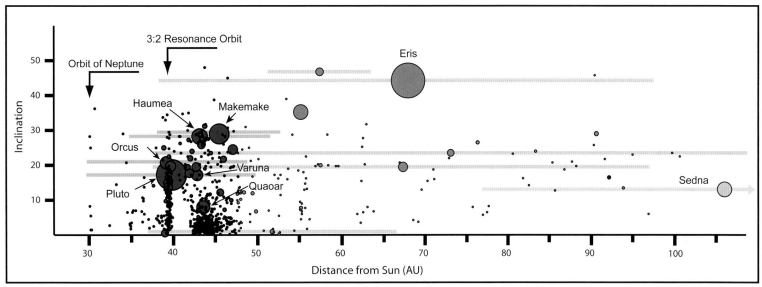

This chart shows all the known Trans-Neptunian objects, or bodies outside the orbit of Neptune. Classical Kuiper Belt objects are shown in red tints; objects in more distant scattered orbits are shown in blue tints. The vertical axis indicates the inclination of the object's orbit. The relative size of large bodies is shown. Objects in 3:2 resonance orbits, about 25% of the total including Pluto, revolve around the Sun twice for every three orbits of Neptune. Colored horizontal lines indicate the minimum and maximum distance of an orbit. Sedna reaches a maximum distance of about 975 Astronomical Units.

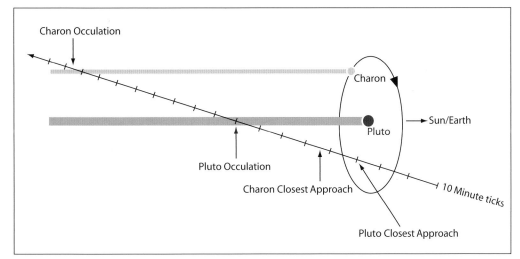

New Horizons will perform a flyby of Pluto and Charon in 2015. The encounter will be brief due to the high velocity of New Horizons.

This artist's conception depicts New Horizons as it encounters Pluto and other Kuiper Belt objects in the middle part of the 2110s.

Space Navigation: Looking to the Stars

For centuries mariners have looked to the stars to cross the oceans. Mariners at sea carried instruments such as cross staffs and sextants to determine the position of celestial objects in the sky. When combined with an accurate time reference, this would allow a marine navigator to determine the position of a ship on the Earth's surface. Similar techniques updated with modern technology can be used in space. Early human missions to the Moon even carried sextants and celestial charts that could be used to determine position.

The art and science of space navigation have continued to be employed to ensure that spacecraft arrive at their destinations. Special tools and techniques have been developed to find the way across the vast distances of the Solar System. Early flyby missions needed only to arrive in the correct vicinity, but more recent missions orbiting other planets required highly precise trajectories to be successful. Performing this type of navigation requires a network of Earth-based communication stations, accurate time-keeping equipment, and many complex calculations.

Probes in the first generation of planetary spacecraft were often equipped with star trackers to maintain attitude and keep antennas pointed at the Earth. Star trackers are small optical devices that maintain a lock on a bright star. The most common star used for this purpose was Canopus, visible in the southern hemisphere. It is the second brightest star in the sky after Sirius, although Sirius is not well-suited for tracking because it is a binary star. The star tracker would signal if a spacecraft drifted away from its correct alignment, and thrusters would be fired to correct the position.

As a spacecraft approaches its intended destination, other kinds of optical techniques are used to refine its position. Cameras on the spacecraft are used to obtain images of nearby planetary bodies with stars in the background. Because the positions of the stars are well known, these images can be used to determine the position of the spacecraft relative to the planetary body. In this way the position of the spacecraft can be determined at higher accuracy than is possible from Earth.

DEEP SPACE NETWORK

Since the early days of space exploration a network of communications stations has been required to track and navigate planetary spacecraft. Goldstone, the first U.S. station for this purpose, became operational in 1958 in the Mojave Desert in California to support the Pioneer missions to the Moon. Stations in Australia, South Africa, and Spain were later added. This array of facilities, known as the Deep Space Network, today consists of three globally distributed stations to enable communication with missions at all times. The Deep Space Network is managed by the Jet Propulsion Laboratory for NASA. Most data from planetary missions are returned through this network, and different missions must share the system.

Each station in the Deep Space Network is equipped with at least four dish antennas used to transmit and receive data from operational spacecraft. The largest antenna at each station is a 70 meter diameter dish. Others are about 30

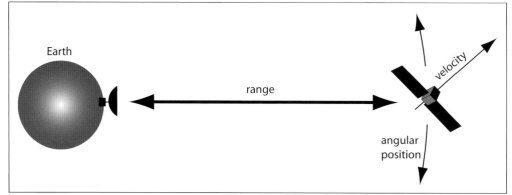

Space navigation requires that a spacecraft's range, angular position, and velocity be determined.

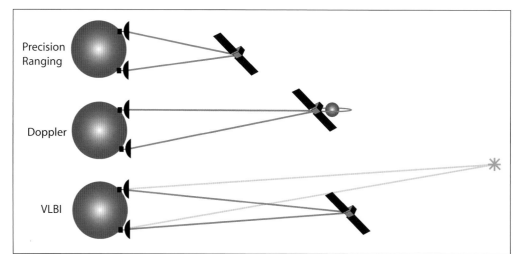

This annotated photograph, taken in August 1959, shows the first large antenna at the Pioneer station at Goldstone. This antenna received telemetry from the Pioneer probes to the Moon. It was used from 1958 to 1981. A boresight telescope was used to assist aiming the antenna. A theodolite was used to survey the position relative to other nearby antenna sites. Although no longer being used, this antenna still stands as a historical site.

Three methods of determining position using two telemetry sites are shown here. All use signals received from spacecraft. In Precision Ranging, the difference in arrival time between two stations is calculated. Telemetry is received at two stations simultaneously and is timed using atomic clocks. By knowing precisely the distance on the Earth between the two stations, it is possible to determine the three dimensional positions of the spacecraft using triangulation. The second method shown uses two stations to determine the difference in Doppler shift. As a spacecraft revolves around a distant planet, it will appear to move in slightly different directions from two points of view on the Earth. Therefore the two stations will detect a slightly different Doppler shift in the transmission. This information can be used to calculate the shape of the orbit. In Very Long Baseline Intererometry, two stations receive transmissions from the spacecraft. Then the two antennas are moved to point at a quasar, a class of extremely distant celestial objects whose positions are very well known. By comparing these signals it is possible to determine the angular position of the spacecraft very accurately.

meters in diameter. Large dishes are needed to concentrate weak signals from distant spacecraft.

Tracking a distant spacecraft from Earth requires predictions to be made of its position. Communications are not maintained around the clock. Instead, the Deep Space Network reacquires a spacecraft at specified times. The spacecraft continues to move between communication sessions, so a prediction must be made to point the antenna at the correct point in the sky. Thousands of measurements of the spacecraft's distance and velocity are made. These are used to update a model predicting the movement of the spacecraft.

NAVIGATION TASKS

One of the first tasks required in space navigation is determining velocity. The speed at which a spacecraft moves can be found by measuring the Doppler shift of its radio transmissions. All spacecraft are designed to transmit at certain radio frequencies. On Earth, the received signal is slightly shifted to a lower frequency because the spacecraft is moving away. This is the same process that causes light from stars and distant galaxies to be "redshifted." Measuring the amount of Doppler shift enables engineers to determine the rate at which the spacecraft is receding.

The range, or distance, of a spacecraft must also be determined. This can also be accomplished using radio transmissions. The amount of time for a signal to travel between Earth, the probe, and back can be used to determine the distance because the speed of light is precisely known. The amount of time required for the signal to be processed on the spacecraft must also be known. This is done by testing engineering copies of the spacecraft radio equipment used for testing. Movements of the Earth between the time of transmission and when the signal was received must also be known.

The angular position of the spacecraft must also be determined. This is a measure of the probe's location as seen from Earth, and along with range and velocity allows the position and movement to be calculated in three dimensions. Angular position can be crudely measured by using pointing information of an Earth-based antenna. More precise measurements are possible by using transmissions received simultaneously at two different Earth-based stations.

TIMING IS EVERYTHING

All the space navigation techniques have one important aspect in common: they rely on accurate timekeeping. Atomic clocks are used at each tracking station. These provide a stable timing reference to maintain constant

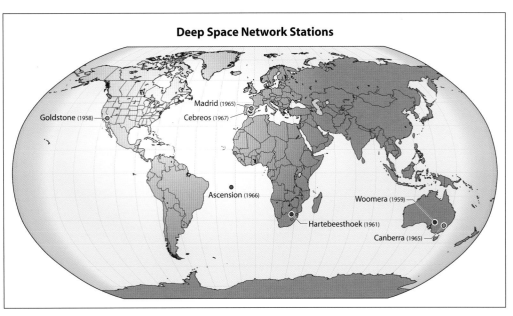

Deep Space Network Stations

The Deep Space Network was constructed to communicate with spacecraft across the Solar System. This map shows the three active stations in blue, inactive stations in red, and the first year of operation for each station. Stations for the Deep Space Network have been constructed at sites that allow for constant communication throughout the Solar System. Almost all missions in space remain near the ecliptic, so that must be visible in the sky at all three locations.

At least three stations spread out in longitude are required to allow constant communication. The Goldstone station in the Mojave Desert of California was the first to begin operations. Stations in Australia, South Africa, Spain, and Ascension Island were later added. Today the stations at Goldstone, Madrid, and Canberra make up the network.

The position of the three stations on the Earth's surface has been surveyed very accurately. The distance between stations, or the baseline, must be known when using two stations to determine the location of a spacecraft.

transmission frequencies and allow data to be combined from more than one station.

To measure the velocity using Doppler shift, frequencies of radio transmissions must be precisely controlled. Onboard spacecraft, ultra-stable oscillators are used to maintain a consistent frequency in radio transmissions. These stable transmissions can be used to determine position, but not with a great deal of accuracy. Highly stable time standards are heavy and consume a great deal of power, so installing them in planetary spacecraft is not an option. This situation is different with GPS satellites, all of which carry their own atomic clocks. To obtain a stable timing reference for planetary spacecraft, a stable time standard known as a hydrogen maser is used to produce a stable transmission frequency on Earth. This signal is sent to a spacecraft, which is then programmed to mathematically alter the frequency and return the signal. This way the velocity of a spacecraft can be determined to an accuracy of a few millimeters per second.

To determine the range, the travel time of a signal must be known to a small fraction of a second. Atomic clocks at the tracking station measure the amount of time required to send and receive signals moving at the speed of light. Atomic clocks are also used to compare signals received at different stations. This allows space navigators to precisely determine the angular position.

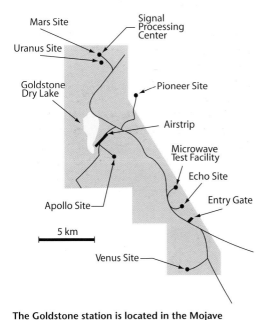

The Goldstone station is located in the Mojave Desert of California. The location was chosen for favorable topography and open space that limited radio interference. Goldstone contains several individual sites, each with its own set of large dish antennas. Each site is commonly named for the mission or destination for which it was first used. The first to begin operation was the Pioneer site, used to receive data from the Pioneer probes to the Moon. The Uranus site was first used to receive data from the Voyager 2 flyby of Uranus.

At the Edge of the Solar System

Five spacecraft are currently leaving the Solar System. Pioneer 10, Pioneer 11, Voyager 1, Voyager 2, and New Horizons were all designed for planetary encounters. In order to visit the outer planets, all five were accelerated to solar escape velocity.

The Pioneer 10 and 11 spacecraft were designed for encounter with Jupiter. Pioneer 11 also visited Saturn on its way out of the Solar System. These spacecraft were spin-stabilized and carried several instruments and an imaging sensor. Pioneer 10 and 11 returned data until 2002 and 1995, respectively, until their power supplies became too weak to support operations.

The two Voyager spacecraft continue to operate, sending data on magnetic fields and energetic particles as they approach interstellar space. The imaging instruments are no longer operated. The two spacecraft have enough electrical power to continue operating until about 2020.

The Voyagers and New Horizons will investigate the interaction between the Sun and interstellar space. Eventually they will leave the heliosphere. This region surrounding the Solar System is dominated by the solar wind, a constant stream of particles emanating from the Sun. Beyond this distance spacecraft will be able to detect fields and particles in interstellar space.

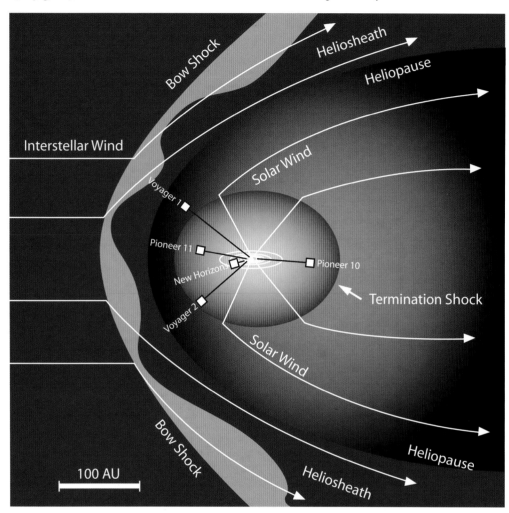

This chart shows the layout of the heliosphere and departing spacecraft. The solar wind pushes outward in all directions, but the interstellar particle stream pushes this envelope of material to one side. Voyager 1 is moving opposite the direction of the interstellar particle stream, in effect moving "upstream." In December 2004 Voyager 1 passed through the termination shock at a distance of 94 Astronomical Units, or 94 times the Sun-Earth distance. Voyager 2 reached this milestone in August 2007. At this point the solar wind slows to subsonic speed under pressure from the interstellar wind.

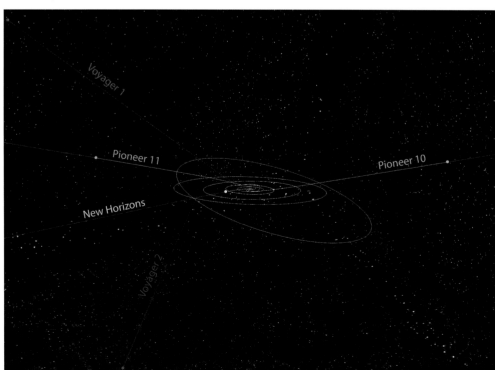

This chart shows the trajectories of the five spacecraft that have reached solar escape velocity. All five will enter interstellar space. Their location in 2009 is marked as dots on trajectory lines.

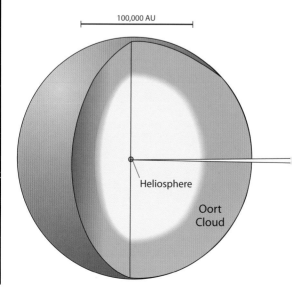

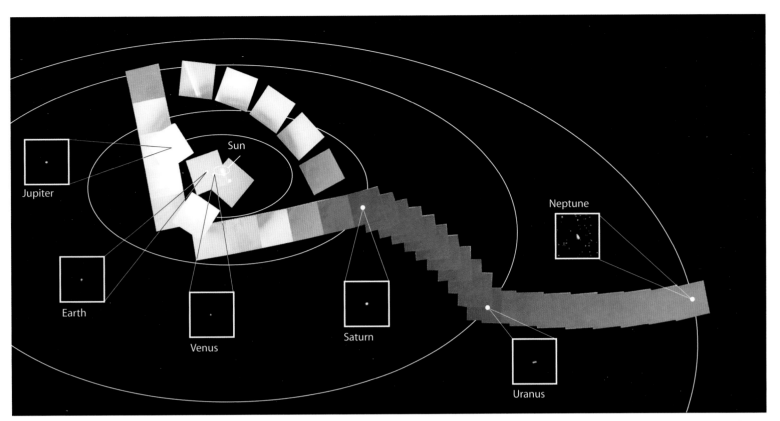

Voyager 1 took this series of images on February 14, 1990, showing all the planets of the Solar System. The mosaic contains more than 60 individual frames, the last images returned by either Voyager spacecraft. At the time, Voyager 1 was located about 4 billion miles from the Sun. At this distance the Sun appears less than 3% its size as seen from the Earth. Voyager 1 is leaving the Solar System at about 32 degrees above the ecliptic plane, making it possible to view all the planets from this point of view. Several planets are shown greatly magnified in the insets. Venus and Earth were smaller than an image pixel, but their relative brightness made them visible. Uranus and Neptune appear "smeared" because Voyager moved during those 15-second exposure times. Mars and Mercury were not visible.

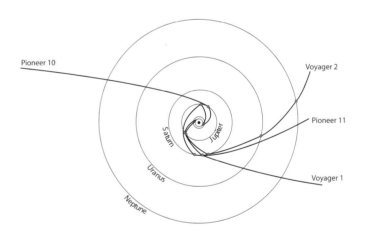

The trajectories of the two Pioneer and two Voyager missions to the outer Solar System were planned to maximize the number of possible visit to different planets. During planning stages, the Voyager missions were often called the "Grand Tour" of the outer planets. Launches were timed to take advantage of a favorable alignment of the outer planets for multiple encounters. After they completed their planetary encounters, Voyager 1 and 2 left the plane of the ecliptic on their way to interstellar space.

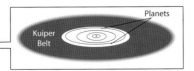

The Oort Cloud is likely the source of comets that appear in hyperbolic orbits. However, none of the objects that make up the Oort Cloud has been observed at great distances. The Oort Cloud is hypothesized to make up a sphere about 100,000 Astronomical Units in radius. This is larger than the heliosphere and almost big enough to reach the nearest star. At the scale of the illustration on the facing page, the realm of the planets would be smaller than the period at the end of this sentence.

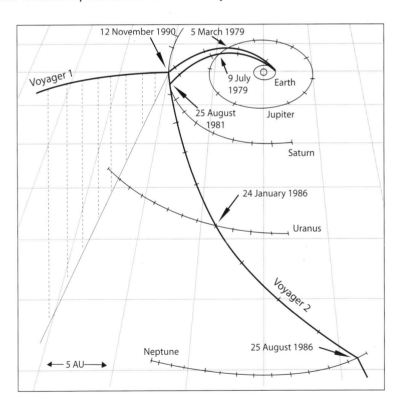

The Voyager 1 and 2 spacecraft followed different paths out of the Solar System. This chart shows their three-dimensional trajectories up to 1990. As the spacecraft receded from Earth, determining their positions accurately was vital to ensure safe encounters with outer planets. As timekeeping technology advanced, greater accuracy was possible during the missions. Voyager 2's flyby of Neptune was the closest encounter of any planet to that point.

To the Stars

Five spacecraft from Earth are currently moving out to the stars. After their operations cease, the spacecraft will continue to coast indefinitely. None of them will come close to any known stars, and it is unlikely they will ever encounter any star systems for at least millions of years.

Voyager 1 and 2 and New Horizons will return data measuring the nature of interstellar space after their planetary missions are completed. By 2009 Voyager 1 reached more than 105 Astronomical Units (AU) from the Sun, or 105 times the Sun-Earth distance. At the same time Voyager 2 reached more than 86 AU from the Sun. After picking up velocity from flybys of Jupiter and Saturn, Voyager 1 has the greatest velocity and is leaving the Solar System at about 3.5 AU per year. Voyager 2 has a slightly lower velocity, at 3.1 annually. New Horizons, after its gravity assist at Jupiter, is approaching the Kuiper Belt at 3.37 AU annually. The two Pioneer probes, although no longer functioning, are leaving the Solar System. Although all of these spacecraft will cease functioning after a few decades, they will continue coasting through the galaxy.

It is very unlikely that any of these spacecraft will ever be seen by any alien civilization, even billions of years in the future. However, four of the outgoing spacecraft contain messages to possible alien space travelers. During planning stages of the Pioneer 10 and 11 missions, it was decided to add a small plaque as a greeting to any alien civilization that may come across the spacecraft in the distant future. The plaque was affixed to the underside of the two spacecraft. The two Voyager spacecraft included a gold-covered phonograph record and a cover with instructions for its use. Encoded on the record are 115 images showing scenes from Earth, audio greetings in several languages, and musical selections. The fifth spacecraft leaving the Solar System, New Horizons, contains several objects including a sample of the ashes of Clyde Tombaugh, the discoverer of Pluto. However, it does not carry any material intended to greet alien civilization.

This diagram shows the position of the nearby stars. The Sun is at the center. Three-dimensional positions are indicated by lines extending above (solid) or below (dashed) the plane of the ecliptic. Also shown are the positions of the five spacecraft currently leaving the Solar System at 200,000 years in the future.

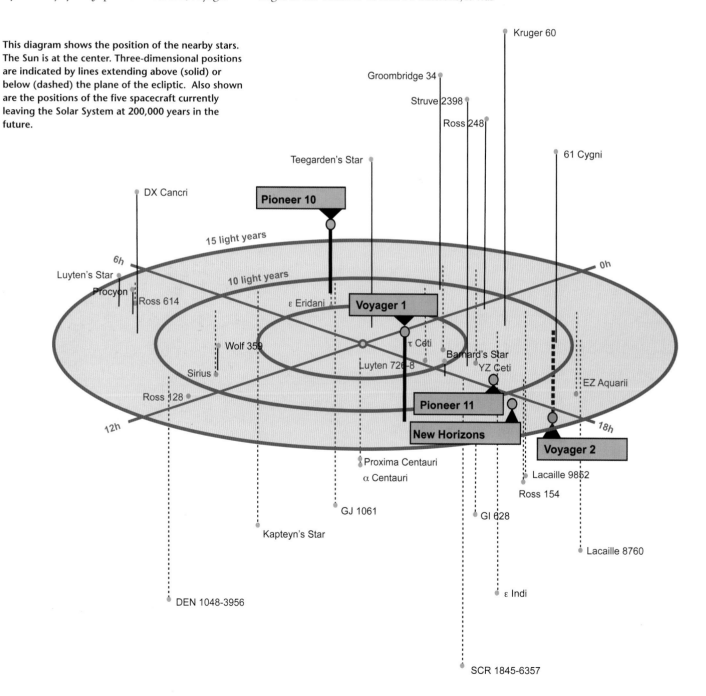

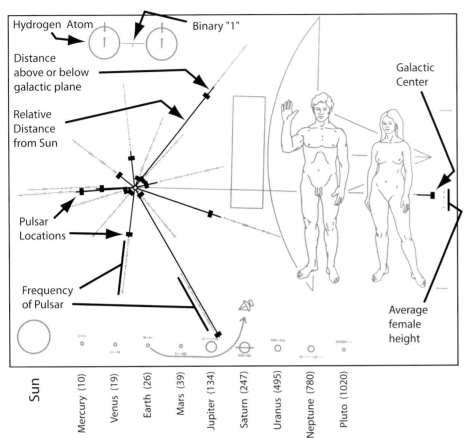

The illustration shown in gray on the left was carried by Pioneer 10 and 11 on metal plaques measuring about 9x6 inches. The spacecraft is drawn behind a human male and female for scale. The solar system appears along the lower edge. Each planet (plus Pluto) is listed with its average relative distance from the Sun. Distances are listed in binary numbers in units of 1/10th the Mercury distance. The diagram uses numerical figures to explain locations and other information. This presents a challenge when attempting to communicate with an alien civilization, which would certainly use numerical and linguistic systems very different to anything with which humans are familiar. The diagram in the upper left shows atomic hydrogen, by far the most abundant element in the universe. It shows a hydrogen atom undergoing a shift in its electron energy level. This change emits electromagnetic radiation, and is the most common such emission in the universe. This is used as a frequency and distance scale represented by the binary number 1. Converging lines in the left show the position of the Sun relative to 14 pulsars in the Milky Way and the center of the galaxy. Pulsars are very dense remnants of exploded giant stars, and they rotate at very stable frequencies. The frequency of each pulsar is listed in binary numerals relative to the frequency of hydrogen emission. The average human height is listed relative to the wavelength of hydrogen emission.

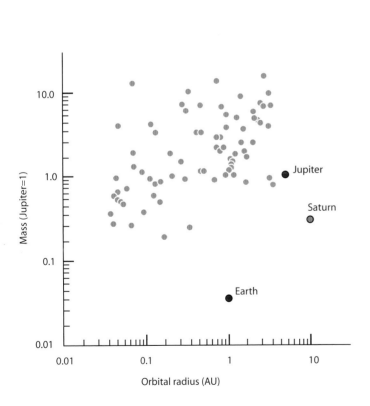

This chart shows the mass and orbital distance of planets discovered orbiting other stars. Jupiter, Saturn, and Earth are shown for comparison. Due to limited ability of ground-based telescopes, most planets discovered so far are large and orbit close to their parent star. This does not mean Earth-like planets do not exist, only that larger or space-based instruments will be needed to find them.

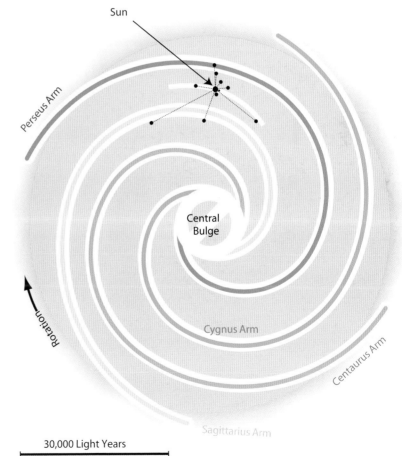

30,000 Light Years

This chart shows a simplified layout of the Milky Way galaxy. The exact nature of the central part of the galaxy is difficult to determine due to the density of dust, but data have suggested that the Milky Way may be a barred spiral. Surrounding the Sun, the location of pulsars on the Pioneer plaque is shown.

Looking into the Past: Mapping Everything

The universe is about 13.7 billion years old and has expanded since its beginning. Because distant objects appear to be receding as the universe expands, the light from them is "stretched" out, altering its wavelength to the red part of the electromagnetic spectrum. This "redshift" can be measured for every object in deep space. The more distant the object, the greater its redshift. The relationship between distance and redshift was described by Edwin Hubble in 1929 and remains fundamental to our understanding of the expanding universe.

Light from distant objects has been traveling toward the Earth for billions of years. In other words, we see distant objects as they appeared when the light left them. It is therefore possible to use telescopes to peer into the past. As astronomers have observed ever more distant objects, it became possible to see into the very early stages of the universe. At the very edge of the observable universe, it is possible to detect electromagnetic radiation in all direction. This cosmic microwave background radiation is the leftover energy from the Big Bang and the origins of our universe. This background radiation is literally the "echo" of the Big Bang.

The chart on the right shows the Local Group of galaxies. This gathering of galaxies is bound together by their mutual gravitational attraction. The largest two galaxies in the Local Group are the Milky Way and Andromeda. These two galaxies are approaching each other. About three billion years in the future they may merge to form a new, larger galaxy. Each galaxy is shown here about three times its actual size.

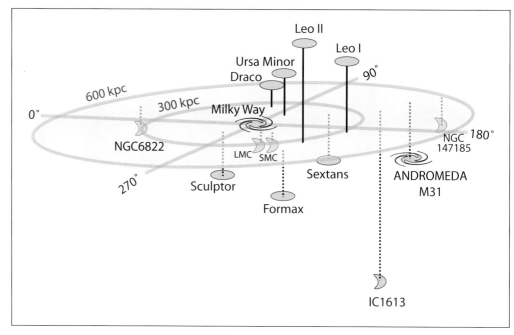

The image below from the Hubble Space Telescope shows a view of the galaxy cluster Abell 2218. In a process known as "gravitational lensing," the gravity of this cluster bends the light from more distant sources. Very distant galaxies are visible as warped arcs of light.

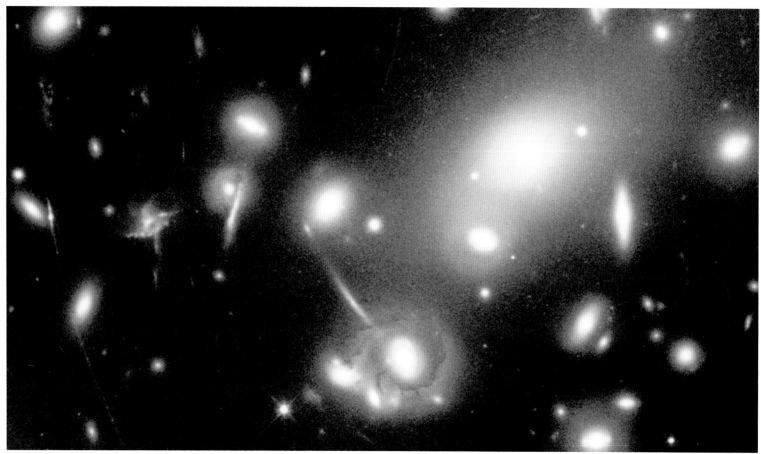

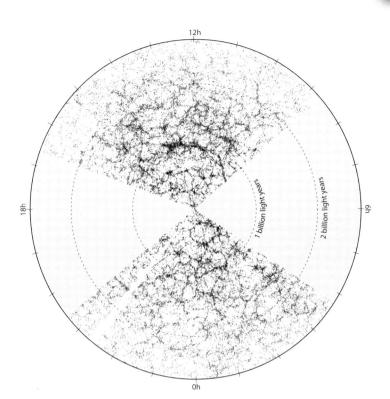

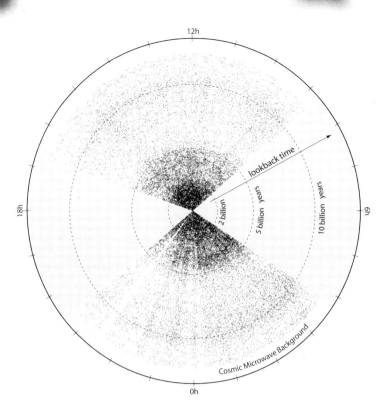

This chart shows data from the Sloan Digital Sky Survey indicating the distribution of galaxies in the universe. The Local Group is at the center of this diagram, but it is too small to be visible at this scale. Dots show the density of galaxies, each consisting of hundreds of billions of stars. The positions were determined by measuring the redshift of each galaxy and their angular position. The gray wedge-shaped areas to the left and right are parts of the sky obscured by material within the Milky Way.

As we peer into greater distances, we are in effect seeing back in time. Telescopes do not show deep space objects as they are—they show objects as they were billions of years ago. Because of this, representations that attempt to show the entire universe need to incorporate time as well as space. As we look out in space, and back in time, vast distances can be referred to as a "lookback time." This chart shows data from the Sloan Digital Sky Survey. Close to the center, small dots show the density of galaxies. Beyond a lookback time of about 5 billion years, most of the dots represent quasars instead of galaxies. Quasars, or "quasi-stellar" objects, are likely the cores of energetic galaxies. The objects were much more plentiful in the early universe and emitted enormous amounts of radiation. Due to their distance only their energetic emissions are visible. At the very edge of what is visible, we can detect the cosmic microwave background.

This chart shows the cosmic background radiation as measured by the Wilkinson Microwave Anisotropy Probe (WMAP). This spacecraft was launched in 2001 into a halo orbit around the L2 libration point beyond Earth's orbit. The cosmic background radiation was emitted about 13.7 billion years ago in the aftermath of the Big Bang, and has been stretched to the microwave part of the electromagnetic spectrum by the expansion of the universe. The colors indicate the intensity of the background radiation, which can be measured as temperatures barely above absolute zero. Reds signify temperatures about 0.0002 degrees Kelvin higher than blue areas. These differences reflect the "clumping" of matter that would later occur in the early history of the universe. This 360-degree view of the night sky has been mapped to a flat surface in the same way a global map of Earth is projected to a sheet of paper.

What Are the Possibilities of Future Spaceflight?

Who knows what the future might hold? Only time will tell. Space exploration provides a window on the universe from which fantastic new discoveries may be made. Humans may well discover extraterrestrial life. They may set their eyes on the image of an Earth-like planet around a nearby star. They may discover some fantastic material that can only be made in a gravity-free realm. Perhaps they may discover some heretofore unknown principle of physics. Maybe they will capture an image of the creation of the universe. That is the true excitement of the endeavor.

The 21st century promises to be an exciting experience for many reasons, but spaceflight offers a uniquely challenging set of possibilities. Each of these may be traced far back in the history of the space age, and have served as perennial issues affecting all outcomes involving an expansive future beyond this planet.

On January 14, 2004, President Bush announced a vision of space exploration that called for humans to reach for the Moon and Mars during the next thirty years. As stated at the time, the fundamental goal of this vision is to advance U.S. scientific, security, and economic interests through a robust space exploration program. In support of this goal, the United States will:

- implement a sustained and affordable human and robotic program to explore the Solar System and beyond;
- extend human presence across the Solar System, starting with a human return to the Moon by the year 2020, in preparation for human exploration of Mars and other destinations;
- develop the innovative technologies, knowledge, and infrastructures both to explore and to support decisions about the destinations for human exploration; and
- promote international and commercial participation in exploration to further U.S. scientific, security, and economic interests.

In so doing the president called for completion of the ISS as a lynchpin for space-based research. NASA would then invest in the enabling technologies necessary to return to the Moon and eventually to Mars, the Constellation program to which the Orion spacecraft and the Ares I and Ares V launchers are critical. By the end of Bush's second term, however, it had become highly uncertain that the initiative as originally explained could be realized.

Since the dawn of the space age, humanity has developed and used effectively the capability to move outward. In the process much has been accomplished, some tragedies have occurred, and several challenges remain. Who knows what transforming discoveries will be made in the first part of the 21st century that will alter the course of the future? Only one feature of spaceflight is inevitable: the unexpected will occur. Space is full of achievements, disappointments, and surprises. By going into space, humans learn what they do not know. Properly conducted, this effort will lead to a hopeful future.

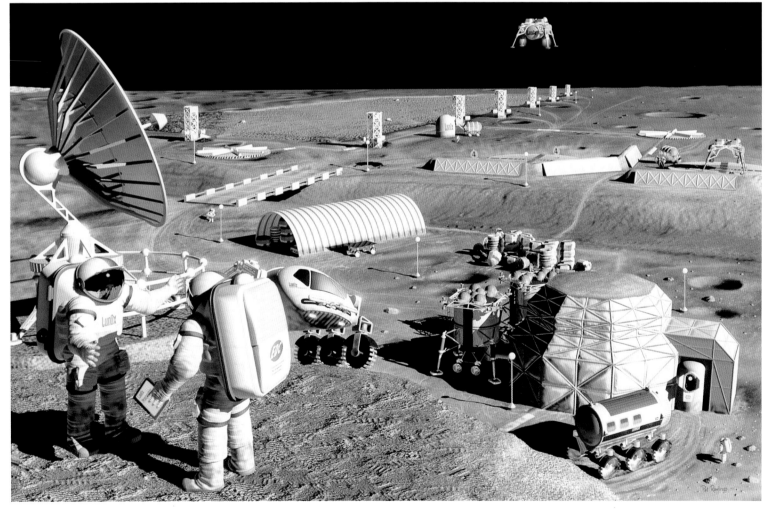

This illustration shows the possible configuration of a future lunar surface base.

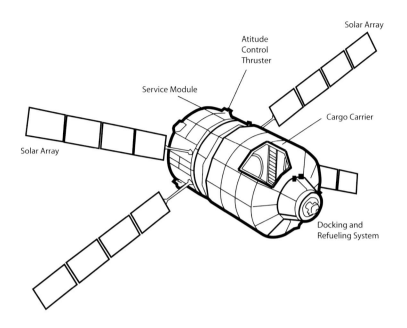

Solar Array

Atitude
Control
Thruster

Service Module

Solar Array

Cargo Carrier

Docking and
Refueling System

This schematic shows the automated Verne module. The European Space Agency designed Verne to autonomously dock with the International Space Station, delivering supplies and fuel.

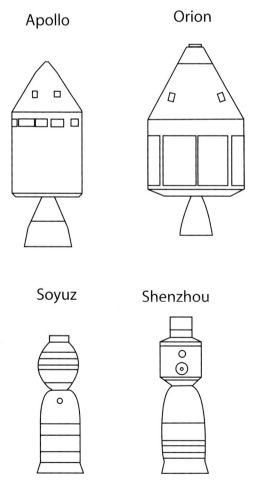

Apollo

Orion

Soyuz

Shenzhou

This comparison of four human spaceflight capsules shows the U.S. Apollo and Orion vehicles, the Soviet/Russian Soyuz, and the similar Chinese Shenzhou.

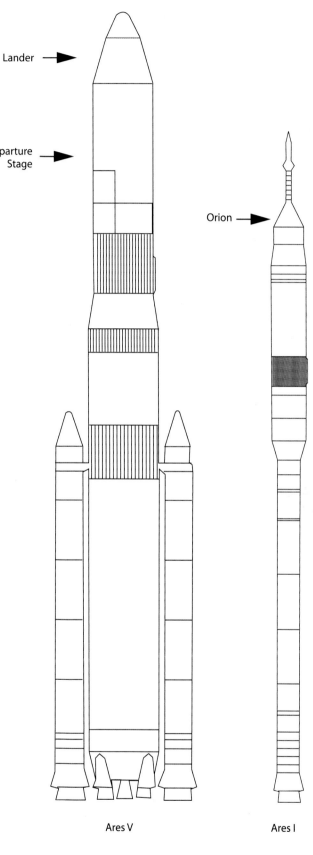

Lander

Departure
Stage

Orion

Ares V

Ares I

The Ares I and Ares V rockets will be used by NASA to launch future human missions. Ares 1 will launch the Orion crew vehicle into Earth orbit. Ares 5 is planned for taking humans on lunar missions.

A Basic Shelf of Readings on the History of Space Exploration

Arnold, David Christopher. *Spying From Space: Constructing America's Satellite Command and Control Systems*. College Station: Texas A&M University Press, 2005. A history of national security space satellite control.

Baker, David. *Spaceflight and Rocketry: A Chronology*. New York: Facts on File, 1996. A basic, single-volume reference on space exploration.

Benson, Michael. *Beyond: Visions of the Interplanetary Probes*. New York: Harry N. Abrams, 2003. Presenting photographs from the history of robotic space exploration, this oversized book provides a visual narrative of the Solar System's planets, moons, and asteroids.

Bille, Matt, and Erika Lishock. *The First Space Race: Launching the World's First Satellites*. College Station: Texas A&M University Press, 2004. A fine historical synthesis of the period between the mid-1950s and the aftermath of Sputnik, focusing on the rivalry between the United States and the Soviet Union to launch the first orbital satellite.

Bilstein, Roger E. *Flight in America: From the Wrights to the Astronauts*. Baltimore, MD: Johns Hopkins University Press, 1984, paperback reprint 1994. A superb synthesis of the origins and development of aerospace activities in America. This is the book to start with in any investigation of air and space activities.

---. *Testing Aircraft, Exploring Space: An Illustrated History of NACA and NASA*. Baltimore, MD: Johns Hopkins University Press, 2003. A general history of NASA.

Boss, Alan. *The Crowded Universe: The Search for Living Planets*. New York: Basic Books, 2009. A useful discussion of the search for planets beyond this Solar System.

Boyce, Joseph M. *The Smithsonian Book of Mars*. Washington, DC: Smithsonian Institution Press, 2003. Provides clear explanations of Mars's atmosphere, climate, surface, and interior from the monumental findings of the different NASA missions.

Burrows, William E. *The Infinite Journey: Eyewitness Accounts of NASA and the Age of Space*. New York: Discovery Books, 2000. A large-format history of spaceflight that includes important discussions of the endeavor by participants.

---. *This New Ocean: The Story of the First Space Age*. New York: Random House, 1998. A strong overview of the history of the space age from Sputnik to 1998.

Cabbage, Michael, and William Harwood. *Comm Check…: The Final Flight of Shuttle Columbia*. New York: Free Press, 2004. This book, by an investigative journalist, seeks to unravel the complex story of the loss of the Space Shuttle Columbia on February 1, 2003, during its return from orbit. It emphasizes relentless political pressure, shrinking budgets, and flawed decision making in NASA.

Caiden, Martin, and Jay Barbree, with Susan Wright. *Destination Mars: In Art, Myth, and Science*. New York: Penguin Studio, 1997. A beautifully illustrated overview of the lure of the red planet throughout humanity's history.

Chaikin, Andrew. *A Man on the Moon: The Voyages of the Apollo Astronauts*. New York: Viking, 1994. One of the best books on Apollo, this work emphasizes the exploration of the Moon by the astronauts between 1968 and 1972.

Clary, David A. *Rocket Man: Robert H. Goddard and the Birth of the Space Age*. New York: Hyperion, 2003. A superior biography of the American rocket pioneer.

Collins, Michael. *Carrying the Fire: An Astronaut's Journeys*. New York: Farrar, Straus and Giroux, 1974. This is the first candid book about life as an astronaut, written by the member of the Apollo 11 crew that remained in orbit around the Moon.

---. *Liftoff: The Story of America's Adventure in Space*. New York: Grove Press, 1988. General history of the U.S. space program for a popular audience written by a former astronaut.

Crosswell, Ken. *Planet Quest: The Epic Discovery of Alien Solar Systems*. New York: Free Press, 1997. A fine discussion of the effort to find planets circling other stars.

Darling, David. *Life Everywhere: The Maverick Science of Astrobiology*. New York: Basic Books, 2001. A study of life in the universe.

Dethloff, Henry C., and Ronald A. Schorn. *Voyager's Grand Tour: To the Outer Planets and Beyond*. Washington, DC: Smithsonian Institution Press, 2003. A fine history of the Voyager mission to the outer planets.

Dick, Steven J. *The Biological Universe: The Twentieth Century Extraterrestrial Life Debate and the Limits of Science*. New York: Cambridge University Press, 1996. The superb history of the possibility of life elsewhere in the universe.

---, Robert Jacobs, Constance Moore, and Bertram Ulrich. Editors. *America in Space: NASA's First Fifty Years*. New York: Abrams, 2007. Some of the best photos from the history of NASA.

Erickson, Mark. *Into the Unknown Together: The DOD, NASA, and Early Spaceflight*. Maxwell AFB, AL: Air University Press, 2005. A history of national security space activities.

Fischer, Daniel. *Mission Jupiter: The Spectacular Journey of the Galileo Spacecraft*. New York: Copernicus Books, 2001. A history of the Galileo spacecraft to Jupiter.

Goldsmith, Donald. *The Hunt for Life on Mars*. New York: E. P. Dutton, 1997. A solid discussion of the study of Mars, especially the search for possible life there from Lowell to the present.

Gruntman, Mike. *Blazing the Trail: The Early History of Spacecraft and Rocketry*. Reston, VA: American Institute for Aeronautics and Astronautics, 2004. Provides an introduction to the history of early rocketry and the subsequent developments that led to the space age.

Hansen, James R. *First Man: The Life of Neil A. Armstrong*. New York: Simon & Schuster, 2005. A superb biography of the first American to set foot on the Moon.

Harrison, Albert A. *Starstruck: Cosmic Visions in Science, Religion, and Folklore*. New York: Berghahn Books, Inc., 2007. Investigates how the explosion in knowledge about the universe has transformed the human perspective on life and the cosmos.

Heppenheimer, T.A. *Countdown: The History of Space Exploration*. New York: John Wiley & Sons, 1997. A general audience history, somewhat quirky but well written and entertaining.

Hitt, David, Owen Garriott, and Joseph P. Kerwin. *Homesteading Space: The Skylab Story*. Lincoln: University of Nebraska Press, 2008. A very fine account of the U.S.'s first space station, written by some of the astronauts who flew aboard it.

Hogan, Thor. *Mars Wars: The Rise and Fall of the Space Exploration Initiative*. Washington, DC: NASA SP-2007-4410, 2007. A provocative book arguing that the failure of President George H. W. Bush's Space Exploration Initiative (SEI) in 1989 was the result of a flawed policy process.

Hunley, J.D. *The Development of Propulsion Technology for U.S. Space-Launch Vehicles, 1926-1991*. College Station: Texas A&M University Press, 2007. In this definitive study, J. D. Hunley traces the development from Robert Goddard's early rockets and the German V-2 missile through the Titan IVA and the propulsion system of the Space Shuttle.

Jenkins, Dennis R. *Space Shuttle: The History of the National Space Transportation System, the First 100 Missions*. North Branch, MN: Speciality Press, 2001, 3rd Edition. By far the best technical history of the Space Shuttle, presenting an overview of the vehicle's development and use.

Johnson-Freese, Joan. *Space as a Strategic Asset*. New York: Columbia University Press, 2007. A policy analysis that explores many current national security space issues and offers solutions to vexing problems.

Kevles, Bettyann Holtzmann. *Almost Heaven: The Story of Women in Space*. New York: Basic Books, 2003. A fascinating account of the experiences of women in space.

Koerner, David, and Simon LeVay. *Here There Be Dragons: The Scientific Quest for Extraterrestrial Life*. New York: Oxford University Press, 2000. A good overview.

Launius, Roger D. *Frontiers of Space Exploration*. Westport, CT: Greenwood Press, 2nd edition, 2003. A collection of essays along with key documents and biographies of actors in the space exploration effort.

---. *Space Stations: Base Camps to the Stars*. Washington, DC: Smithsonian Books, 2003. A history of space stations—real and imagined—as cultural icons, fully illustrated with rare and evocative imagery.

---, and Howard E. McCurdy. *Imagining Space: Achievements, Predictions, Possibilities, 1950-2050*. San Francisco, CA: Chronicle Books, 2001. A large-format book sweeping from the past to the future of spaceflight.

---, *Robots in Space: Technology, Evolution, and Interplanetary Travel*. Baltimore, MD: Johns Hopkins University Press, 2008. A history of the debate over whether to send humans or robots to explore space.

Lemonick, Michael D. *Echo of the Big Bang*. Princeton, NJ: Princeton University Press, 2003. An excellent discussion on the current state of cosmology and why.

---. *Other Worlds: The Search for Life in the Universe*. New York: Simon & Schuster, 1998. A strong analysis of whether or not there is life on other planets in the universe and the efforts under way to find it.

Leverington, David. *New Cosmic Horizons: Space Astronomy from the V-2 to the Hubble Space Telescope*. New York: Cambridge University Press, 2001. An outstanding history of this subject.

Linehan, Dan. *SpaceShipOne: An Illustrated History*. New York: Zenith Press, 2008. Chronicles the development of the world's first commercial crewed space program that won the Ansari X-Prize in 2004.

Lipartito, Kenneth, and Orville R. Butler. *A History of the Kennedy Space Center*. Gainesville: University Press of Florida, 2007. This first comprehensive history of the Kennedy Space Center, NASA's famous launch facility located at Cape Canaveral, Florida, demonstrated the vital but largely unknown work that takes place before the rocket is lit.

Logsdon, John M. General Editor. *Exploring the Unknown: Selected Documents in the History of the U.S. Civil Space Program*. 7 Vols. Washington, DC: NASA Special Publication-4407, 1995-2008. An essential reference work, these volumes print more than 550 key documents in space policy and its development throughout the twentieth century.

Lord, M.G. *Astro Turf: The Private Life of Rocket Science*. New York: Walker and Co., 2005. An inventive account of the cult of the rocket with forays into science fiction and pop culture.

Lorenz, Ralph, and Jacqueline Mitton. *Titan Unveiled: Saturn's Mysterious Moon Explored*. Princeton, NJ: Princeton University Press, 2008. This is one of the first general-interest books to reveal the startling new discoveries that have been made since the arrival of the Cassini-Huygens mission to Saturn and Titan.

Mackowski, Maura Phillips. *Testing the Limits: Aviation Medicine and the Origins of Manned Space Flight*. College Station: Texas A&M University Press, 2005. A solid discussion of the manner in which the U.S. pursued the knowledge required to live and work in space.

Markley, Robert. *Dying Planet: Mars in Science and the Imagination*. Durham, NC: Duke University Press, 2005. About Mars and its place in the popular culture.

Mather, John, and John Boslough. *The Very First Light: The True Inside Story of the Scientific Journey Back to the Dawn of the Universe*. New York: Basic

Books, 1996. An account of NASA's Cosmic Background Explorer (COBE), written by the project's chief scientist and recent Nobel Laureate.

McCurdy, Howard E. *Space and the American Imagination*. Washington, DC: Smithsonian Institution Press, 1997. A significant analysis of the relationship between popular culture and public policy.

McDougall, Walter A. *The Heavens and the Earth: A Political History of the Space Age*. New York: Basic Books, 1985. Reprint edition, Baltimore, MD: Johns Hopkins University Press, 1997. This Pulitzer Prize–winning book analyzes the space race to the Moon in the 1960s. The author argues that Apollo prompted the space program to stress engineering over science, competition over cooperation, civilian over military management, and international prestige over practical applications.

Michaud, Michael A.G. *Contact with Alien Civilizations: Our Hopes and Fears about Encountering Extraterrestrials*. New York: Copernicus Books, 2007. Explores the political and social consequences of interstellar contact with extraterrestrials and how our species should be prepared.

Mindell, David A. *Digital Apollo: Human, Machine, and Space*. Cambridge, MA: MIT Press, 2008. A superb account of the manner in which humanity found its way to the Moon during the Apollo program.

Morton, Oliver. *Mapping Mars: Science, Imagination, and the Birth of a World*. New York: Picador USA, 2003. Tells the story of the landscapes of Mars, and introduces the reader to the visionaries who devoted themselves to understanding Mars.

Murray, Bruce C. *Journey into Space: The First Three Decades of Space Exploration*. New York: W.W. Norton and Co., 1989. This book is an excellent discussion of the planetary science program written by the former director of the Jet Propulsion Laboratory.

Murray, Charles A., and Catherine Bly Cox. *Apollo: The Race to the Moon*. New York: Simon and Schuster, 1989. Perhaps the best general account of the lunar program, this history uses interviews and documents to reconstruct the stories of the people who participated in Apollo.

Neal, Valerie, Cathleen S. Lewis, and Frank H. Winter. *Spaceflight: A Smithsonian Guide*. New York: Macmillan, 1995. This book provides, with numerous illustrations, a basic history of space exploration by the United States.

Neufeld, Michael J. *Von Braun: Dreamer of Space, Engineer of War*. New York: Alfred A. Knopf, 2007. The definitive biography of the German-American rocket pioneer.

North, John. *Cosmos: An Illustrated History of Astronomy and Cosmology*. Revised Edition. Chicago: University of Chicago Press, 2008. Offers a sweeping historical survey of the two sciences that help define our place in the universe: astronomy and cosmology.

Reeves-Stevens, Judith, Garfield Reeves-Stevens, and Brian K. Muirhead. *Going to Mars: The Untold Story of Mars Pathfinder and NASA's Bold New Missions for the 21st Century*. New York: Pocket Books, 2003. An excellent account of the recent and future missions to the red planet.

Sagan, Carl. *Pale Blue Dot: A Vision of the Human Future in Space*. New York: Random House, 1994. Probably the most sophisticated articulation of the exploration imperative to appear since Wernher von Braun's work of the 1950s and 1960s.

Schmitt, Harrison H. *Return to the Moon*. New York: Copernicus-Praxis, 2005. Argues that helium-3 fusion power will make possible the opening of Moon to human activity. Schmitt believes that an ideally funded business plan for lunar exploitation would require about $15 billon and fifteen years.

Schrunk, David, Burton Sharpe, Bonnie L. Cooper, and Madhu Thangavelu. *The Moon: Resources, Future Development and Settlement*, 2nd edition. Chichester, United Kingdom: Springer-Praxis, 2007. Tells the story of the feasible transformation of the Moon into an inhabited sister body of Earth in the coming century.

Sheehan, William. *The Planet Mars: A History of Observation & Discovery*. Tucson: University of Arizona Press, 1996. An excellent survey of how humans have acquired knowledge about the red planet from antiquity to the present. It concentrates on the work of Earth-based astronomers but also includes succinct narratives of the Mariner 4 mission and the Viking project of the 1970s.

Siddiqi, Asif A. *The Soviet Space Race with Apollo and Sputnik and the Soviet Space Challenge*. Gainesville: University Press of Florida, 2003. A superb two-volume history of the Soviet space program through the Moon race.

Singh, Simon. *Big Bang: The Origin of the Universe*. New York: Fourth Estate, 2005. A popular account of the manner in which the Big Bang became the dominant theory explaining the origins of the universe.

Squyres, Steve. *Roving Mars: Spirit, Opportunity, and the Exploration of the Red Planet*. New York: Hyperion, 2005. Written by the Cornell University scientist who is the principal investigator on the Mars missions that landed the rovers Spirit and Opportunity in January 2004, this book tells how the rovers operated.

Stern, Alan. Editor. *Worlds Beyond: The Thrill of Planetary Exploration*. New York: Cambridge University Press, 2003. An excellent account of planetary exploration.

Stooke, Philip J. *The International Atlas of Lunar Exploration*. New York: Cambridge University Press, 2007. A comprehensive reference on lunar exploration.

Tompkins, Philip K. *Apollo, Challenger, Columbia: The Decline of the Space Program, A Study in Organizational Communication*. Los Angeles, California: Roxbury Publishing Company, 2005. Presents a lesson in organization dynamics and communication strategies.

Tucker, Wallace H., and Karen Tucker. *Revealing the Universe: The Making of the Chandra X-Ray Observatory*. New York: Harvard University Press, 2001. An important history of a major recent NASA space science effort.

Tyson, Neil de Grasse. *Universe: Down to Earth*. New York: Columbia University Press, 1995. An up-to-date analysis of the basic evolution of the universe using scientific information gleaned from research from all sources, including space exploration missions.

Weitekamp, Margaret A. *Right Stuff, Wrong Sex: America's First Women in Space Program*. Baltimore, MD: Johns Hopkins University Press, 2004. On June 17, 1963, Soviet cosmonaut Valentina Tereshkova became the first woman in space. Unlike every previous milestone in the space race, however, this event did not spur NASA to put an American woman into orbit. American women did not escape Earth's orbit for another thirty years.

Westwick, Peter J. *Into the Black: JPL and the American Space Program, 1976-2004*. New Haven, CT: Yale University Press, 2006. A history of NASA's leading planetary science organization.

Wolverton, Mark. *The Depths of Space: The Pioneer Planetary Probes*. Washington, DC: Joseph Henry Press, 2004. A history of Pioneers 10 and 11.

Zimmerman, Robert. *The Universe in a Mirror: The Saga of the Hubble Space Telescope and the Visionaries Who Built It*. Princeton, NJ: Princeton University Press, 2008. A readable account of the history of the Hubble Space Telescope.

Zubrin, Robert, and Richard Wagner. *The Case for Mars: The Plan to Settle the Red Planet and Why*. New York: The Free Press, 1996. A critically important description of the "Mars Direct" strategy for reaching Mars with humans.

Illustration Credits

Unless otherwise noted, all images and graphics are courtesy of Smithsonian National Air and Space Museum.

111: Surveyor 7 photomosaic, NASA
114: Saturn V launch schematic, NASA
115: Apollo orbital tracks, Analytical Graphics Inc.
115: Saturn V configuration, NASA
116: Saturn 1B stack in wind tunnel, NASA
116: Saturn V first stages, NASA
117: Saturn V first stage at test stand, NASA
119: Lunar rover, NASA
120: Apollo 11 campers, NASA
120: Buzz Aldrin on lunar surface, NASA
121: Sea of Tranquillity map, NASA
122: Apollo 12 panorama, NASA
122: Preliminary map of Apollo EVAs, NASA
123: Technician at lunar landscape mock-up, NASA
125: Apollo 15 LM and Rover, NASA
125: Apollo 15 astronaut and LRV, NASA
127: Apollo 16 flag salute, NASA
127: Apollo 17 panorama, NASA
128: Lunar orbital tracks, Analytical Graphics Inc.
129: Clementine topographic map of Moon, LPI
129: Kaguya image of Moon and Earth, JAXA/ NHK
129: Clementine Topographic Map of the Moon, NASA
130: Clementine image of Moon-Saturn-Mars-Mercury, NASA
132: Planet formation, NASA
133: Terrestrial planets, NASA
133: SOHO image of Sun, NASA
134: Mars topographic maps, NASA
135: Hemispheres of Mars, US Geological Survey
136: Mariner 4 at Mars, NASA
136: Mariner 4 images and LBJ, NASA
137: Mariner 4 image, NASA/JPL
137: Mariner Crater from Mars Global Surveyor, NASA/JPL
139: Olympus Mons from Mariner 9, NASA/ JPL
140: Mars 2–5 and Mariner 9, Analytical Graphics Inc.
140: Viking orbits, Analytical Graphics Inc.
141: Mars orbital missions, Analytical Graphics Inc.
142: Mars global topography, NASA/JPL
143: MGS water seepage, MSSS
144: Mars Odyssey in orbit, NASA
145: Mars Reconnaissance Orbiter, NASA
145: Mars volcano map and image, NASA
146: Viking 1 landing pad, NASA
148: Mars surface from Viking 2, NASA
149: Viking image of Big Joe, NASA/JPL
150: Mars Pathfinder panorama, NASA
151: Phoenix Lander image, NASA/JPL
152: Sunset on Mars, NASA/JPL
153: MER artist's conception, NASA/JPL
155: MER schematic, NASA/JPL image data
155: Opportunity panorama, NASA/JPL
156: Venus transit time series, courtesy of a private collection

157: Venus hemispheres from Magellan, NASA/ JPL
158: Venus from Pioneer Venus Orbiter, NASA/ JPL
159: Venus orbits, Analytical Graphics Inc.
160: Magellan orbits, Analytical Graphics Inc.
160: Mariner 2, NASA/JPL
161: Plains of Venus, NASA/JPL
162: Venera 13 on surface of Venus, NASM/ NASA/JPL
163: Venera 14 landing site, (c) SovFoto
164: MESSENGER image of Mercury, NASA/ Johns Hopkins University APL/Carnegie Institute of Washington
165: Mercury from Mariner 10, NASA/JPL
166: MESSENGER photomosaic of Mercury, NASA/Johns Hopkins University APL/ Carnegie Institute of Washington
167: Mercury from MESSENGER, NASA/ Johns Hopkins University APL/Carnegie Institute of Washington
168: Mosaic of planets and four large moons of Jupiter, NASA/JPL
170: Artist's concept for hypothetical Solar System, NASA/JPL
171: Saturn from Cassini, NASA/JPL
173: Solar probe orbits (Genesis-Hinode), Analytical Graphics Inc.
174: Sun from SOHO, NASA/JPL
174: SOHO-EIT image, NASA
174: STEREO-B image, NASA/JPL
175: Pioneer orbits, Analytical Graphics Inc.
176: Wild 2 Comet from Stardust, NASA/JPL
176: Halley's Comet from Giotto, courtesy ESA
177: Comet Halley from Kuiper Airborne Observatory, NASA
177: Stardust encountering Comet Wild 2, NASA/JPL
178: ICE-Vegas-Giotto trajectories, Analytical Graphics Inc.
178: DS1-Rosetta trajectories, Analytical Graphics Inc.
178: Stardust-Deep Impact trajectories, Analytical Graphics Inc.
180: Galileo-Cassini trajectories, Analytical Graphics Inc.
180: Dawn-DS1-NEAR trajectories, Analytical Graphics Inc.
181: Asteroid Steins from Rosetta, courtesy ESA
181: Dawn Spacecraft, NASA
182: NEAR-Shoemaker images of Eros, NASA/JPL
183: Asteroid Itokawa from Hayabusa, courtesy JAXA/NHK
183: Hayabusa, courtesy JAXA/NHK
183: Hayabusa and Minerva surface hopper, courtesy JAXA/NHK
184: Jupiter from New Horizons spacecraft, NASA/JPL
186: Europa, NASA/JPL
186: Four Galilean satellites, NASA/JPL
187: Io, NASA/JPL

188: Callisto map, US Geological Survey image data
188: Ganymede map, US Geological Survey image data
188: Ganymede close-up, NASA/JPL
189: Europa, Ganymede, Callisto surface comparison, NASA/JPL image data
189: Europa map, US Geological Survey image data
189: Io map, NASA/JPL/USGS image data
190: Shoemaker-Levy 9 impact images, NASA
190: Shoemaker-Levy 9 impact from Hubble, NASA
192: Saturn by Cassini, NASA/JPL
193: Saturn false-color image from Cassini, NASA/JPL
195: Titan surface from Huygens, NASA/ESA
196: Dione map, US Geological Survey image data
196: Enceledus map, US Geological Survey image data
196: Iapatus map, US Geological Survey image data
196: Mimas map, US Geological Survey image data
196: Tethys map, US Geological Survey image data
196: Rhea map, US Geological Survey image data
197: Iapatus, NASA/JPL
198: Atlas, NASA/JPL
198: Calypso, NASA/JPL
198: Helene, NASA/JPL
198: Janus, NASA/JPL
199: Hyperion, NASA/JPL
199: Phoebe, NASA/JPL
200: Uranus's five largest moons, NASA/JPL image data
200: Miranda, NASA/JPL
201: Uranus from Voyager 2, NASA/JPL
202: Miranda close-up, NASA/JPL
202: Titania, NASA/JPL
202: Oberon, NASA/JPL
203: Umbriel, NASA/JPL
203: Uranus from Hubble Space Telescope, NASA
204: Neptune from Voyager 2, NASA/JPL
205: Triton, NASA/JPL
207: New Horizons at Pluto, NASA/JPL
208: Goldstone antenna, NASA/JPL
210: Heliosphere and departing spacecraft, Analytical Graphics Inc.
211: Solar System portrait from Voyager 1, NASA/JPL
214: Galaxy cluster Abell 2218 from Hubble Space Telescope, NASA/STScI
215: Background radiation, NASA/WMAP Science Team
216: Possible future Moon base, NASA

ACKNOWLEDGMENTS

The authors would like to acknowledge the support of:
National Aeronautics and Space Administration, grant NNX08AQ76G
Analytical Graphics Incorporated

Photo Researcher: Joan Mathys

Graphics Design Assistance: Stephanie Markgraf

Graphics Interns: Meleta Buckstaff
Jessica Kirsch
Hermes Marticio
Ngoc Tran
Heather van Werkhooven

**Visualization Support, for
Analytical Graphics Incorporated:**
Jeff Baxter
Kel Elkins
Marc Hoffman
Kenneth Kawahara
Jonathan Lowe
Jens Ramrath

**Design and Layout,
for Sterling Hill Productions:**
Peter Holm
Abrah Griggs

Whenever writers take on a project such as this they stand squarely on the shoulders of earlier investigators and incur a good many intellectual debts. The authors would like to acknowledge the assistance of several individuals who aided in the preparation of this book. It was only through the assistance of several key people that we have been able to assemble the maps and illustrations for this volume. For their many contributions in completing this project we wish especially to thank Jane Odom and her staff archivists at the NASA History Division who helped track down information and correct inconsistencies, as well as Steve Dick, Steve Garber, Glen Asner, and Nadine Andreassen at NASA; the staffs of the NASA Headquarters Library and the Scientific and

Technical Information Program who provided assistance in locating materials; Marilyn Graskowiak and her staff at the NASM Archives; and many archivists and scholars throughout NASA and other space organizations. The National Aeronautics and Space Administration provided a generous grant to make this work possible, and we thank it for this assistance.

Patricia Graboske, head of publications at the National Air and Space Museum, provided important guidance for this project. Thanks to Tom Watters of the National Air and Space Museum for providing Mercury MESSENGER imagery, and to Jim Zimbelman for allowing the use of Mars geologic maps. Thanks also to Ross Anderson for his assistance. Our thanks are multifold to Mark Brender and Val Webb at GeoEye for allowing use of IKONOS satellite imagery. Special thanks to Jonathan Lowe, Michael Limcangco, and others at Analytical Graphics Inc. for producing graphics showing three-dimensional paths of spacecraft in Earth and planetary orbits. We also thank Ib Bellew at Bunker Hill Publishing for agreeing to pursue this work, and to Peter Holm, Sterling Hill Productions, for designing the book. Our deep thanks are due to all of these fine people.

In addition to these individuals, we wish to acknowledge the following individuals who aided in a variety of ways: Debbora Battaglia, David Brandt, William E. Burrows, Bruce Campbell, Erik Conway, Bob Craddock, Tom D. Crouch, Gen. John R. Dailey, David H. DeVorkin, Robert Farquhar, Jens Feeley, James Rodger Fleming, James Garvin, Lori B. Garver, Michael H. Gorn, John Grant, G. Michael Green, Barton C. Hacker, James R. Hansen, Wes Huntress, Peter Jakab, Dennis R. Jenkins, Violet Jones-Bruce, Sylvia K. Kraemer, John Krige, Alan M. Ladwig, W. Henry Lambright, Jennifer Levasseur, John M. Logsdon, W. Patrick McCray, Howard E. McCurdy, Jonathan C. McDowell, Karen McNamara, Ted Maxwell, Valerie Neal, Allan A. Needell, Michael J. Neufeld, Frederick I. Ordway III, Scott Pace, Robert Poole, Anthony M. Springer, Alan Stern, Harley Thronson, and Margaret Weitekamp. Our greatest debts are to the women in our lives, whose names grace the dedication page. All of these people would disagree with some of the materials and observations made here, but such is both the boon and the bane of scholarly inquiry.

Roger D. Launius
Andrew K. Johnston
Washington, D.C

Index